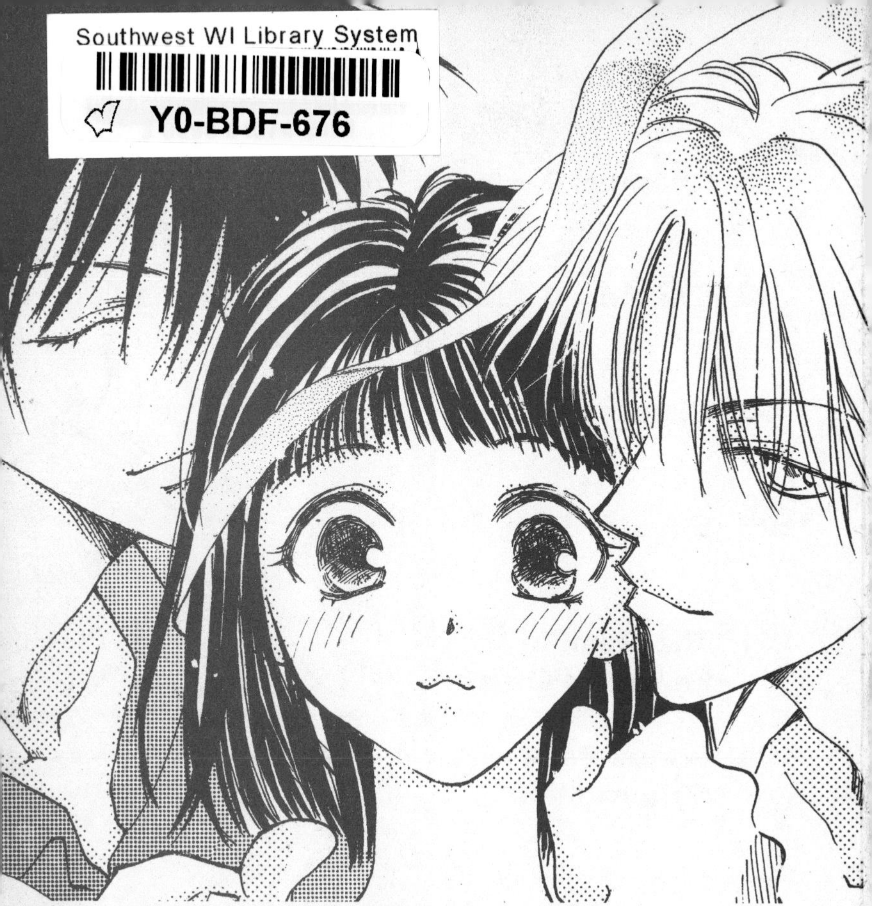

Land of the Blindfolded

Volume 2

By Sakura Tsukuba

CONTENTS

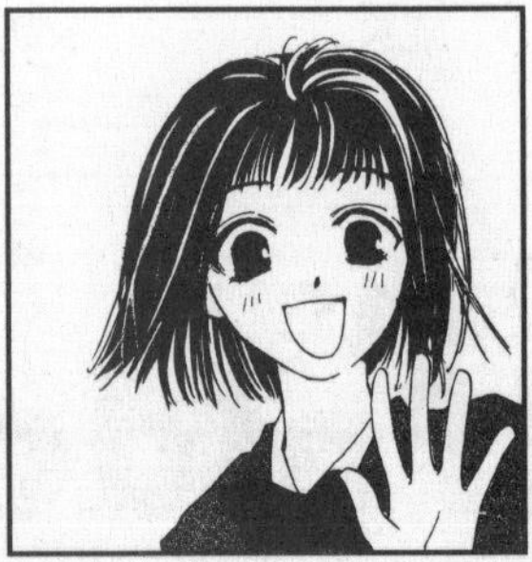

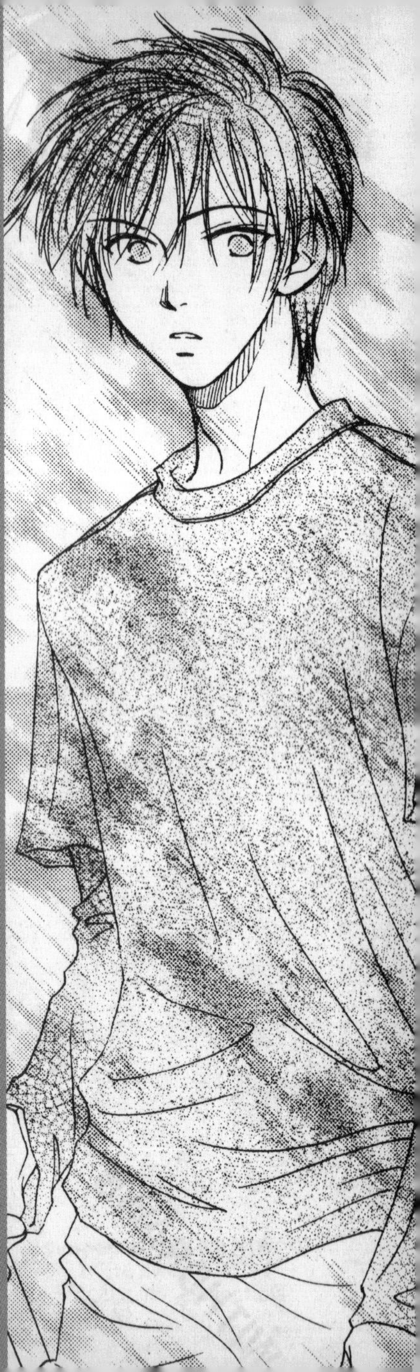

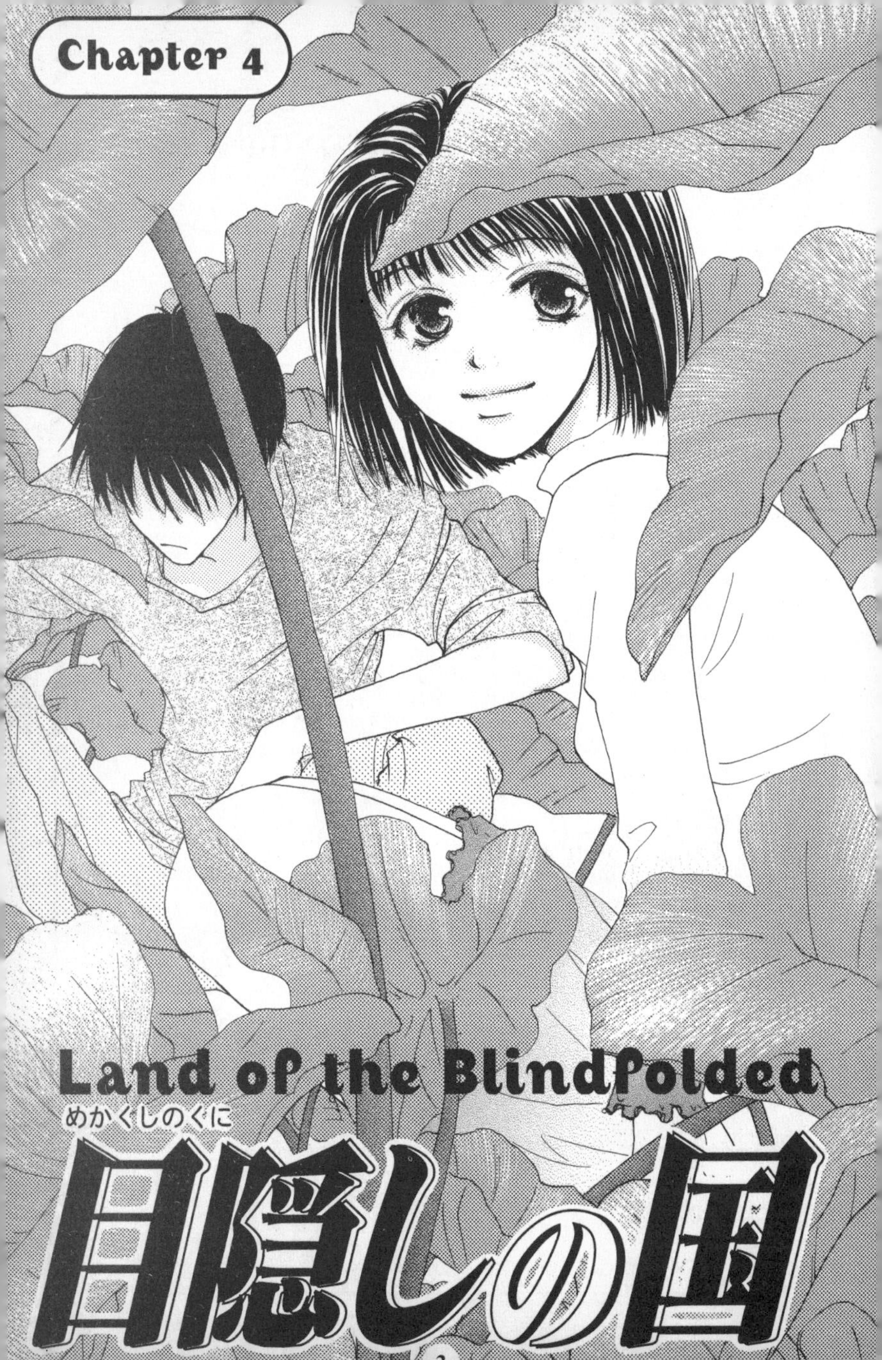
Chapter 4
Land of the Blindfolded
めかくしのくに
目隠しの国

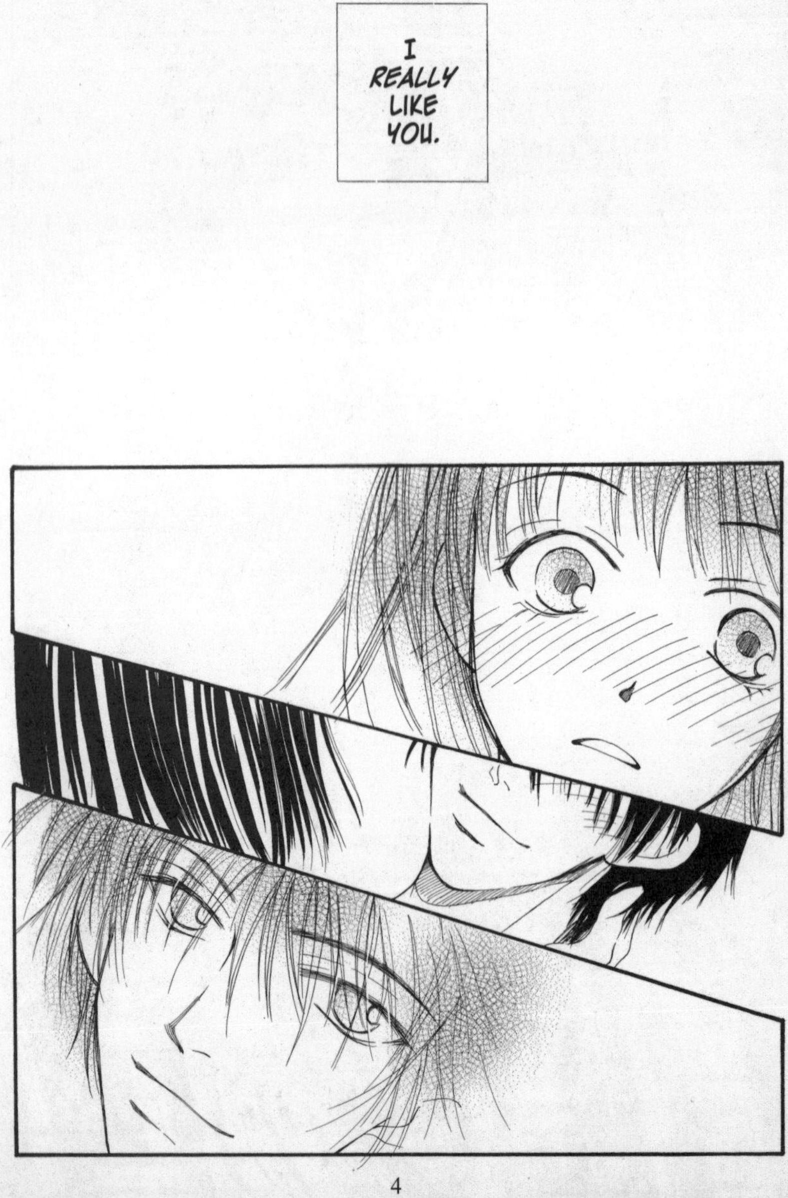
I REALLY LIKE YOU.

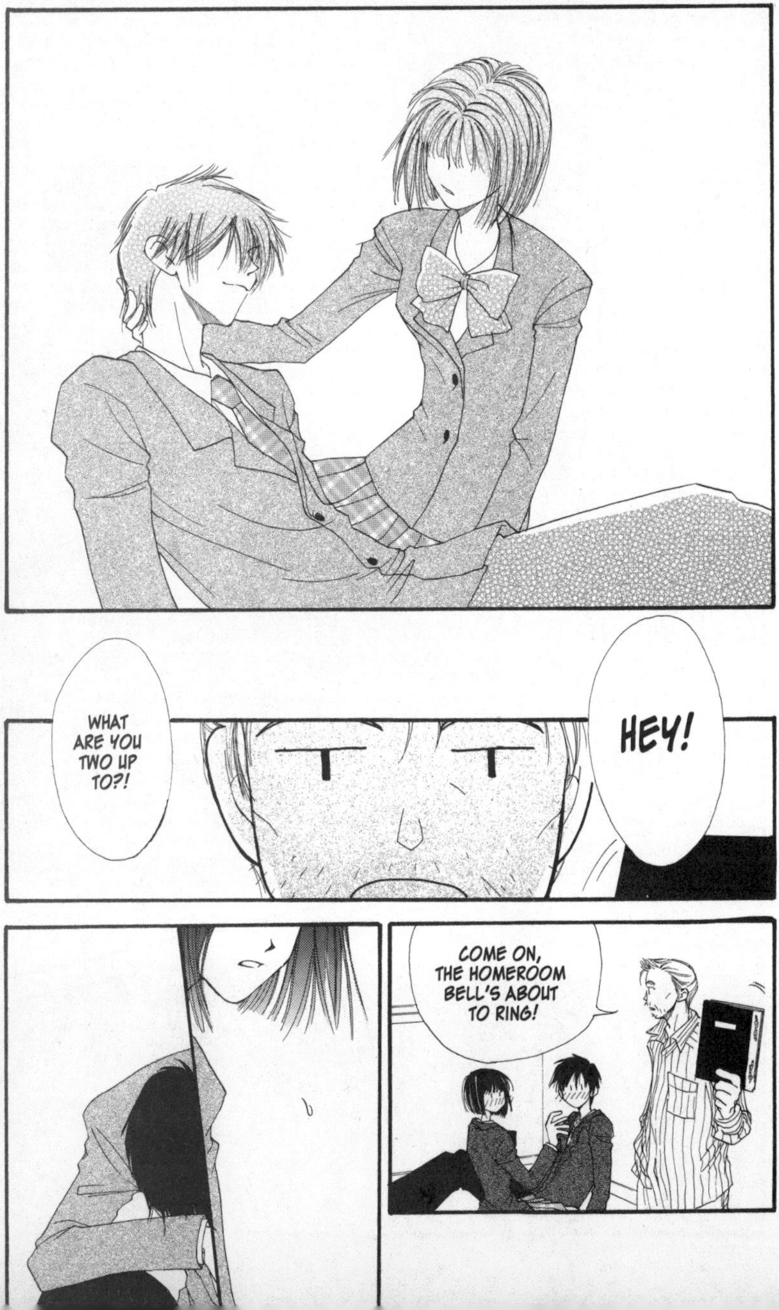
HEY!
WHAT ARE YOU TWO UP TO?!
COME ON, THE HOMEROOM BELL'S ABOUT TO RING!

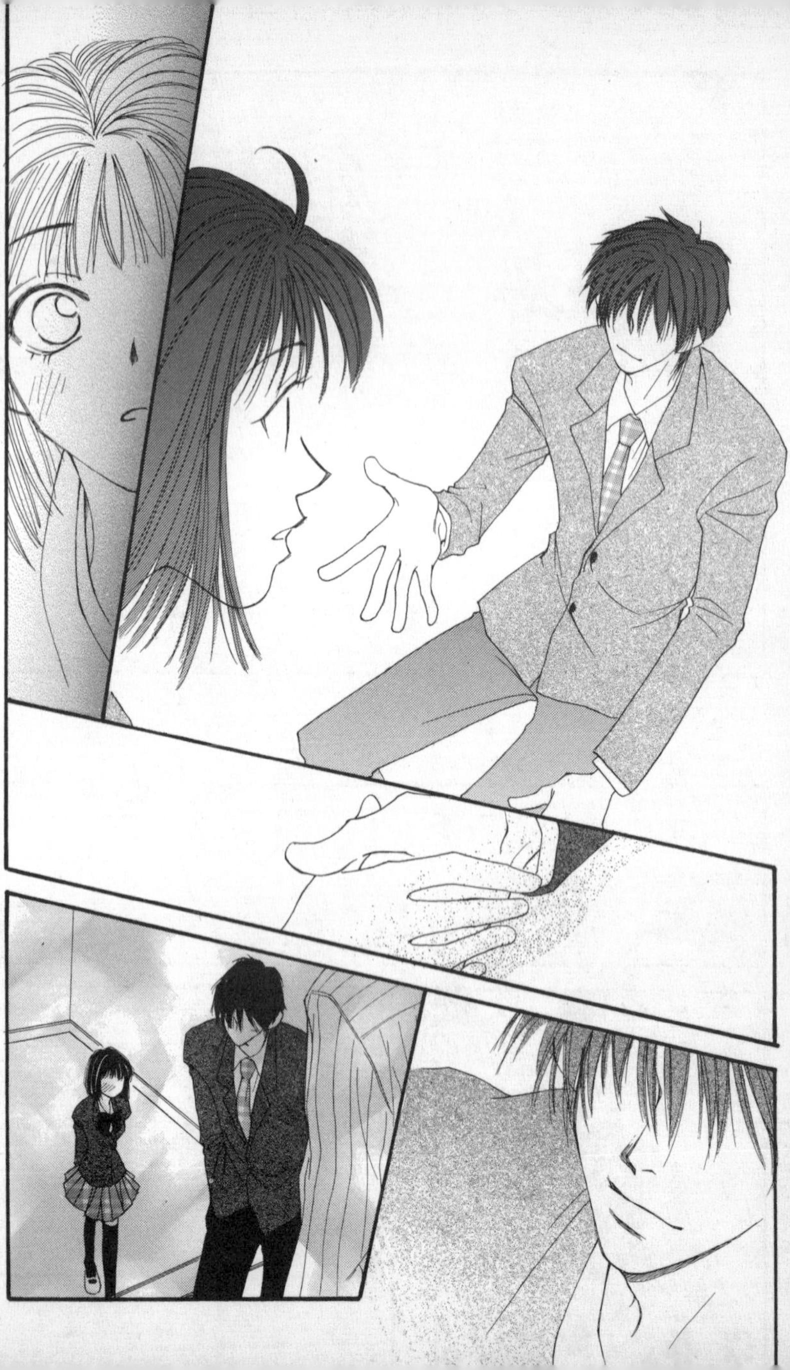

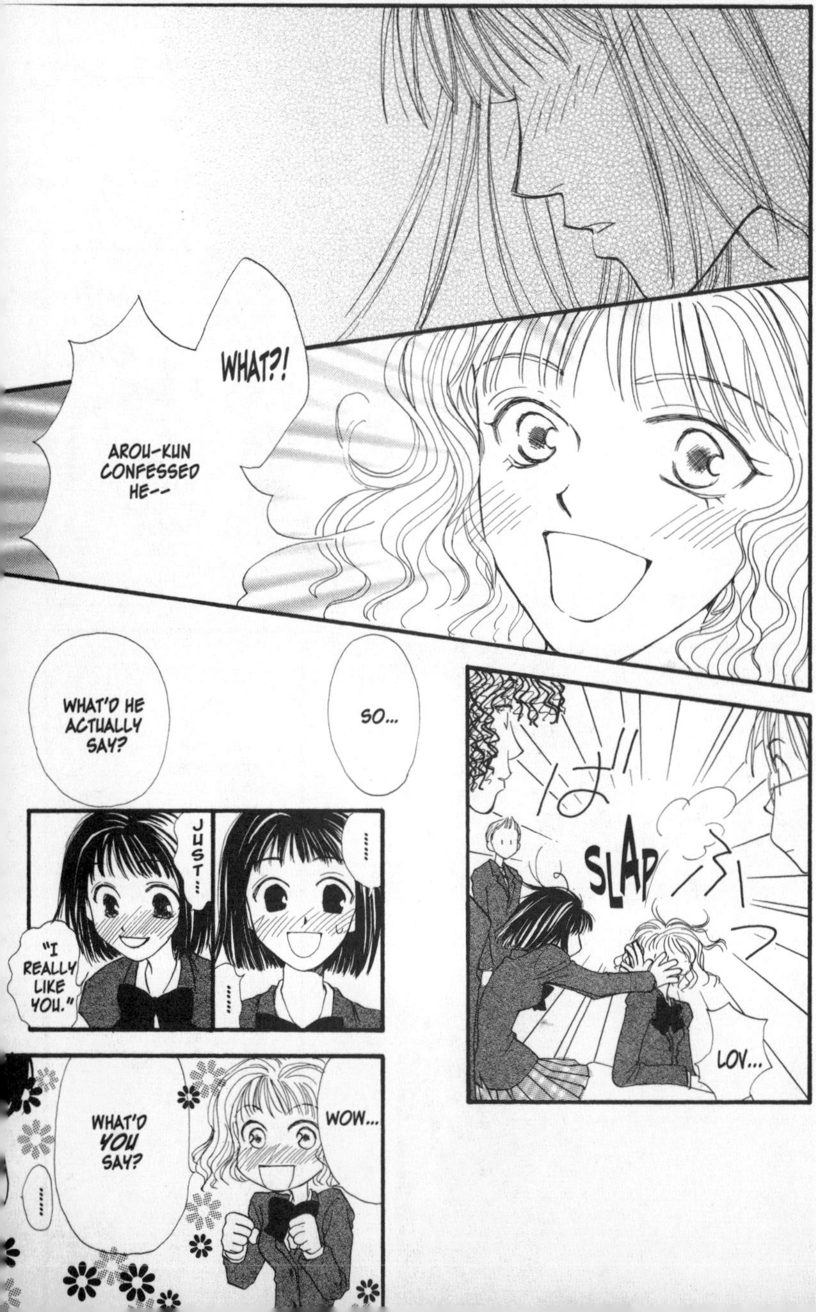
WHAT?!
AROU-KUN CONFESSED HE--
SLAP
LOV...
SO...
WHAT'D HE ACTUALLY SAY?
.....
.....
JUST...
"I REALLY LIKE YOU."
WOW...
WHAT'D *YOU* SAY?
.....

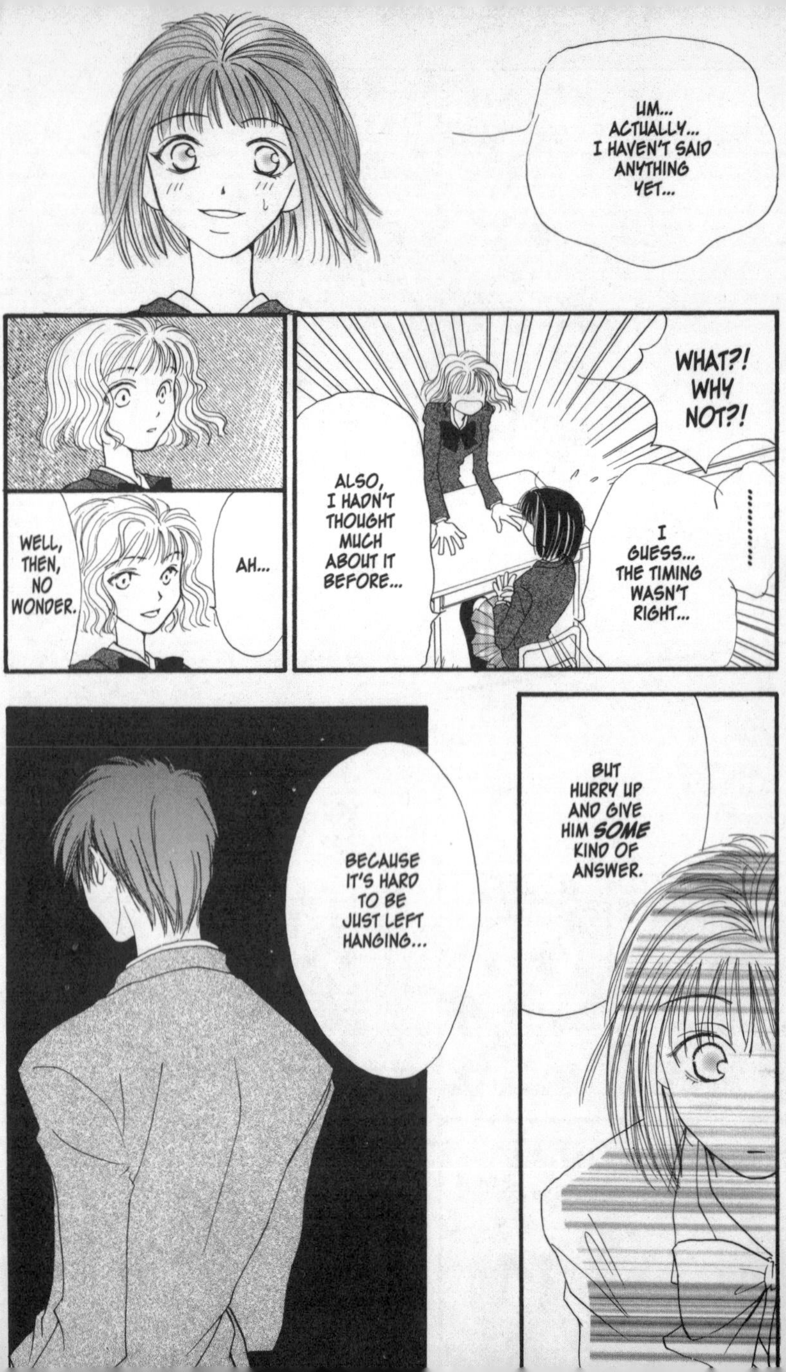
UM... ACTUALLY... I HAVEN'T SAID ANYTHING YET...
WHAT?! WHY NOT?!
......
I GUESS... THE TIMING WASN'T RIGHT...
ALSO, I HADN'T THOUGHT MUCH ABOUT IT BEFORE...
AH...
WELL, THEN, NO WONDER.
BUT HURRY UP AND GIVE HIM *SOME* KIND OF ANSWER.
BECAUSE IT'S HARD TO BE JUST LEFT HANGING...

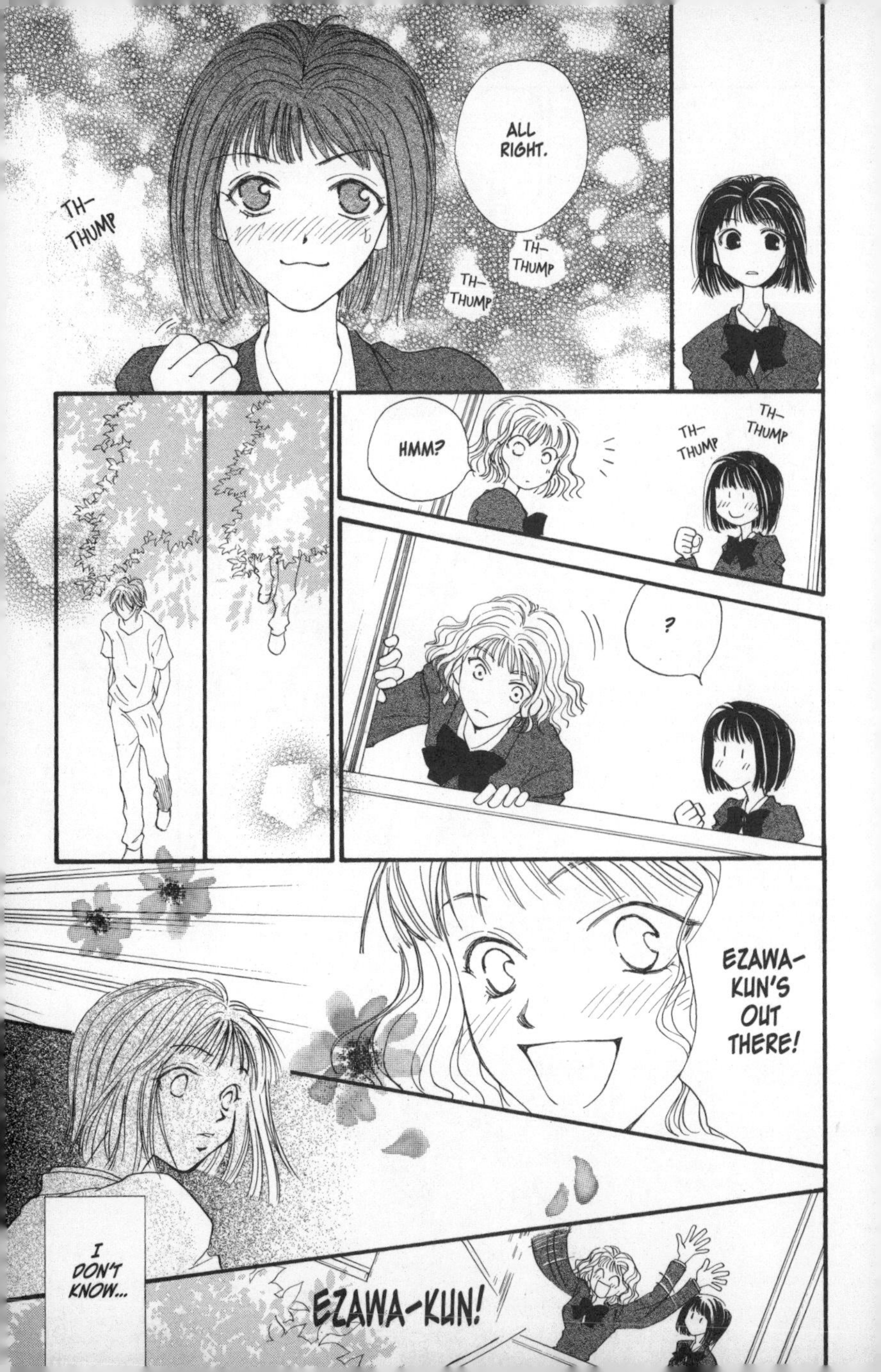

ALL RIGHT.
TH-THUMP
TH-THUMP
TH-THUMP
TH-THUMP
TH-THUMP
HMM?
?
EZAWA-KUN'S OUT THERE!
I DON'T KNOW...
EZAWA-KUN!

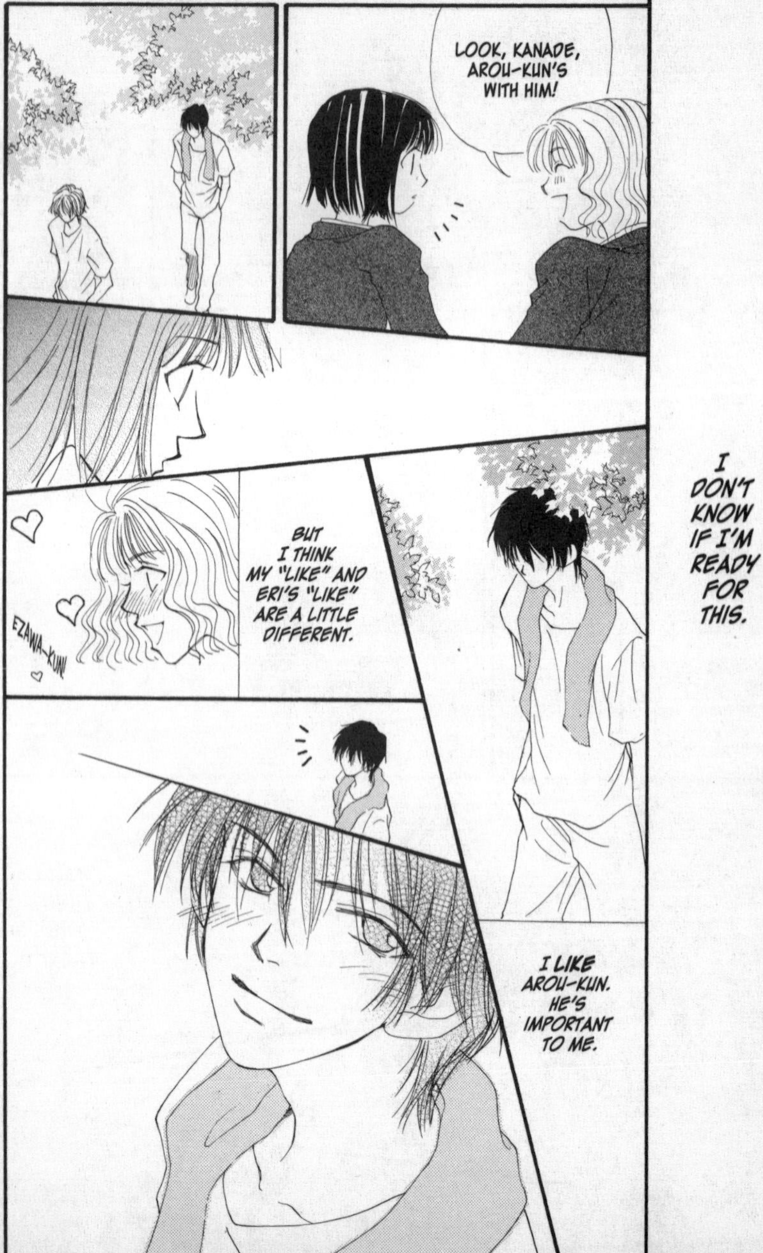
LOOK, KANADE, AROU-KUN'S WITH HIM!
I DON'T KNOW IF I'M READY FOR THIS.
BUT I THINK MY "LIKE" AND ERI'S "LIKE" ARE A LITTLE DIFFERENT.
EZAWA-KUN!
I LIKE AROU-KUN. HE'S IMPORTANT TO ME.

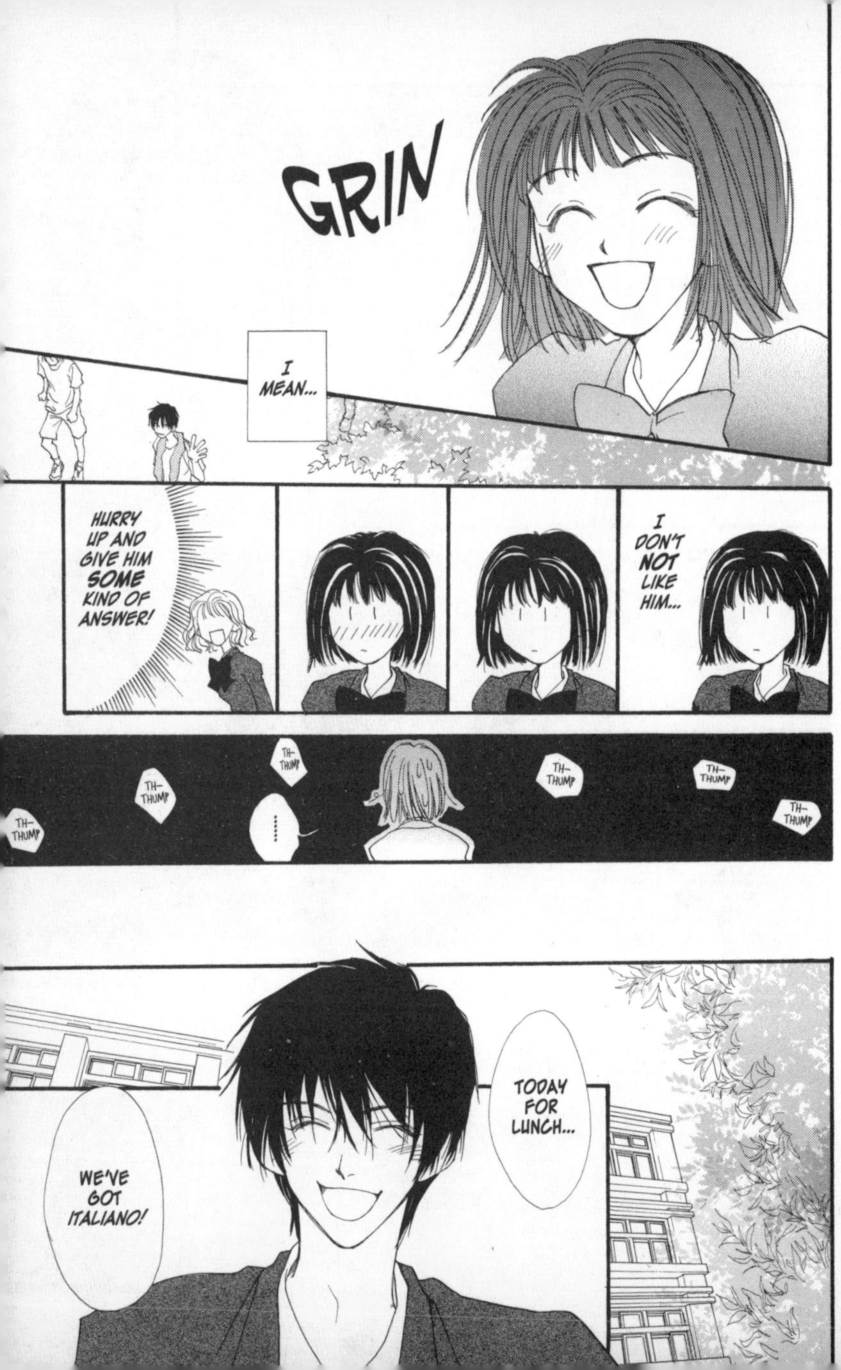
GRIN
I MEAN...
I DON'T NOT LIKE HIM...
HURRY UP AND GIVE HIM SOME KIND OF ANSWER!
TH-THUMP
TH-THUMP
TH-THUMP
TH-THUMP
......
TH-THUMP
TH-THUMP
TODAY FOR LUNCH...
WE'VE GOT ITALIANO!

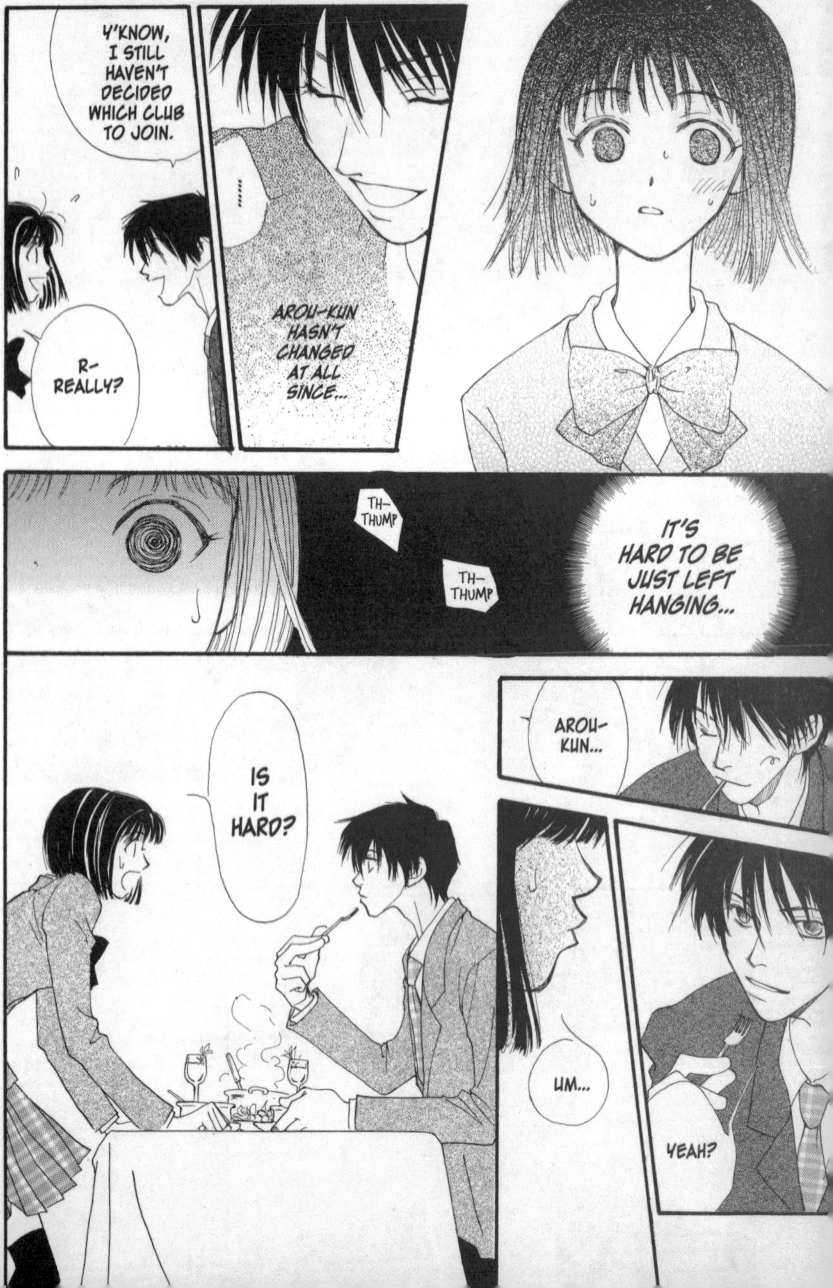
......
AROU-KUN HASN'T CHANGED AT ALL SINCE...
Y'KNOW, I STILL HAVEN'T DECIDED WHICH CLUB TO JOIN.
R-REALLY?
IT'S HARD TO BE JUST LEFT HANGING...
TH-THUMP
TH-THUMP
AROU-KUN...
YEAH?
UM...
IS IT HARD?

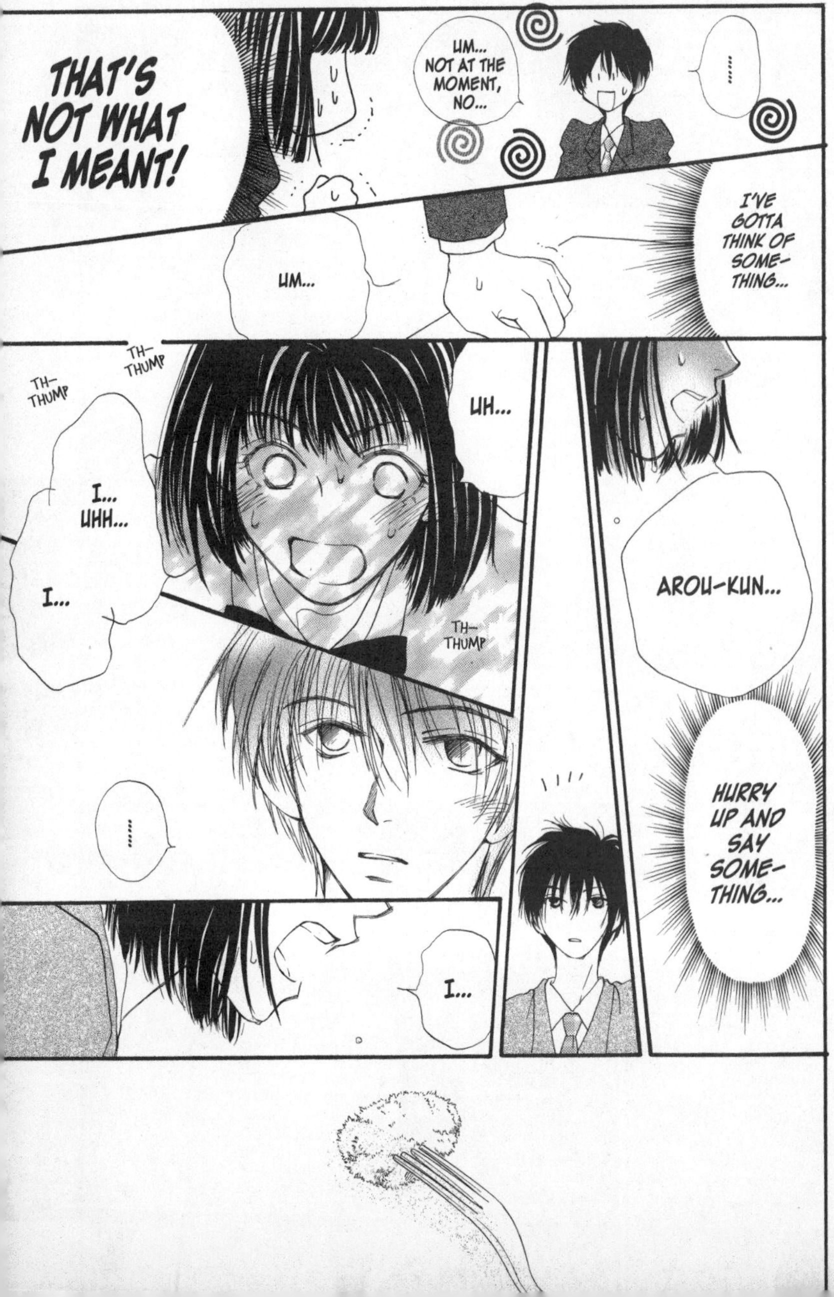
......
UM... NOT AT THE MOMENT, NO...
THAT'S NOT WHAT I MEANT!
I'VE GOTTA THINK OF SOME-THING...
UM...
AROU-KUN...
HURRY UP AND SAY SOME-THING...
TH-THUMP
TH-THUMP
UH...
I... UHH...
I...
TH-THUMP
......
I...

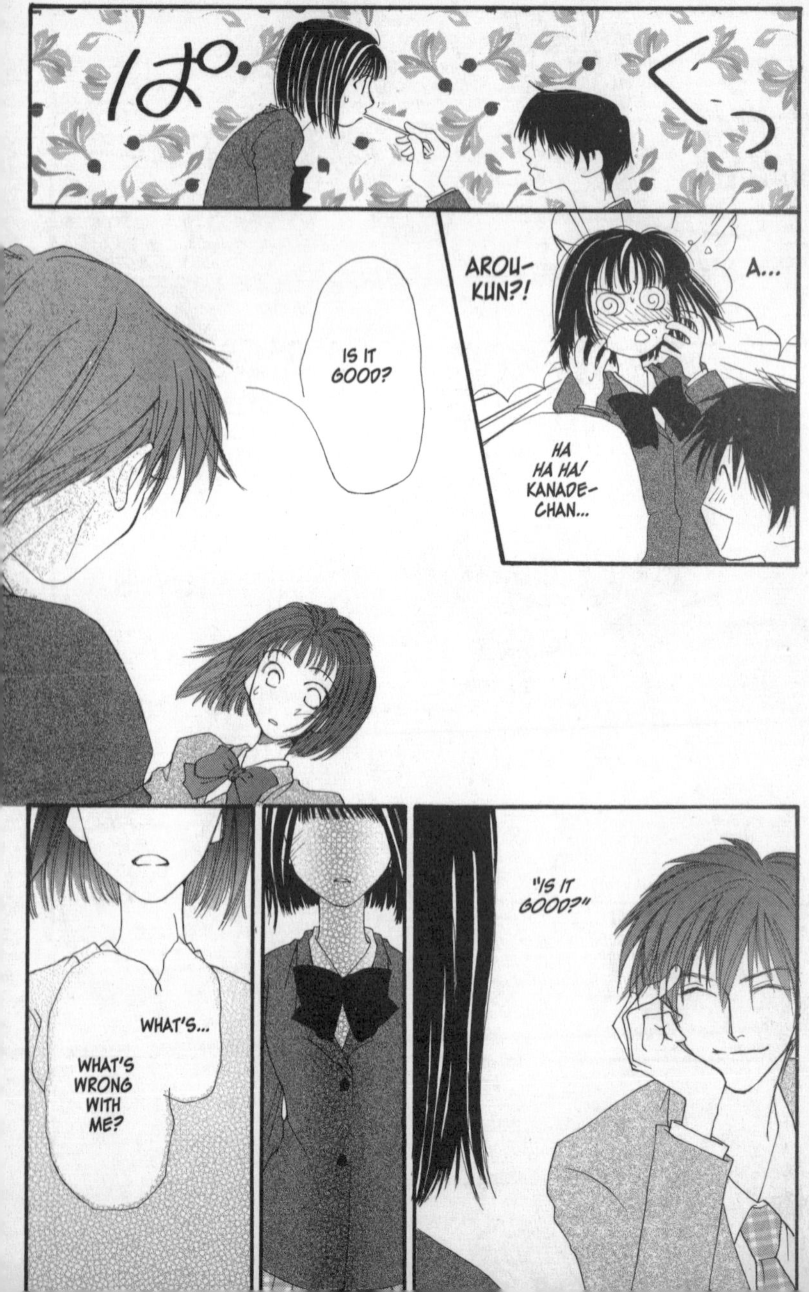
ぱくっ
A...
AROU-KUN?!
HA HA HA! KANADE-CHAN...
IS IT GOOD?
"IS IT GOOD?"
WHAT'S...
WHAT'S WRONG WITH ME?

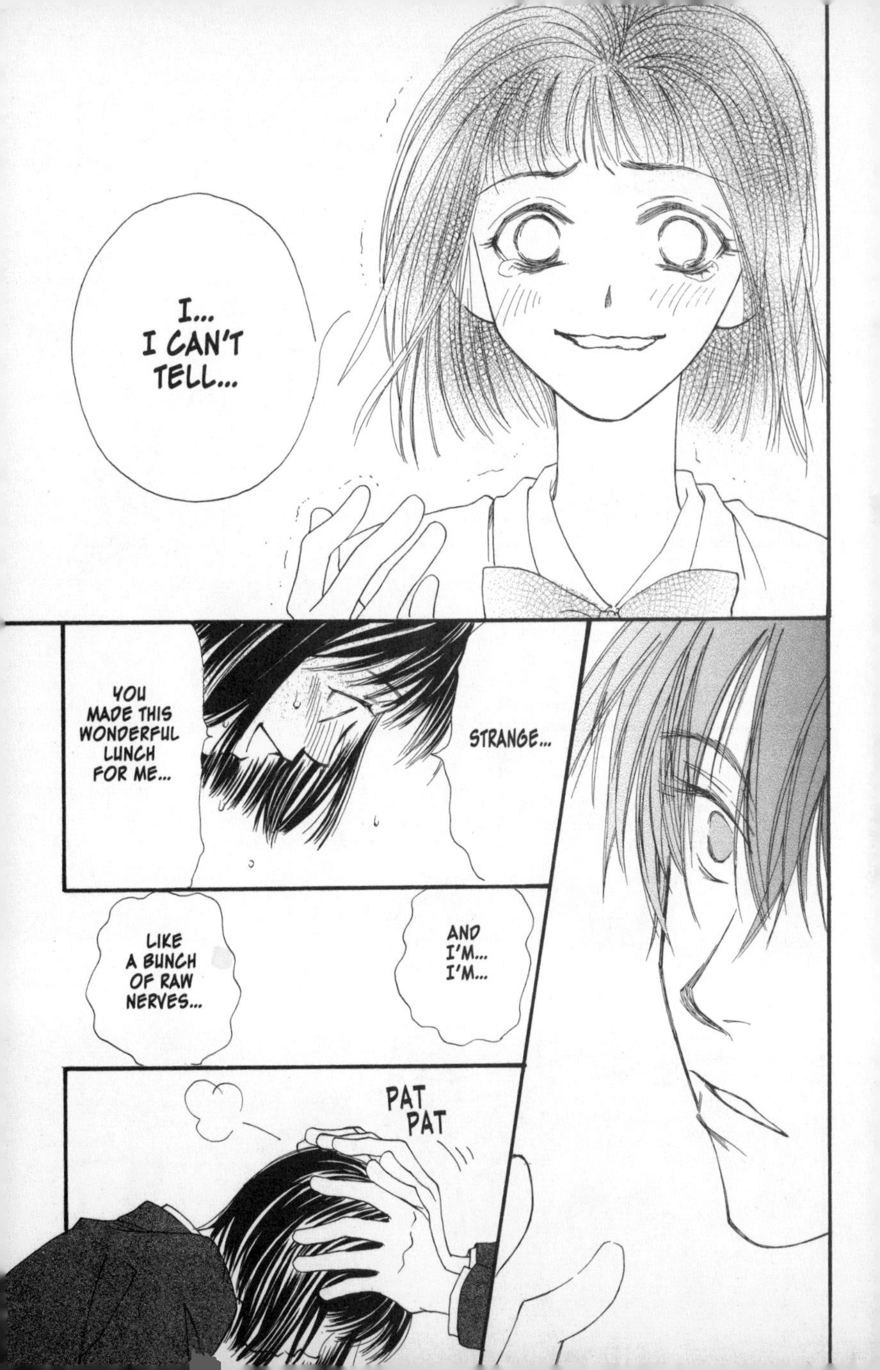
I... I CAN'T TELL...
STRANGE...
YOU MADE THIS WONDERFUL LUNCH FOR ME...
AND I'M... I'M...
LIKE A BUNCH OF RAW NERVES...
PAT PAT

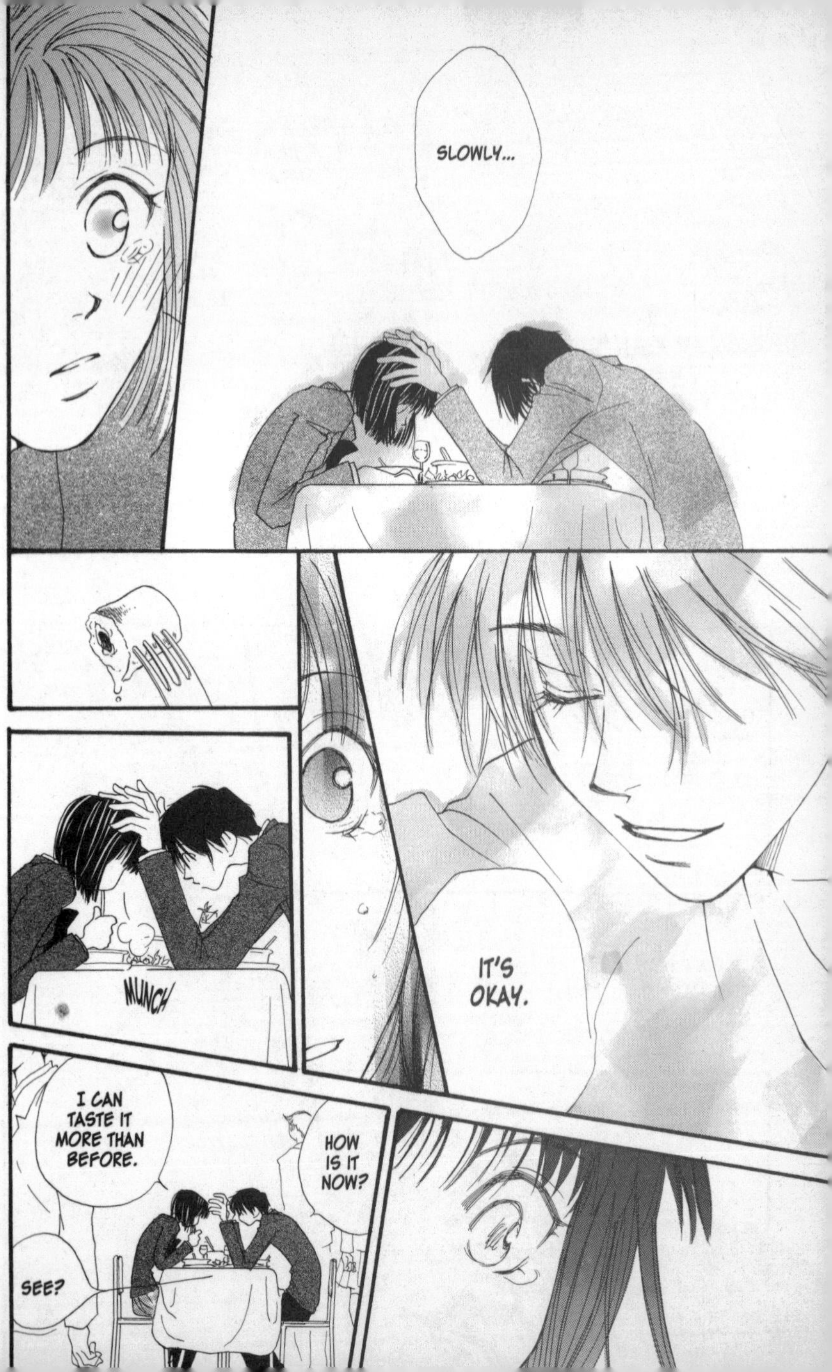
SLOWLY...
IT'S OKAY.
MUNCH
HOW IS IT NOW?
I CAN TASTE IT MORE THAN BEFORE.
SEE?

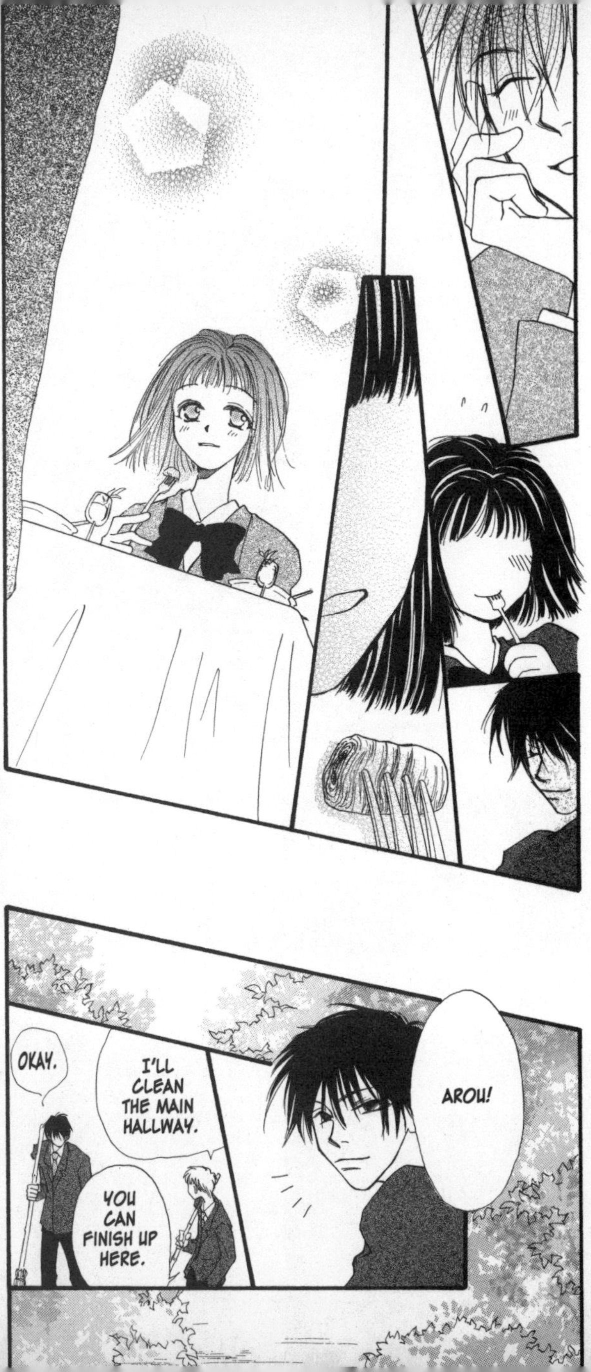
AROU!
I'LL CLEAN THE MAIN HALLWAY.
OKAY.
YOU CAN FINISH UP HERE.

1/4 Sakura Mail

その1

This episode is the first one I've ever written that's been continued from the previous story. Kind of makes me feel privileged to be allowed to write a "continuing series." (Thank you!) As one way of showing my appreciation, I thought I'd better flesh out Arou-kun's character more... so "flesh him out" I did, and I had a wickedly fun time drawing it for this story. Gasp!

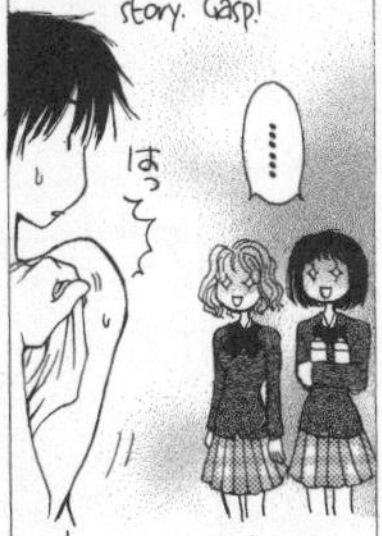
はっ
......

Of course, I took care to make sure his chest-baring fit in with the flow of the story, but... (I didn't just do it because I have a dirty mind, did I?!) Anyway, this is one of those times where I got to project both my own feelings and "interests" onto the story. I feel ashamed and pleased with myself at the same time.

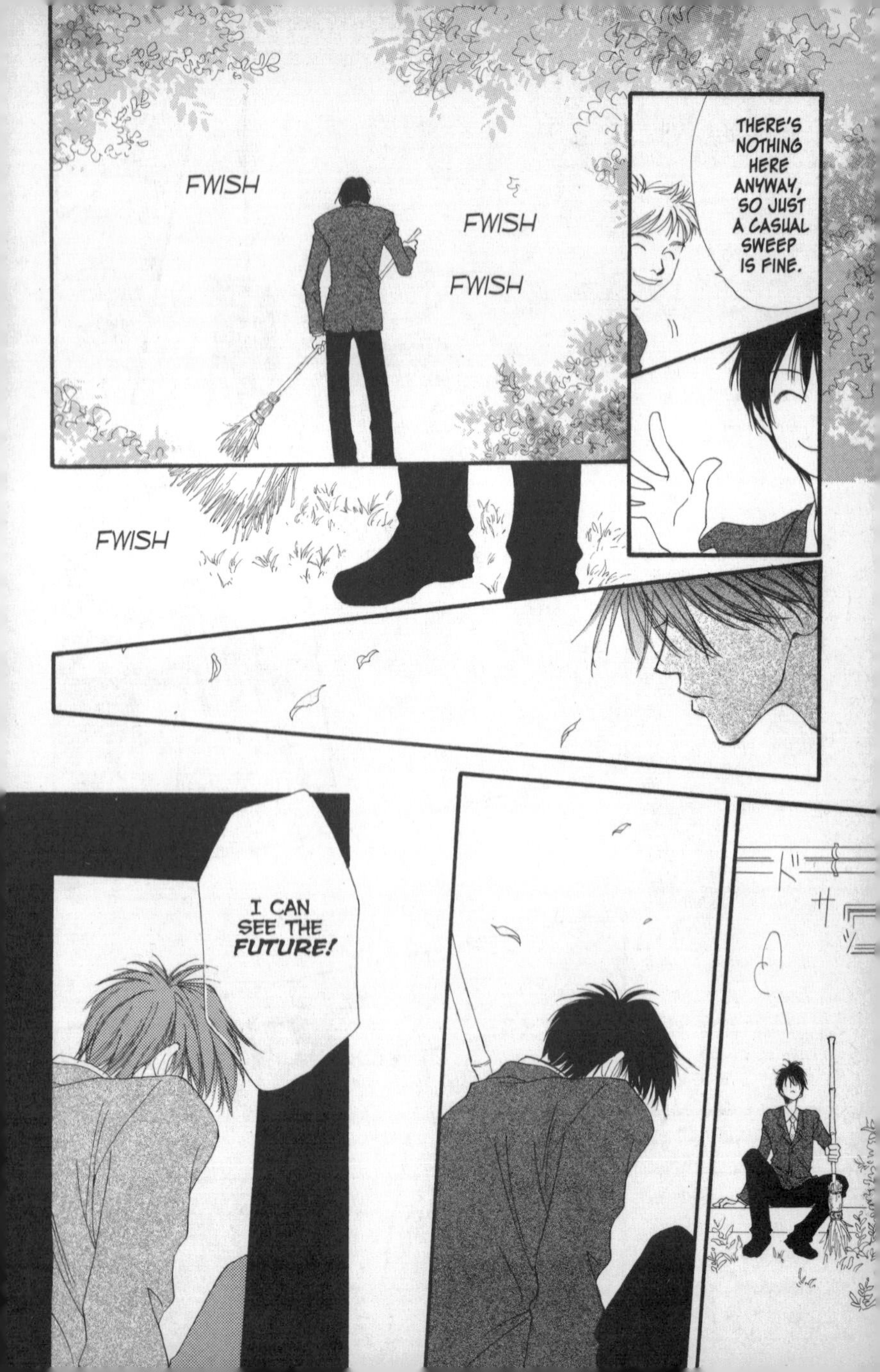
THERE'S NOTHING HERE ANYWAY, SO JUST A CASUAL SWEEP IS FINE.
FWISH
FWISH
FWISH
FWISH
I CAN SEE THE *FUTURE!*

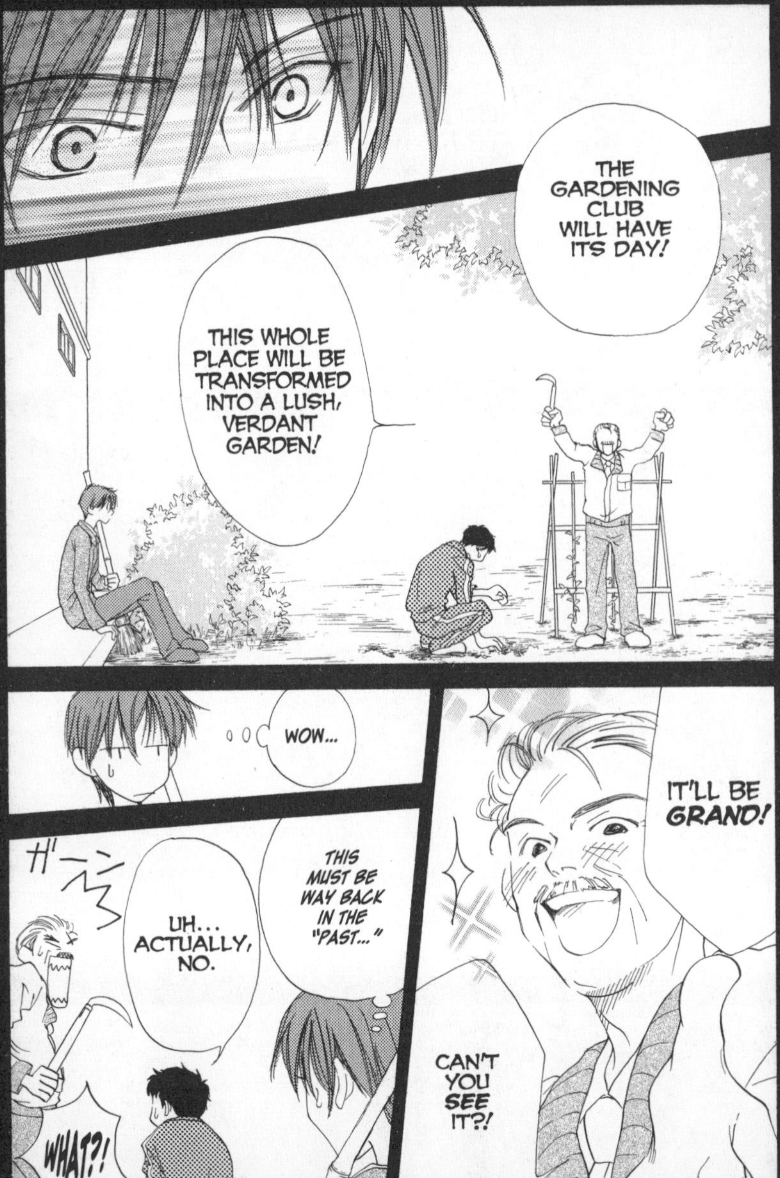
THE GARDENING CLUB WILL HAVE ITS DAY!
THIS WHOLE PLACE WILL BE TRANSFORMED INTO A LUSH, VERDANT GARDEN!
IT'LL BE GRAND!
CAN'T YOU SEE IT?!
WOW...
THIS MUST BE WAY BACK IN THE "PAST..."
UH... ACTUALLY, NO.
ガーン
WHAT?!

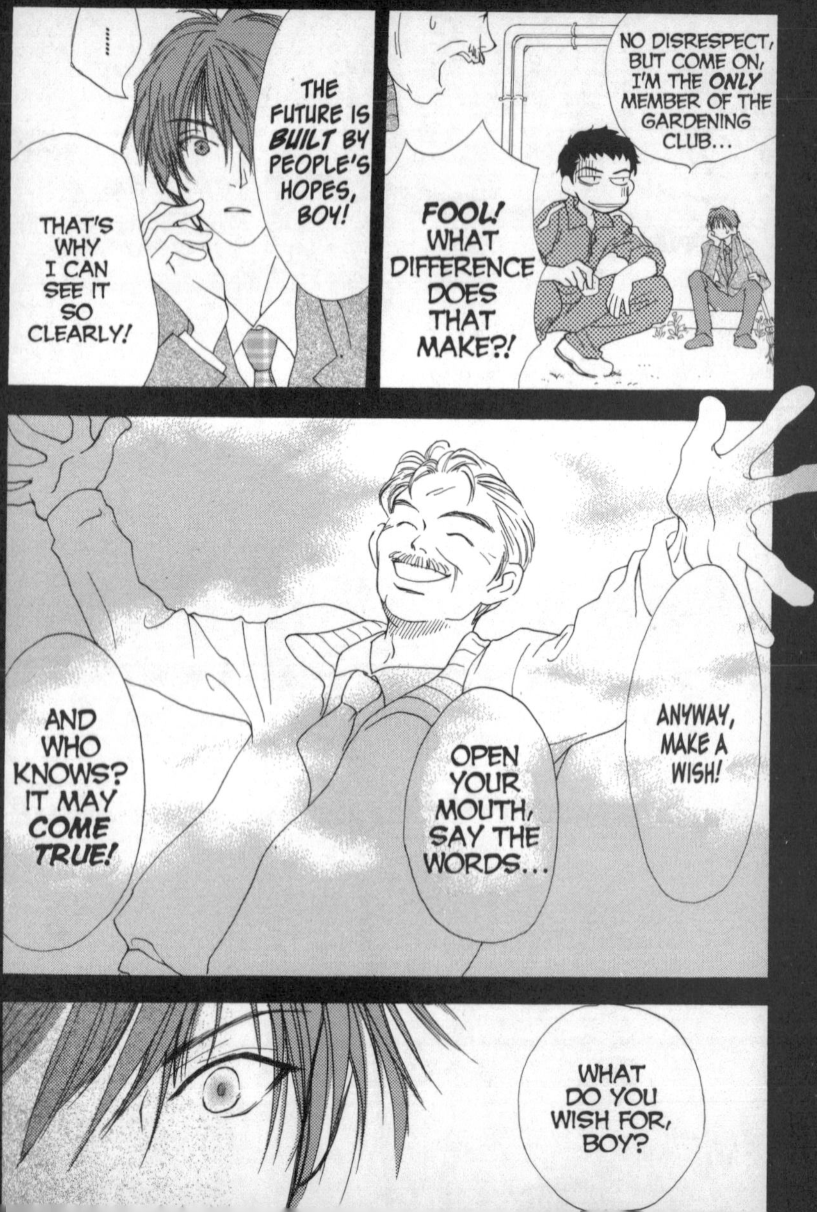
NO DISRESPECT, BUT COME ON, I'M THE ONLY MEMBER OF THE GARDENING CLUB...
FOOL! WHAT DIFFERENCE DOES THAT MAKE?!
THE FUTURE IS BUILT BY PEOPLE'S HOPES, BOY!
......
THAT'S WHY I CAN SEE IT SO CLEARLY!
ANYWAY, MAKE A WISH!
OPEN YOUR MOUTH, SAY THE WORDS...
AND WHO KNOWS? IT MAY COME TRUE!
WHAT DO YOU WISH FOR, BOY?

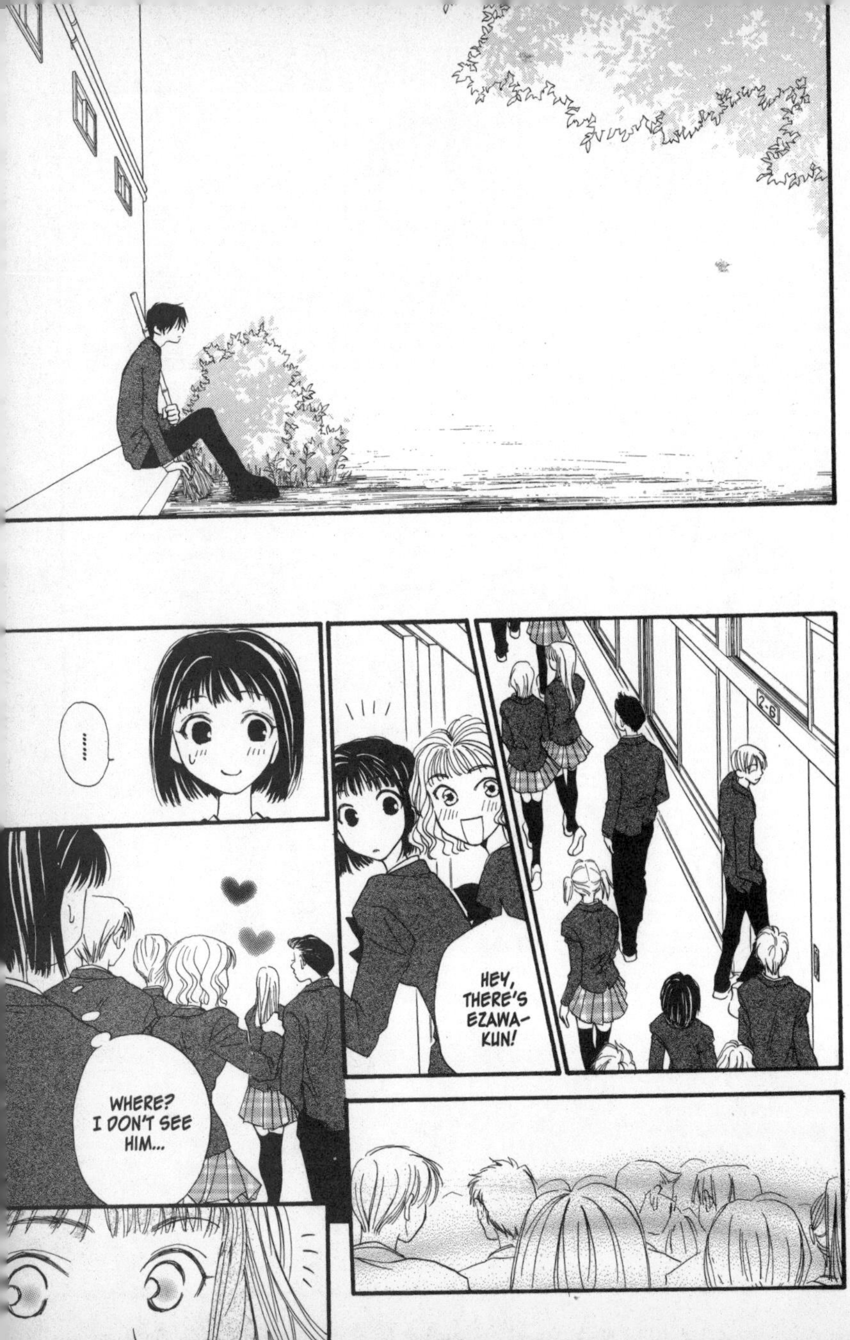
HEY, THERE'S EZAWA-KUN!
......
WHERE? I DON'T SEE HIM...

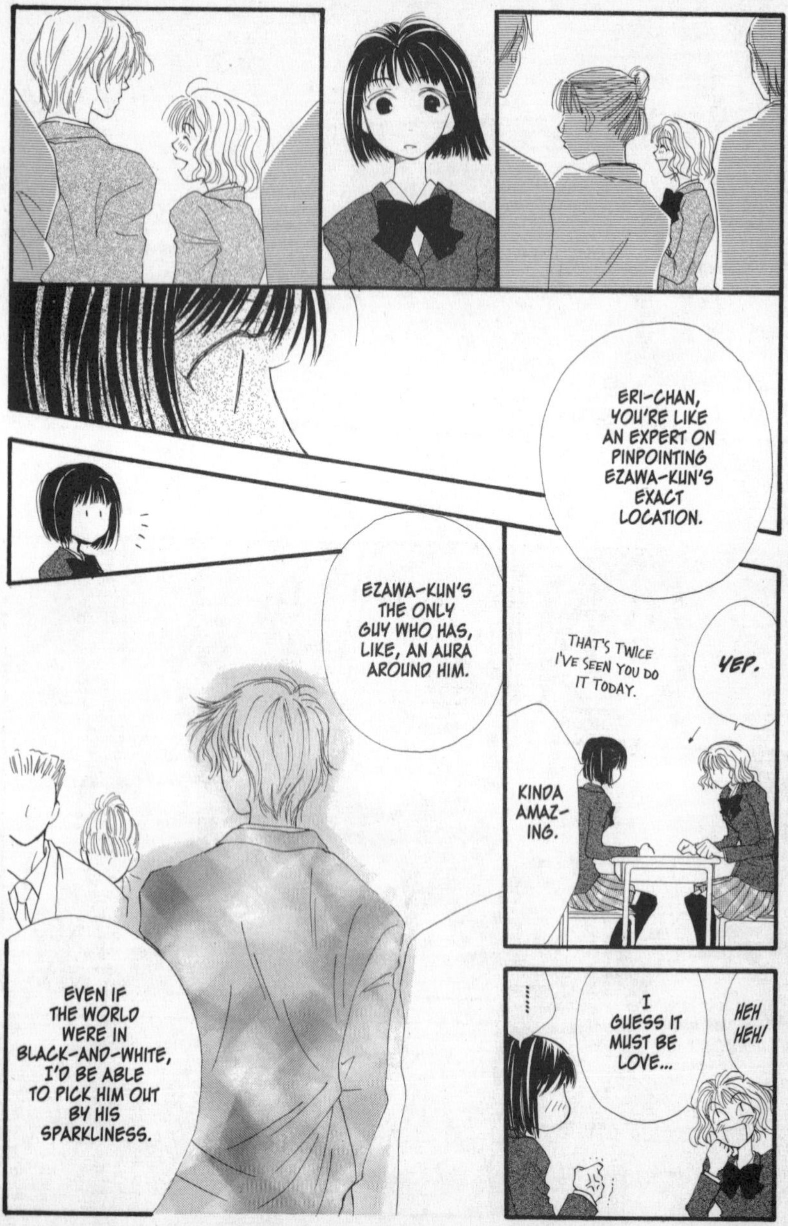
ERI-CHAN, YOU'RE LIKE AN EXPERT ON PINPOINTING EZAWA-KUN'S EXACT LOCATION.
YEP.
THAT'S TWICE I'VE SEEN YOU DO IT TODAY.
KINDA AMAZ-ING.
EZAWA-KUN'S THE ONLY GUY WHO HAS, LIKE, AN AURA AROUND HIM.
EVEN IF THE WORLD WERE IN BLACK-AND-WHITE, I'D BE ABLE TO PICK HIM OUT BY HIS SPARKLINESS.
I GUESS IT MUST BE LOVE...
HEH HEH!
......

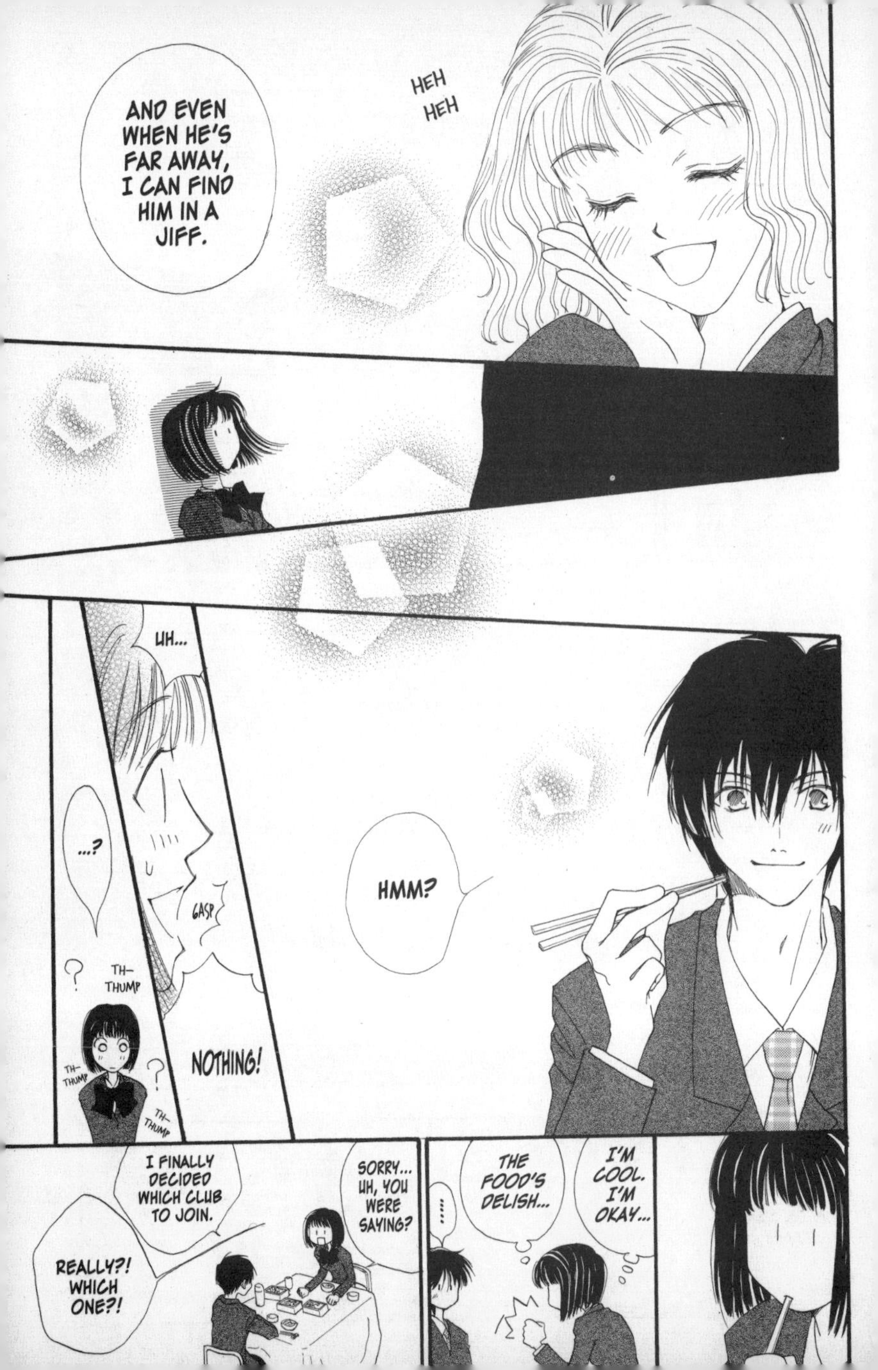
HEH HEH
AND EVEN WHEN HE'S FAR AWAY, I CAN FIND HIM IN A JIFF.
HMM?
UH...
GASP
NOTHING!
...?
TH-THUMP
TH-THUMP
TH-THUMP
I'M COOL. I'M OKAY...
THE FOOD'S DELISH...
....
SORRY... UH, YOU WERE SAYING?
I FINALLY DECIDED WHICH CLUB TO JOIN.
REALLY?! WHICH ONE?!

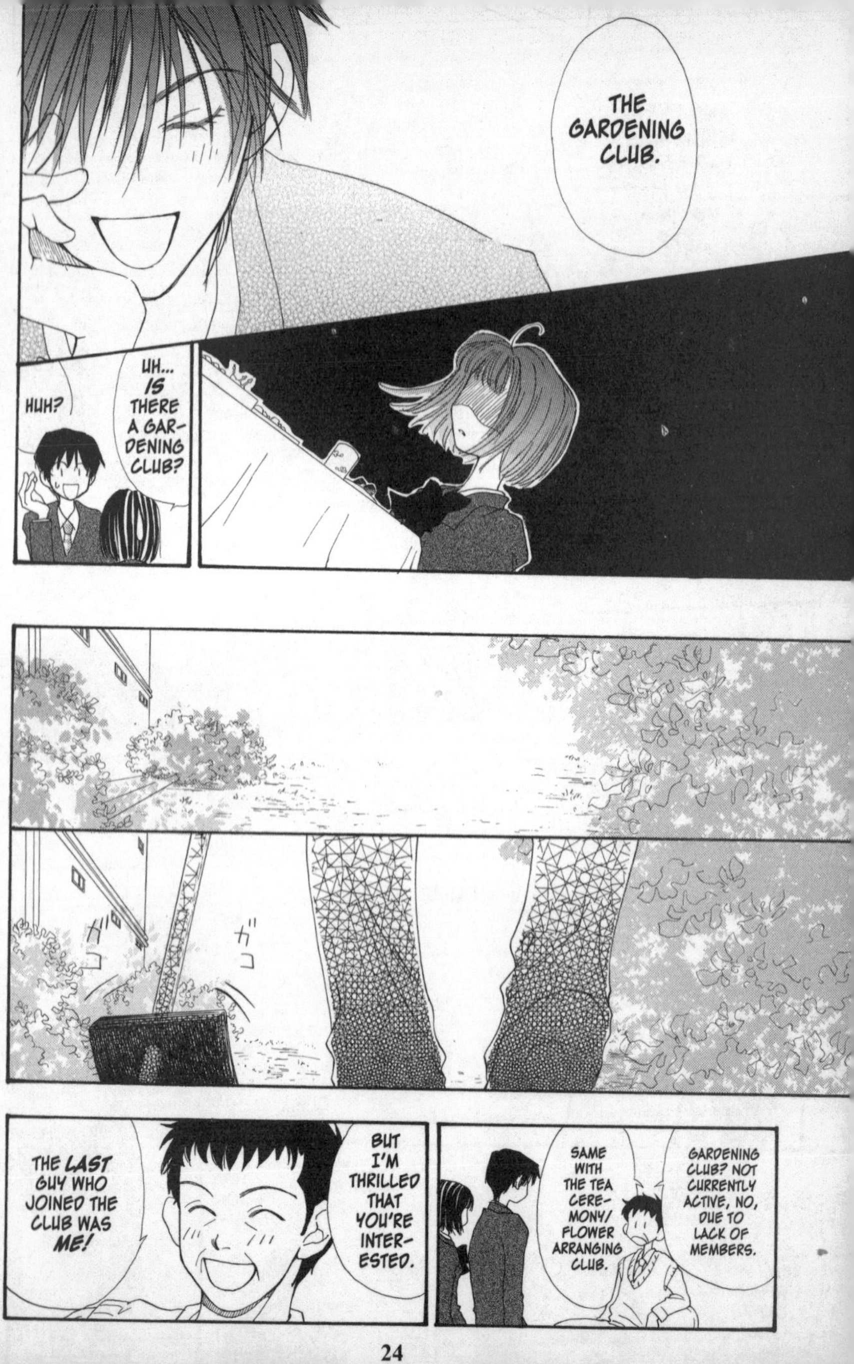
THE GARDENING CLUB.
UH... *IS* THERE A GARDENING CLUB?
HUH?
ガコ
ガコ
GARDENING CLUB? NOT CURRENTLY ACTIVE, NO, DUE TO LACK OF MEMBERS.
SAME WITH THE TEA CEREMONY/ FLOWER ARRANGING CLUB.
BUT I'M THRILLED THAT YOU'RE INTERESTED.
THE *LAST* GUY WHO JOINED THE CLUB WAS *ME!*

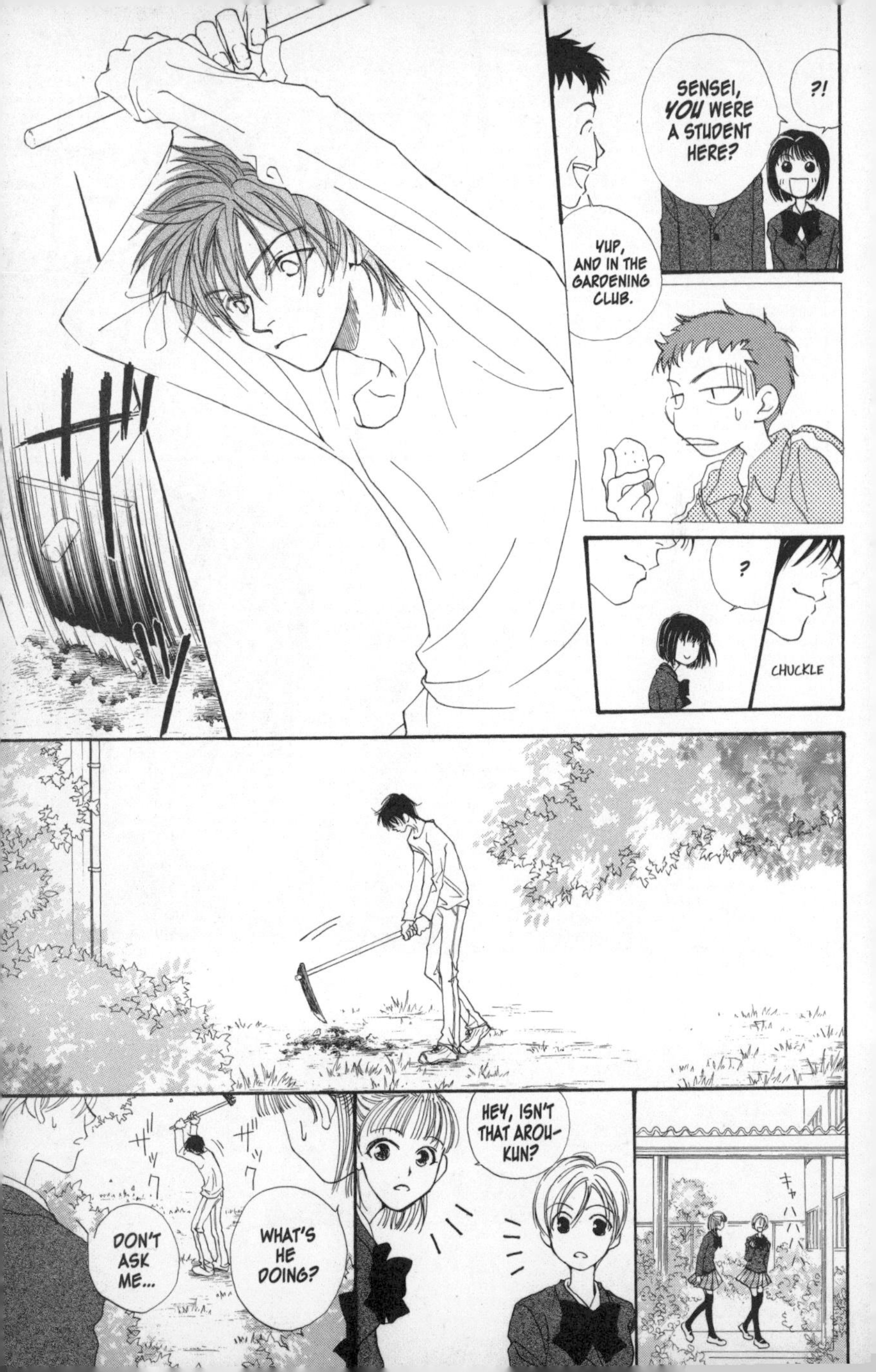
?!
SENSEI, YOU WERE A STUDENT HERE?
YUP, AND IN THE GARDENING CLUB.
?
CHUCKLE
キャハハハ
HEY, ISN'T THAT AROU-KUN?
ザック
ザック
WHAT'S HE DOING?
DON'T ASK ME...

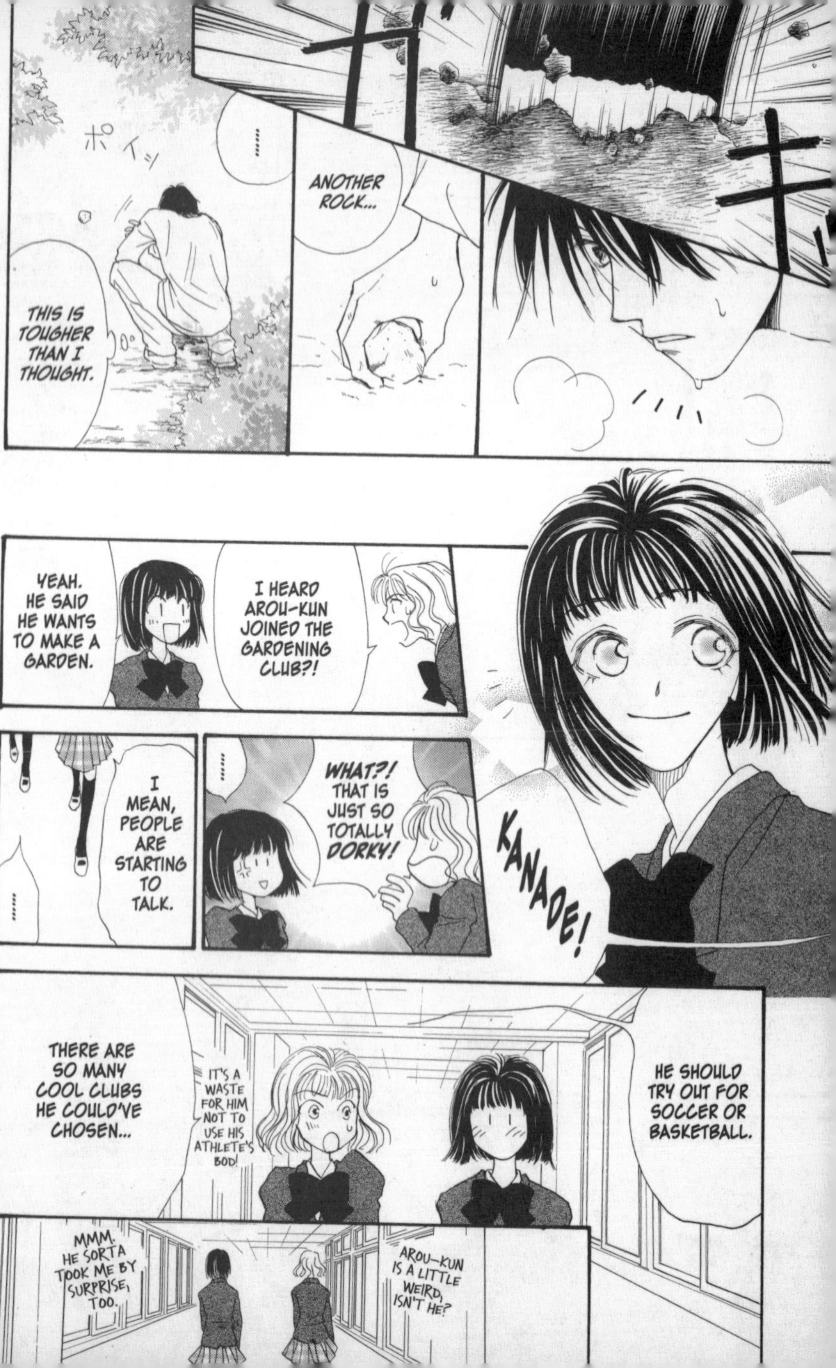
ガキッ
......
ANOTHER ROCK...
ポイッ
THIS IS TOUGHER THAN I THOUGHT.
KANADE!
I HEARD AROU-KUN JOINED THE GARDENING CLUB?!
YEAH. HE SAID HE WANTS TO MAKE A GARDEN.
......
WHAT?! THAT IS JUST SO TOTALLY DORKY!
I MEAN, PEOPLE ARE STARTING TO TALK.
......
HE SHOULD TRY OUT FOR SOCCER OR BASKETBALL.
IT'S A WASTE FOR HIM NOT TO USE HIS ATHLETE'S BOD!
THERE ARE SO MANY COOL CLUBS HE COULD'VE CHOSEN...
AROU-KUN IS A LITTLE WEIRD, ISN'T HE?
MMM. HE SORTA TOOK ME BY SURPRISE, TOO.

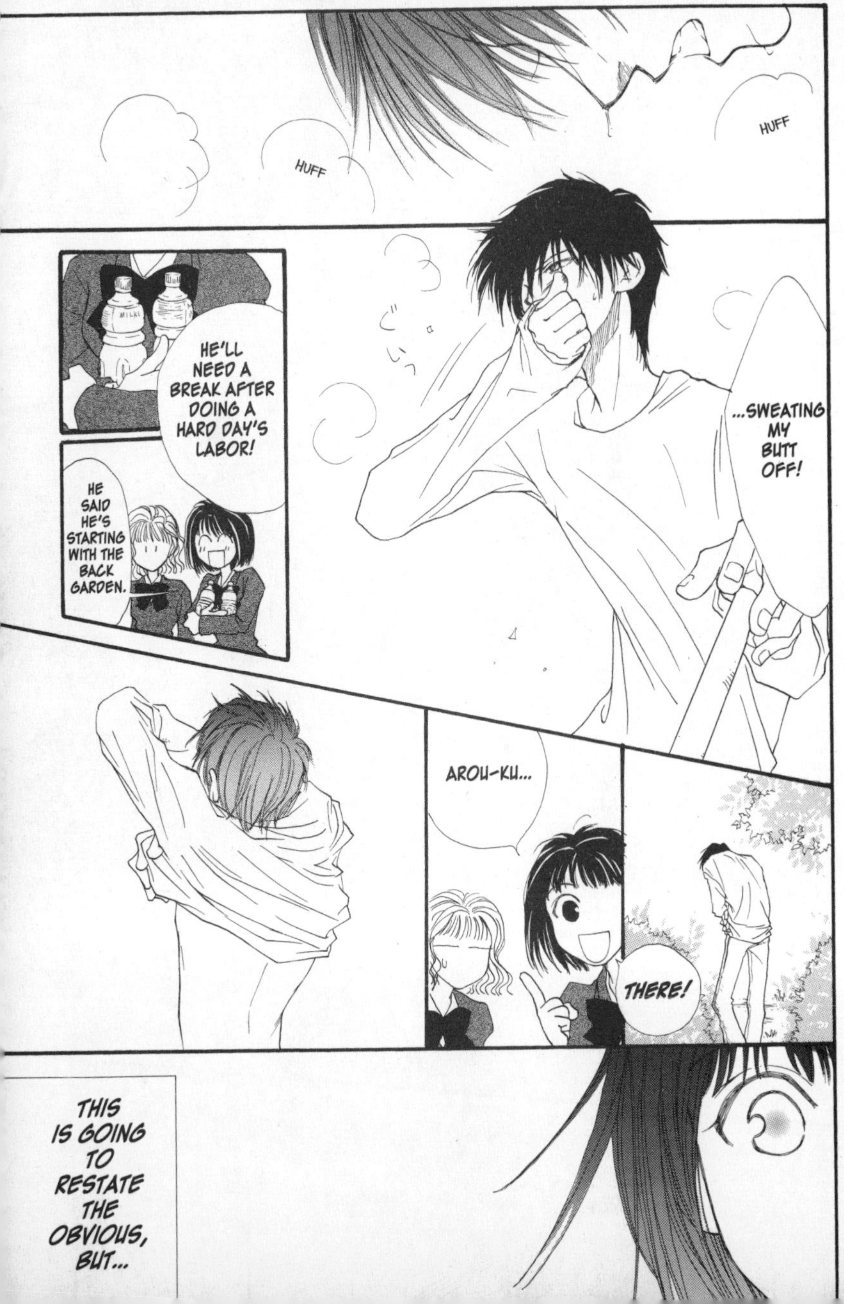
HUFF
HUFF
...SWEATING MY BUTT OFF!
ごしっ
HE'LL NEED A BREAK AFTER DOING A HARD DAY'S LABOR!
HE SAID HE'S STARTING WITH THE BACK GARDEN.
THERE!
AROU-KU...
THIS IS GOING TO RESTATE THE OBVIOUS, BUT...

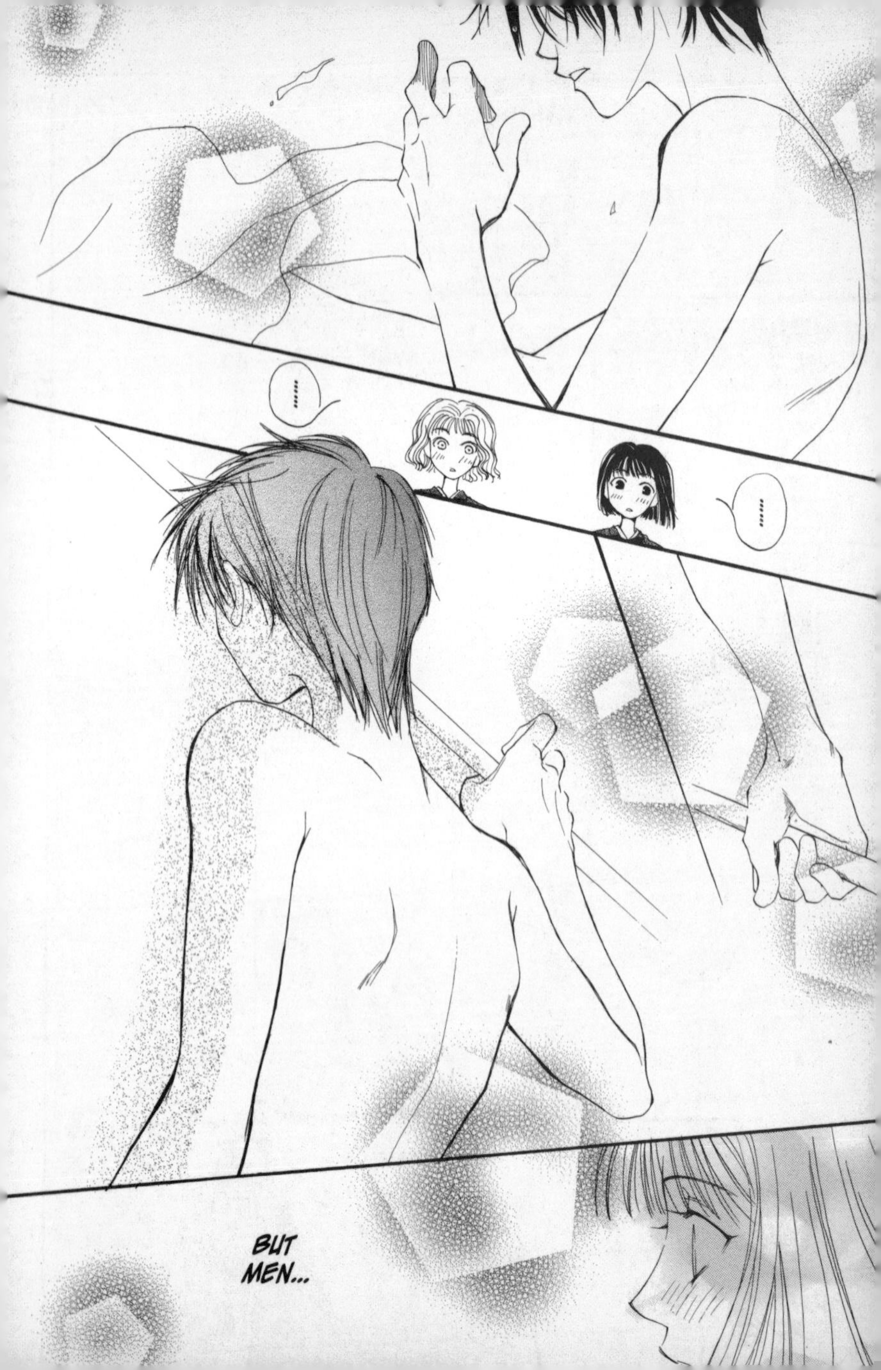
......
......
BUT MEN...

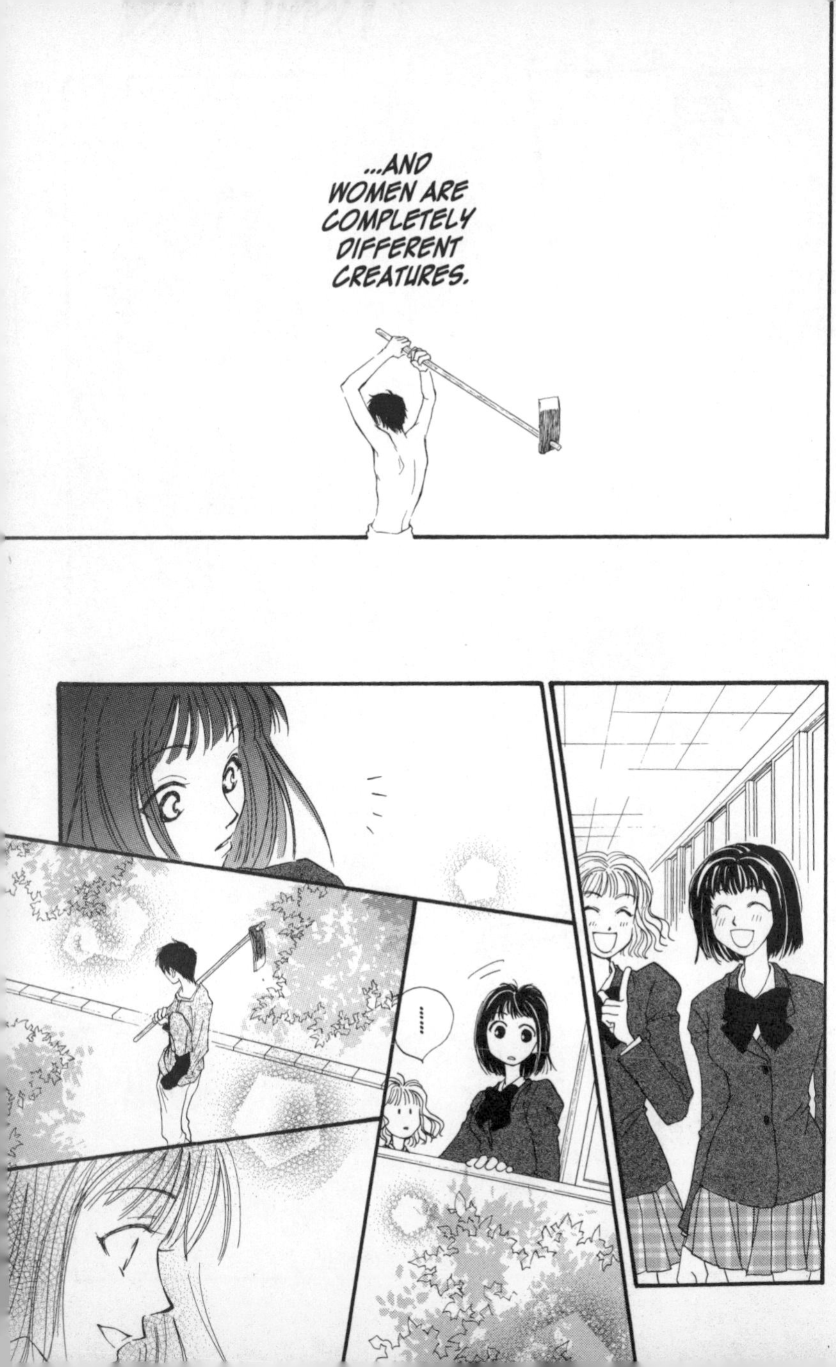
...AND WOMEN ARE COMPLETELY DIFFERENT CREATURES.
......

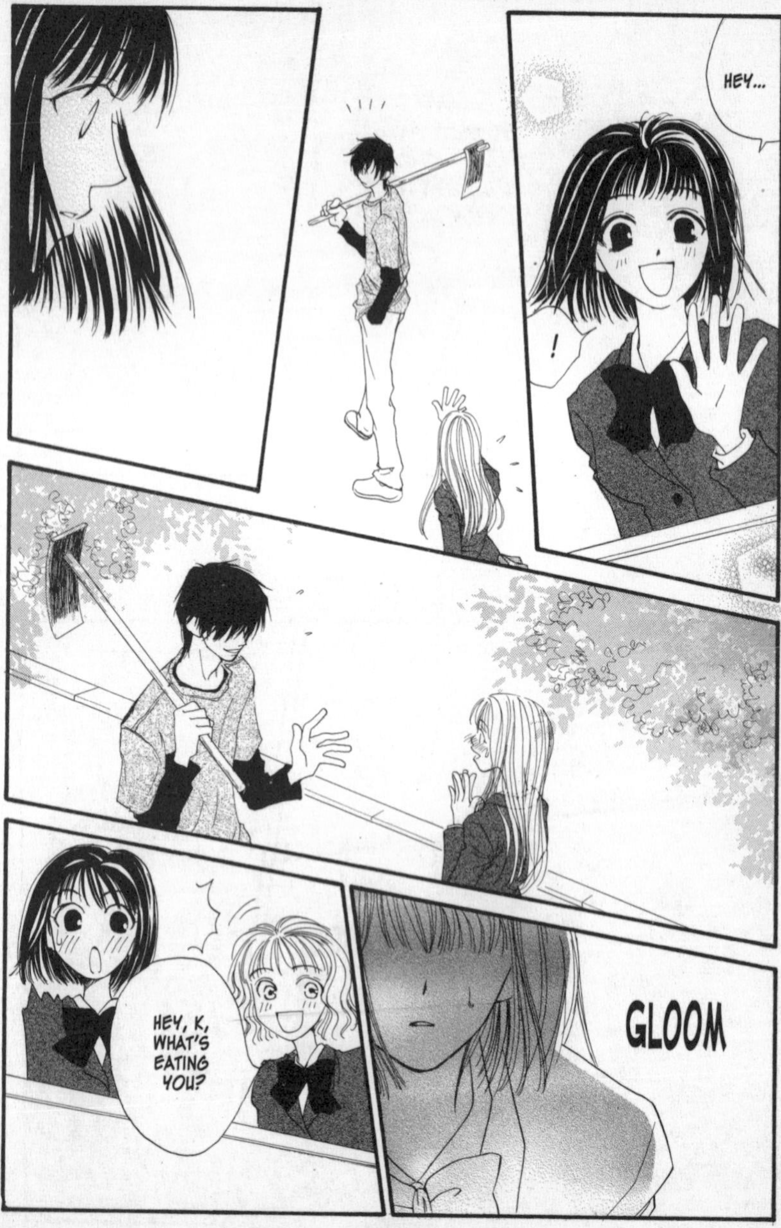
HEY...
!
GLOOM
HEY, K, WHAT'S EATING YOU?

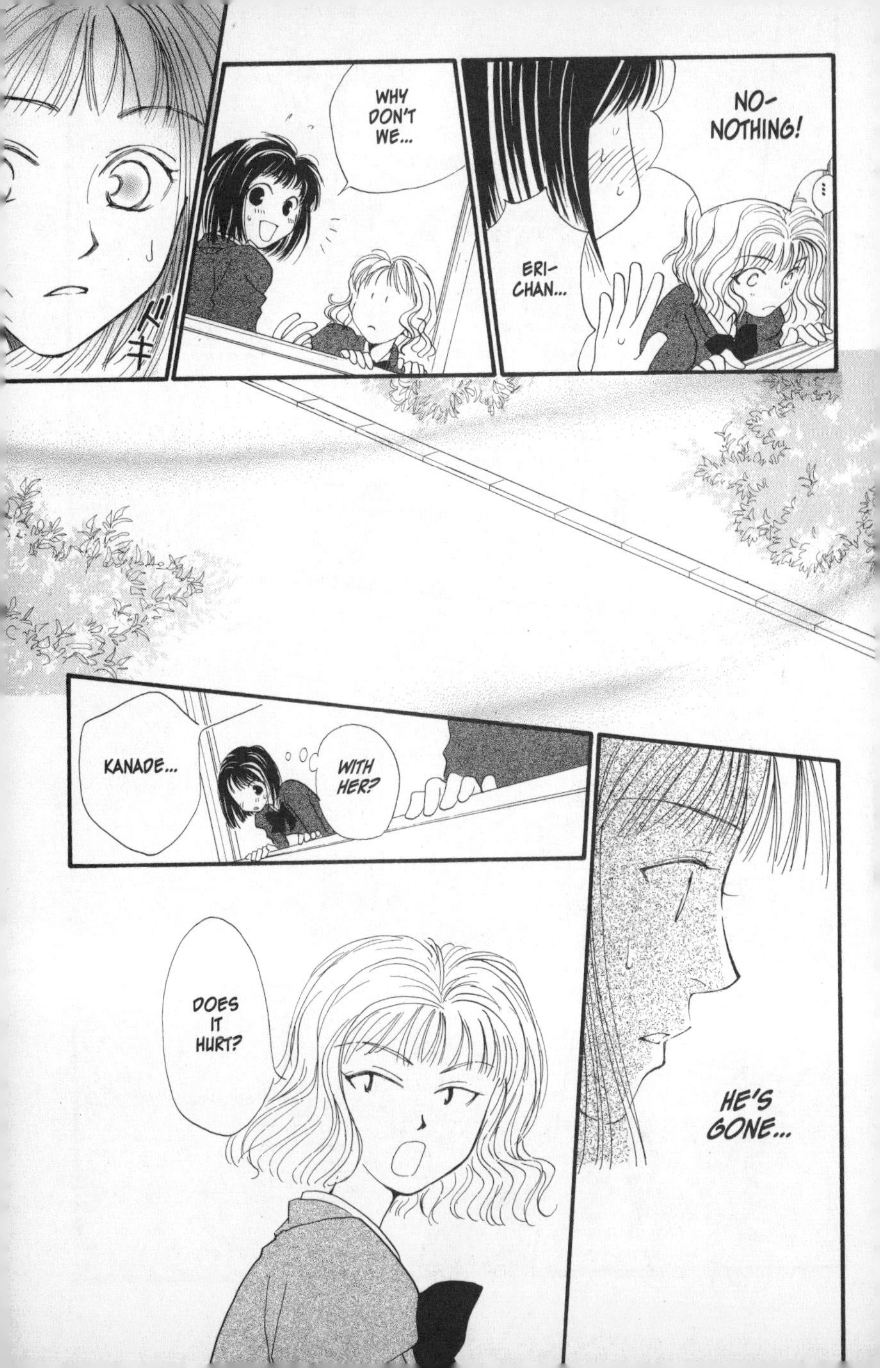
NO-NOTHING!
...
ERI-CHAN...
WHY DON'T WE...
HE'S GONE...
KANADE...
WITH HER?
DOES IT HURT?

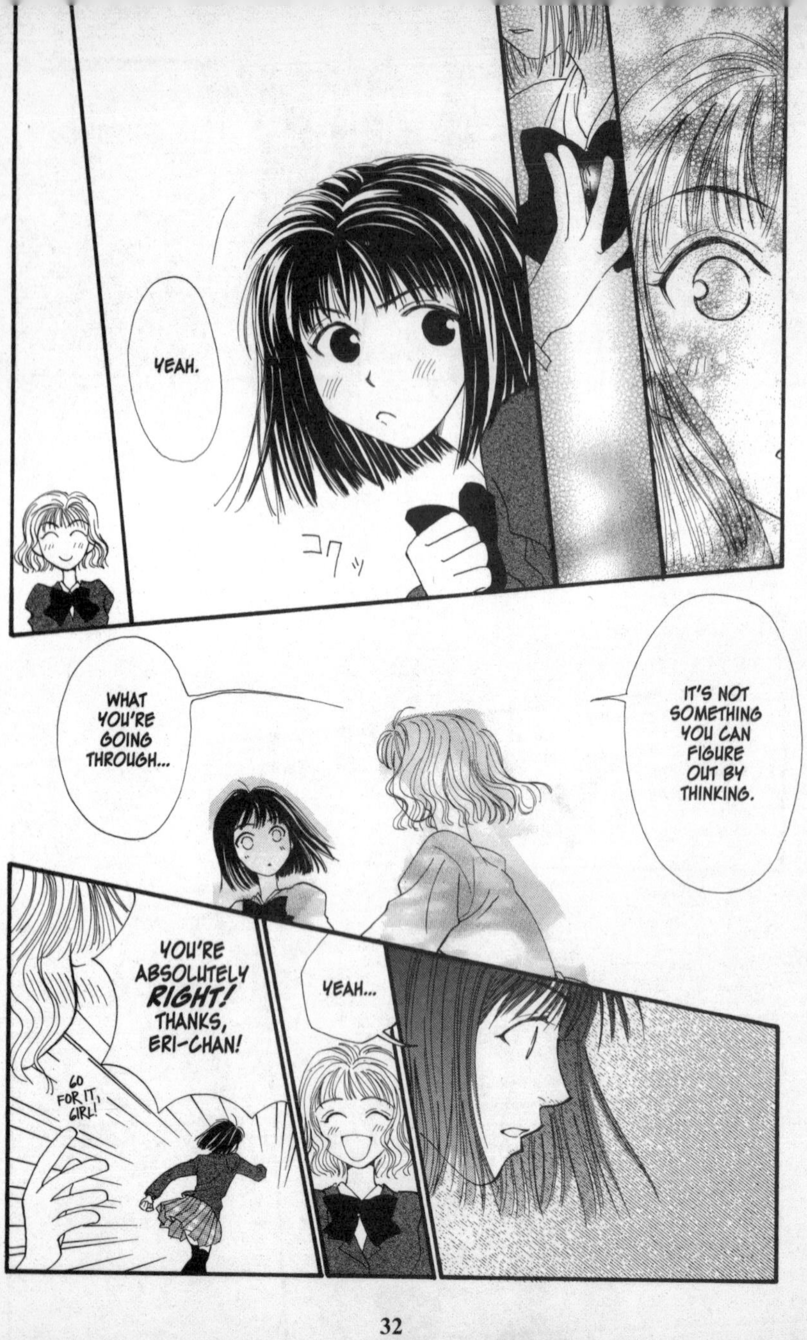
YEAH.
コクッ
IT'S NOT SOMETHING YOU CAN FIGURE OUT BY THINKING.
WHAT YOU'RE GOING THROUGH...
YEAH...
YOU'RE ABSOLUTELY **RIGHT!** THANKS, ERI-CHAN!
GO FOR IT, GIRL!

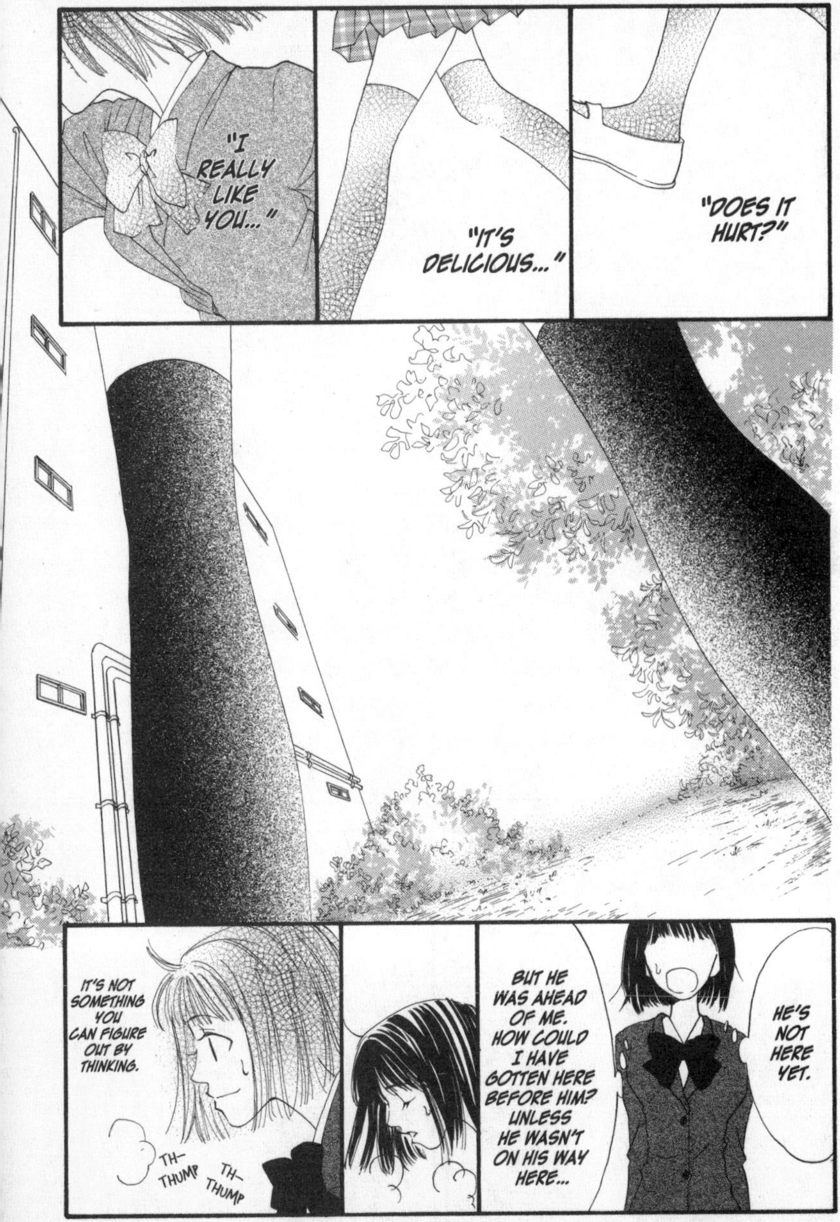
"DOES IT HURT?"
"IT'S DELICIOUS..."
"I REALLY LIKE YOU..."
HE'S NOT HERE YET.
BUT HE WAS AHEAD OF ME. HOW COULD I HAVE GOTTEN HERE BEFORE HIM? UNLESS HE WASN'T ON HIS WAY HERE...
IT'S NOT SOMETHING YOU CAN FIGURE OUT BY THINKING.
TH-THUMP TH-THUMP

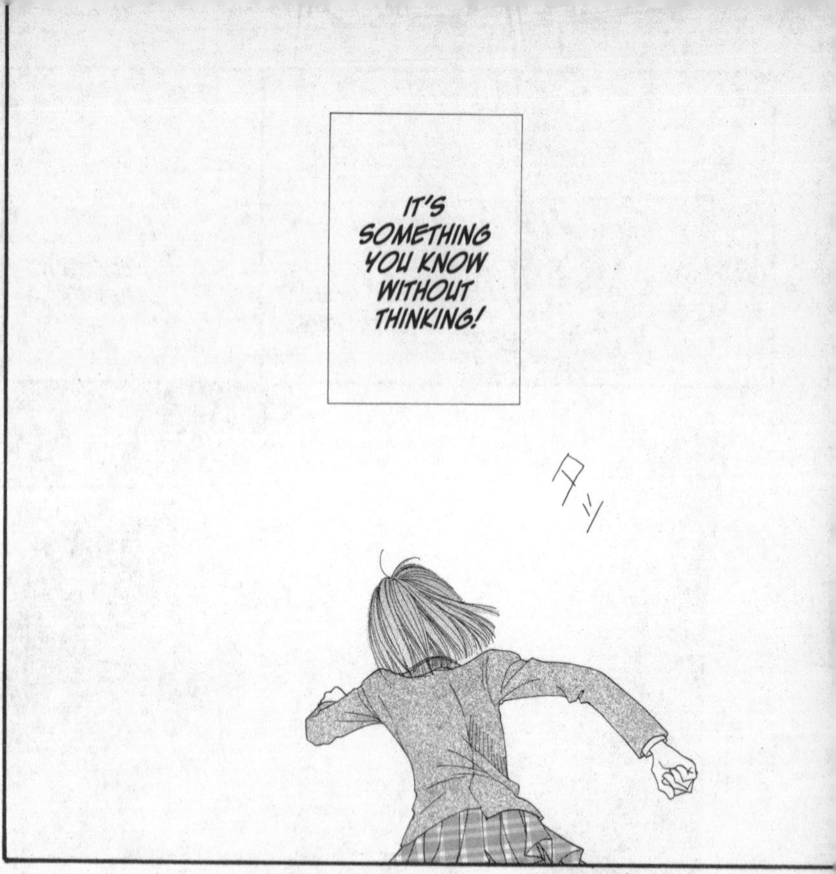
IT'S SOMETHING YOU KNOW WITHOUT THINKING!
タッ
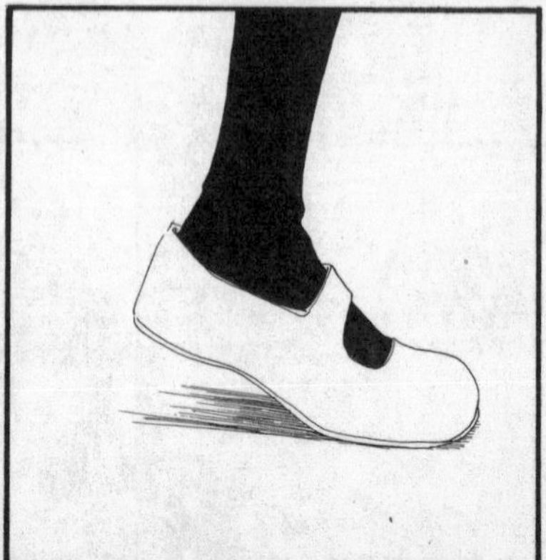
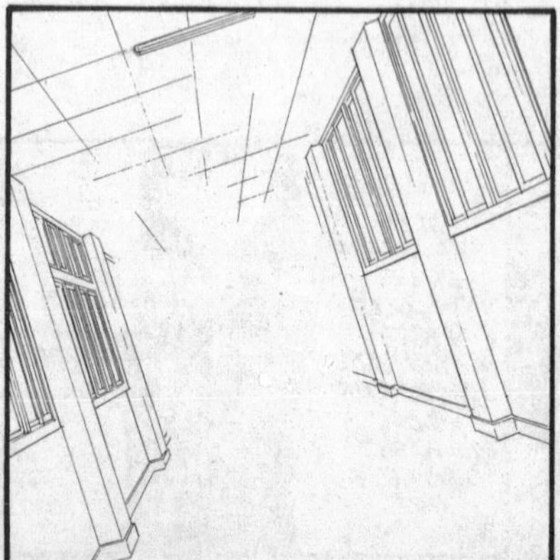

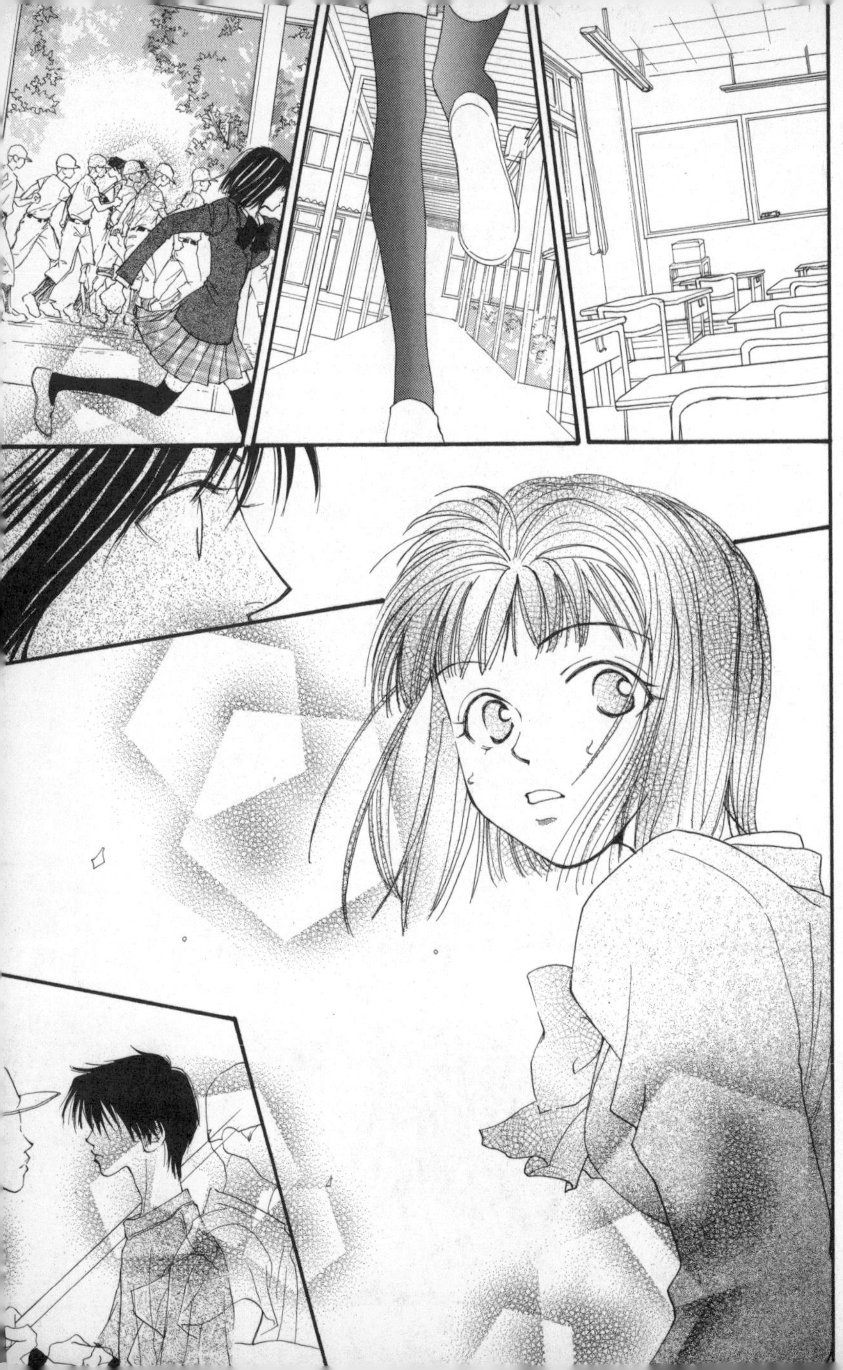

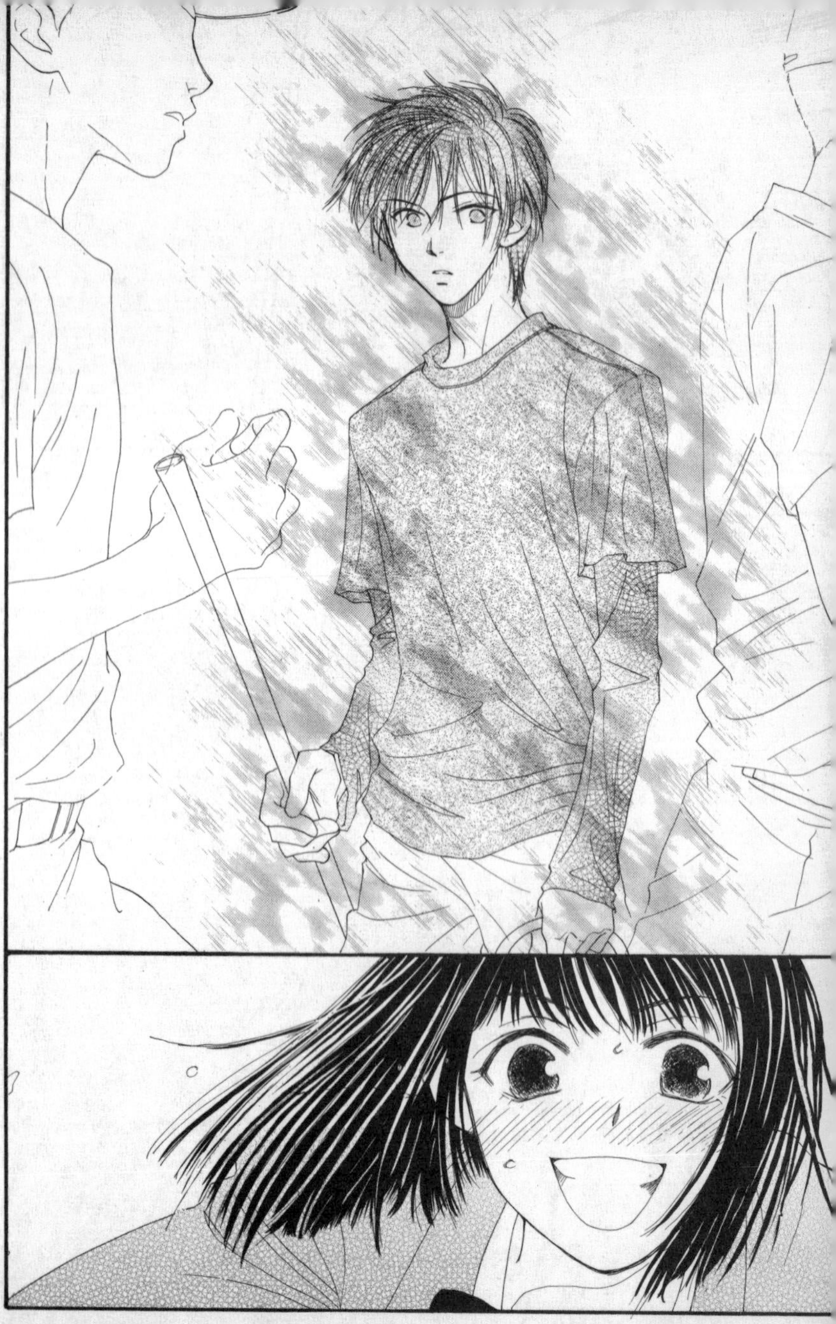

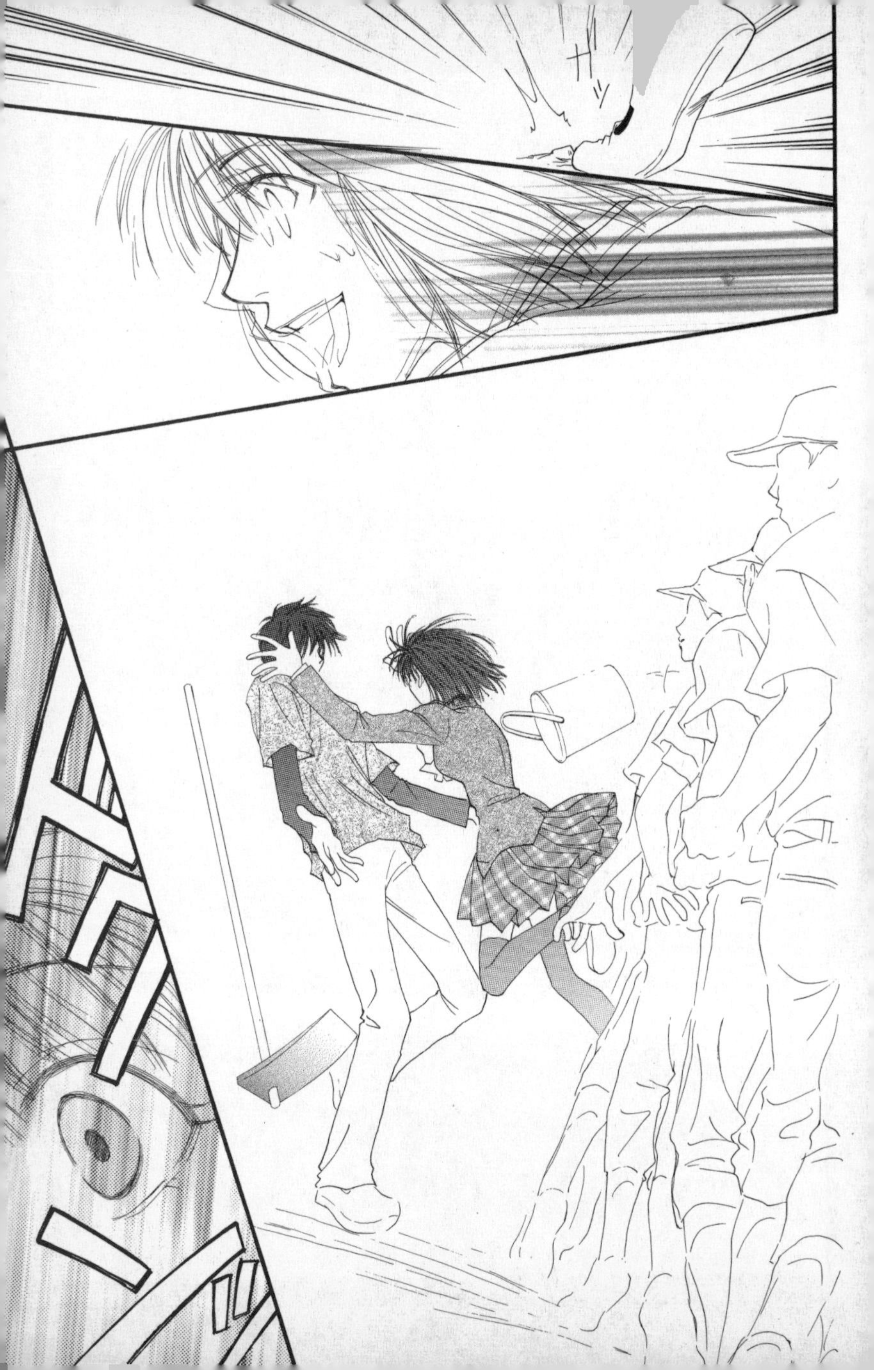

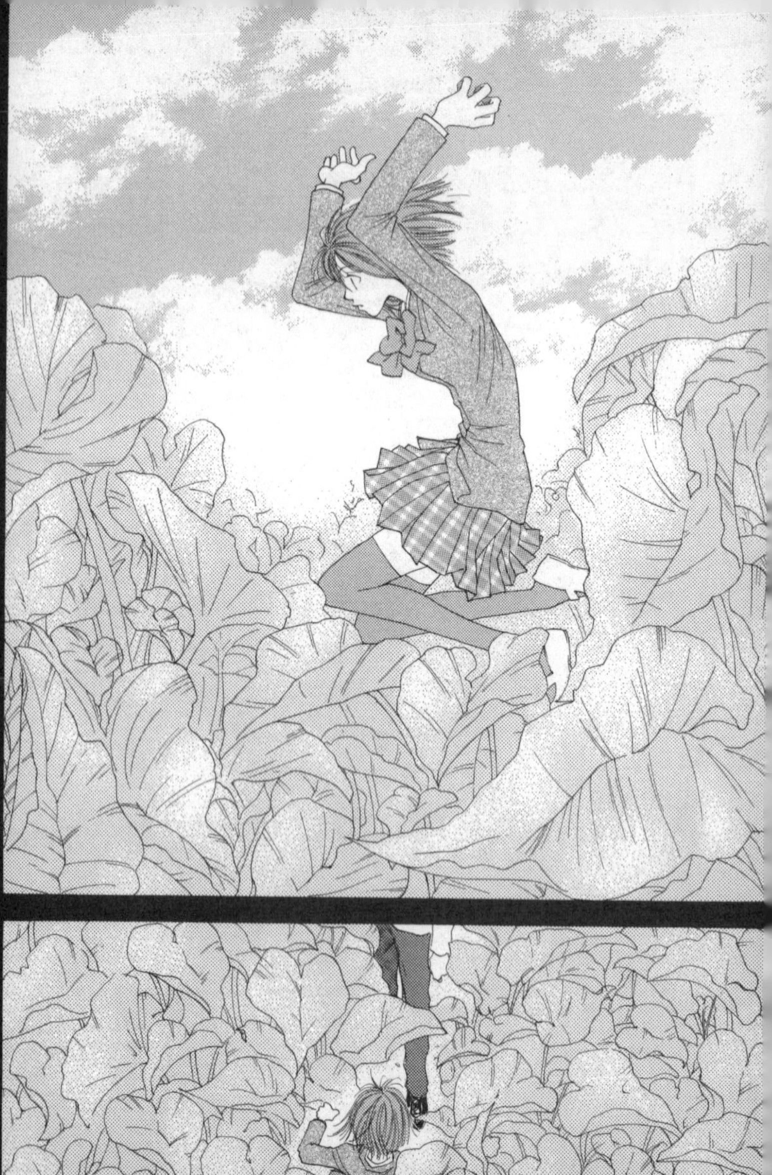

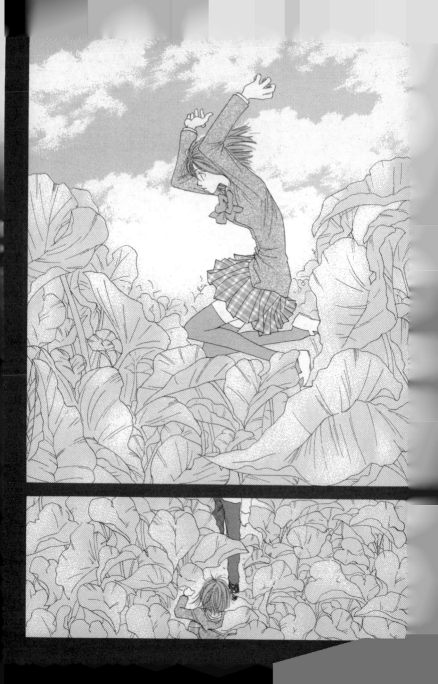

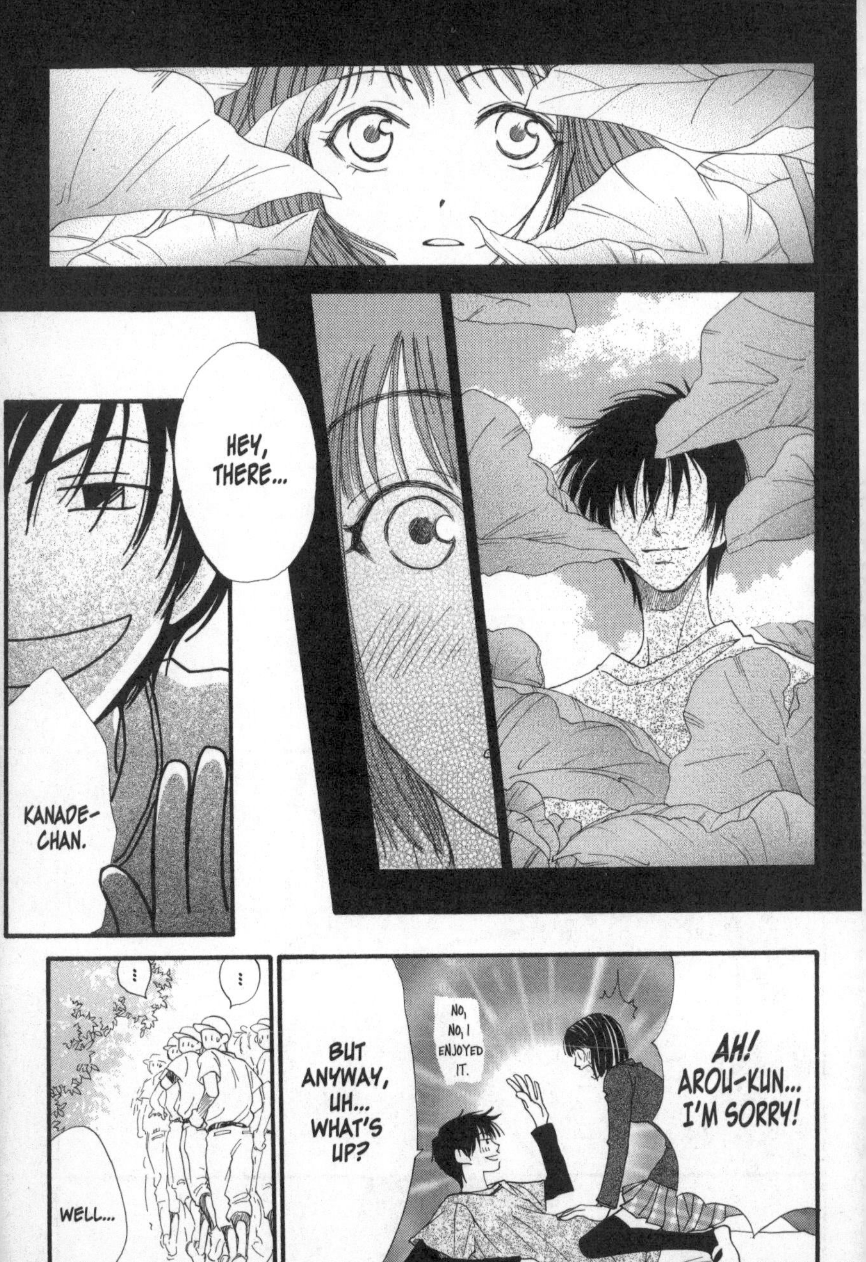
HEY, THERE...
KANADE-CHAN.
AH! AROU-KUN... I'M SORRY!
NO, NO, I ENJOYED IT.
BUT ANYWAY, UH... WHAT'S UP?
...
...
WELL...

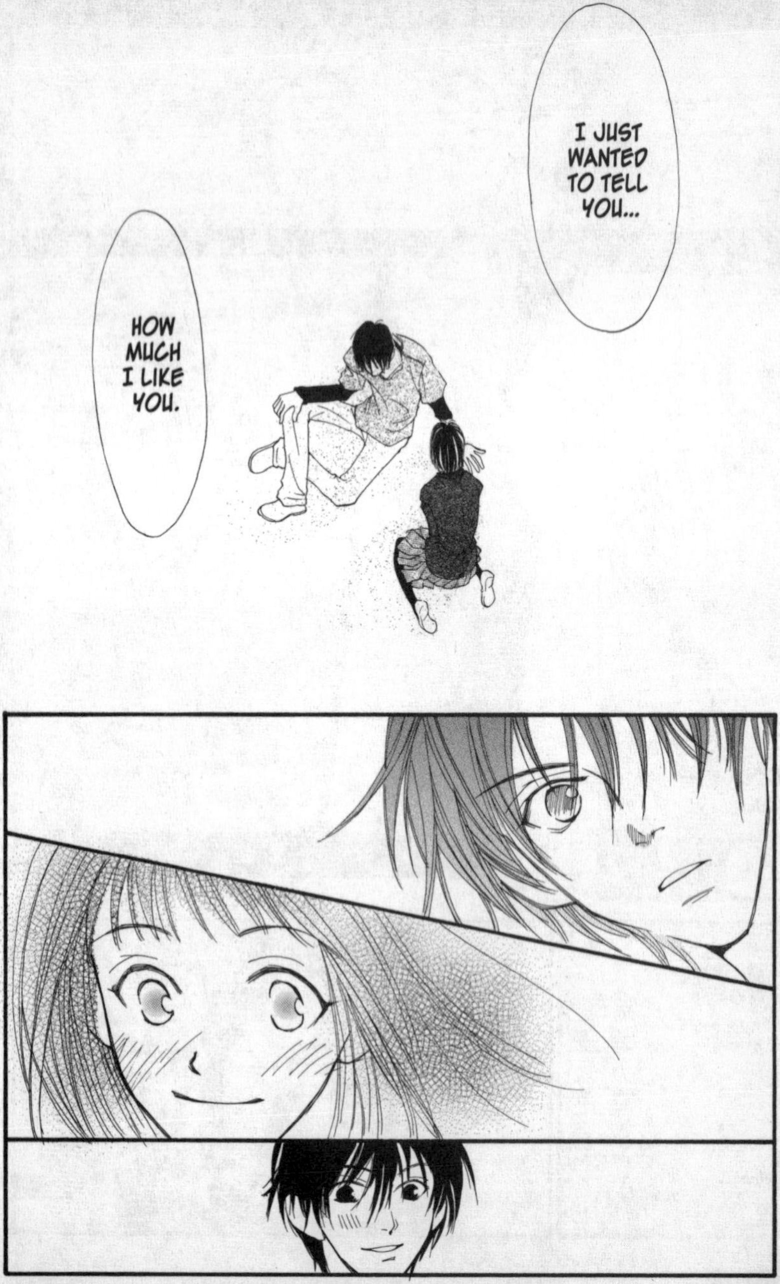
I JUST WANTED TO TELL YOU...
HOW MUCH I LIKE YOU.

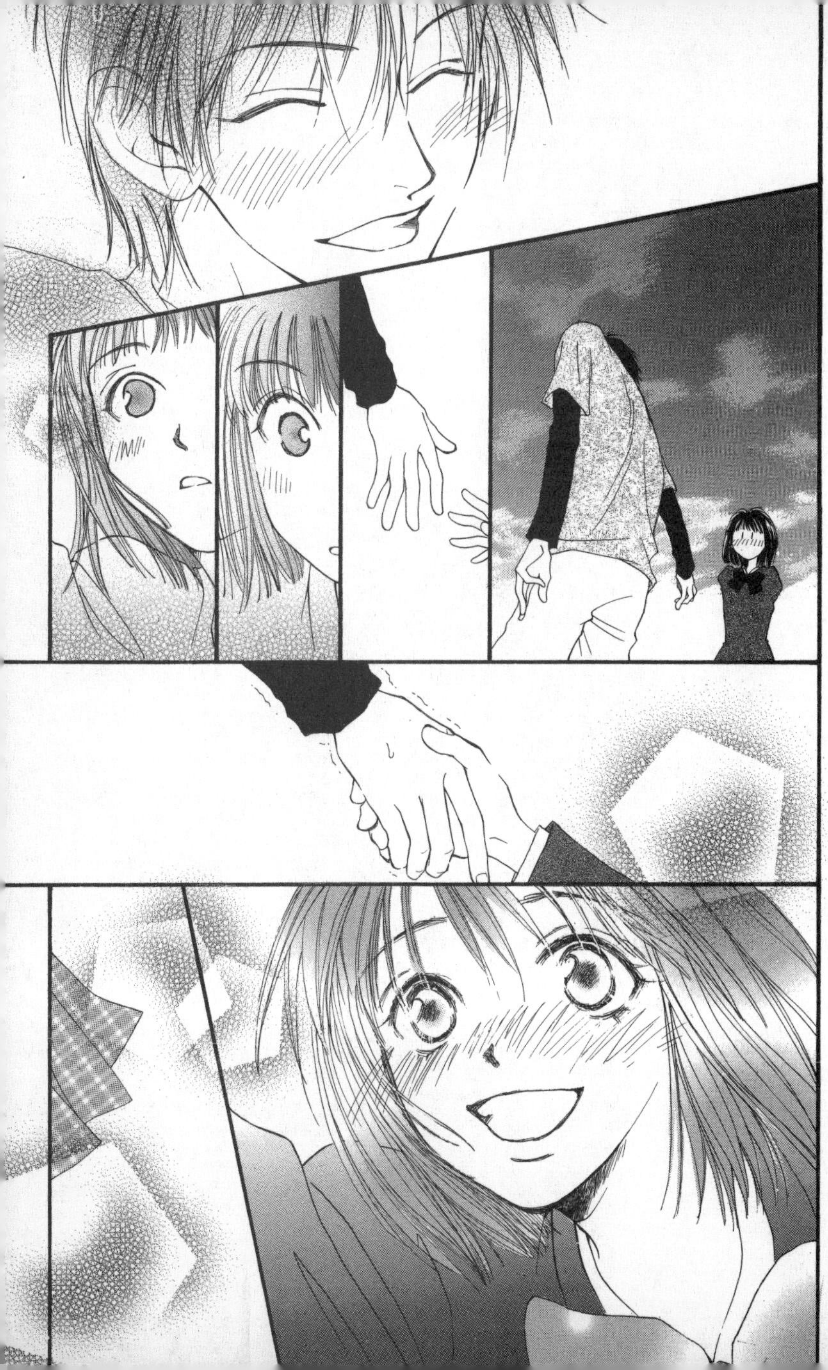

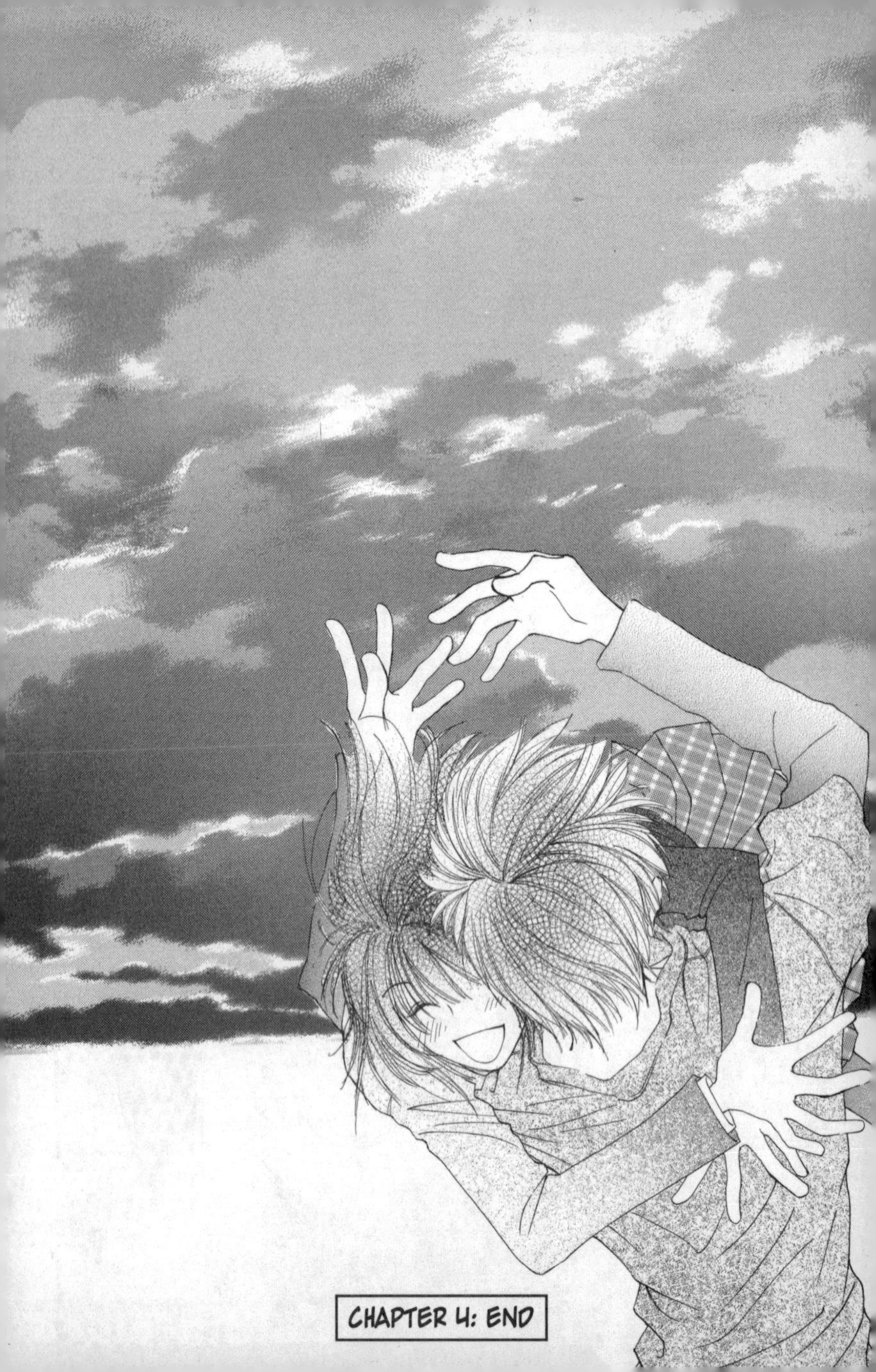
CHAPTER 4: END

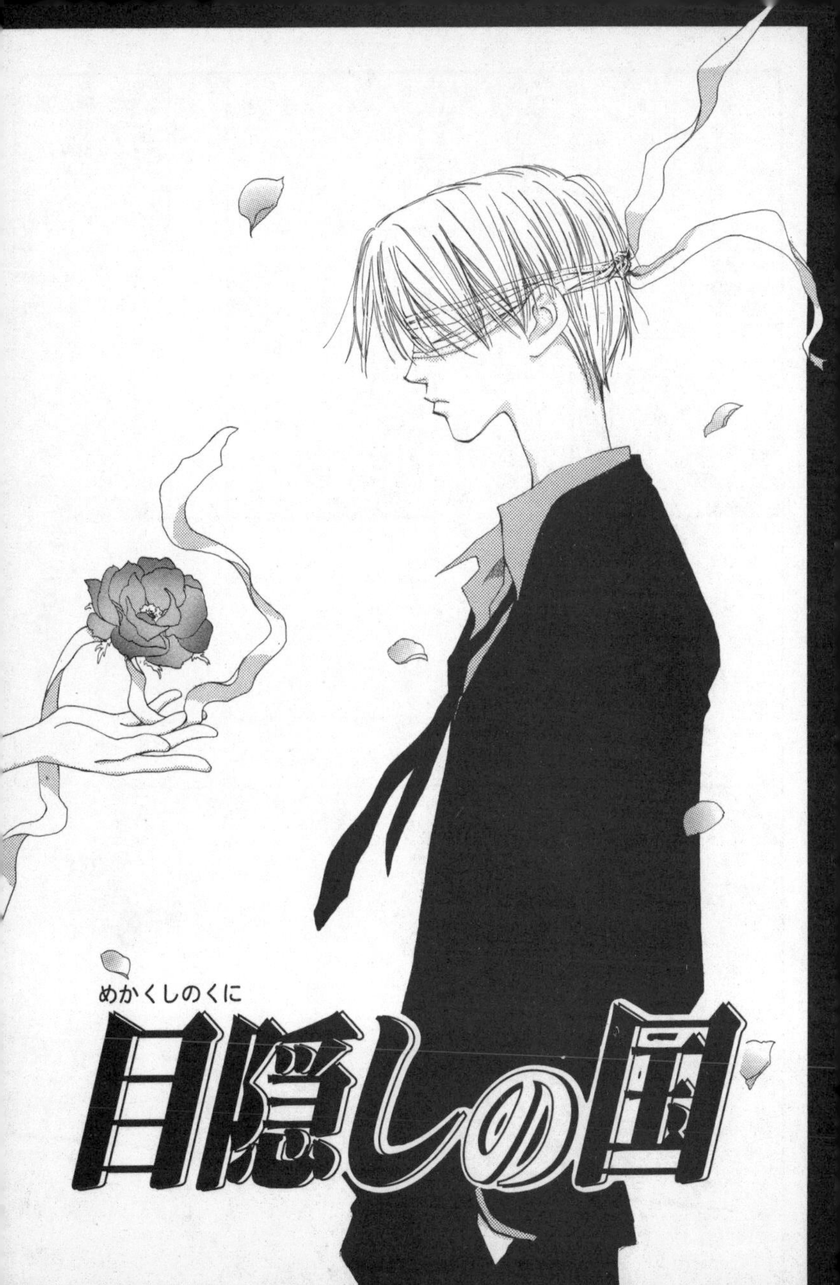
めかくしのくに
目隠しの国

Chapter 5 Land of the Blindfolded

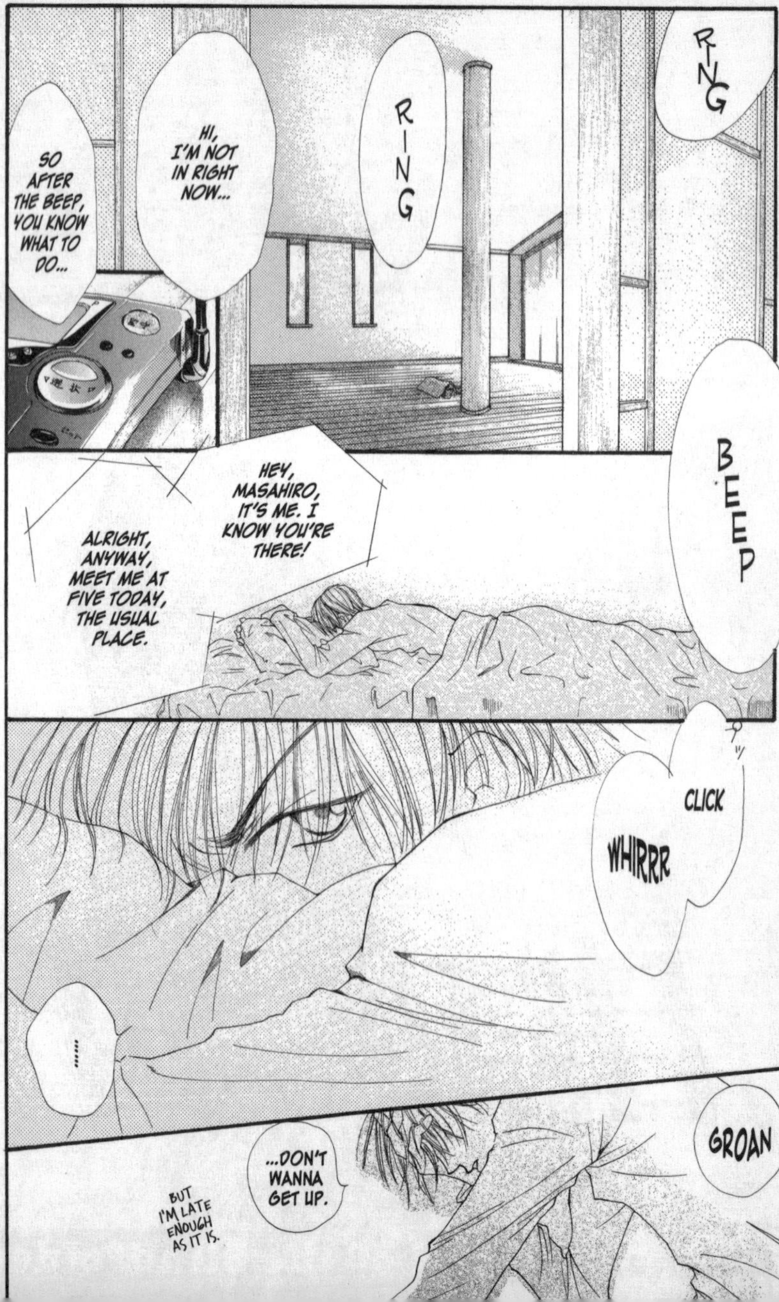
RING
RING
HI, I'M NOT IN RIGHT NOW...
SO AFTER THE BEEP, YOU KNOW WHAT TO DO...
BEEP
HEY, MASAHIRO, IT'S ME. I KNOW YOU'RE THERE!
ALRIGHT, ANYWAY, MEET ME AT FIVE TODAY, THE USUAL PLACE.
CLICK
WHIRRR
......
GROAN
...DON'T WANNA GET UP.
BUT I'M LATE ENOUGH AS IT IS.

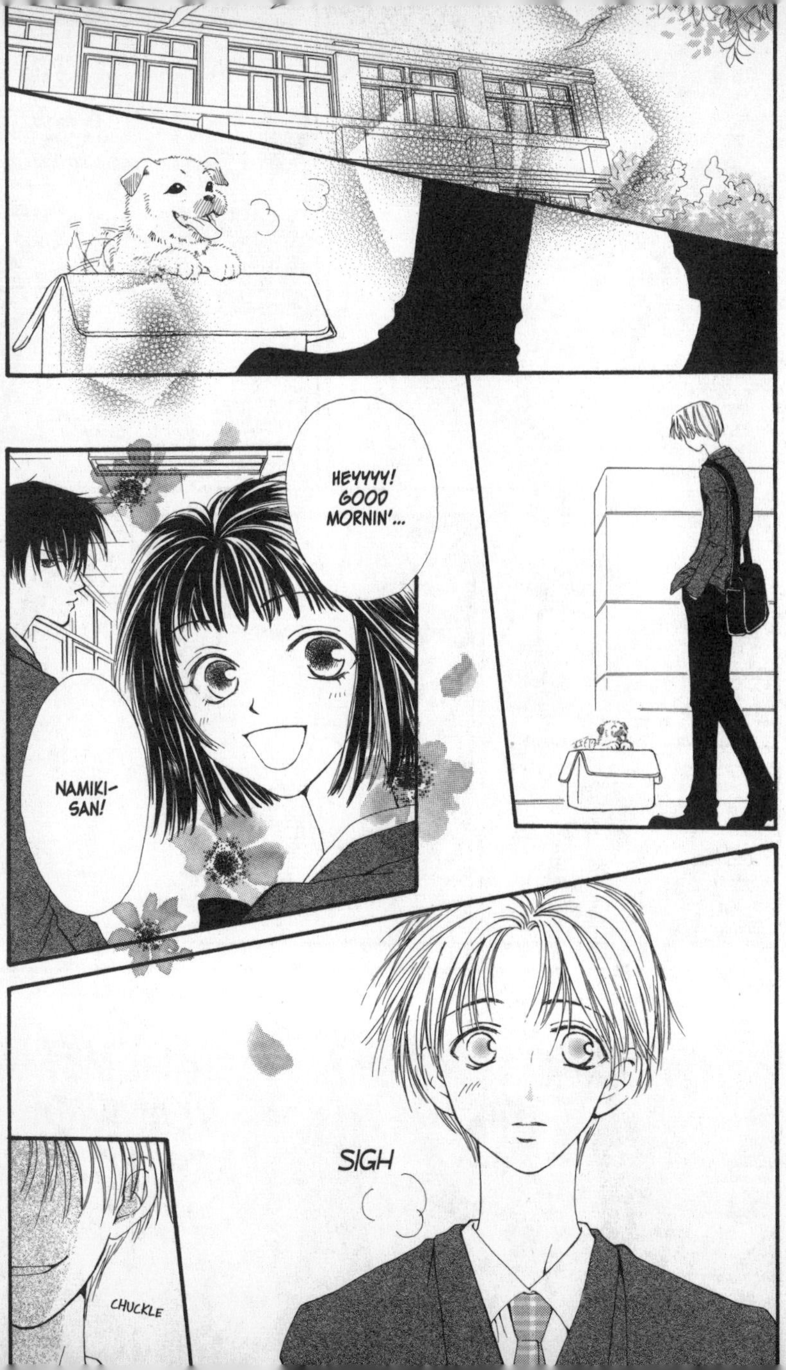
HEYYYY! GOOD MORNIN'...
NAMIKI-SAN!
SIGH
CHUCKLE

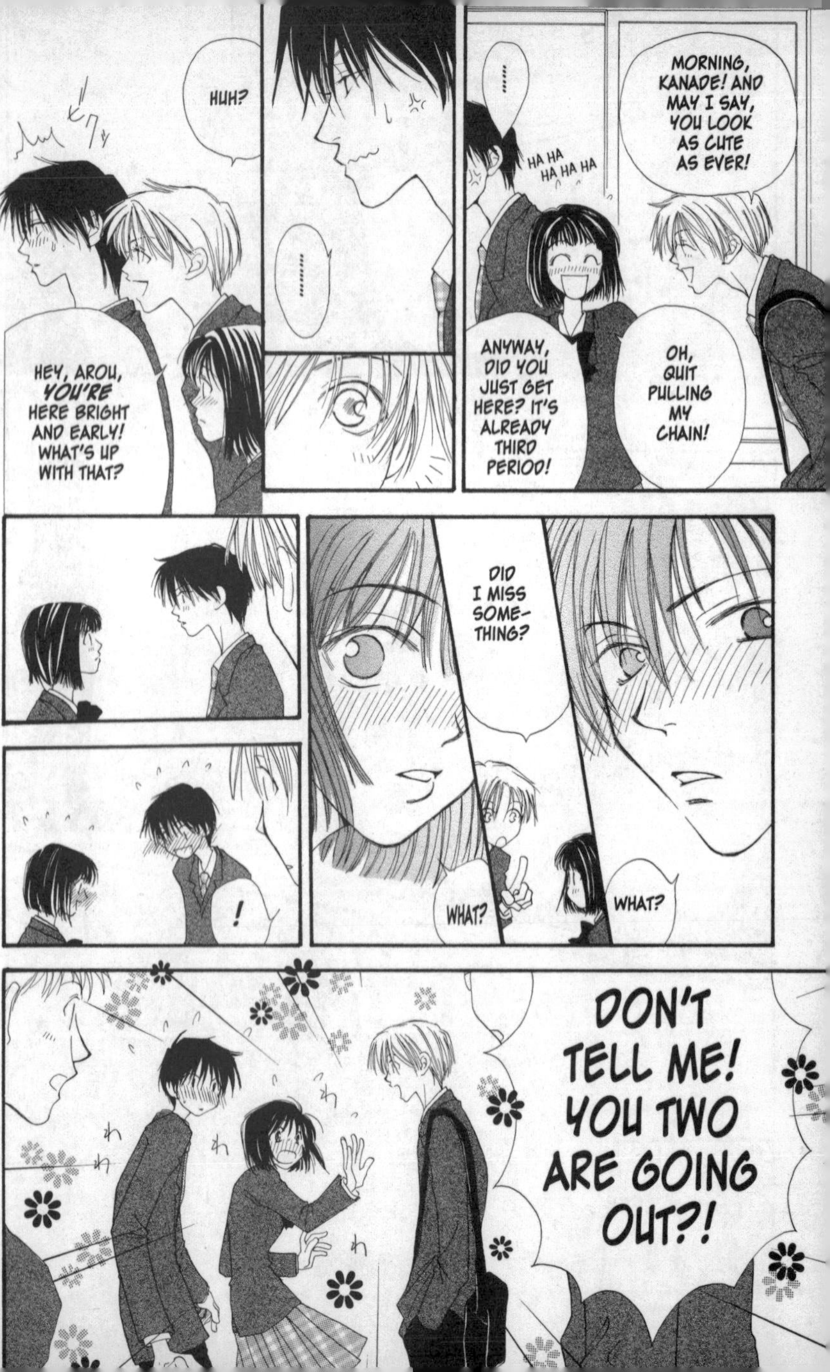
MORNING, KANADE! AND MAY I SAY, YOU LOOK AS CUTE AS EVER!
HA HA HA HA HA
OH, QUIT PULLING MY CHAIN!
ANYWAY, DID YOU JUST GET HERE? IT'S ALREADY THIRD PERIOD!
......
......
HUH?
HEY, AROU, *YOU'RE* HERE BRIGHT AND EARLY! WHAT'S UP WITH THAT?
DID I MISS SOME-THING?
WHAT?
WHAT?
!
DON'T TELL ME! YOU TWO ARE GOING OUT?!

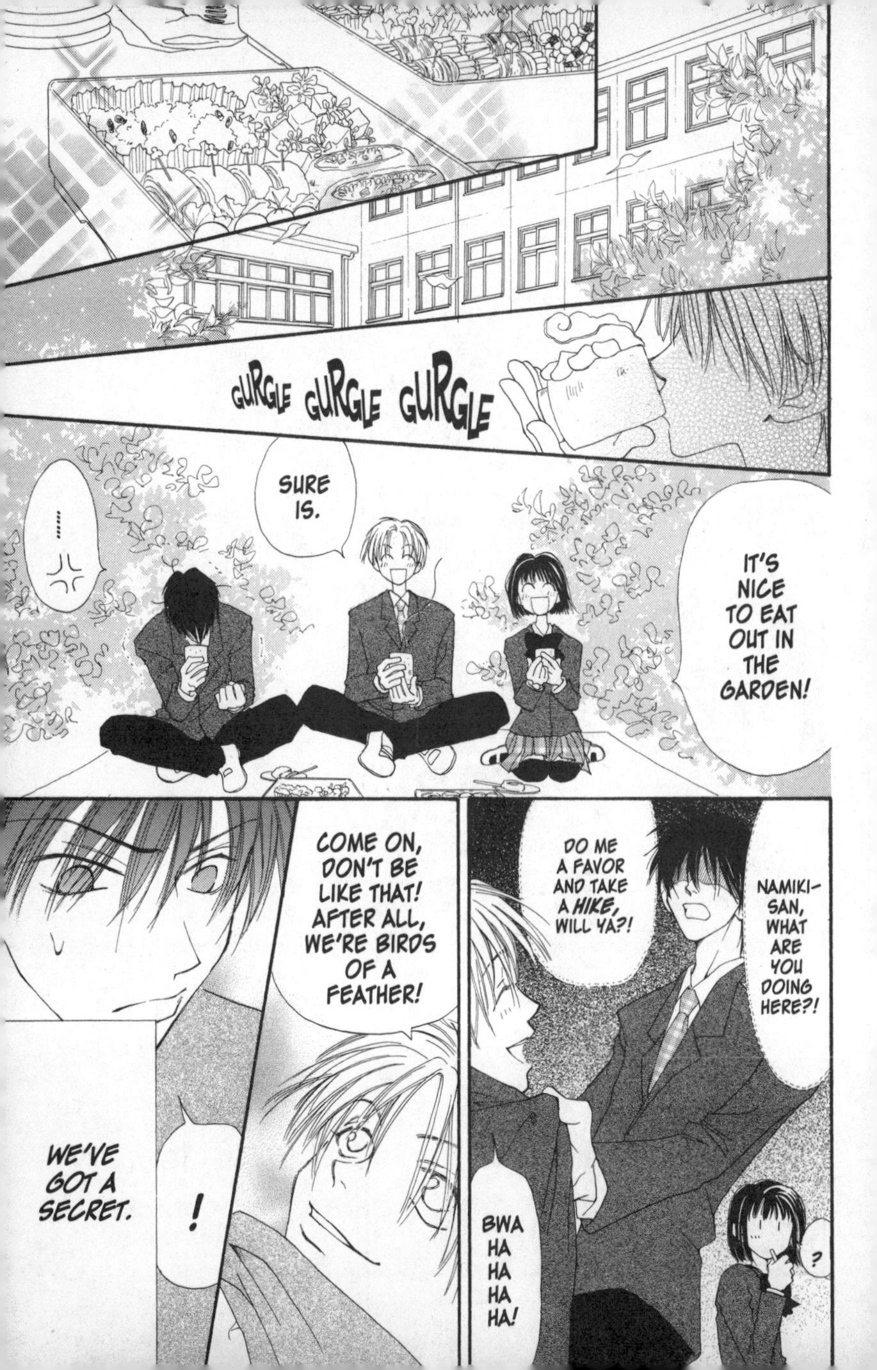
GURGLE GURGLE GURGLE
IT'S NICE TO EAT OUT IN THE GARDEN!
SURE IS.
......
NAMIKI-SAN, WHAT ARE YOU DOING HERE?!
DO ME A FAVOR AND TAKE A *HIKE*, WILL YA?!
BWA HA HA HA HA HA!
?
COME ON, DON'T BE LIKE THAT! AFTER ALL, WE'RE BIRDS OF A FEATHER!
!
WE'VE GOT A SECRET.

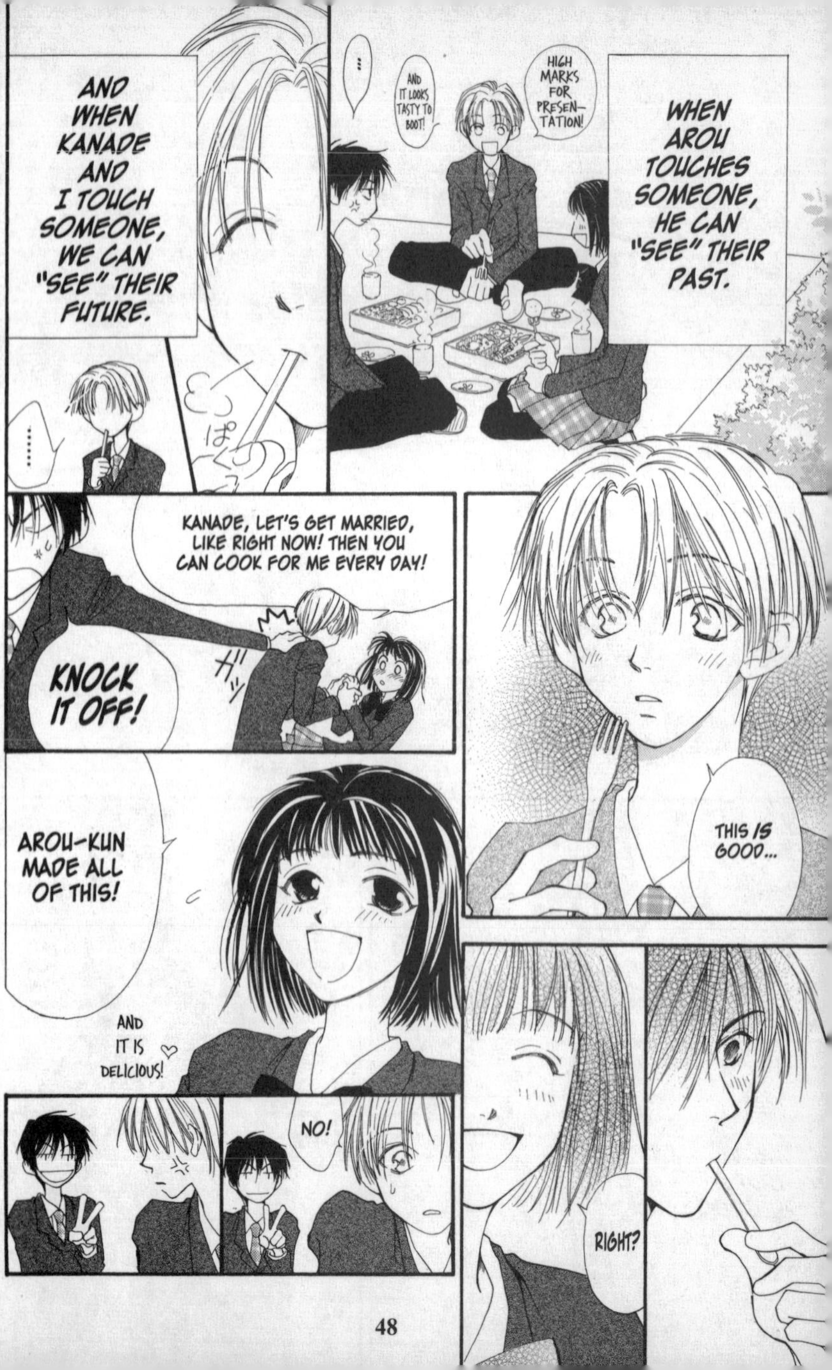
WHEN AROU TOUCHES SOMEONE, HE CAN "SEE" THEIR PAST.
HIGH MARKS FOR PRESEN-TATION!
AND IT LOOKS TASTY TO BOOT!
...
AND WHEN KANADE AND I TOUCH SOMEONE, WE CAN "SEE" THEIR FUTURE.
......
THIS IS GOOD...
KANADE, LET'S GET MARRIED, LIKE RIGHT NOW! THEN YOU CAN COOK FOR ME EVERY DAY!
KNOCK IT OFF!
AROU-KUN MADE ALL OF THIS!
AND IT IS DELICIOUS!
RIGHT?
NO!

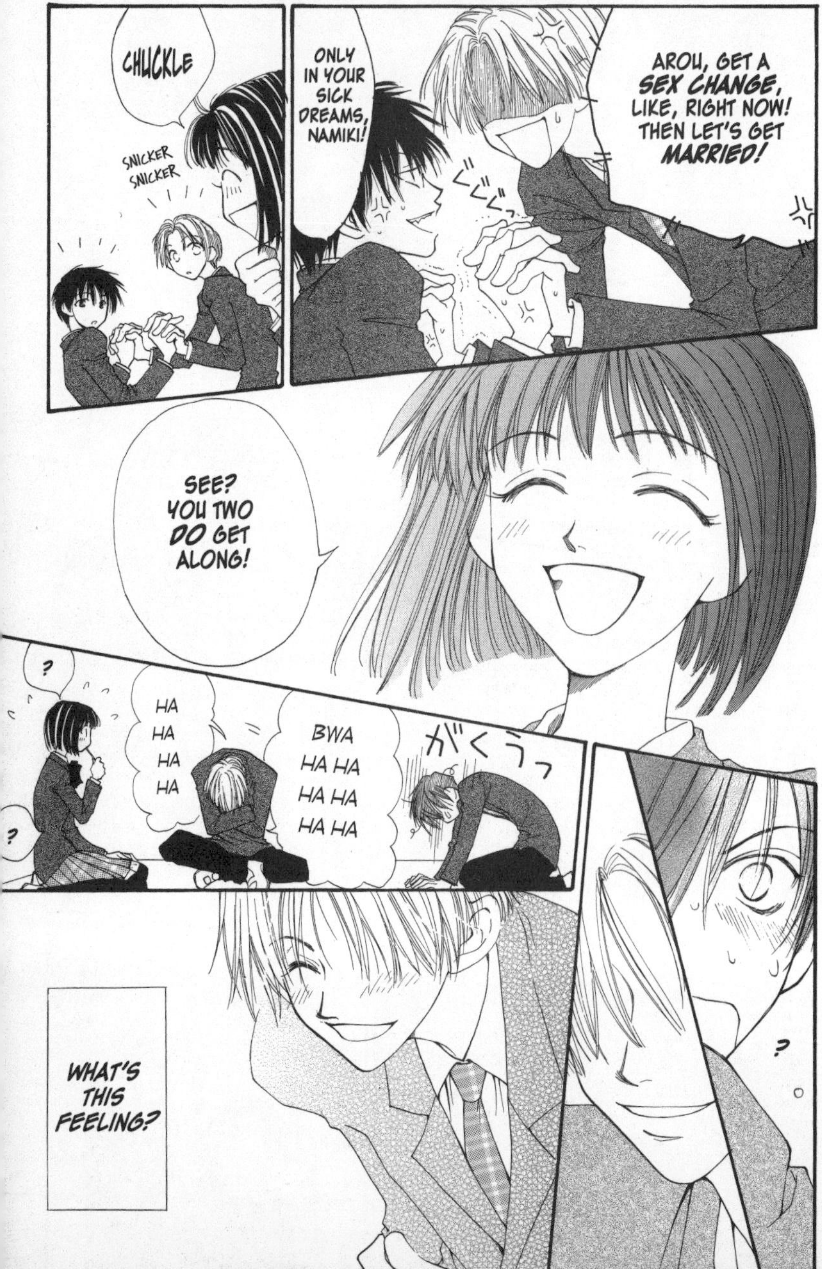

AROU, GET A SEX CHANGE, LIKE, RIGHT NOW! THEN LET'S GET MARRIED!
ONLY IN YOUR SICK DREAMS, NAMIKI!
ぐぐぐっ
CHUCKLE
SNICKER SNICKER
SEE? YOU TWO DO GET ALONG!
?
がくうっ
BWA HA HA HA HA HA HA
HA HA HA HA
?
?
WHAT'S THIS FEELING?

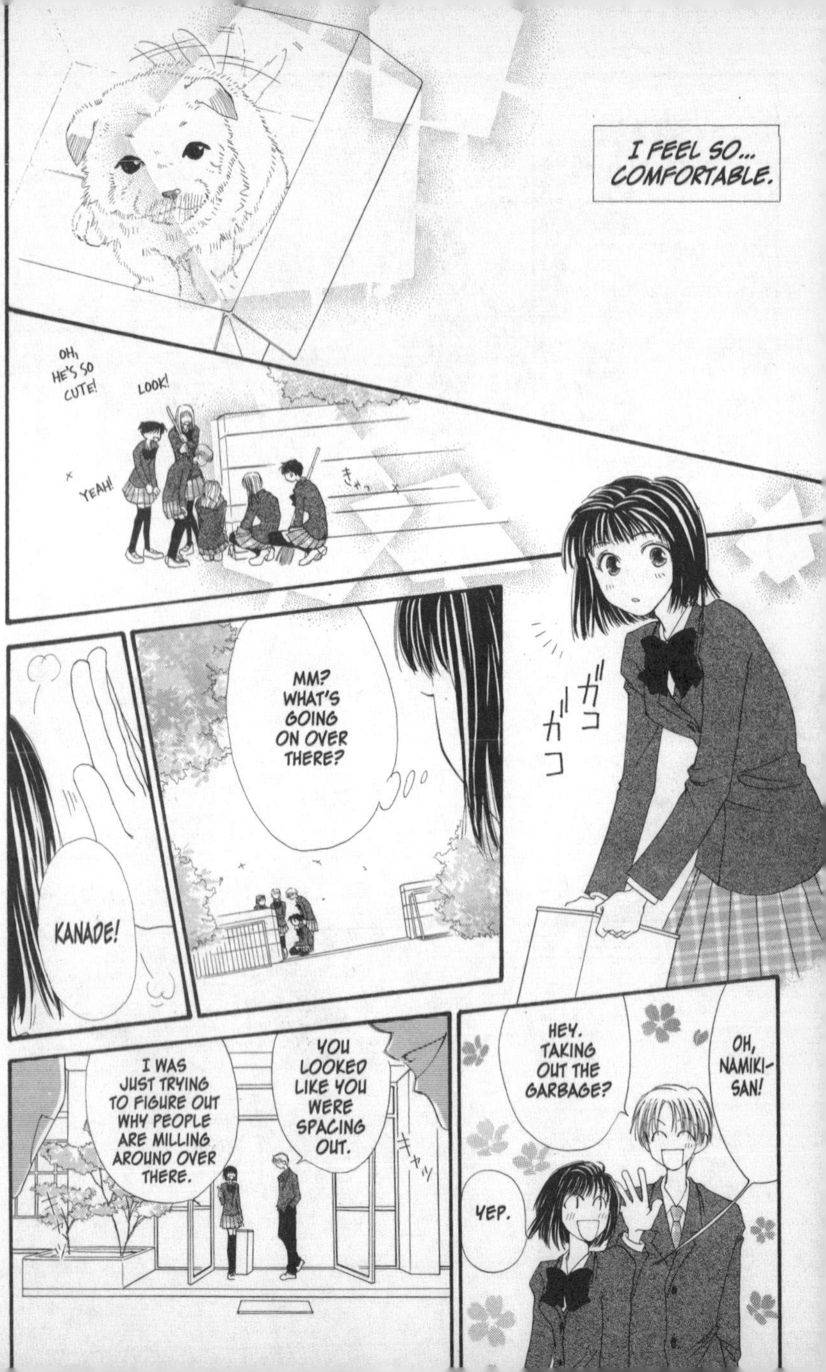
I FEEL SO... COMFORTABLE.
LOOK!
OH, HE'S SO CUTE!
YEAH!
ガコ ガコ
MM? WHAT'S GOING ON OVER THERE?
KANADE!
OH, NAMIKI-SAN!
HEY. TAKING OUT THE GARBAGE?
YEP.
キャッ
YOU LOOKED LIKE YOU WERE SPACING OUT.
I WAS JUST TRYING TO FIGURE OUT WHY PEOPLE ARE MILLING AROUND OVER THERE.

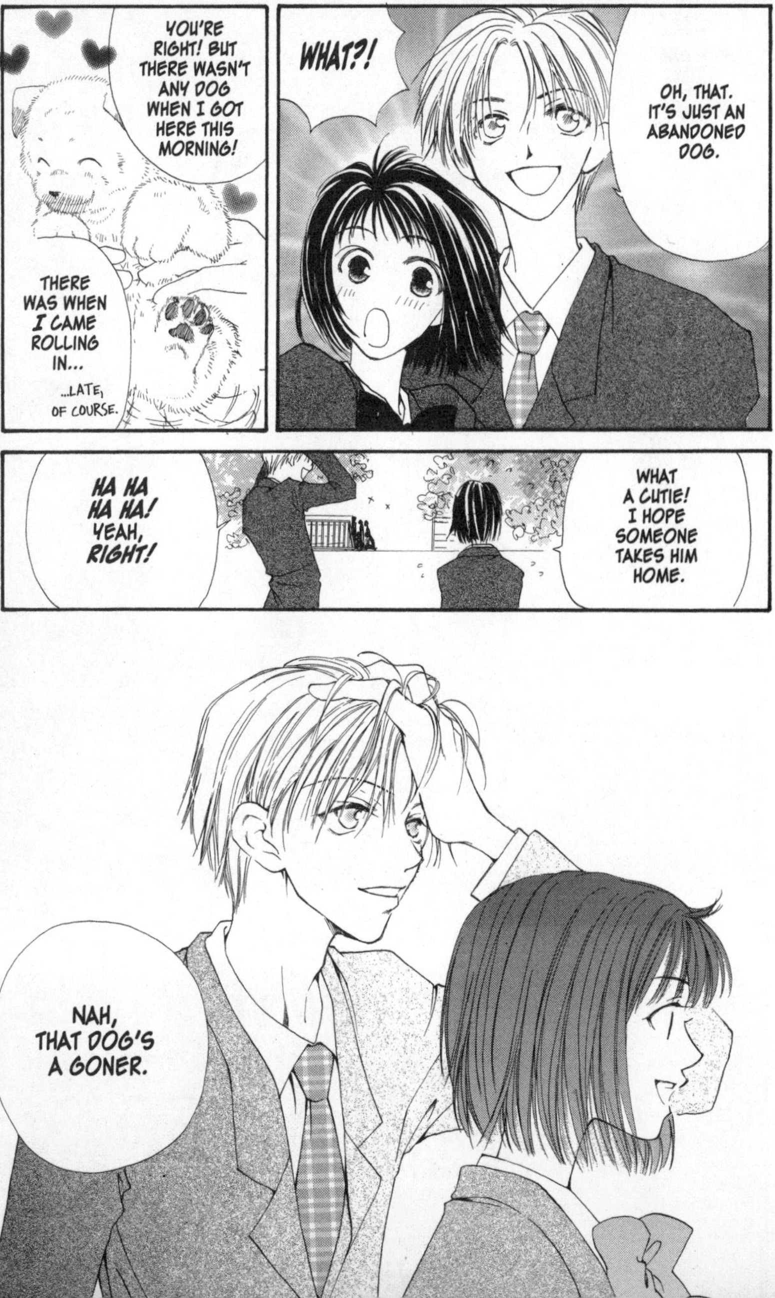
OH, THAT. IT'S JUST AN ABANDONED DOG.
WHAT?!
YOU'RE RIGHT! BUT THERE WASN'T ANY DOG WHEN I GOT HERE THIS MORNING!
THERE WAS WHEN *I* CAME ROLLING IN...
...LATE, OF COURSE.
WHAT A CUTIE! I HOPE SOMEONE TAKES HIM HOME.
HA HA HA HA! YEAH, RIGHT!
NAH, THAT DOG'S A GONER.

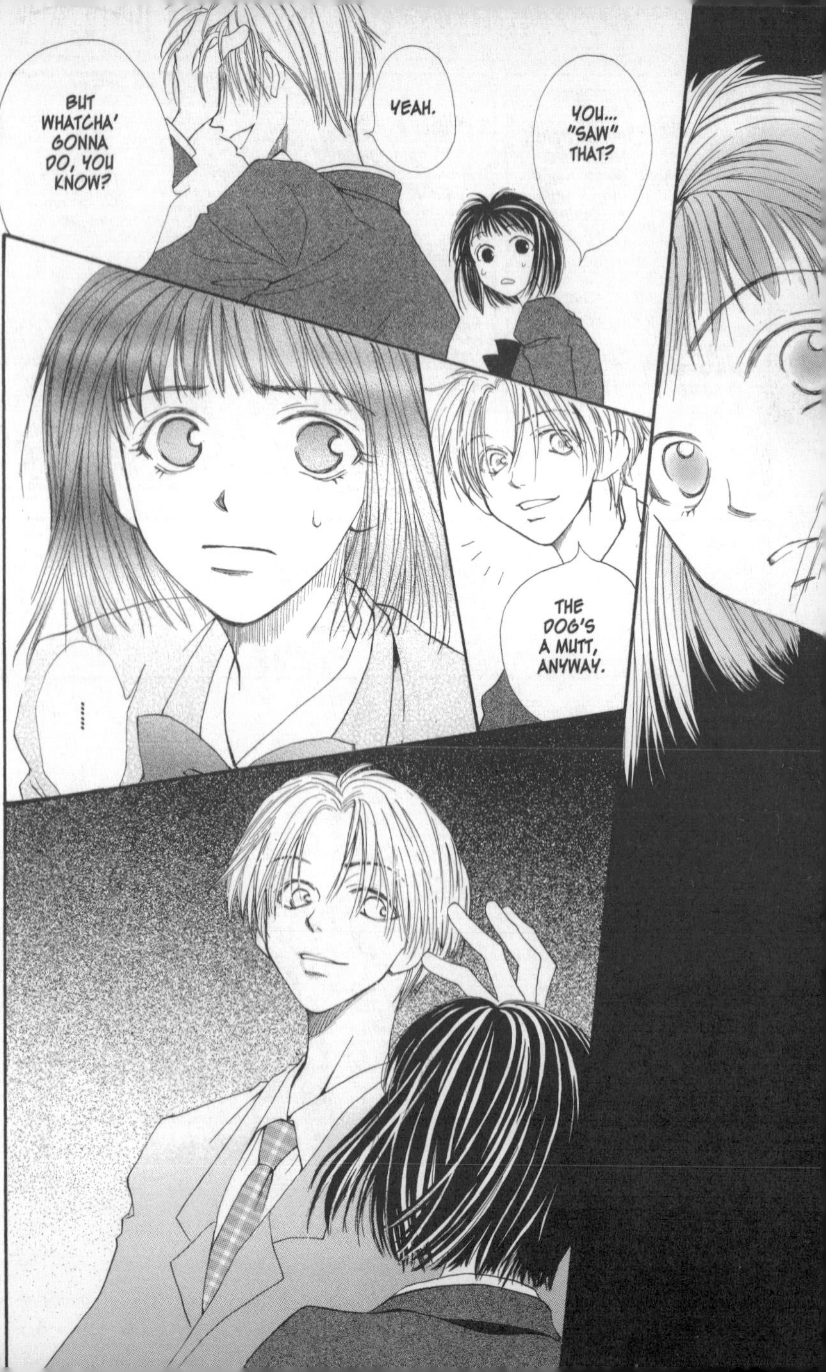
YOU... "SAW" THAT?
YEAH.
BUT WHATCHA' GONNA DO, YOU KNOW?
THE DOG'S A MUTT, ANYWAY.
......

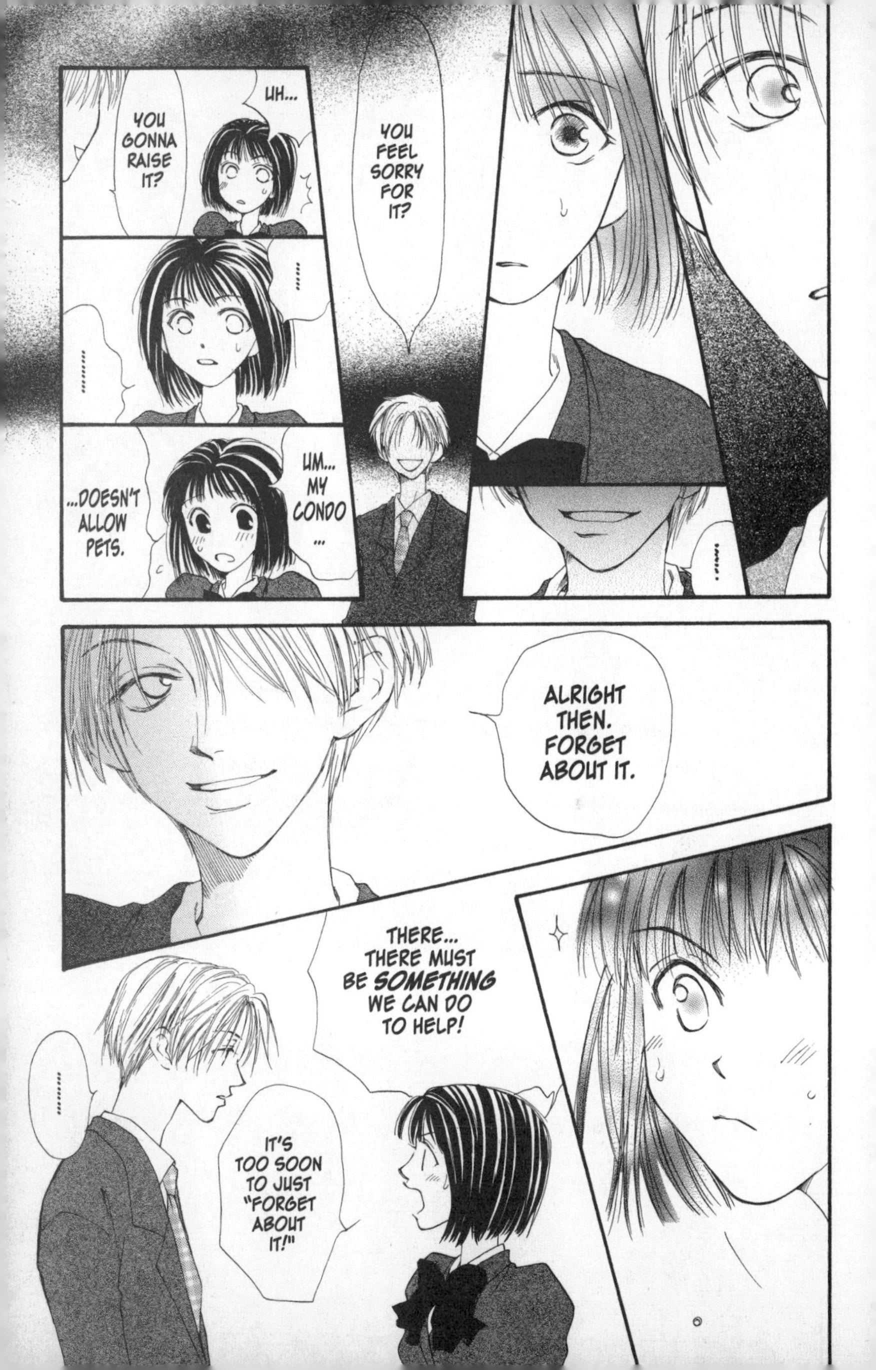
.....
YOU FEEL SORRY FOR IT?
UH...
YOU GONNA RAISE IT?
......
......
UM... MY CONDO ...
...DOESN'T ALLOW PETS.
ALRIGHT THEN. FORGET ABOUT IT.
THERE... THERE MUST BE SOMETHING WE CAN DO TO HELP!
IT'S TOO SOON TO JUST "FORGET ABOUT IT!"
......

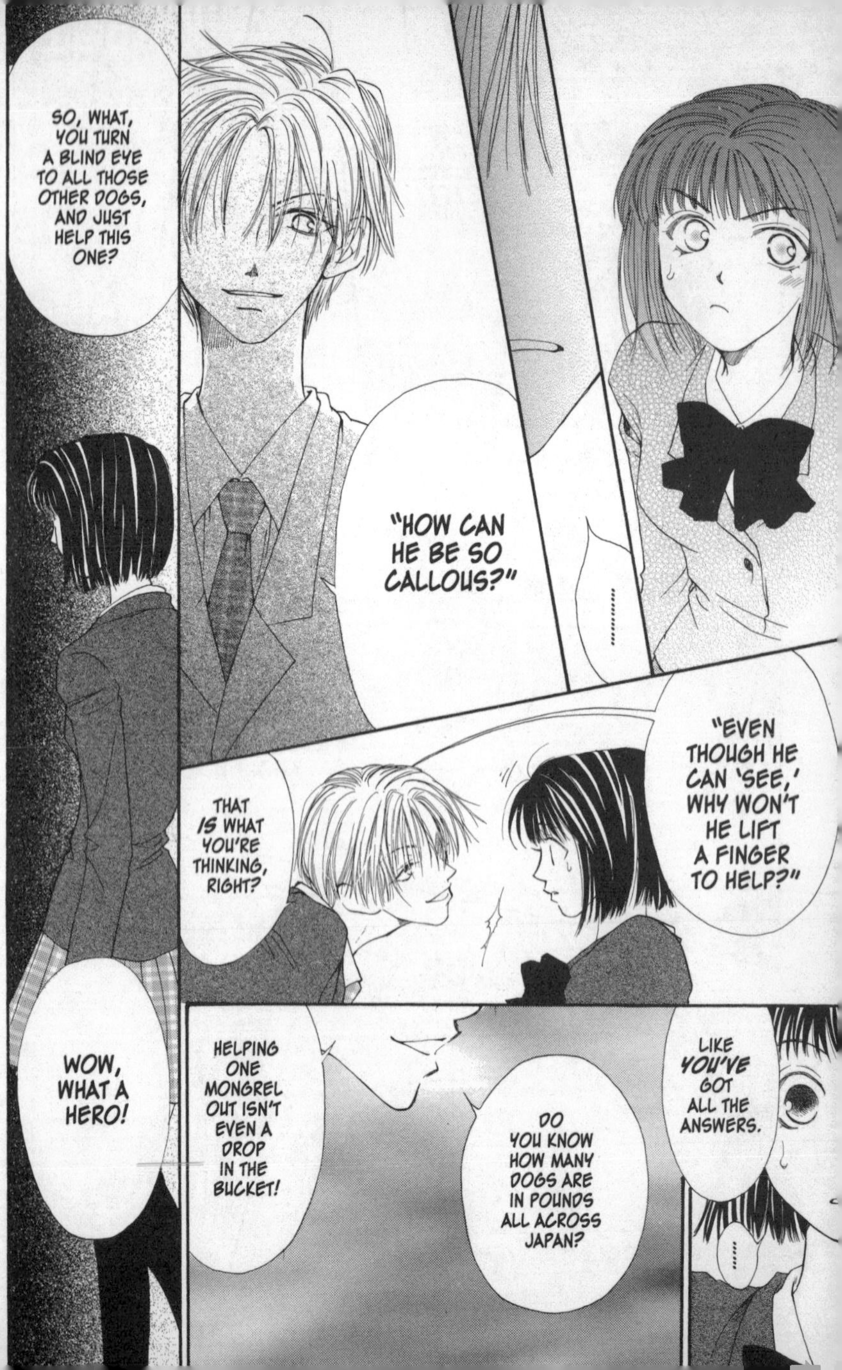
......
"HOW CAN HE BE SO CALLOUS?"
"EVEN THOUGH HE CAN 'SEE,' WHY WON'T HE LIFT A FINGER TO HELP?"
THAT *IS* WHAT YOU'RE THINKING, RIGHT?
LIKE *YOU'VE* GOT ALL THE ANSWERS.
......
HELPING ONE MONGREL OUT ISN'T EVEN A DROP IN THE BUCKET!
DO YOU KNOW HOW MANY DOGS ARE IN POUNDS ALL ACROSS JAPAN?
SO, WHAT, YOU TURN A BLIND EYE TO ALL THOSE OTHER DOGS, AND JUST HELP THIS ONE?
WOW, WHAT A HERO!

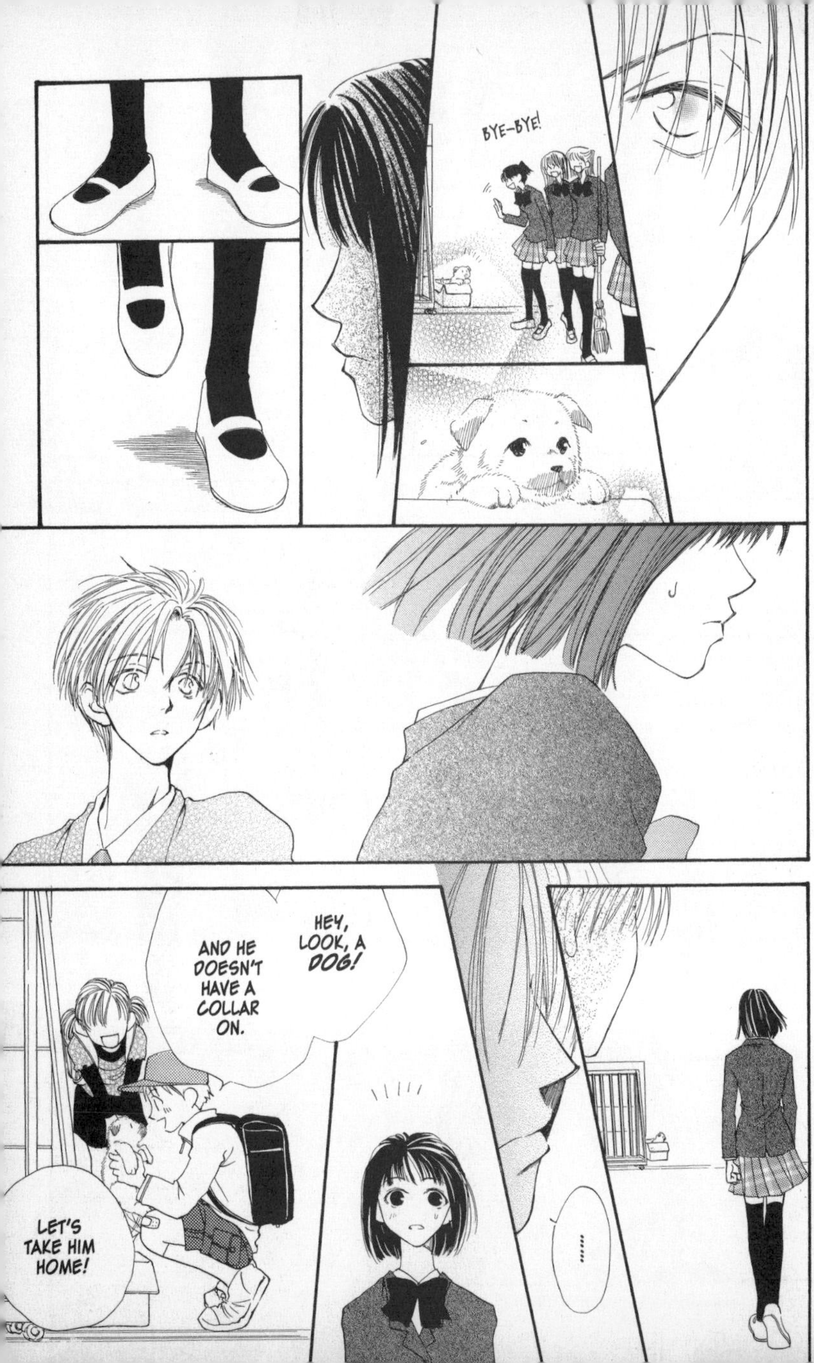
BYE-BYE!
......
HEY, LOOK, A DOG!
AND HE DOESN'T HAVE A COLLAR ON.
LET'S TAKE HIM HOME!

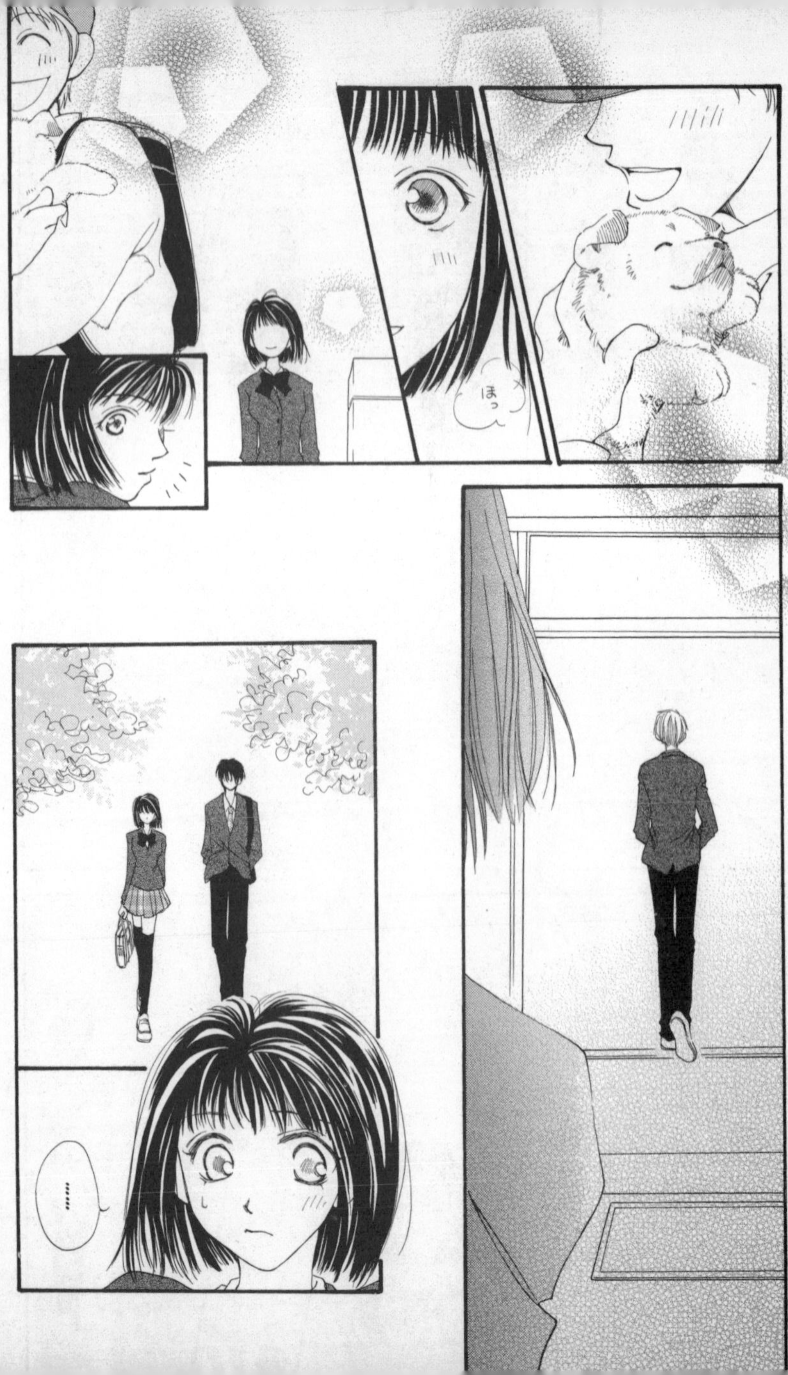
ほっ
……

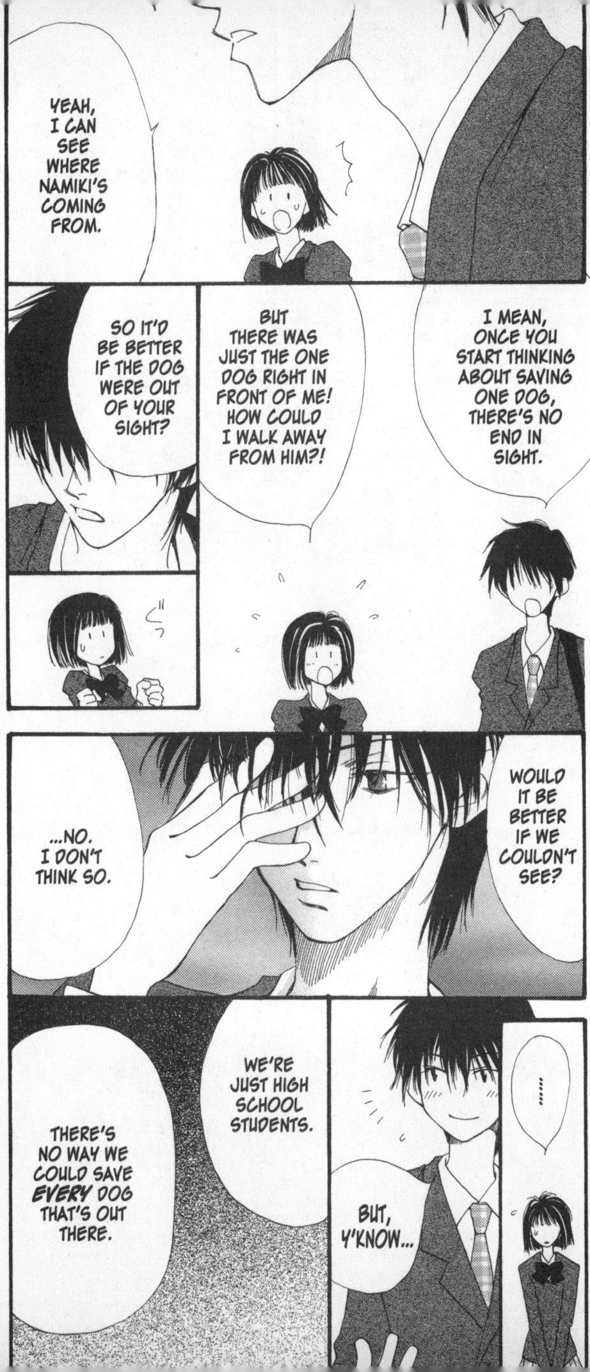
YEAH, I CAN SEE WHERE NAMIKI'S COMING FROM.
I MEAN, ONCE YOU START THINKING ABOUT SAVING ONE DOG, THERE'S NO END IN SIGHT.
BUT THERE WAS JUST THE ONE DOG RIGHT IN FRONT OF ME! HOW COULD I WALK AWAY FROM HIM?!
SO IT'D BE BETTER IF THE DOG WERE OUT OF YOUR SIGHT?
WOULD IT BE BETTER IF WE COULDN'T SEE?
...NO. I DON'T THINK SO.
......
BUT, Y'KNOW...
WE'RE JUST HIGH SCHOOL STUDENTS.
THERE'S NO WAY WE COULD SAVE *EVERY* DOG THAT'S OUT THERE.

1/4 Sakura Mail

No. 2

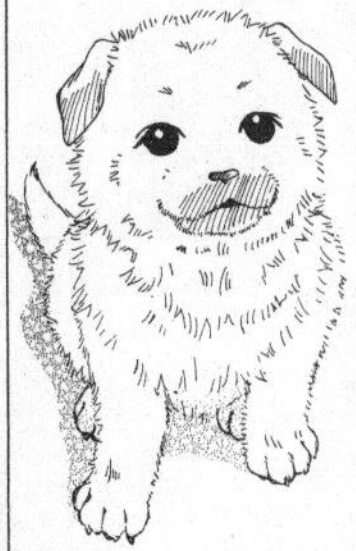

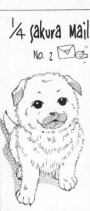

Namiki-san is the star of this story. I think his power is the most useful of the three main characters. But because of that, I wanted him to have a twisted personality and be burdened with the pressure of using his ability to make money, facilitated by Namiki's dark-suited acquaintance, who sort of acts as his "agent."
Even the fat-legged dog has more get-up-and-go spirit than Namiki, who, as I've grown to love, I feel compelled to alternately torment and comfort. But it's just part of the suffering that all my characters have to go through.

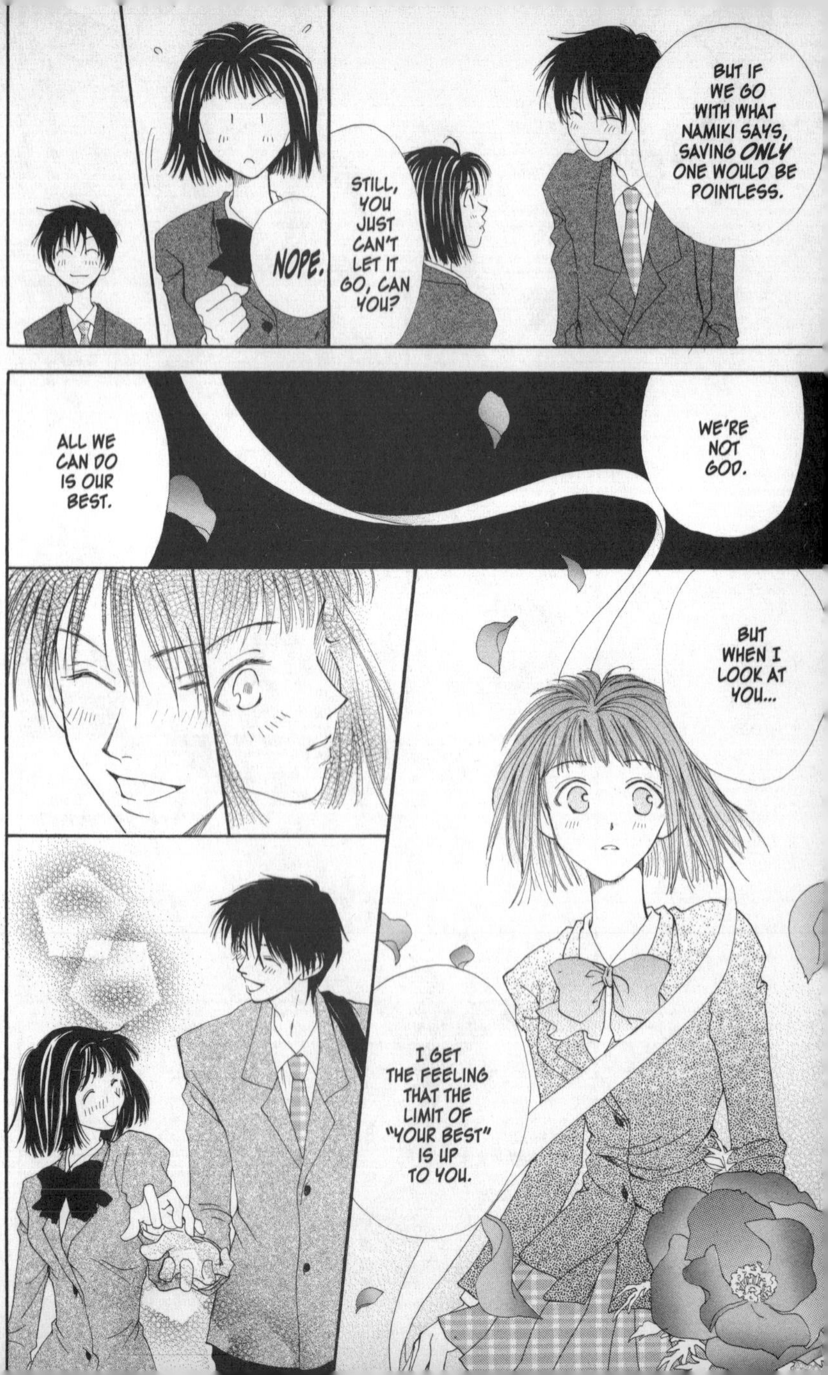
BUT IF WE GO WITH WHAT NAMIKI SAYS, SAVING ONLY ONE WOULD BE POINTLESS.
STILL, YOU JUST CAN'T LET IT GO, CAN YOU?
NOPE.
WE'RE NOT GOD.
ALL WE CAN DO IS OUR BEST.
BUT WHEN I LOOK AT YOU...
I GET THE FEELING THAT THE LIMIT OF "YOUR BEST" IS UP TO YOU.

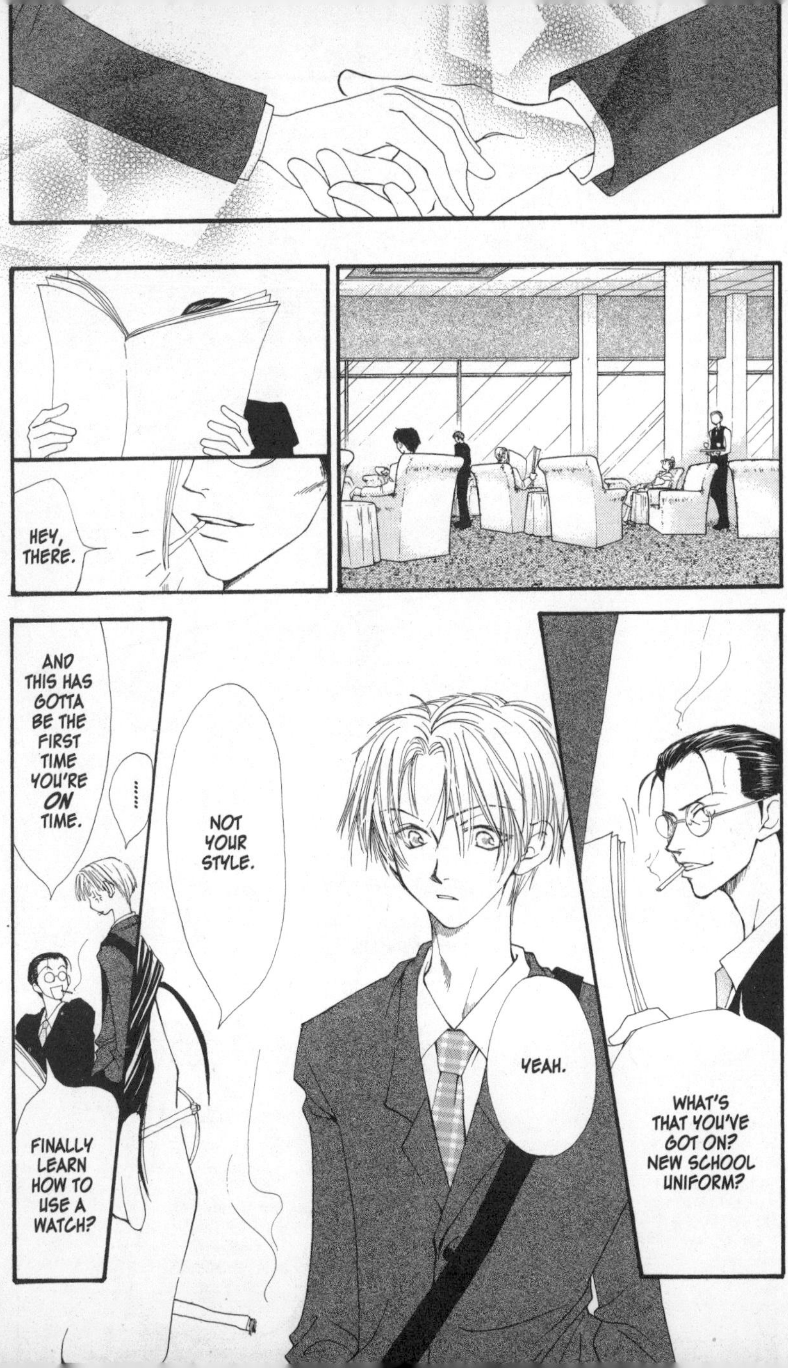
HEY, THERE.
WHAT'S THAT YOU'VE GOT ON? NEW SCHOOL UNIFORM?
YEAH.
NOT YOUR STYLE.
AND THIS HAS GOTTA BE THE FIRST TIME YOU'RE ON TIME.
......
FINALLY LEARN HOW TO USE A WATCH?

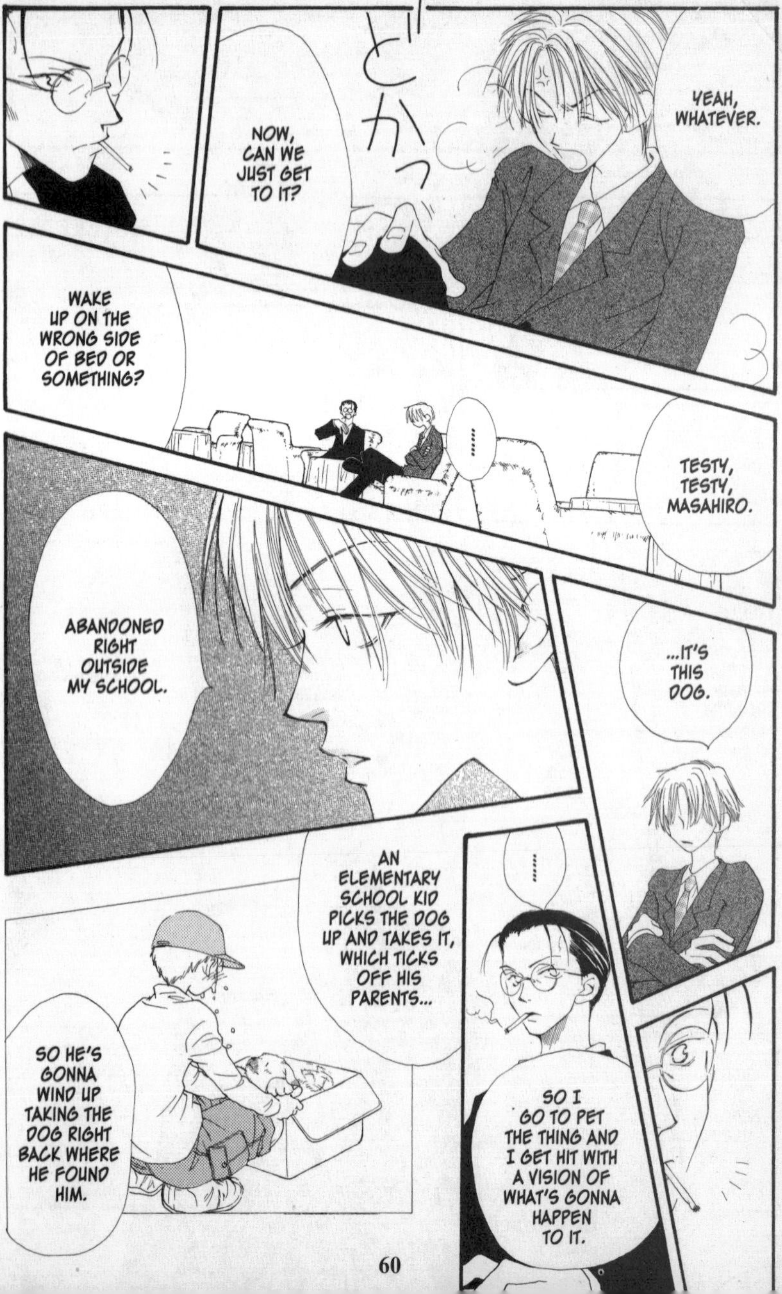
YEAH, WHATEVER.
どかっ
NOW, CAN WE JUST GET TO IT?
WAKE UP ON THE WRONG SIDE OF BED OR SOMETHING?
......
TESTY, TESTY, MASAHIRO.
...IT'S THIS DOG.
ABANDONED RIGHT OUTSIDE MY SCHOOL.
......
SO I GO TO PET THE THING AND I GET HIT WITH A VISION OF WHAT'S GONNA HAPPEN TO IT.
AN ELEMENTARY SCHOOL KID PICKS THE DOG UP AND TAKES IT, WHICH TICKS OFF HIS PARENTS...
SO HE'S GONNA WIND UP TAKING THE DOG RIGHT BACK WHERE HE FOUND HIM.

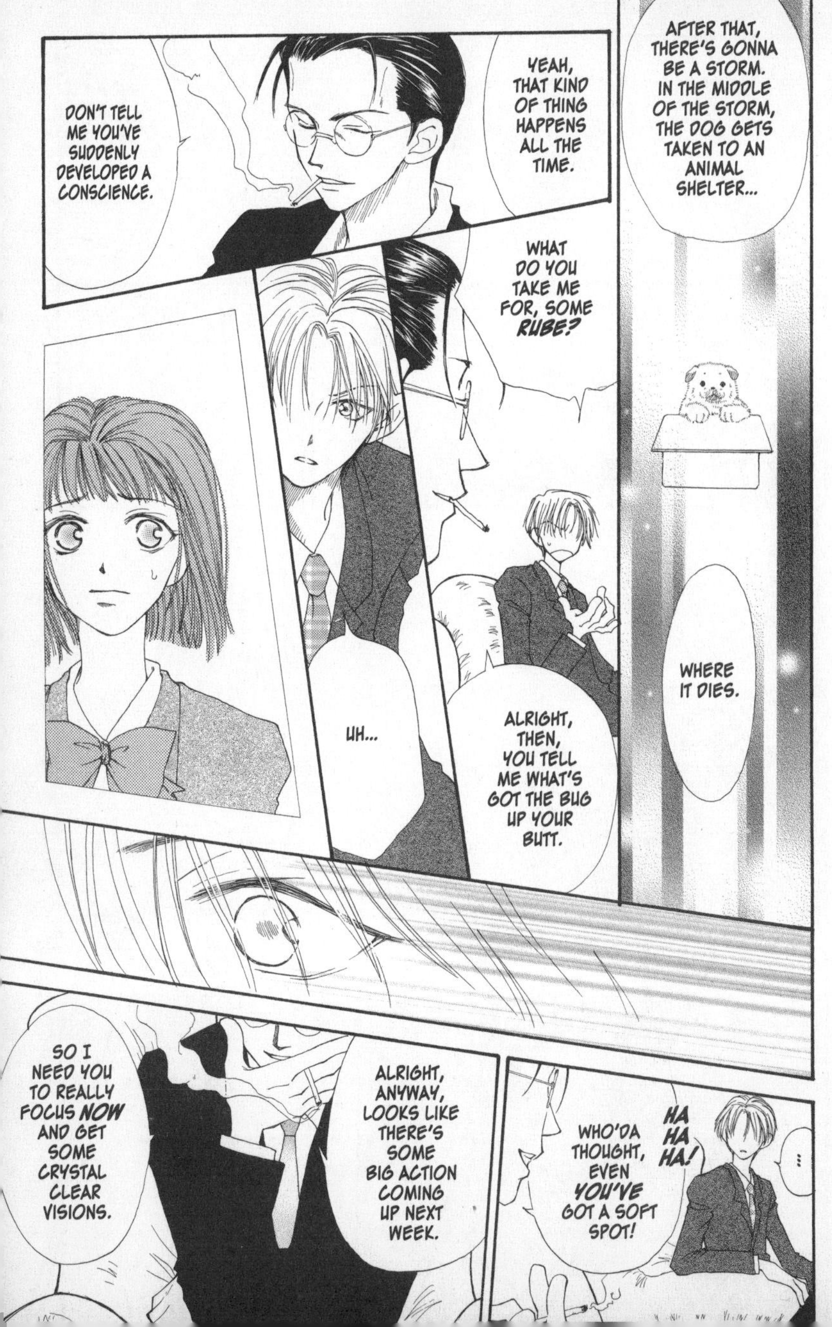
AFTER THAT, THERE'S GONNA BE A STORM. IN THE MIDDLE OF THE STORM, THE DOG GETS TAKEN TO AN ANIMAL SHELTER...
WHERE IT DIES.
YEAH, THAT KIND OF THING HAPPENS ALL THE TIME.
DON'T TELL ME YOU'VE SUDDENLY DEVELOPED A CONSCIENCE.
WHAT DO YOU TAKE ME FOR, SOME *RUBE?*
ALRIGHT, THEN, YOU TELL ME WHAT'S GOT THE BUG UP YOUR BUTT.
UH...
...
HA HA HA!
WHO'DA THOUGHT, EVEN *YOU'VE* GOT A SOFT SPOT!
ALRIGHT, ANYWAY, LOOKS LIKE THERE'S SOME BIG ACTION COMING UP NEXT WEEK.
SO I NEED YOU TO REALLY FOCUS *NOW* AND GET SOME CRYSTAL CLEAR VISIONS.

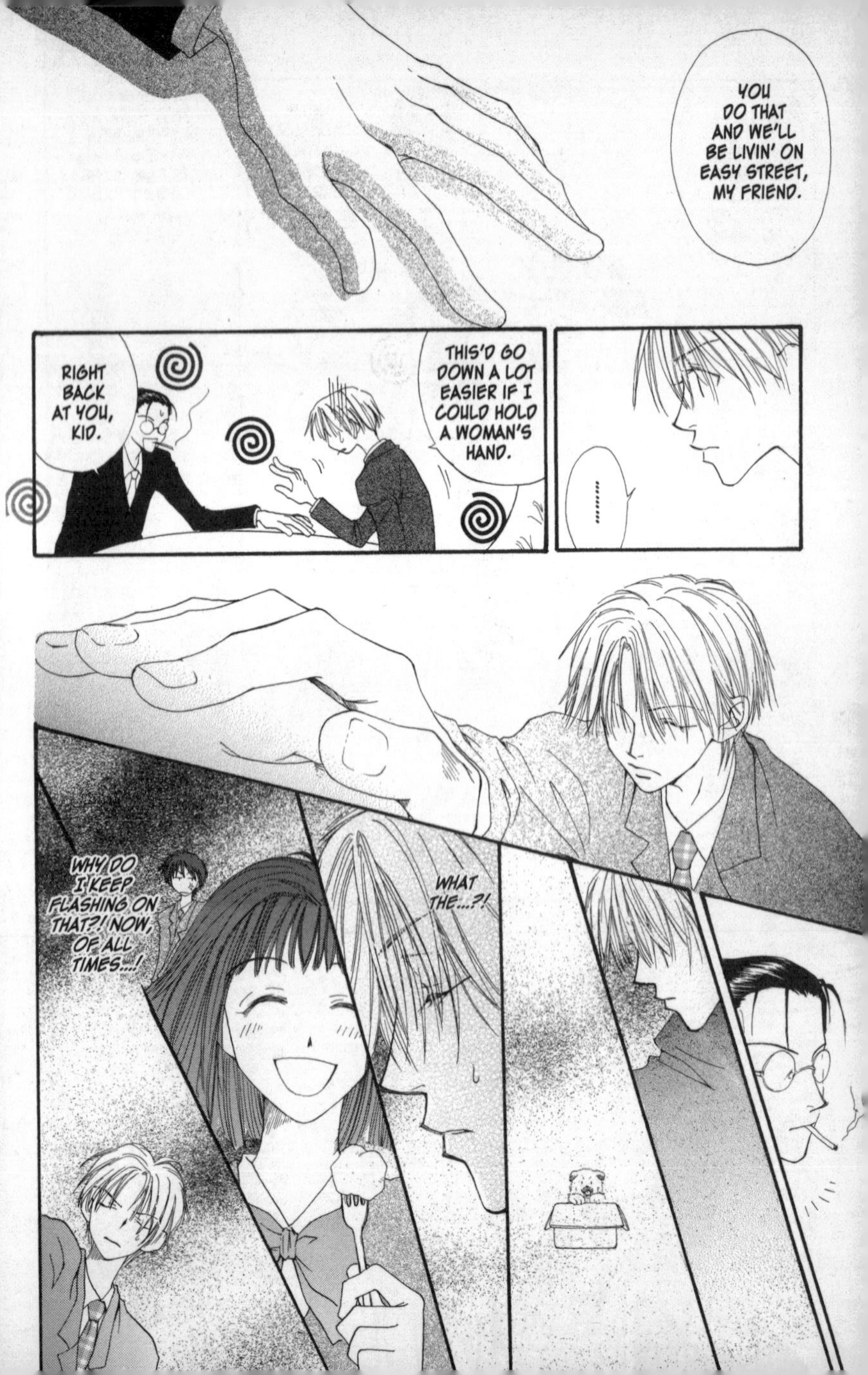
YOU DO THAT AND WE'LL BE LIVIN' ON EASY STREET, MY FRIEND.
......
THIS'D GO DOWN A LOT EASIER IF I COULD HOLD A WOMAN'S HAND.
RIGHT BACK AT YOU, KID.
WHAT THE...?!
WHY DO I KEEP FLASHING ON THAT?! NOW, OF ALL TIMES...!

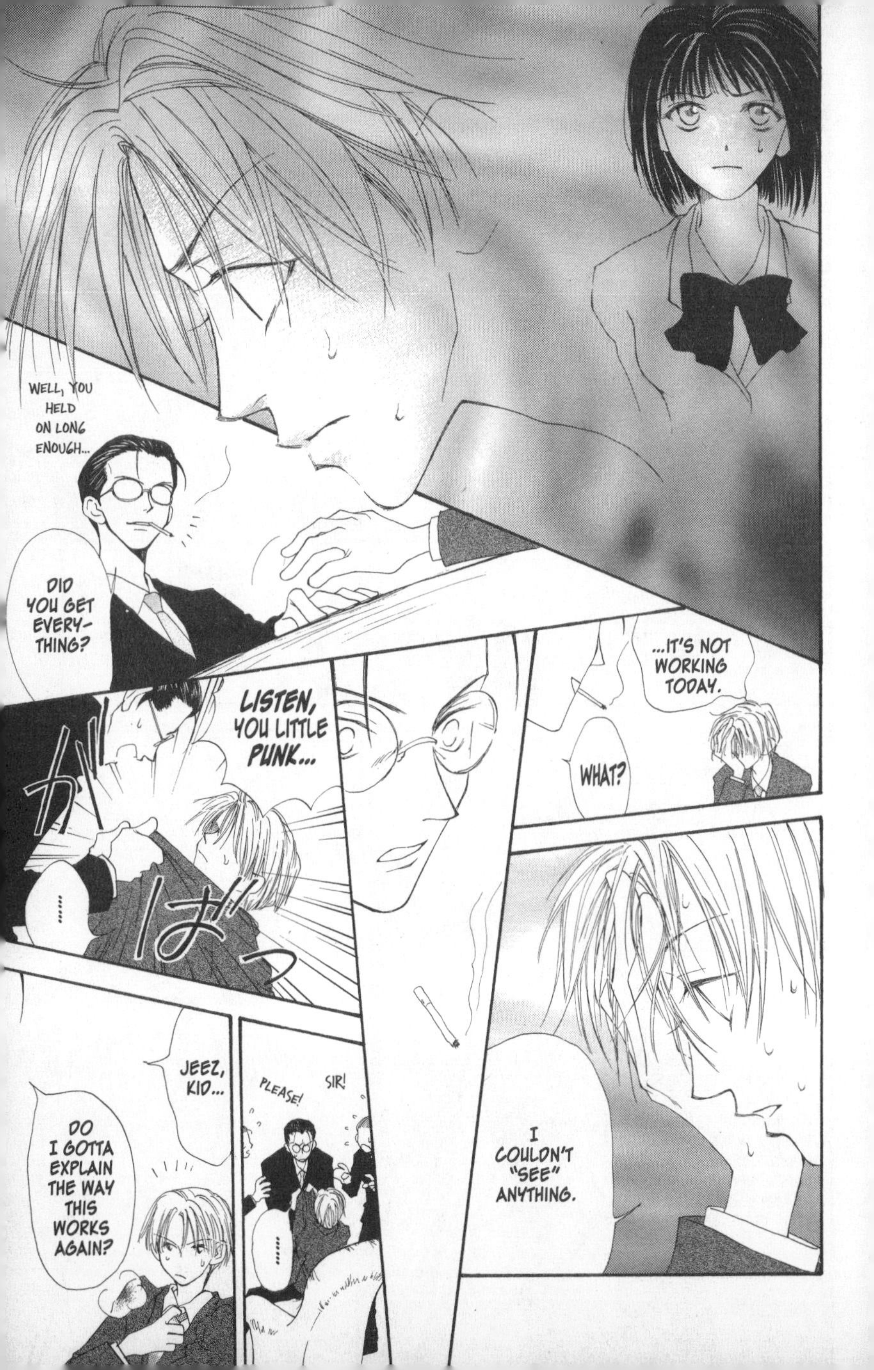
WELL, YOU HELD ON LONG ENOUGH...
DID YOU GET EVERY-THING?
...IT'S NOT WORKING TODAY.
WHAT?
LISTEN, YOU LITTLE PUNK...
......
I COULDN'T "SEE" ANYTHING.
SIR!
PLEASE!
......
JEEZ, KID...
DO I GOTTA EXPLAIN THE WAY THIS WORKS AGAIN?

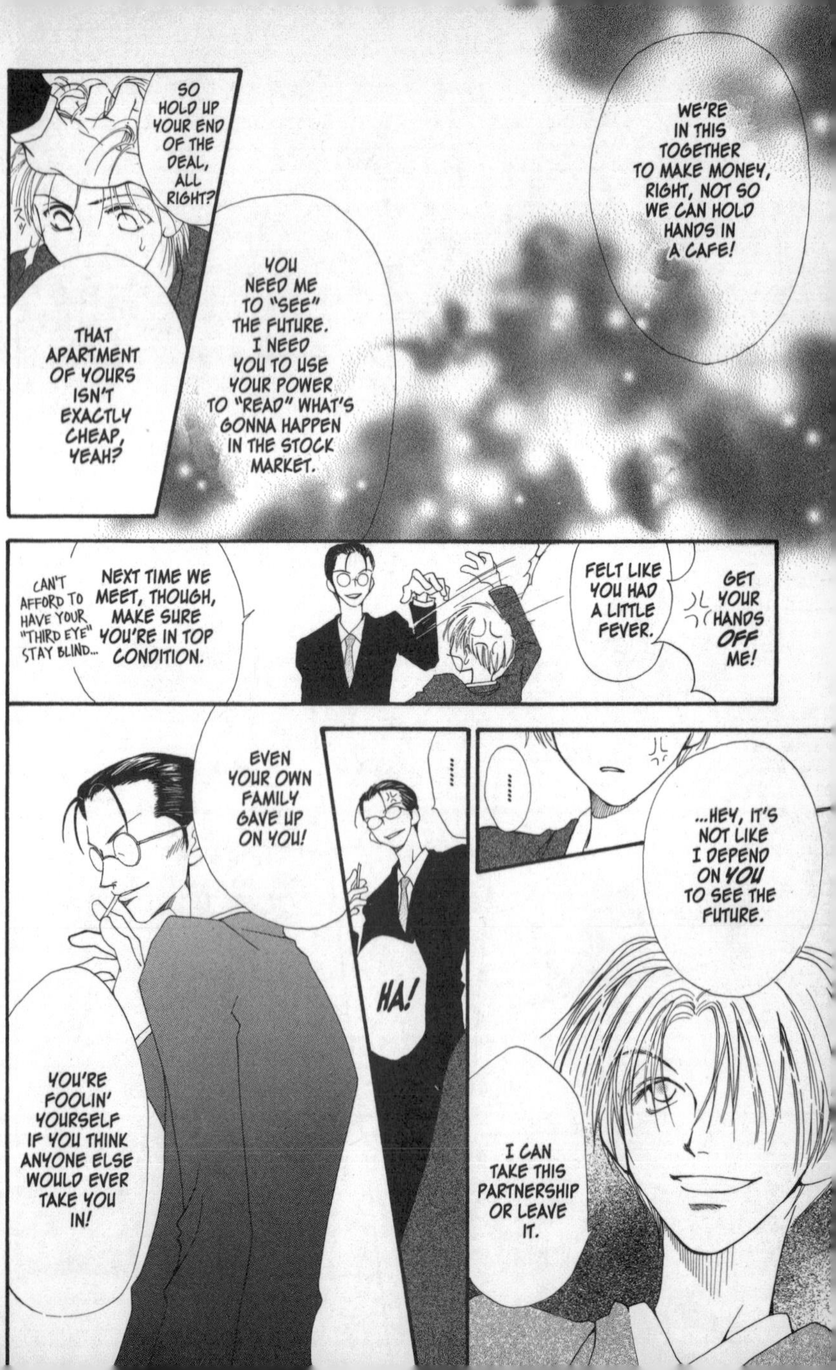

WE'RE IN THIS TOGETHER TO MAKE MONEY, RIGHT, NOT SO WE CAN HOLD HANDS IN A CAFE!
YOU NEED ME TO "SEE" THE FUTURE. I NEED YOU TO USE YOUR POWER TO "READ" WHAT'S GONNA HAPPEN IN THE STOCK MARKET.
SO HOLD UP YOUR END OF THE DEAL, ALL RIGHT?
THAT APARTMENT OF YOURS ISN'T EXACTLY CHEAP, YEAH?
GET YOUR HANDS OFF ME!
FELT LIKE YOU HAD A LITTLE FEVER.
NEXT TIME WE MEET, THOUGH, MAKE SURE YOU'RE IN TOP CONDITION.
CAN'T AFFORD TO HAVE YOUR "THIRD EYE" STAY BLIND...
......
...HEY, IT'S NOT LIKE I DEPEND ON YOU TO SEE THE FUTURE.
I CAN TAKE THIS PARTNERSHIP OR LEAVE IT.
......
HA!
EVEN YOUR OWN FAMILY GAVE UP ON YOU!
YOU'RE FOOLIN' YOURSELF IF YOU THINK ANYONE ELSE WOULD EVER TAKE YOU IN!

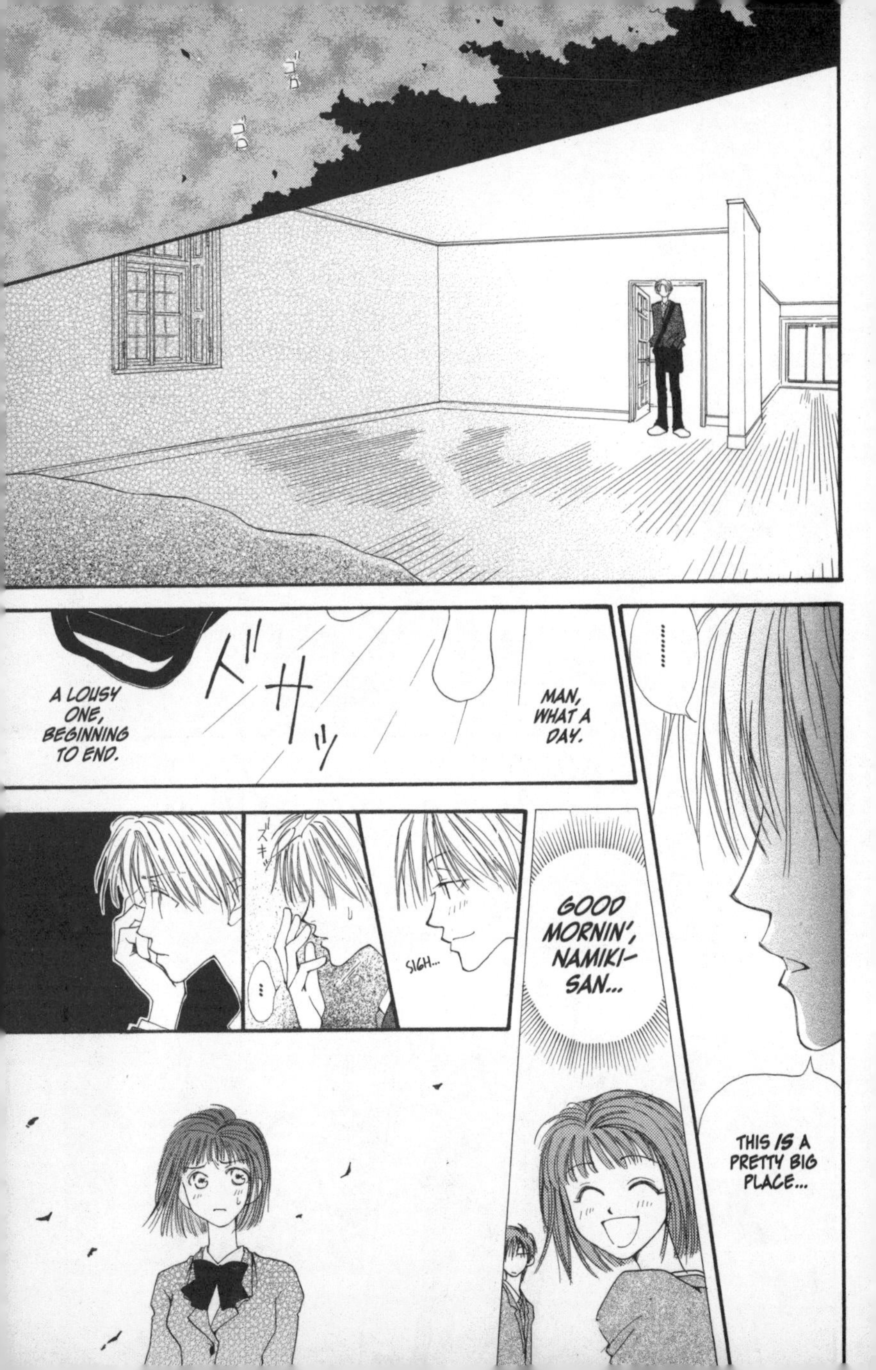
ゴロ
ゴロ
......
THIS *IS* A PRETTY BIG PLACE...
MAN, WHAT A DAY.
ドサッ
A LOUSY ONE, BEGINNING TO END.
GOOD MORNIN', NAMIKI-SAN...
SIGH...
ズキッ
...

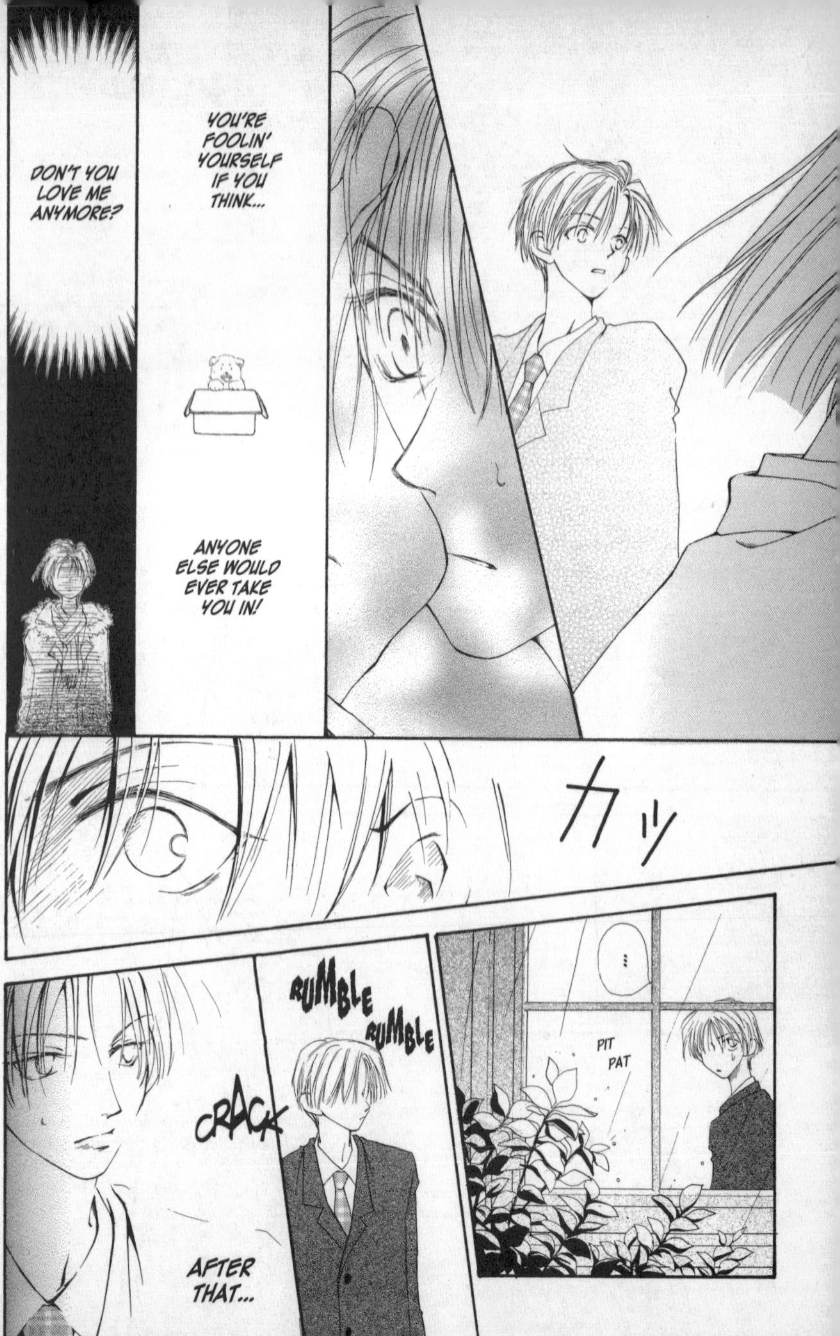
YOU'RE FOOLIN' YOURSELF IF YOU THINK...
ANYONE ELSE WOULD EVER TAKE YOU IN!
DON'T YOU LOVE ME ANYMORE?
カッ
...
PIT PAT
RUMBLE RUMBLE
CRACK
AFTER THAT...

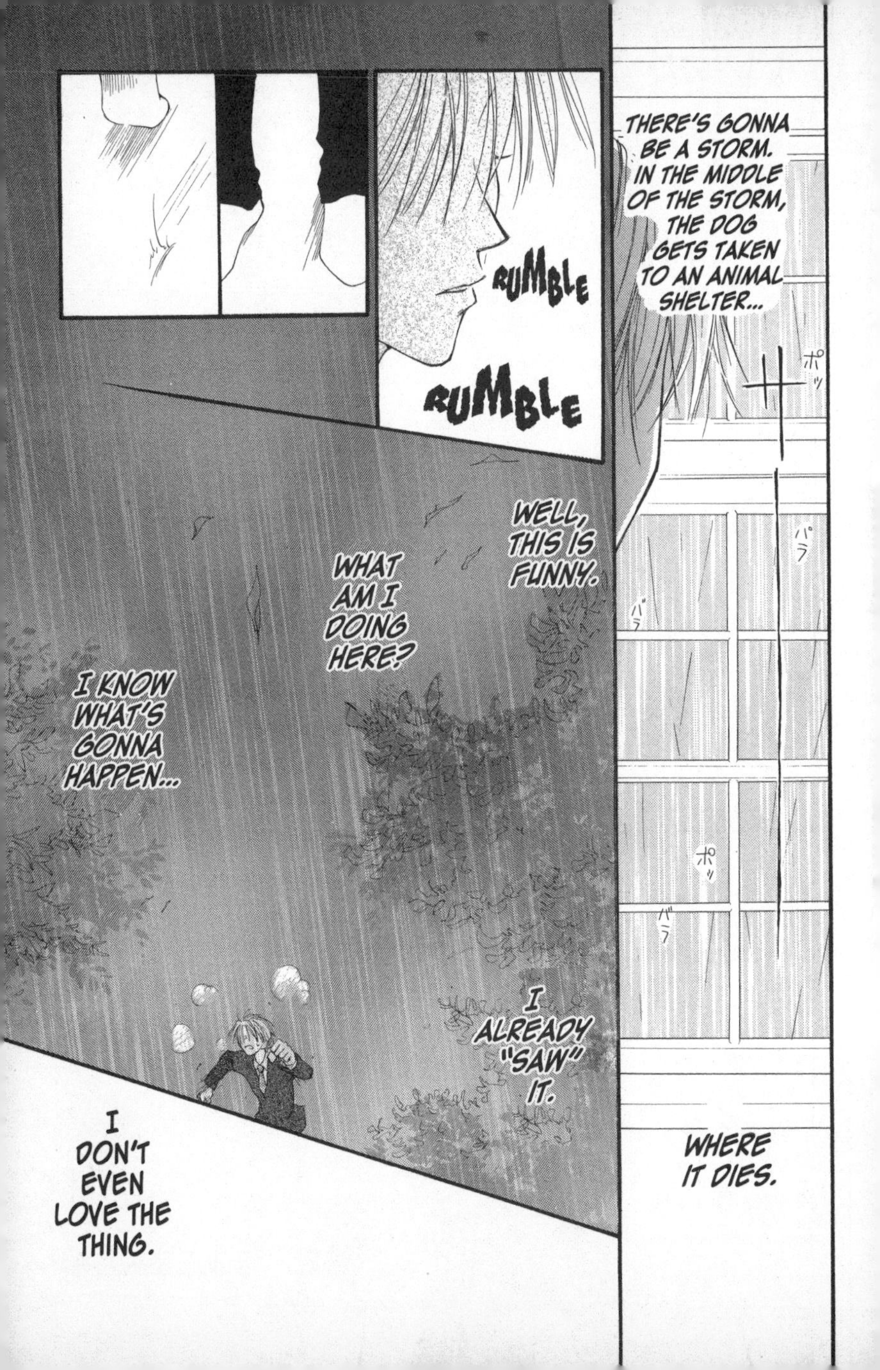
THERE'S GONNA BE A STORM. IN THE MIDDLE OF THE STORM, THE DOG GETS TAKEN TO AN ANIMAL SHELTER...
ポツ
パラ
パラ
ポツ
パラ
WHERE IT DIES.
RUMBLE
RUMBLE
WELL, THIS IS FUNNY.
WHAT AM I DOING HERE?
I KNOW WHAT'S GONNA HAPPEN...
I ALREADY "SAW" IT.
I DON'T EVEN LOVE THE THING.

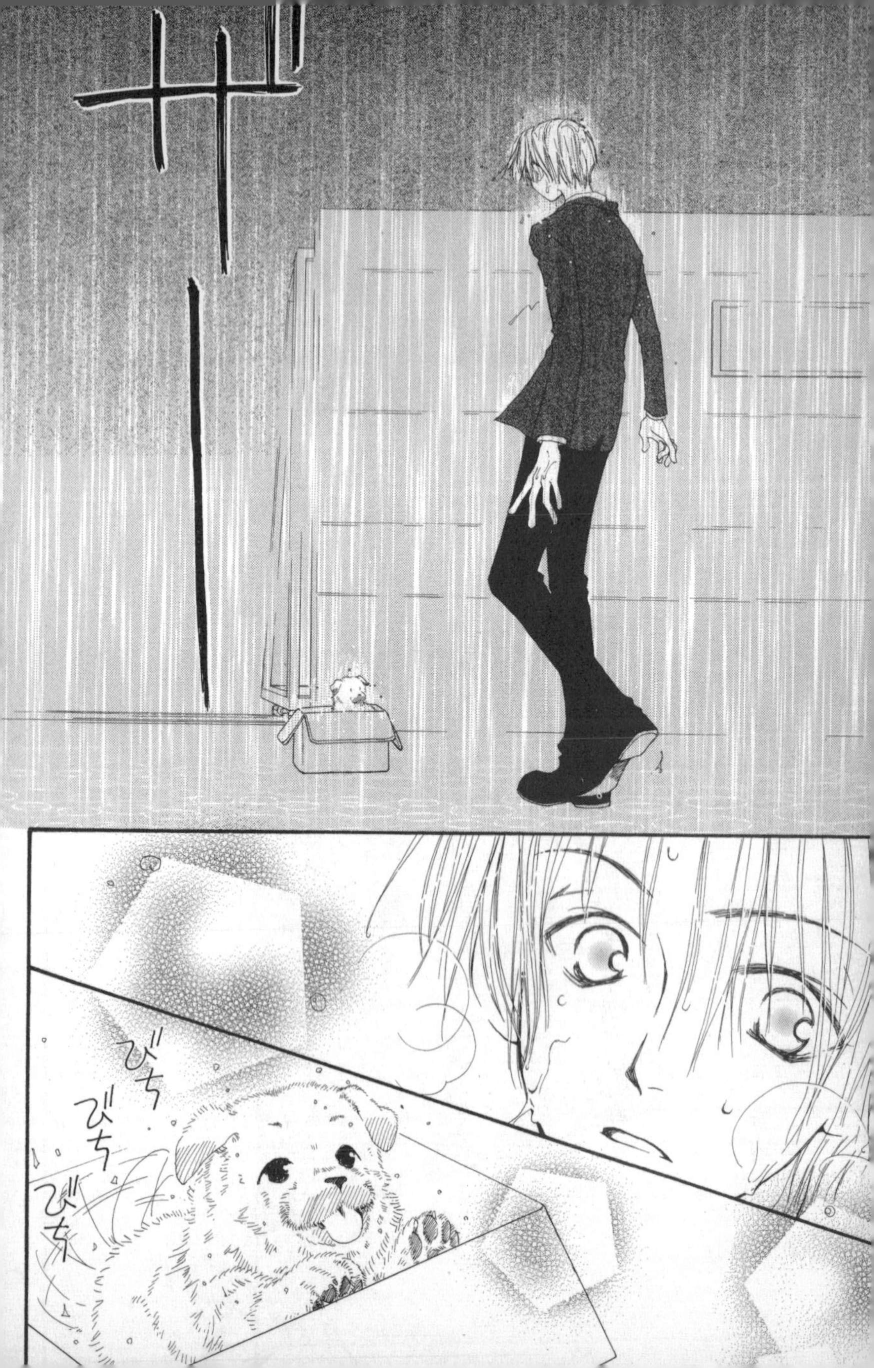
ザー
ぴち
ぴち
ぴち

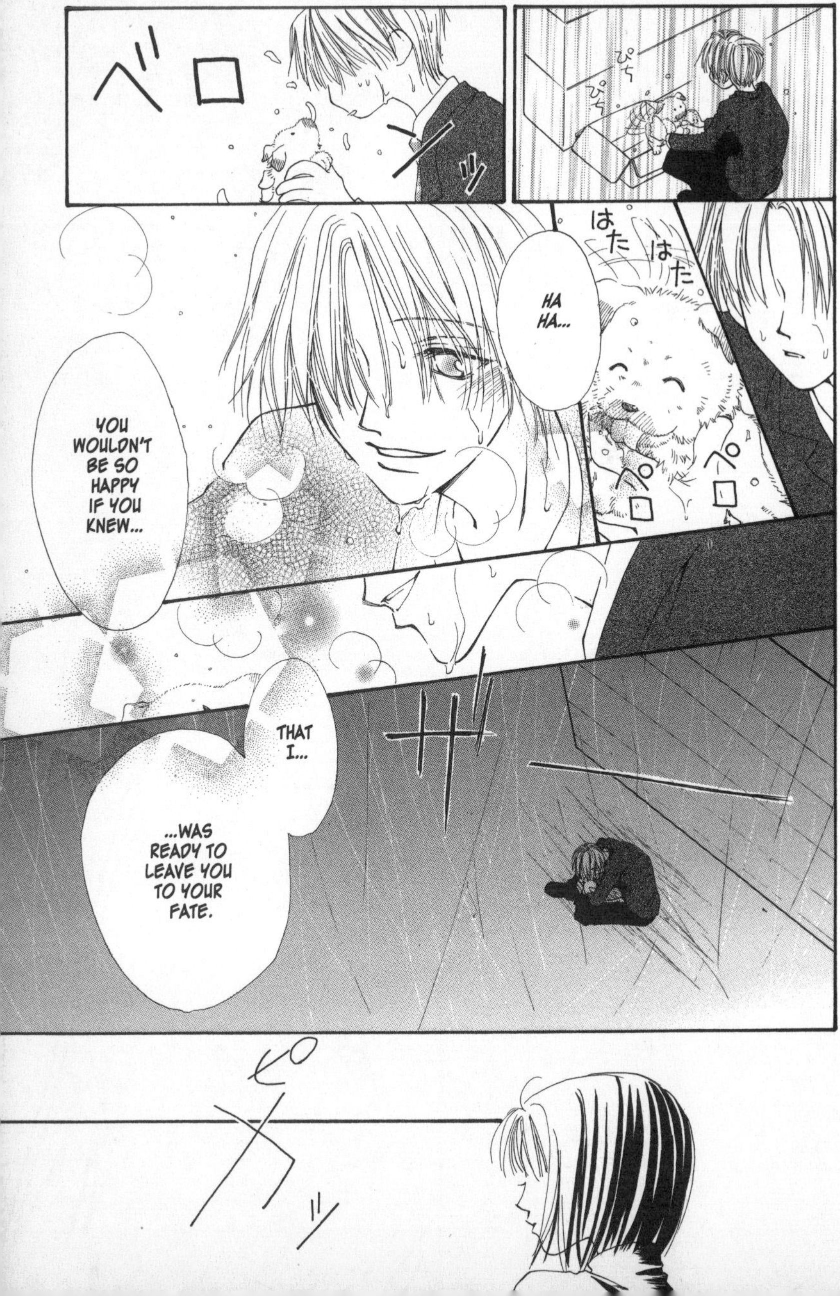
ぴち
ぴち
ベロ
ッ
はた はた
HA HA...
ポロ ポロ
YOU WOULDN'T BE SO HAPPY IF YOU KNEW...
THAT I...
...WAS READY TO LEAVE YOU TO YOUR FATE.
ピクッ

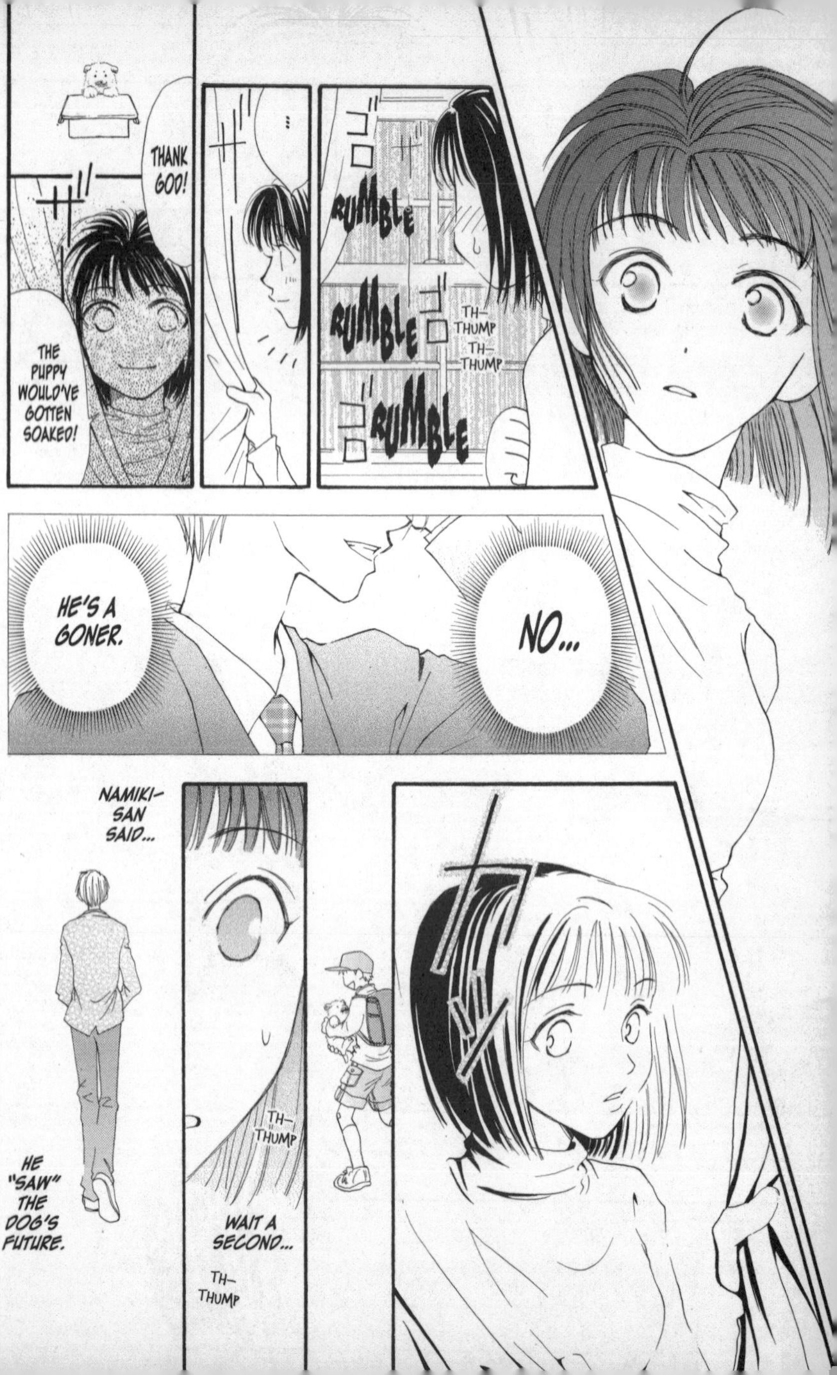
RUMBLE
RUMBLE
RUMBLE
TH-THUMP
TH-THUMP
...
THANK GOD!
THE PUPPY WOULD'VE GOTTEN SOAKED!
NO...
HE'S A GONER.
TH-THUMP
WAIT A SECOND...
TH-THUMP
NAMIKI-SAN SAID...
HE "SAW" THE DOG'S FUTURE.

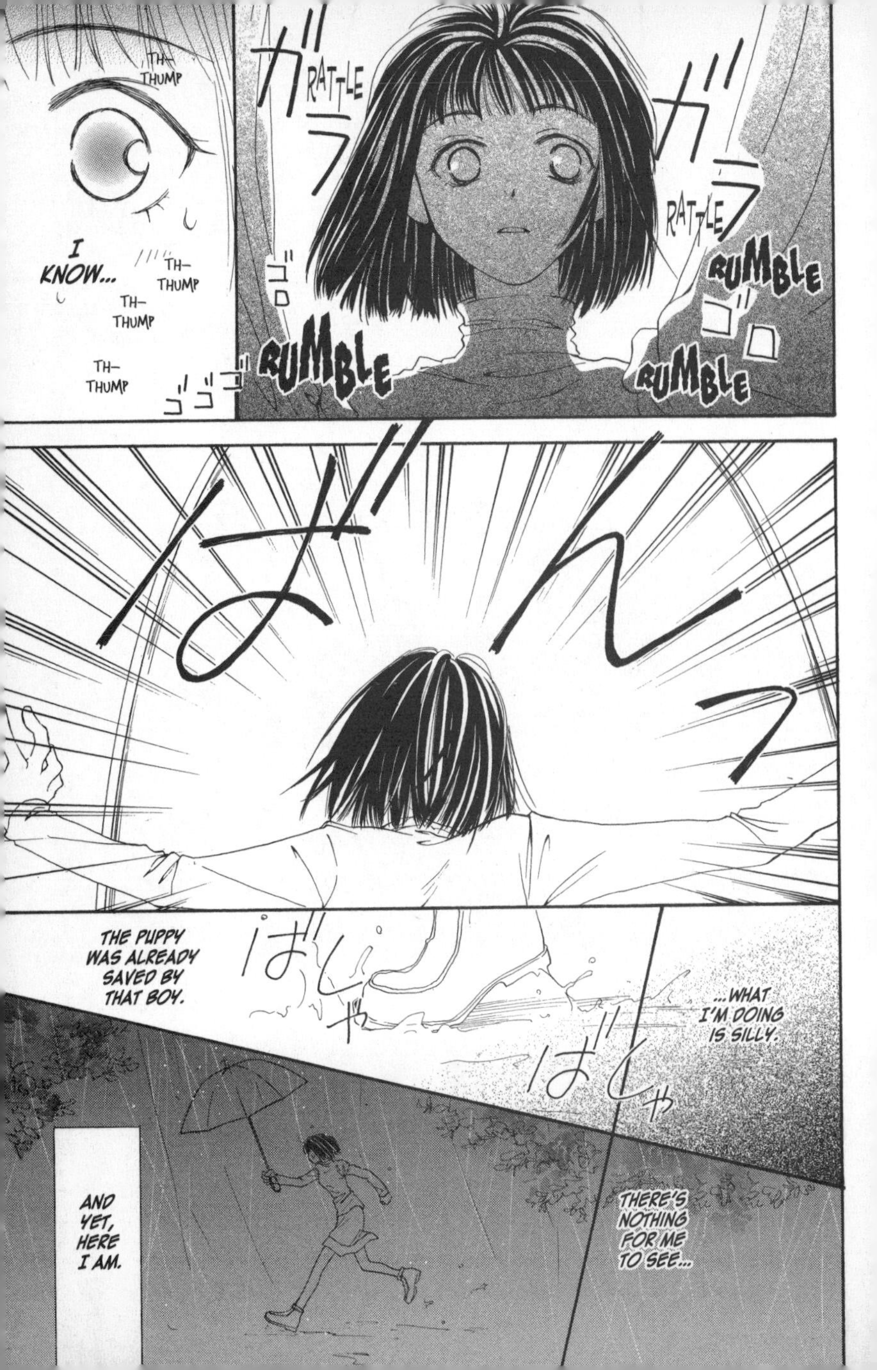
ガラ
RATTLE
ガラ
RATTLE
RUMBLE
ゴロ
RUMBLE
ゴロ
RUMBLE
TH-THUMP
I KNOW...
TH-THUMP
TH-THUMP
TH-THUMP
ゴゴゴ
ばんっ
...WHAT I'M DOING IS SILLY.
ばしゃ
ばしゃ
THE PUPPY WAS ALREADY SAVED BY THAT BOY.
THERE'S NOTHING FOR ME TO SEE...
AND YET, HERE I AM.

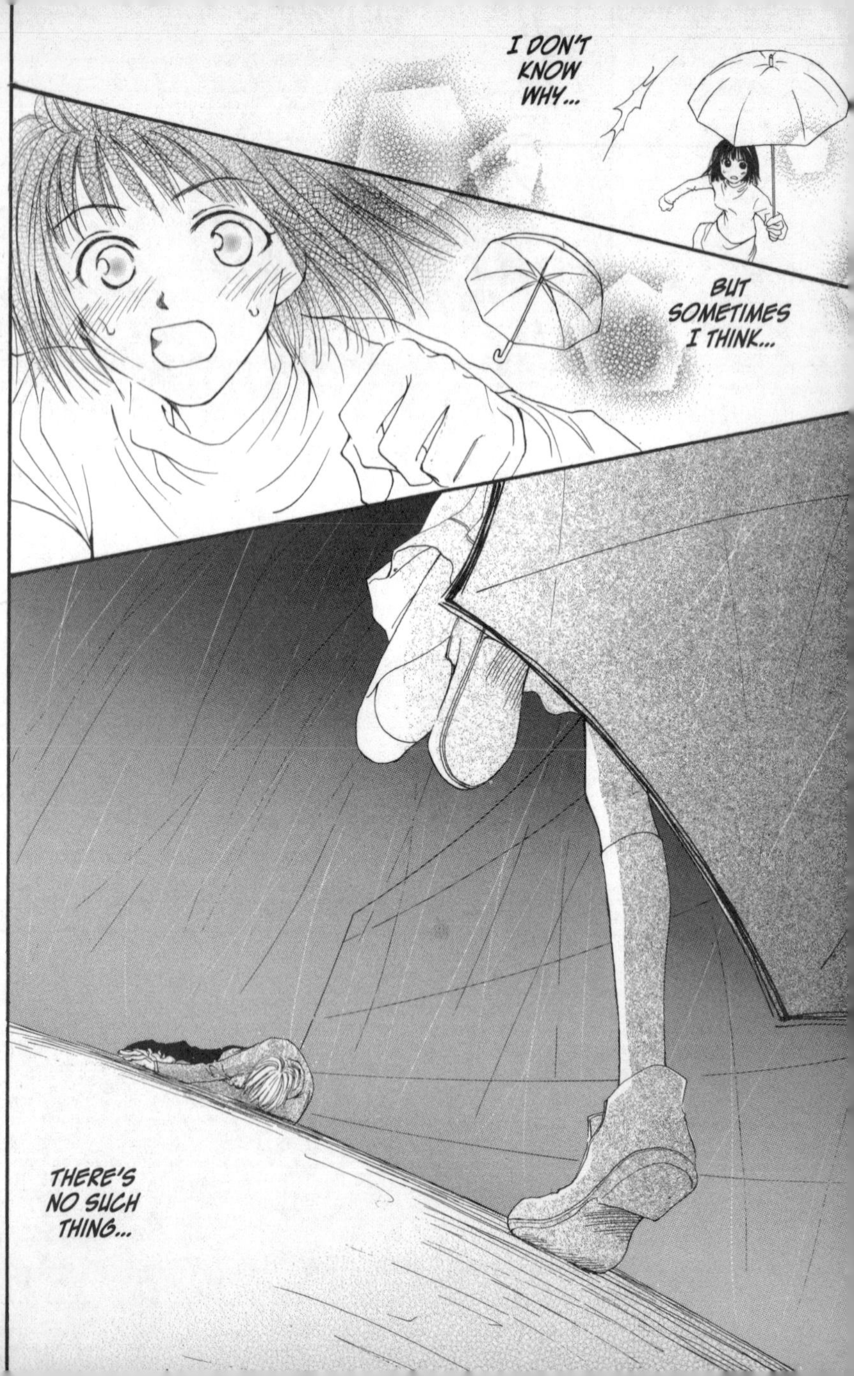
I DON'T KNOW WHY...
BUT SOMETIMES I THINK...
THERE'S NO SUCH THING...

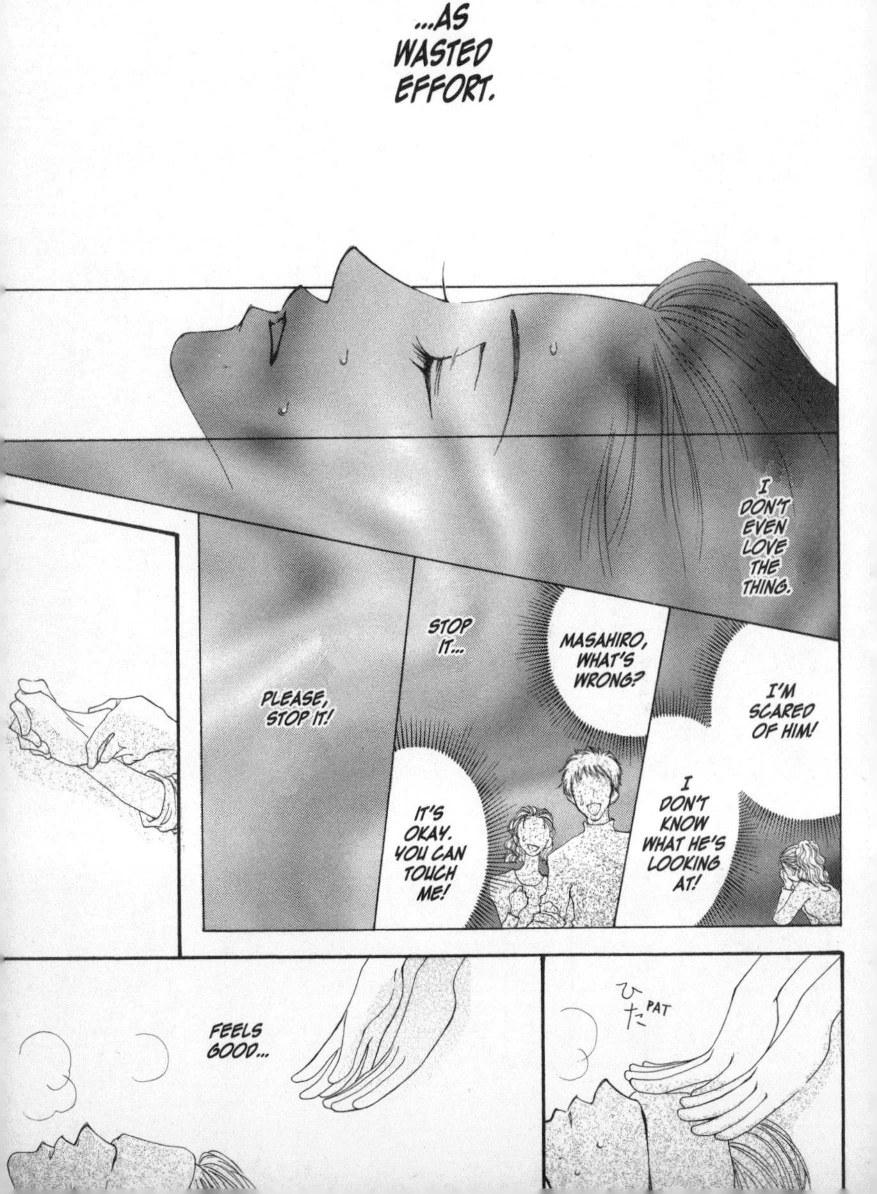
...AS WASTED EFFORT.
I DON'T EVEN LOVE THE THING.
I'M SCARED OF HIM!
I DON'T KNOW WHAT HE'S LOOKING AT!
MASAHIRO, WHAT'S WRONG?
IT'S OKAY. YOU CAN TOUCH ME!
STOP IT...
PLEASE, STOP IT!
ひた
PAT
FEELS GOOD...

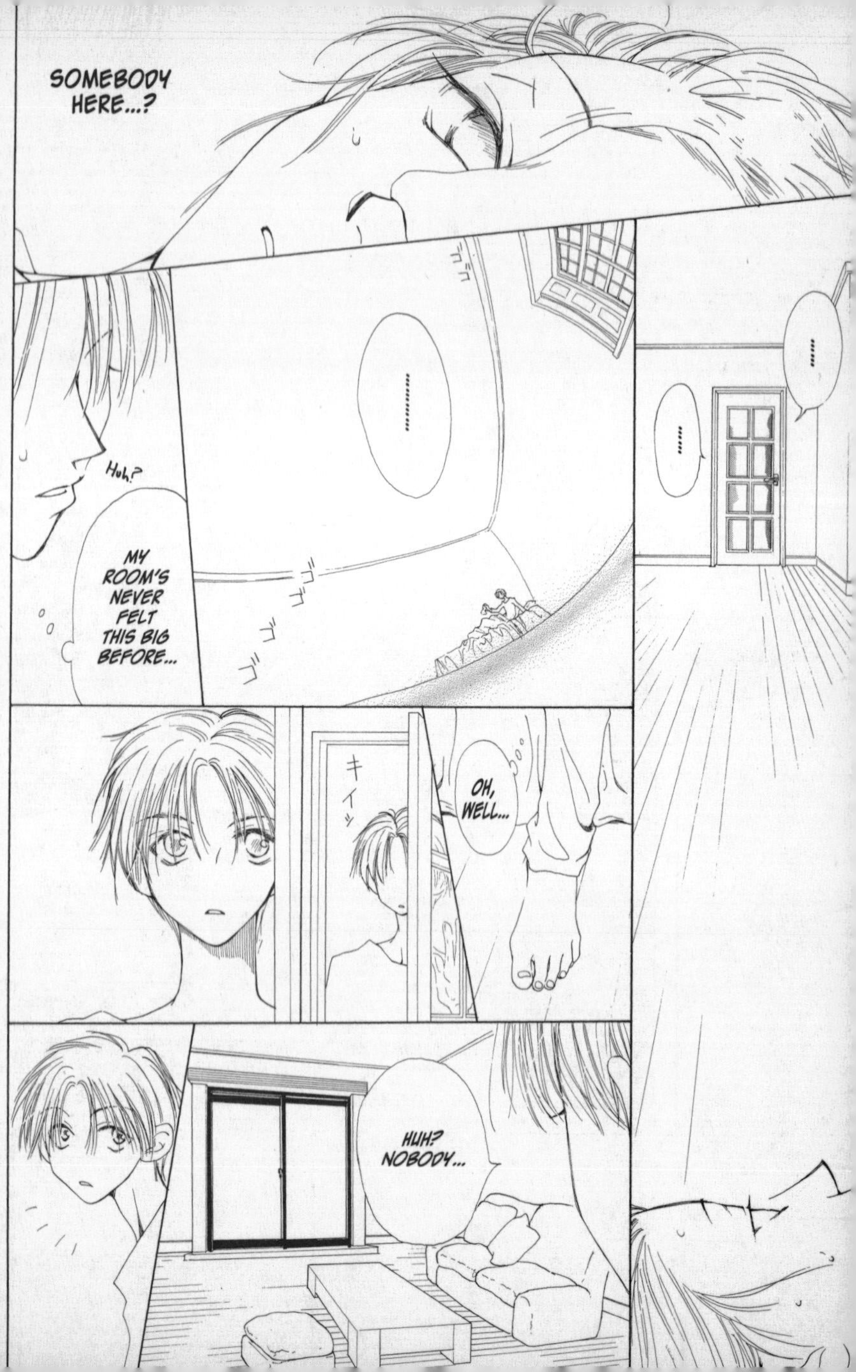
SOMEBODY HERE...?
......
......
ゴゴ
....
ゴゴゴゴ
Huh?
MY ROOM'S NEVER FELT THIS BIG BEFORE...
OH, WELL...
キイッ
HUH? NOBODY...

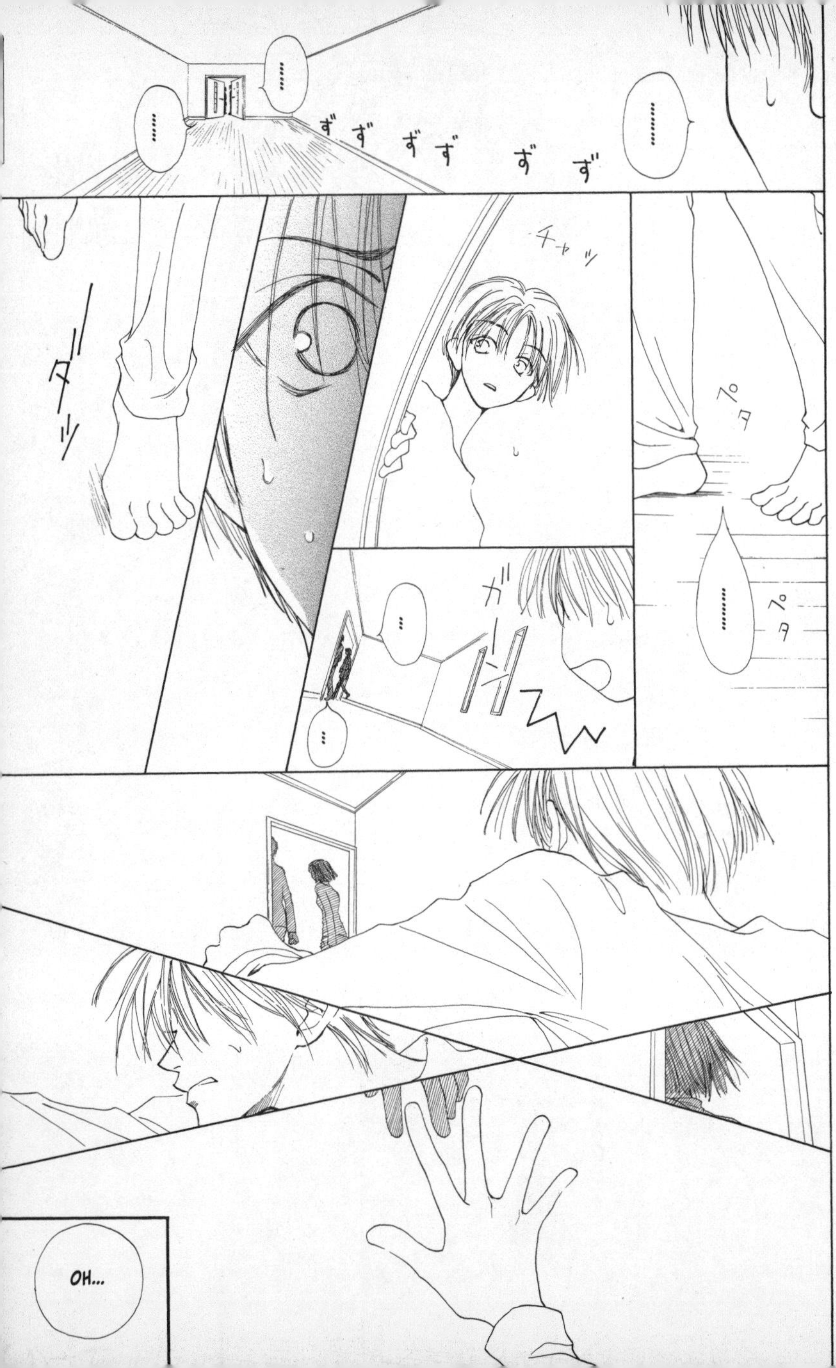
……
ずずずずずず
……
……
パタ
……
パタ
チャッ
…
…
ガーン
ダーッ
OH...

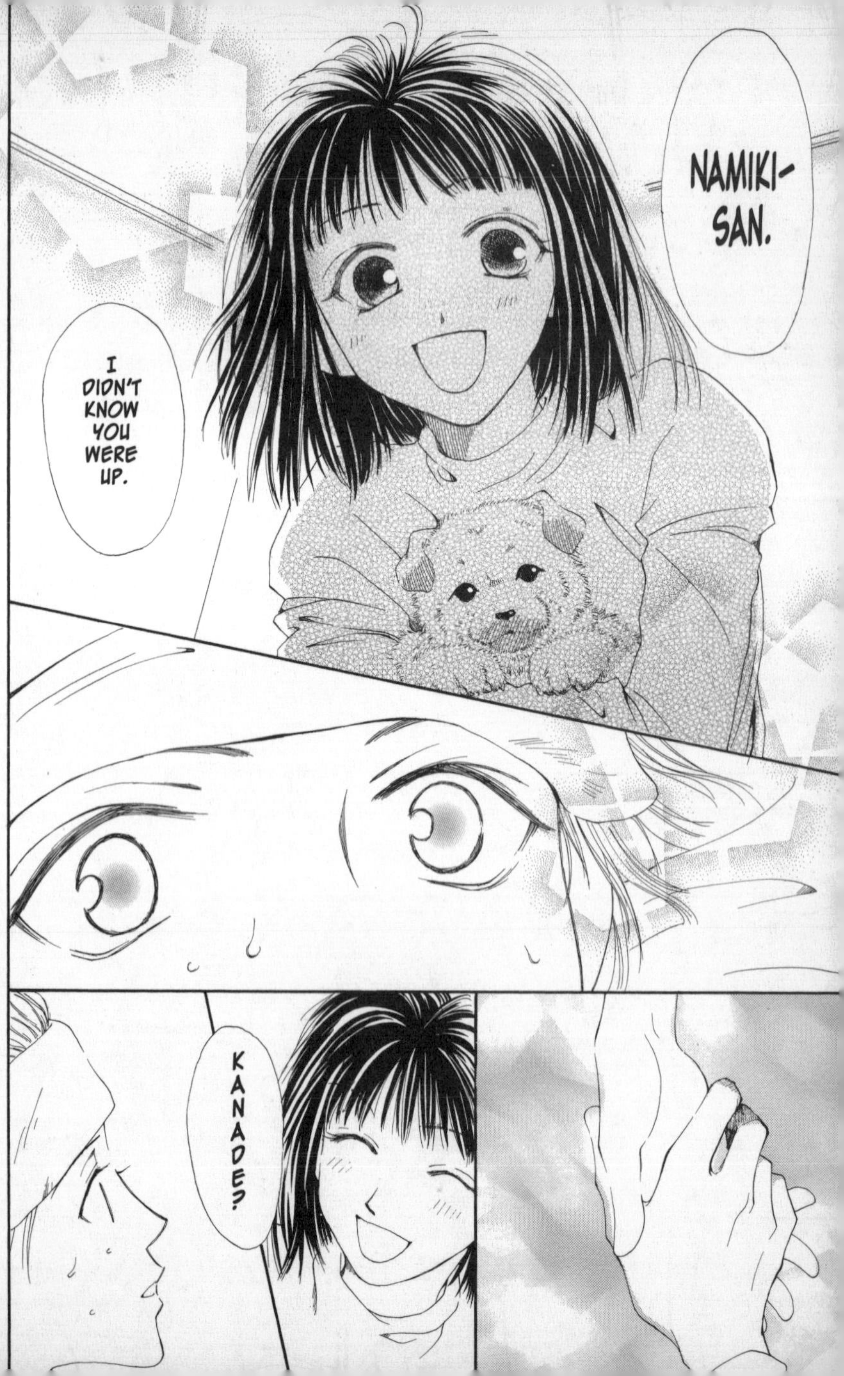
NAMIKI-SAN.
I DIDN'T KNOW YOU WERE UP.
KANADE?

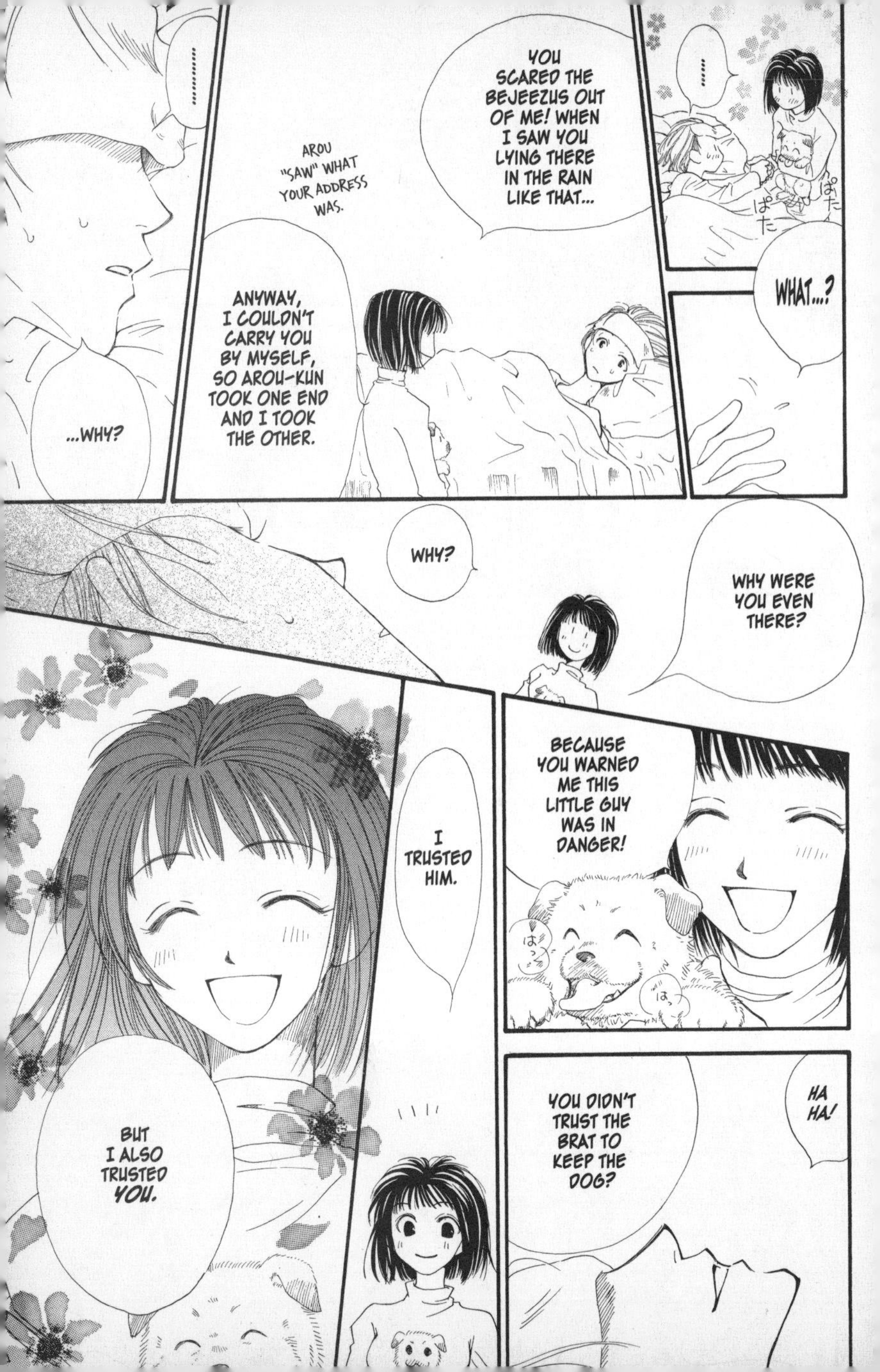
......
ぱた
ぱた
WHAT...?
YOU SCARED THE BEJEEZUS OUT OF ME! WHEN I SAW YOU LYING THERE IN THE RAIN LIKE THAT...
AROU "SAW" WHAT YOUR ADDRESS WAS.
ANYWAY, I COULDN'T CARRY YOU BY MYSELF, SO AROU-KUN TOOK ONE END AND I TOOK THE OTHER.
......
...WHY?
WHY?
WHY WERE YOU EVEN THERE?
BECAUSE YOU WARNED ME THIS LITTLE GUY WAS IN DANGER!
はっ
はっ
HA HA!
YOU DIDN'T TRUST THE BRAT TO KEEP THE DOG?
I TRUSTED HIM.
BUT I ALSO TRUSTED YOU.

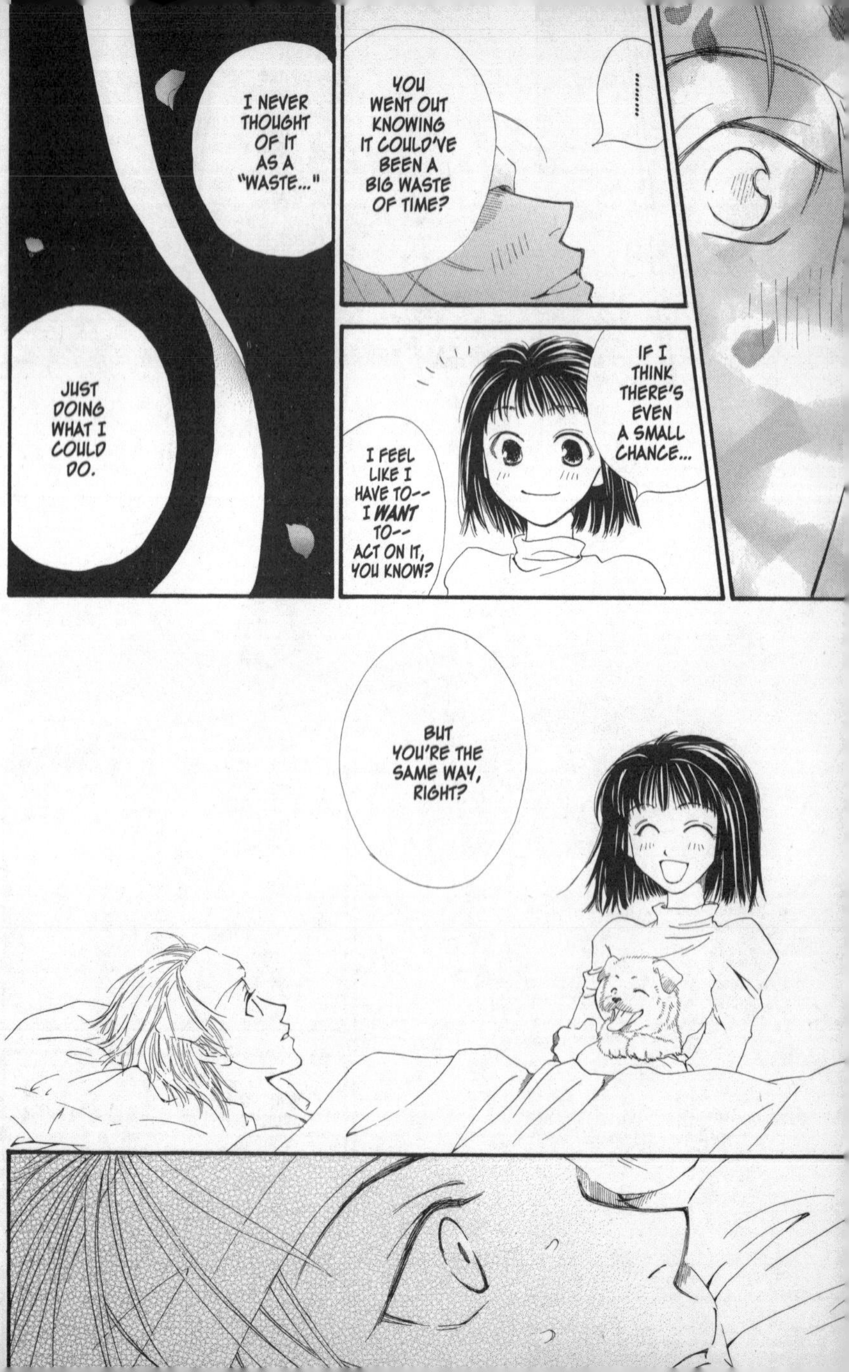
......
YOU WENT OUT KNOWING IT COULD'VE BEEN A BIG WASTE OF TIME?
IF I THINK THERE'S EVEN A SMALL CHANCE...
I FEEL LIKE I HAVE TO-- I *WANT* TO-- ACT ON IT, YOU KNOW?
I NEVER THOUGHT OF IT AS A "WASTE..."
JUST DOING WHAT I COULD DO.
BUT YOU'RE THE SAME WAY, RIGHT?

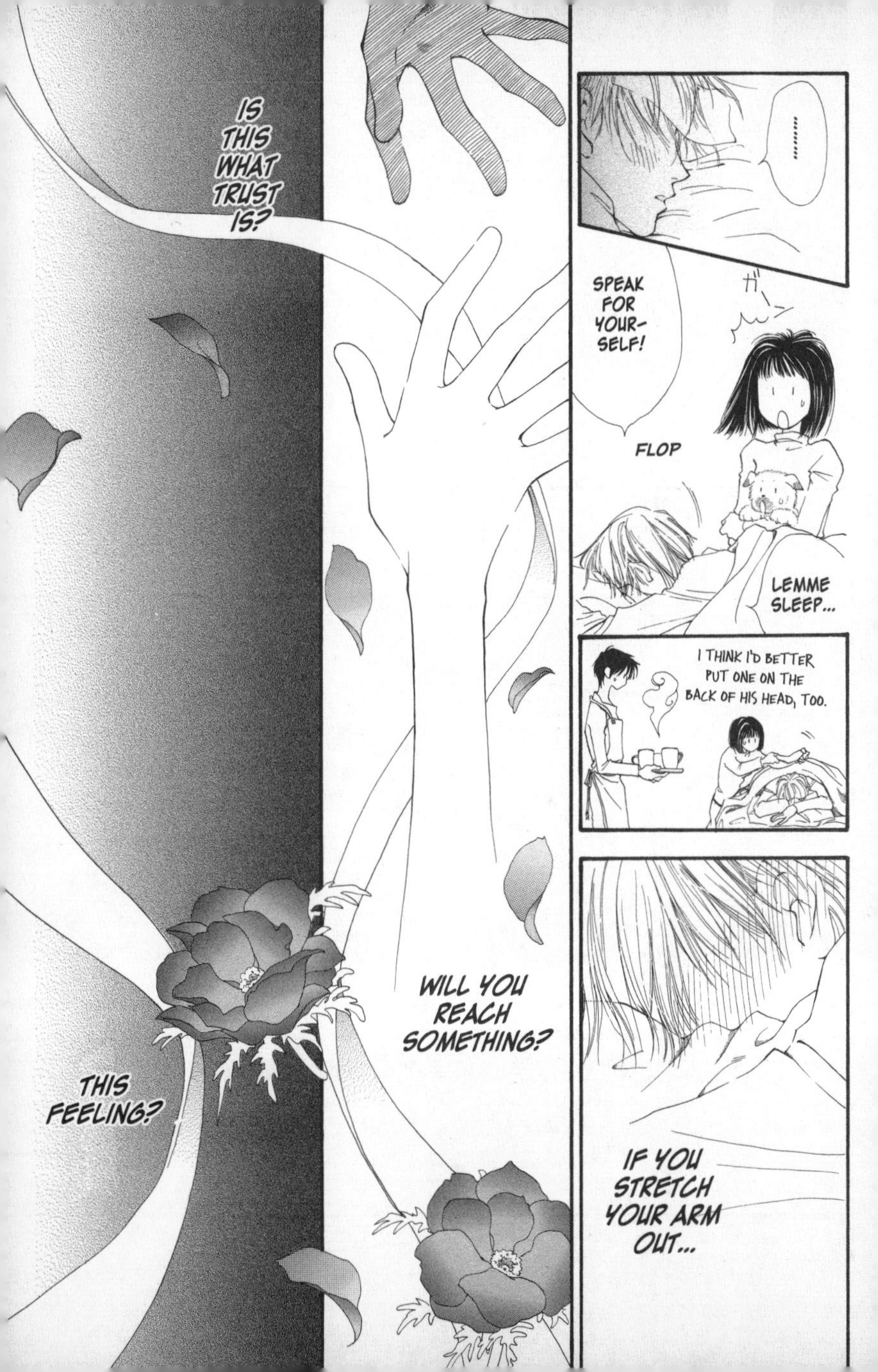
......
SPEAK FOR YOUR-SELF!
ガーン
FLOP
LEMME SLEEP...
I THINK I'D BETTER PUT ONE ON THE BACK OF HIS HEAD, TOO.
IF YOU STRETCH YOUR ARM OUT...
WILL YOU REACH SOMETHING?
IS THIS WHAT TRUST IS?
THIS FEELING?

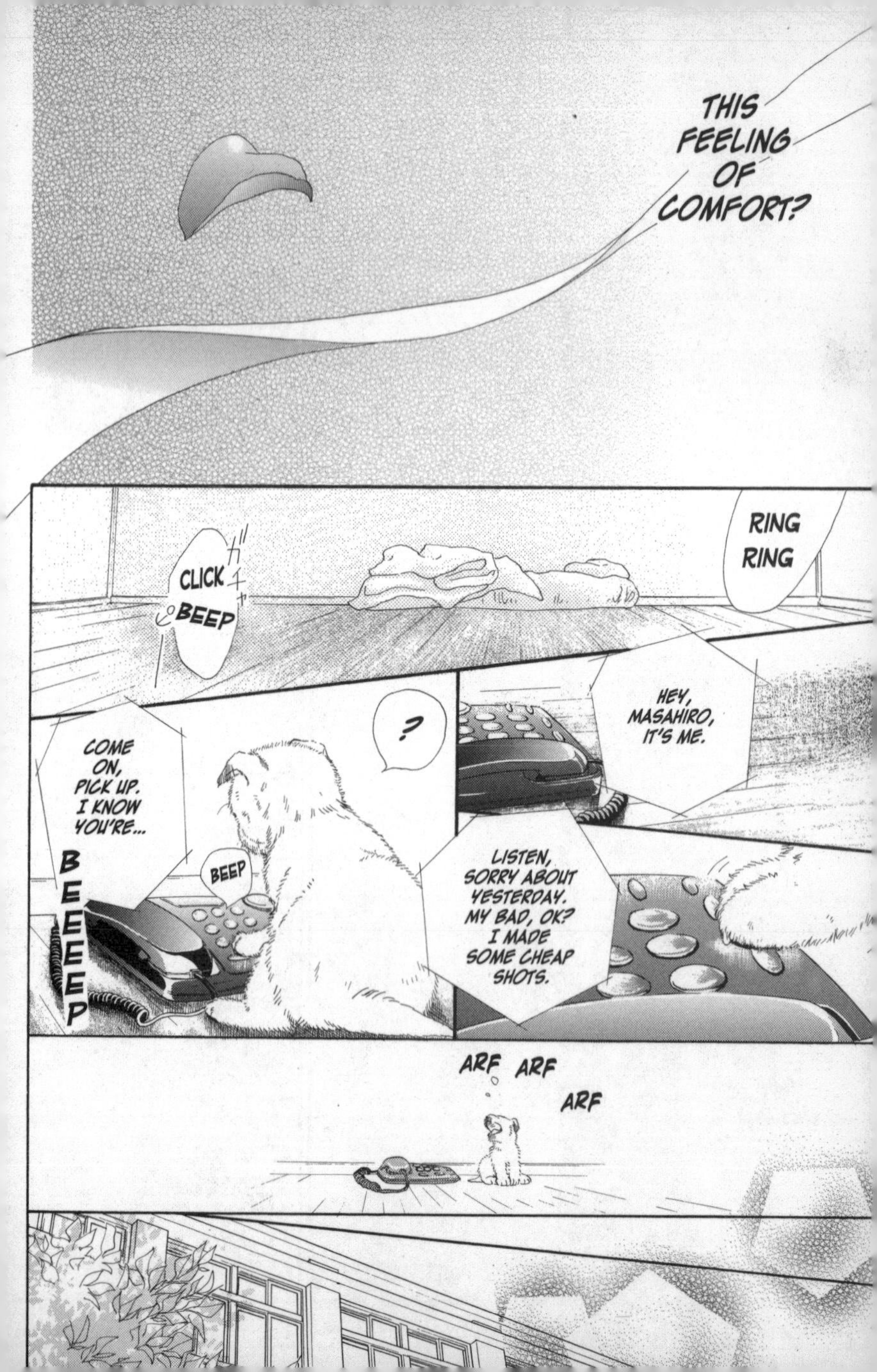
THIS FEELING OF COMFORT?
RING RING
CLICK
ガチャ
BEEP
ピ
HEY, MASAHIRO, IT'S ME.
LISTEN, SORRY ABOUT YESTERDAY. MY BAD, OK? I MADE SOME CHEAP SHOTS.
?
COME ON, PICK UP. I KNOW YOU'RE...
BEEP
BEEEEEP
ARF ARF
ARF

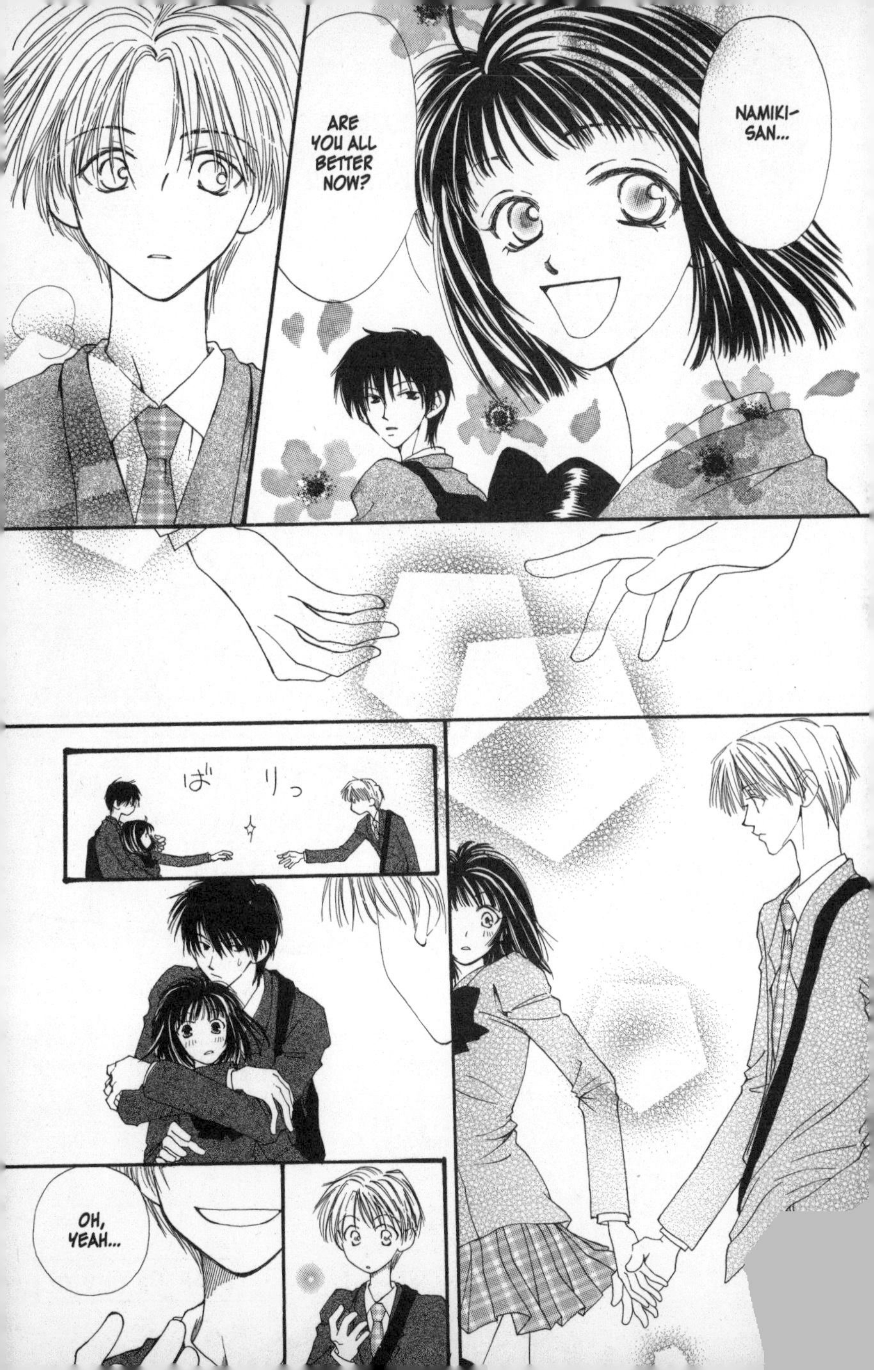
NAMIKI-SAN...
ARE YOU ALL BETTER NOW?
ばりっ
OH, YEAH...

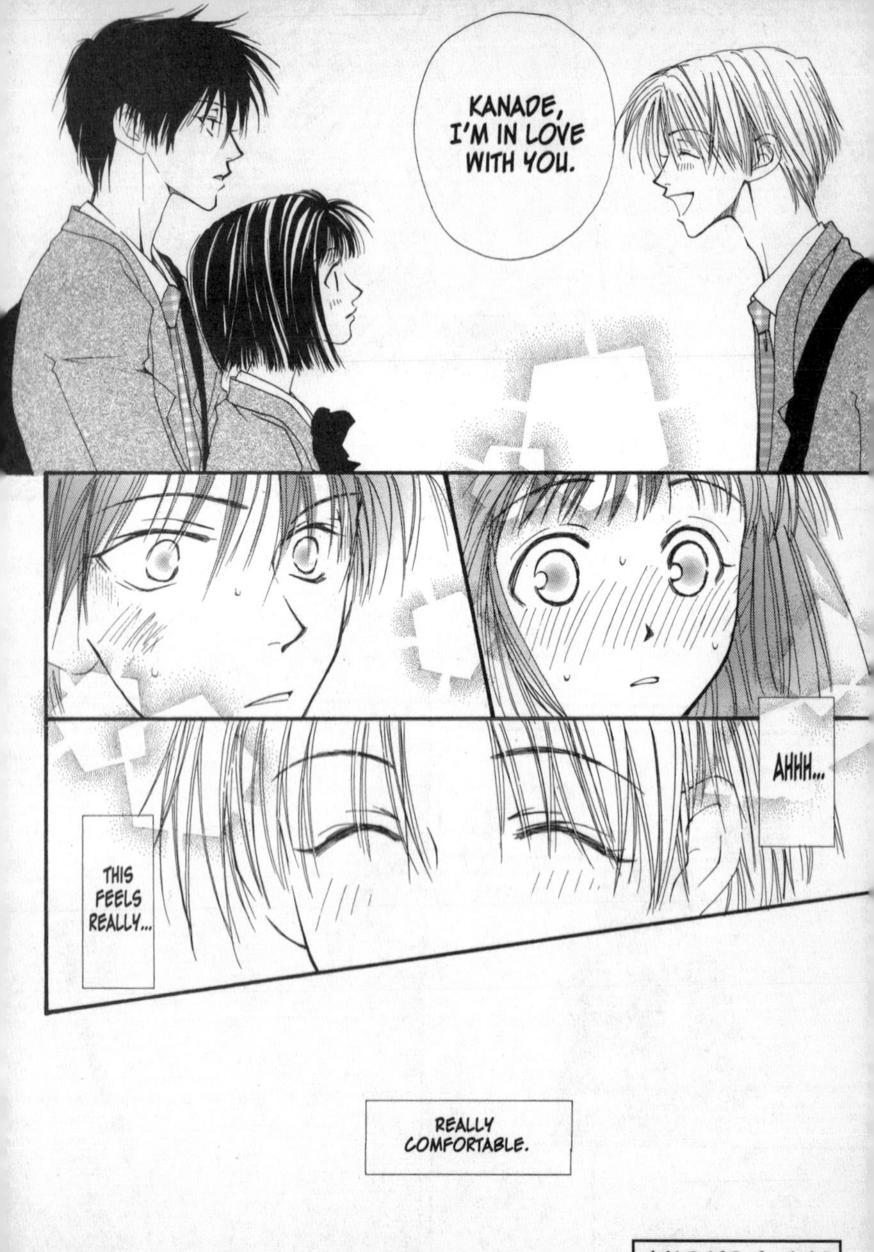
KANADE, I'M IN LOVE WITH YOU.
AHHH...
THIS FEELS REALLY...
REALLY COMFORTABLE.
CHAPTER 5: END

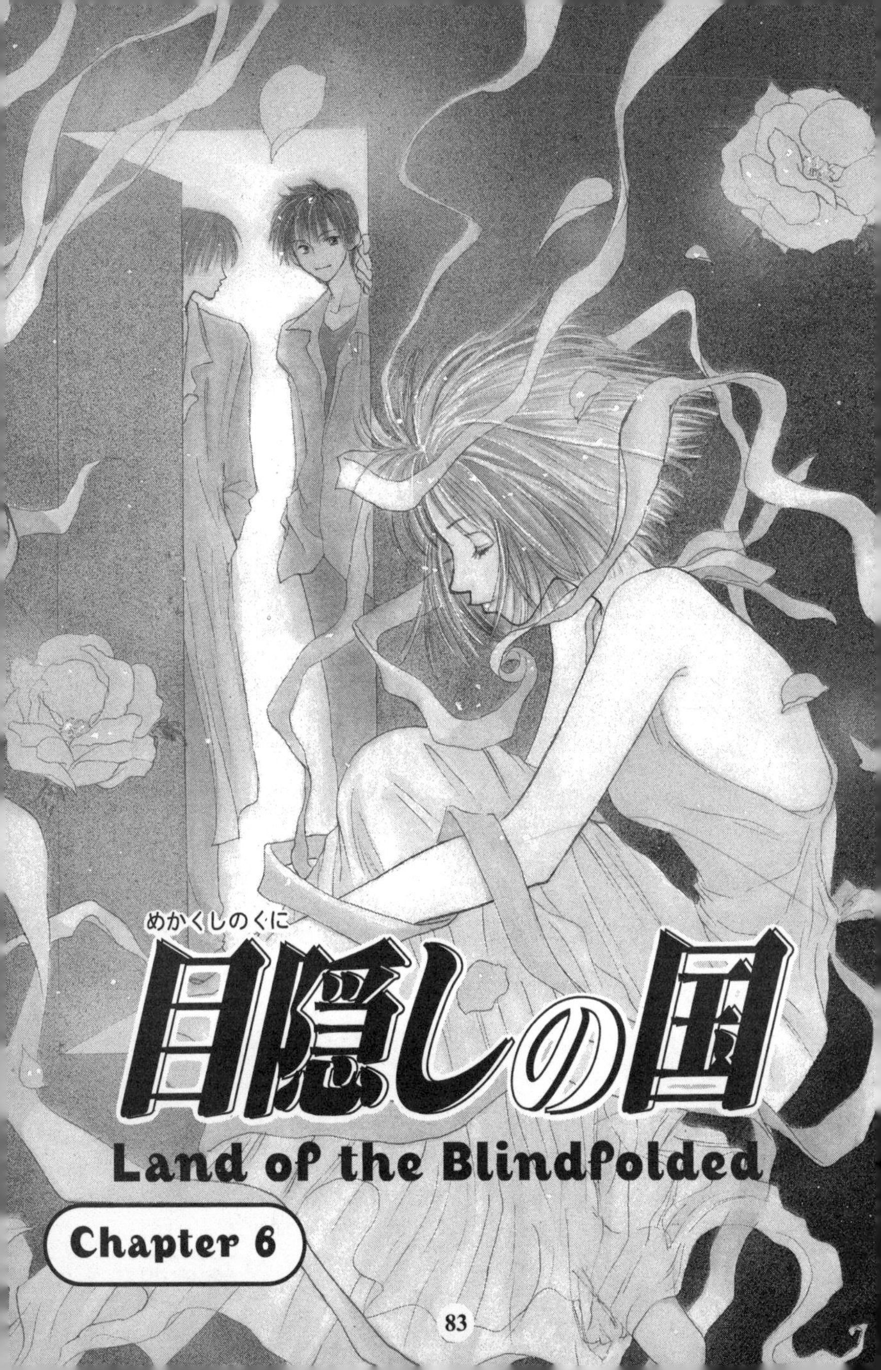
めかくしのくに
目隠しの国
Land of the Blindfolded
Chapter 6

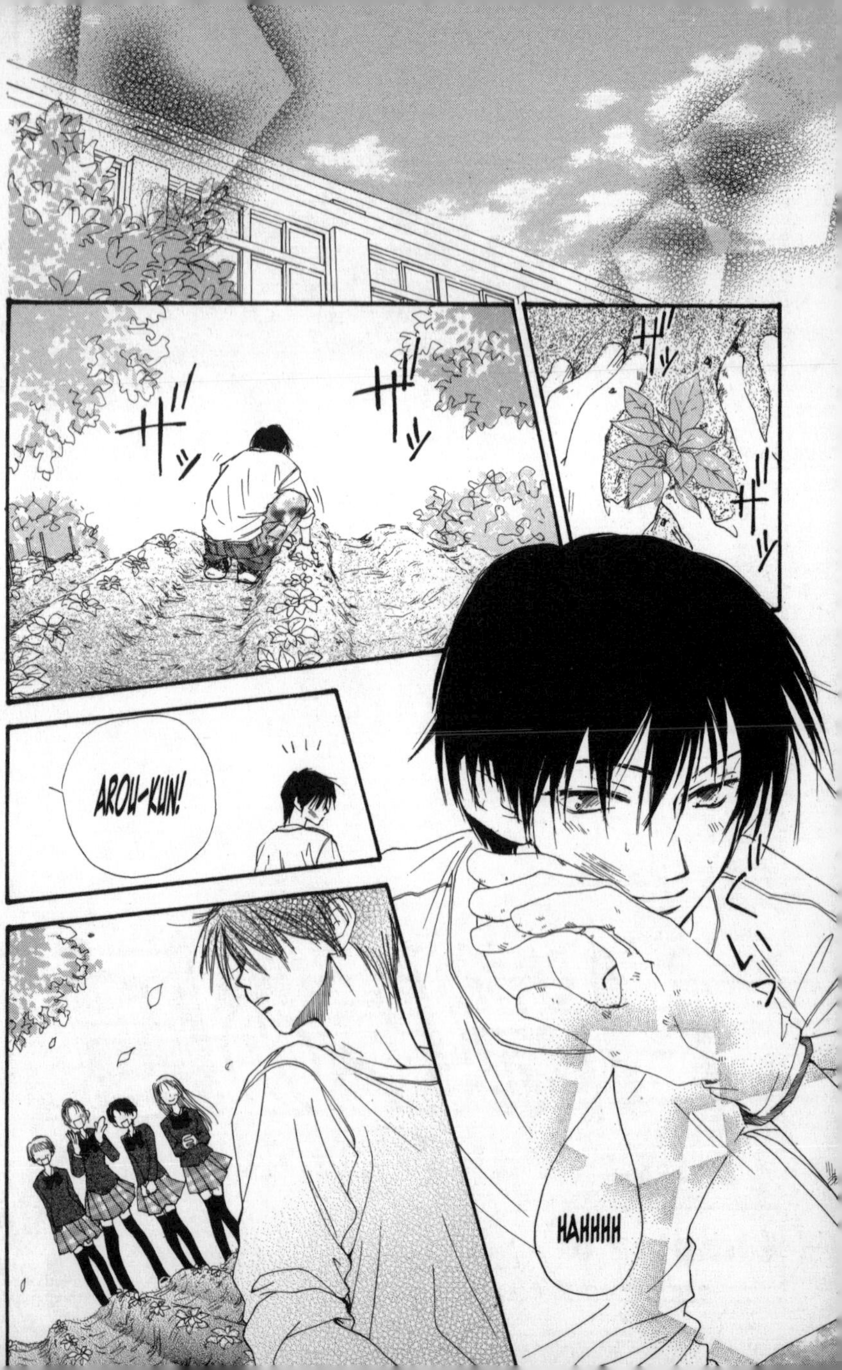
ザッ
ザッ
ザッ
ザッ
ぐいっ
HAHHHH
AROU-KUN!

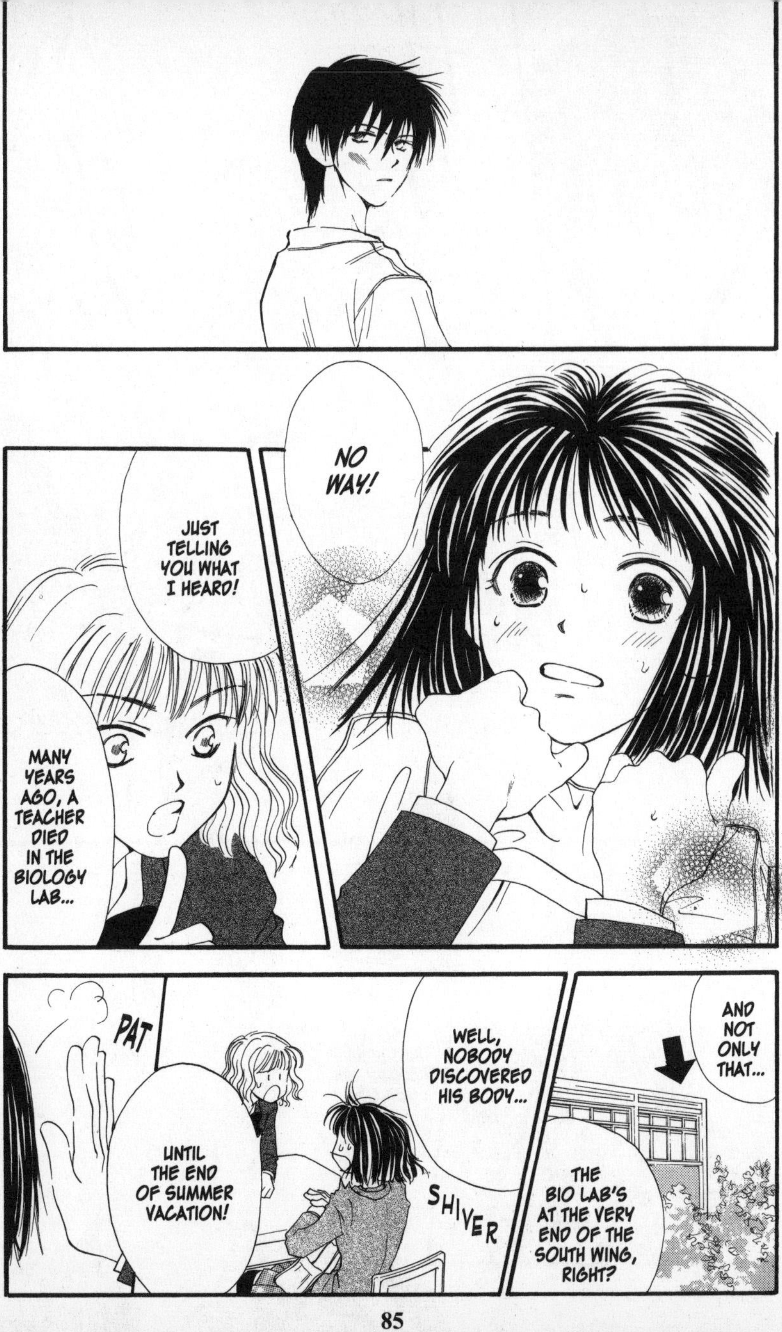
NO WAY!
JUST TELLING YOU WHAT I HEARD!
MANY YEARS AGO, A TEACHER DIED IN THE BIOLOGY LAB...
AND NOT ONLY THAT...
THE BIO LAB'S AT THE VERY END OF THE SOUTH WING, RIGHT?
WELL, NOBODY DISCOVERED HIS BODY...
SHIVER
UNTIL THE END OF SUMMER VACATION!
PAT

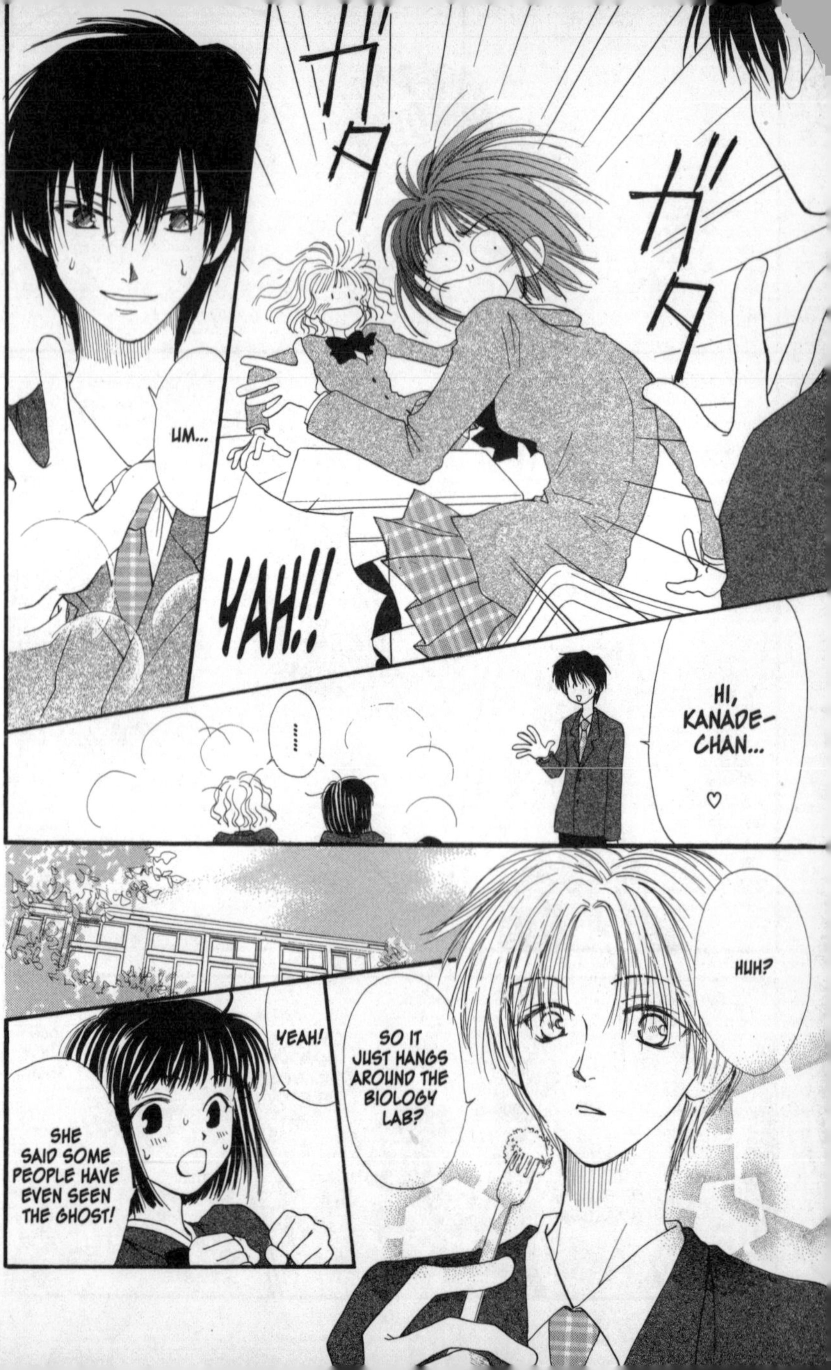
ガタ
ガタ
YAH!!
UM...
HI, KANADE-CHAN... ♡
......
HUH?
SO IT JUST HANGS AROUND THE BIOLOGY LAB?
YEAH!
SHE SAID SOME PEOPLE HAVE EVEN SEEN THE GHOST!

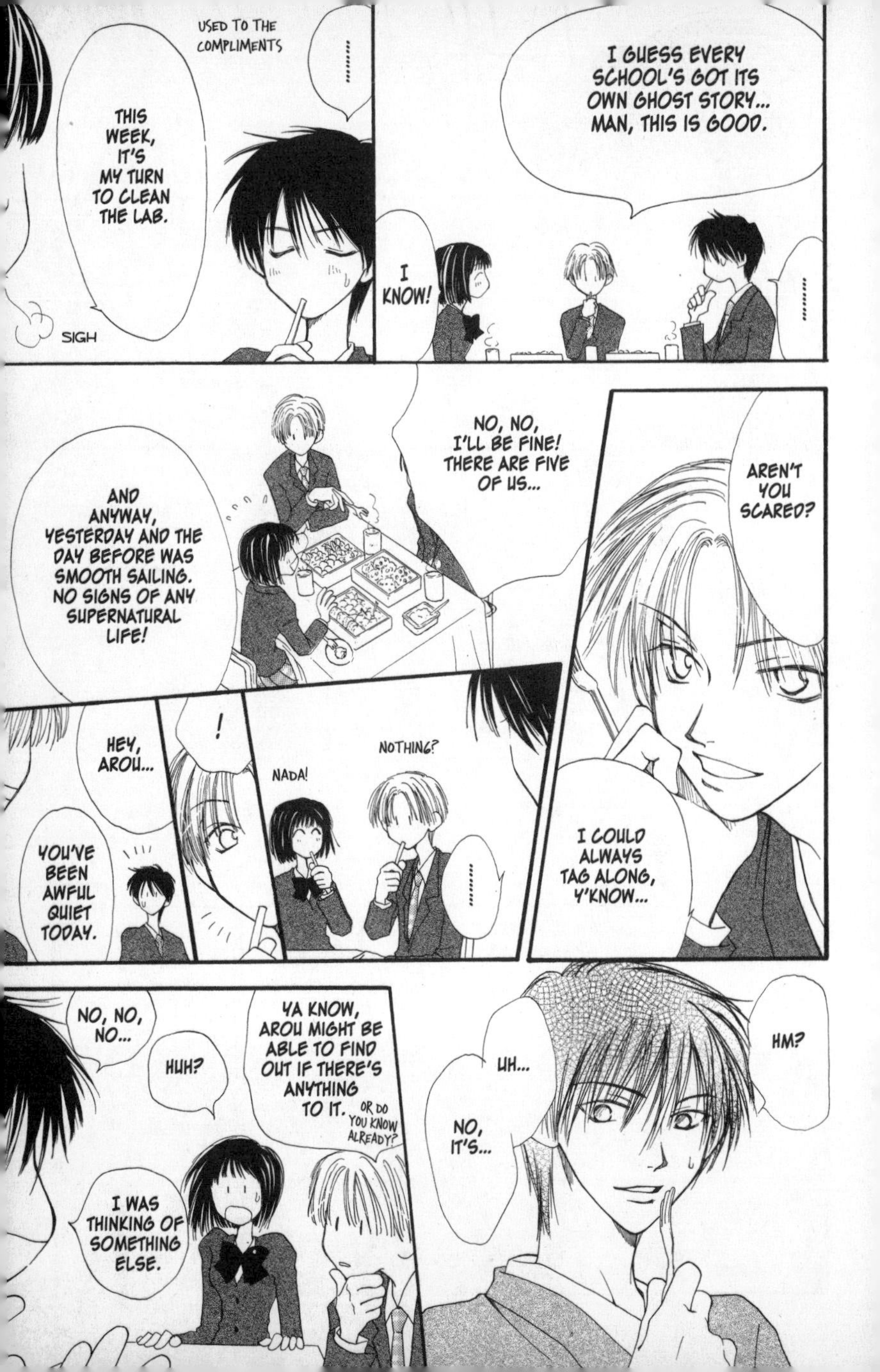
I GUESS EVERY SCHOOL'S GOT ITS OWN GHOST STORY... MAN, THIS IS GOOD.
......
I KNOW!
......
USED TO THE COMPLIMENTS
THIS WEEK, IT'S MY TURN TO CLEAN THE LAB.
SIGH
AREN'T YOU SCARED?
I COULD ALWAYS TAG ALONG, Y'KNOW...
NO, NO, I'LL BE FINE! THERE ARE FIVE OF US...
AND ANYWAY, YESTERDAY AND THE DAY BEFORE WAS SMOOTH SAILING. NO SIGNS OF ANY SUPERNATURAL LIFE!
NOTHING?
......
NADA!
!
HEY, AROU...
YOU'VE BEEN AWFUL QUIET TODAY.
HM?
UH...
NO, IT'S...
YA KNOW, AROU MIGHT BE ABLE TO FIND OUT IF THERE'S ANYTHING TO IT.
OR DO YOU KNOW ALREADY?
HUH?
NO, NO, NO...
I WAS THINKING OF SOMETHING ELSE.

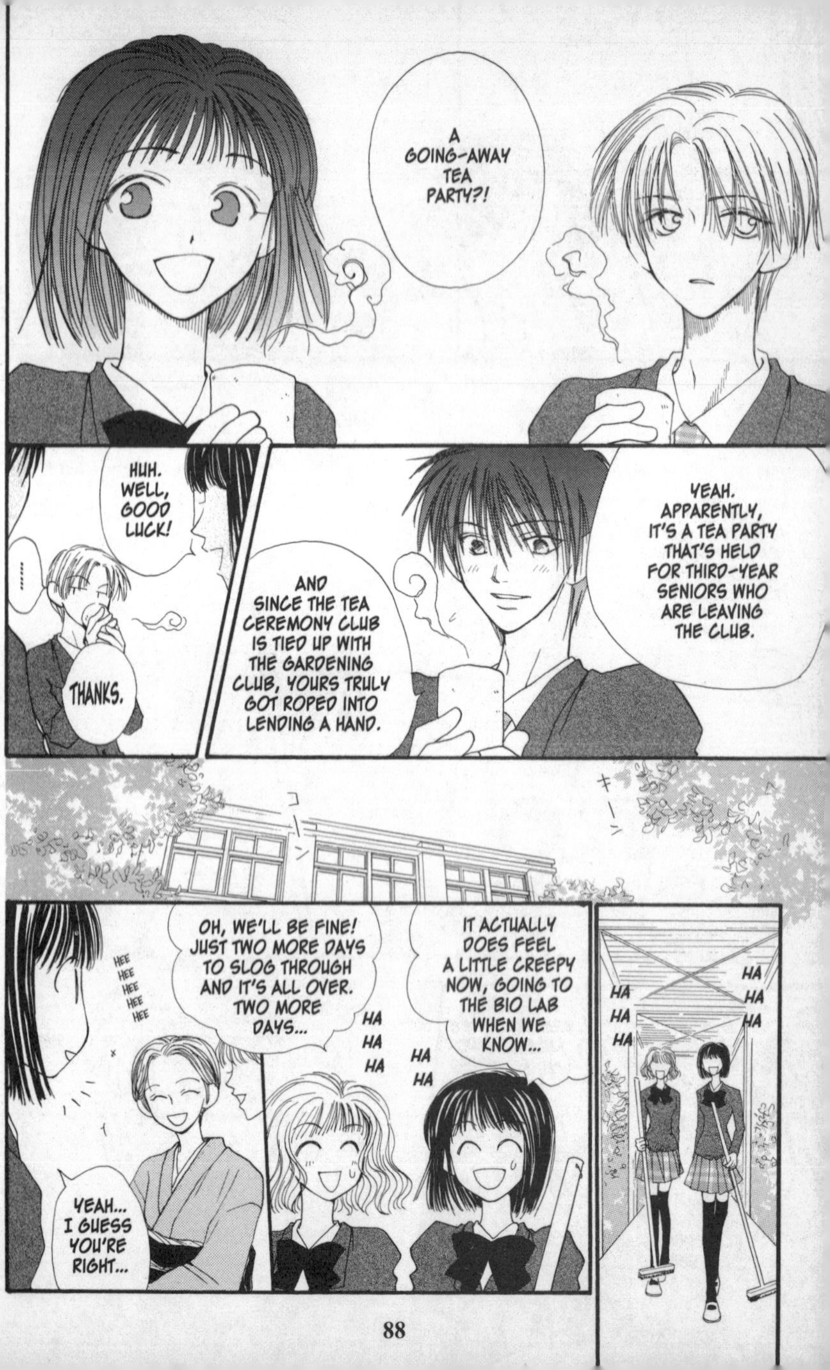
A GOING-AWAY TEA PARTY?!
YEAH. APPARENTLY, IT'S A TEA PARTY THAT'S HELD FOR THIRD-YEAR SENIORS WHO ARE LEAVING THE CLUB.
AND SINCE THE TEA CEREMONY CLUB IS TIED UP WITH THE GARDENING CLUB, YOURS TRULY GOT ROPED INTO LENDING A HAND.
HUH. WELL, GOOD LUCK!
......
THANKS.
キーン
コーン
HA HA HA
HA HA HA
IT ACTUALLY DOES FEEL A LITTLE CREEPY NOW, GOING TO THE BIO LAB WHEN WE KNOW...
OH, WE'LL BE FINE! JUST TWO MORE DAYS TO SLOG THROUGH AND IT'S ALL OVER. TWO MORE DAYS...
HA HA
HA HA HA
HEE HEE HEE HEE HEE
YEAH... I GUESS YOU'RE RIGHT...

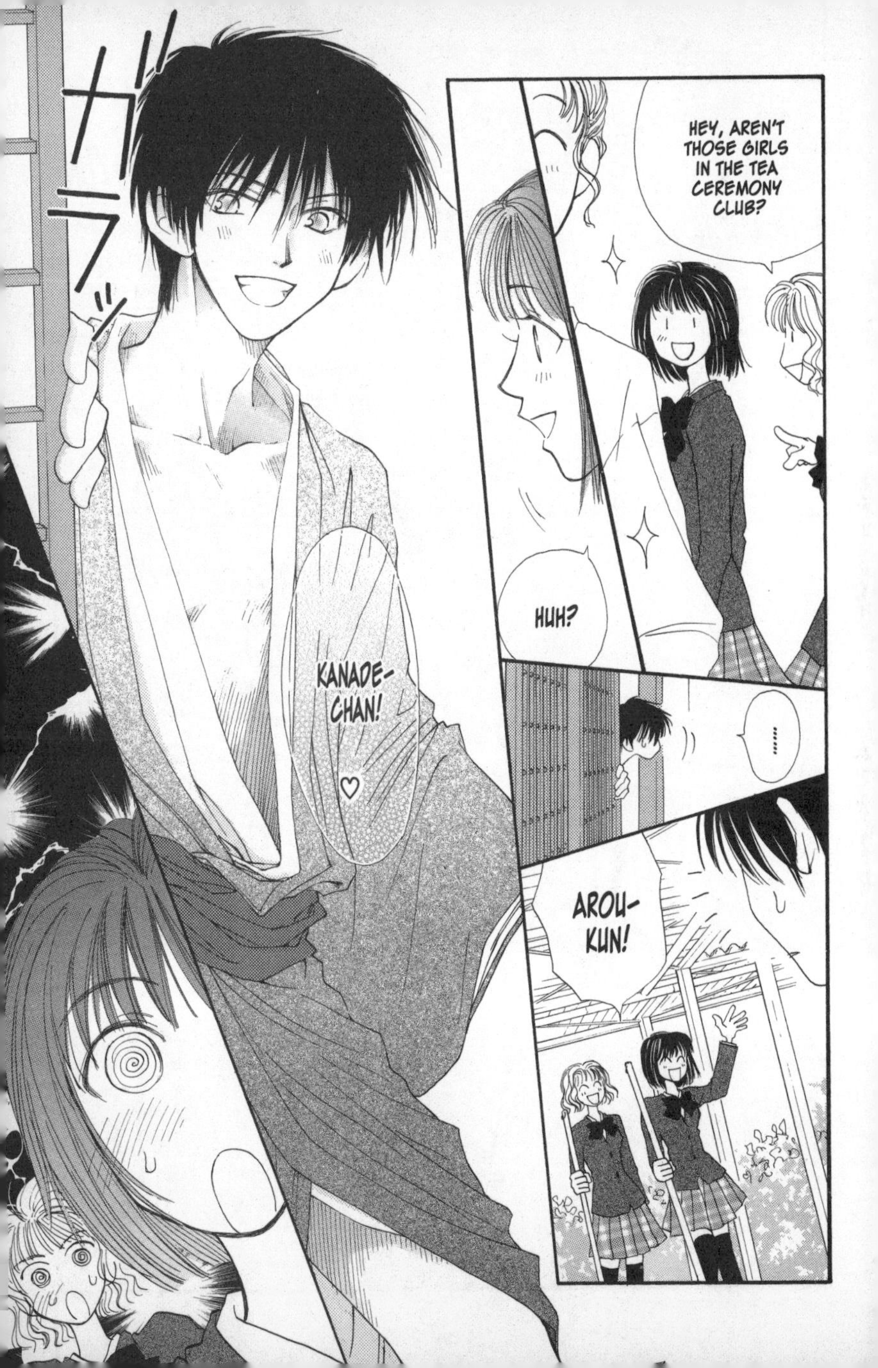
HEY, AREN'T THOSE GIRLS IN THE TEA CEREMONY CLUB?
HUH?
......
AROU-KUN!
ガラッ
KANADE-CHAN! ♡

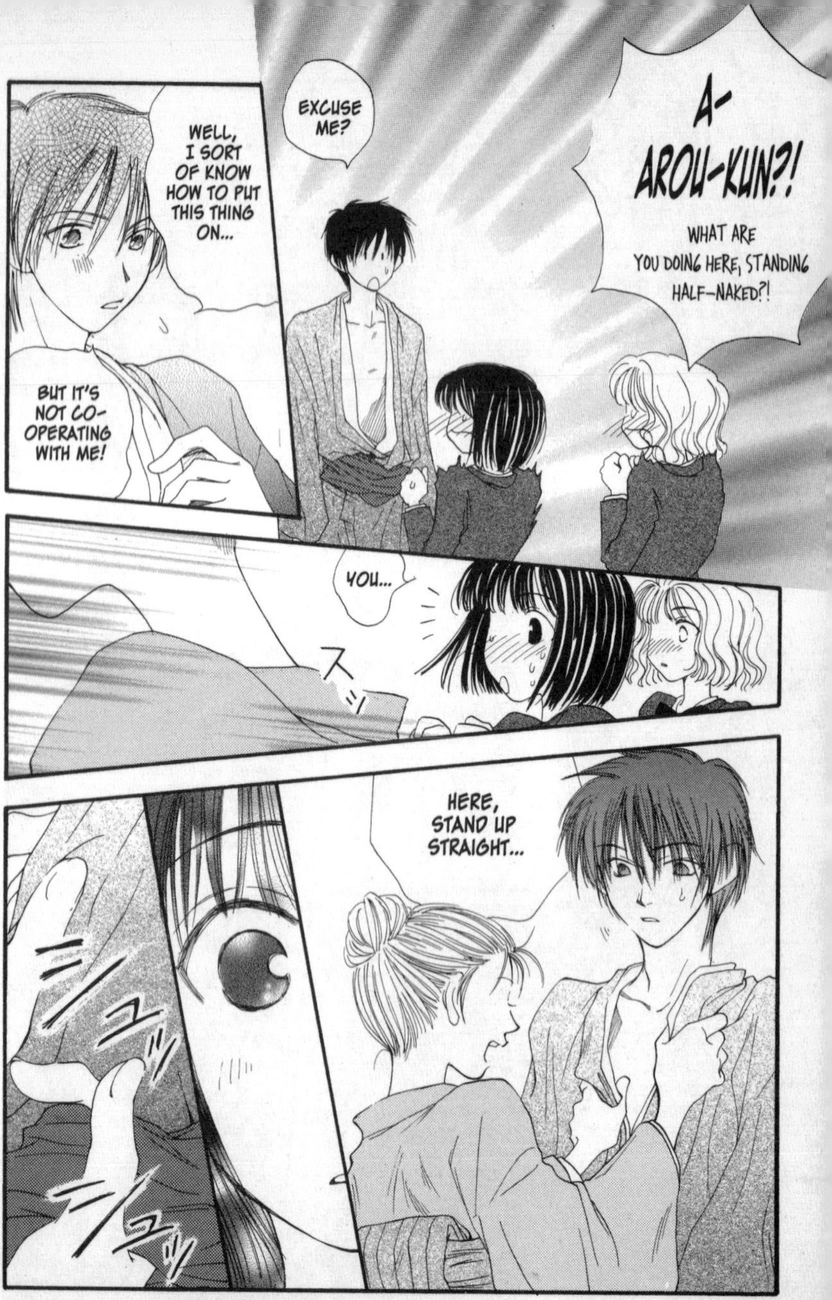
A-AROU-KUN?!
WHAT ARE YOU DOING HERE, STANDING HALF-NAKED?!
EXCUSE ME?
WELL, I SORT OF KNOW HOW TO PUT THIS THING ON...
BUT IT'S NOT CO-OPERATING WITH ME!
YOU...
HERE, STAND UP STRAIGHT...

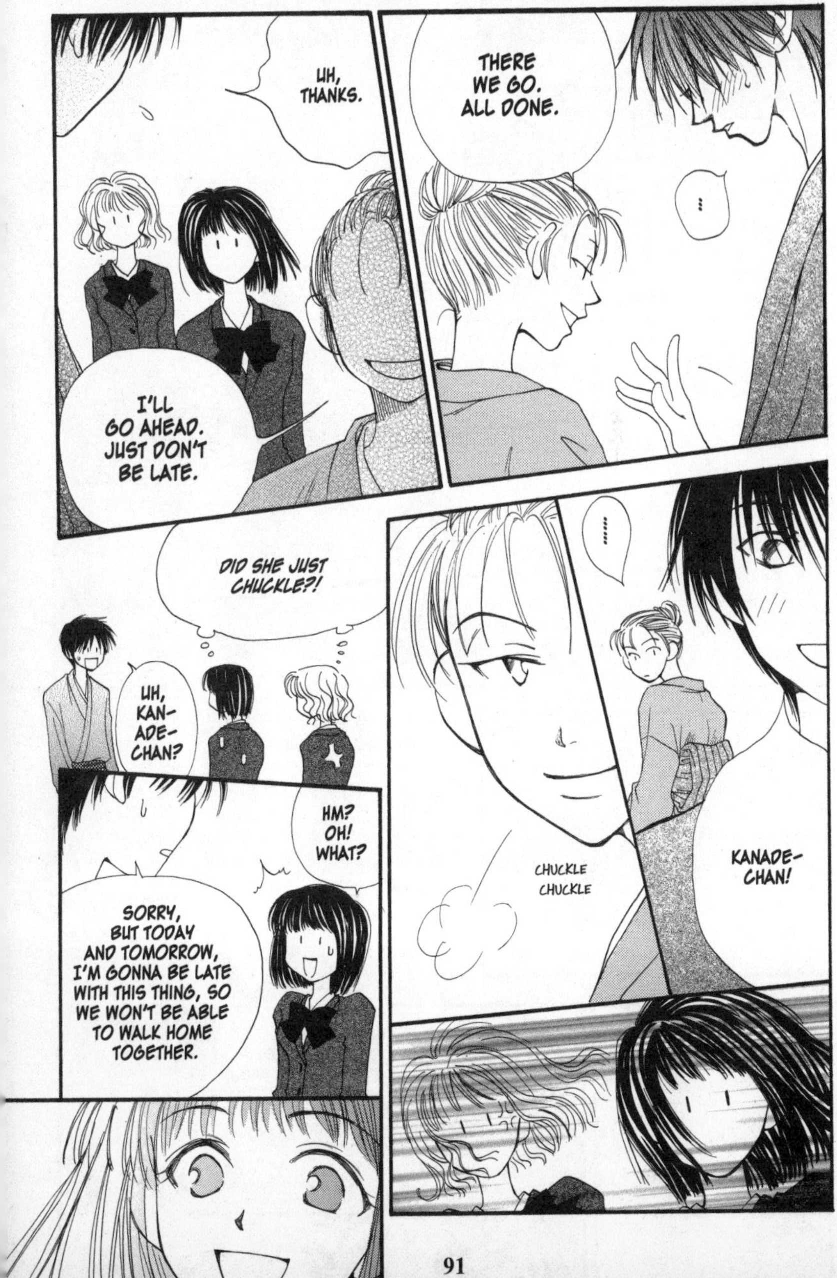
THERE WE GO. ALL DONE.
...
UH, THANKS.
I'LL GO AHEAD. JUST DON'T BE LATE.
......
KANADE-CHAN!
CHUCKLE CHUCKLE
DID SHE JUST CHUCKLE?!
UH, KAN-ADE-CHAN?
HM? OH! WHAT?
SORRY, BUT TODAY AND TOMORROW, I'M GONNA BE LATE WITH THIS THING, SO WE WON'T BE ABLE TO WALK HOME TOGETHER.

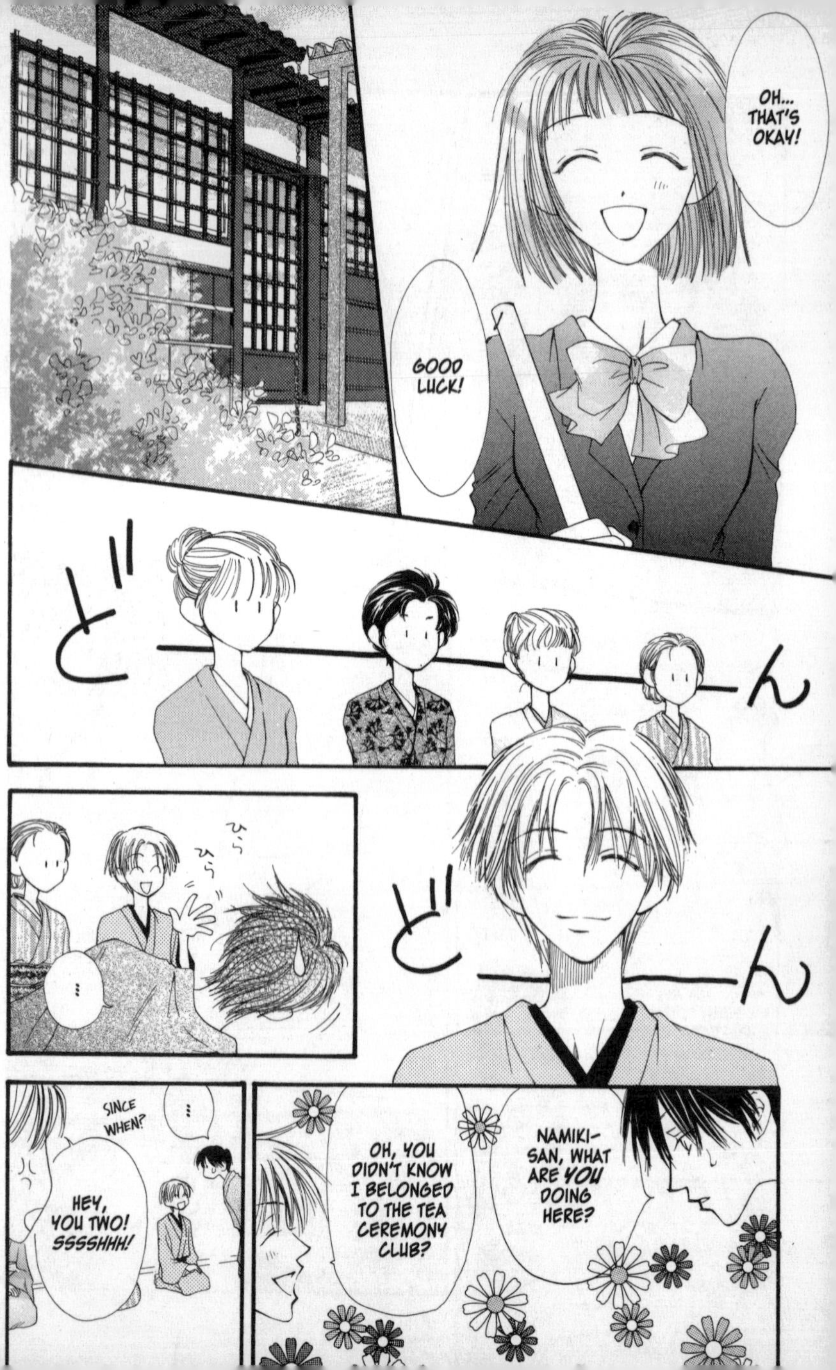
OH... THAT'S OKAY!
GOOD LUCK!
どーーーん
どーーん
ひら ひら
...
NAMIKI-SAN, WHAT ARE YOU DOING HERE?
OH, YOU DIDN'T KNOW I BELONGED TO THE TEA CEREMONY CLUB?
...
SINCE WHEN?
HEY, YOU TWO! SSSSHHH!

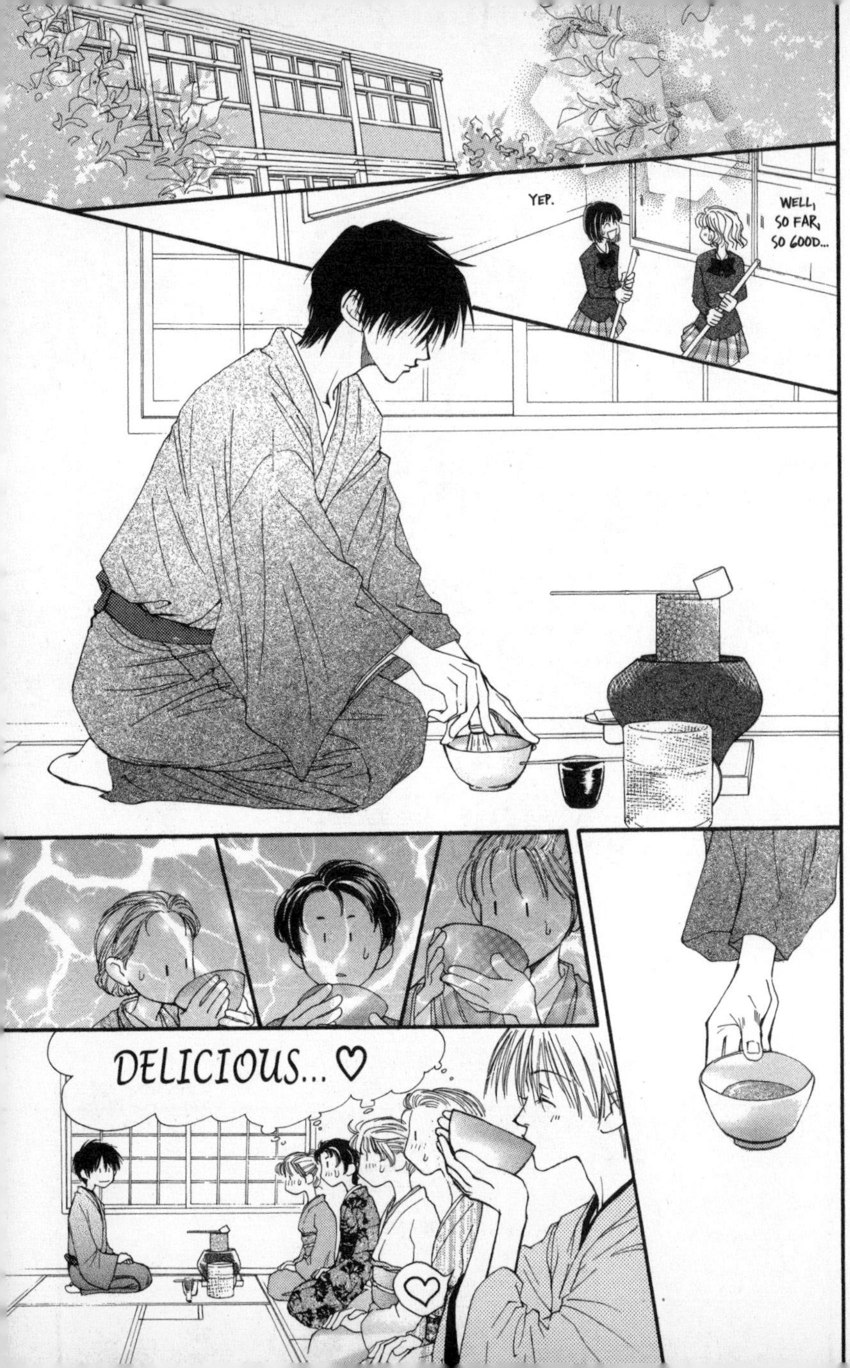
WELL, SO FAR, SO GOOD...
YEP.
DELICIOUS... ♡

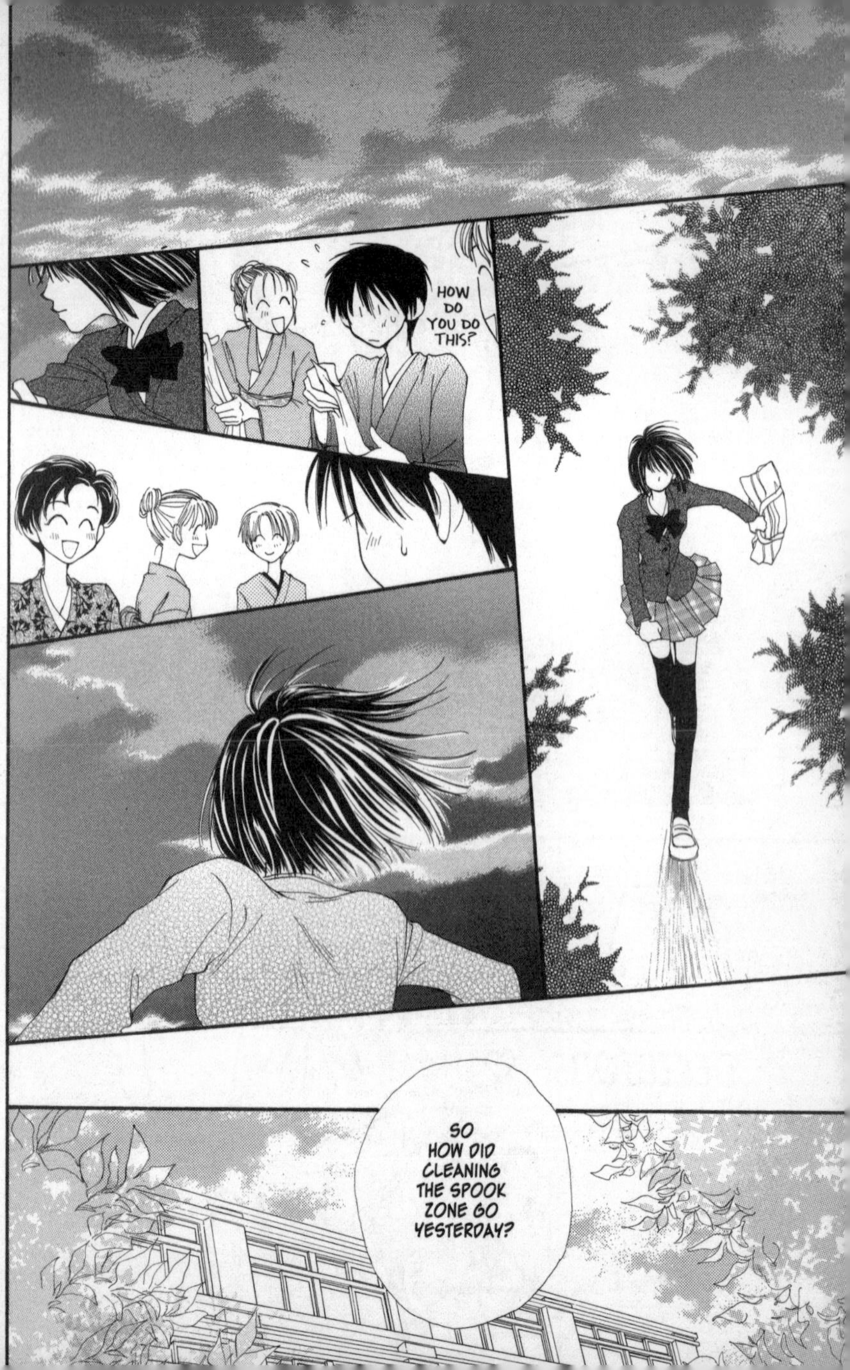
HOW DO YOU DO THIS?
SO HOW DID CLEANING THE SPOOK ZONE GO YESTERDAY?

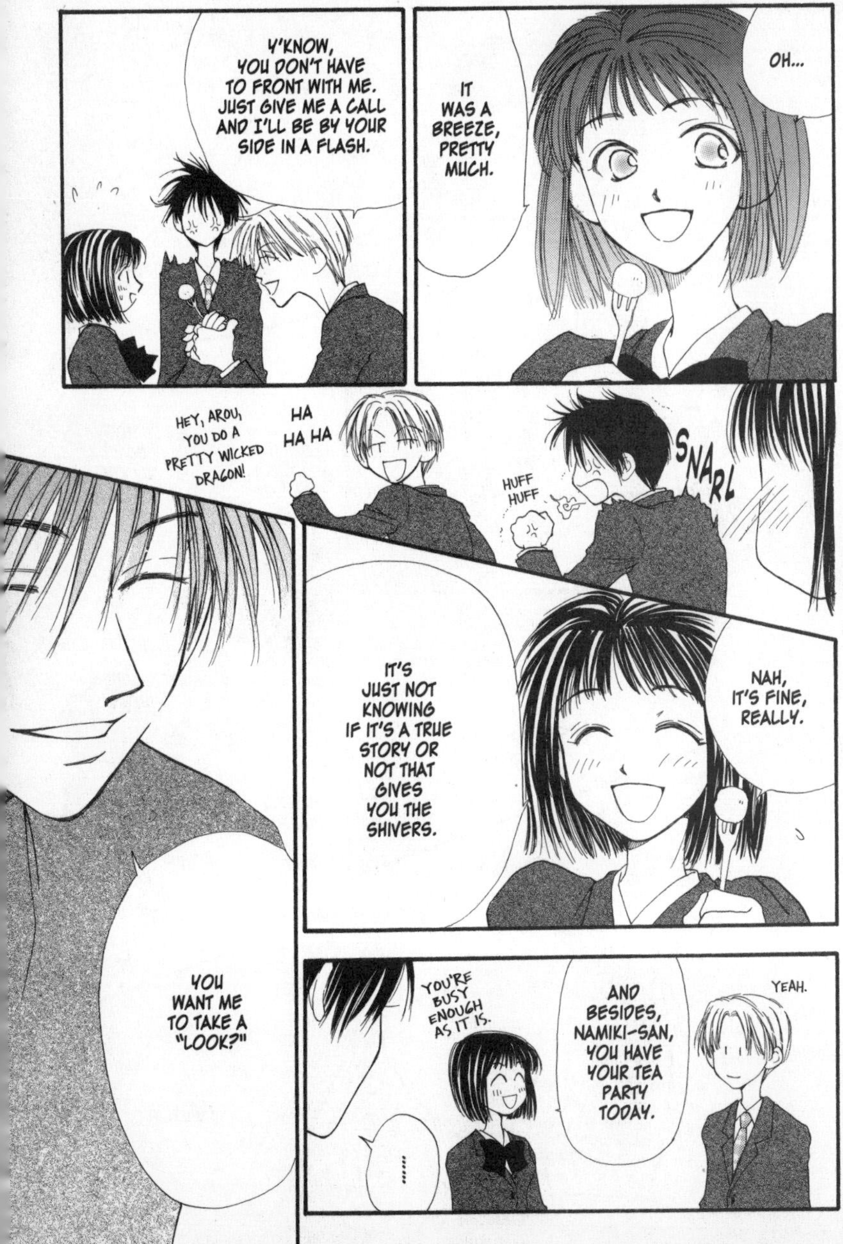
OH...
IT WAS A BREEZE, PRETTY MUCH.
Y'KNOW, YOU DON'T HAVE TO FRONT WITH ME. JUST GIVE ME A CALL AND I'LL BE BY YOUR SIDE IN A FLASH.
HEY, AROU, YOU DO A PRETTY WICKED DRAGON!
HA HA HA
HUFF HUFF
SNARL
NAH, IT'S FINE, REALLY.
IT'S JUST NOT KNOWING IF IT'S A TRUE STORY OR NOT THAT GIVES YOU THE SHIVERS.
YEAH.
AND BESIDES, NAMIKI-SAN, YOU HAVE YOUR TEA PARTY TODAY.
YOU'RE BUSY ENOUGH AS IT IS.
......
YOU WANT ME TO TAKE A "LOOK?"

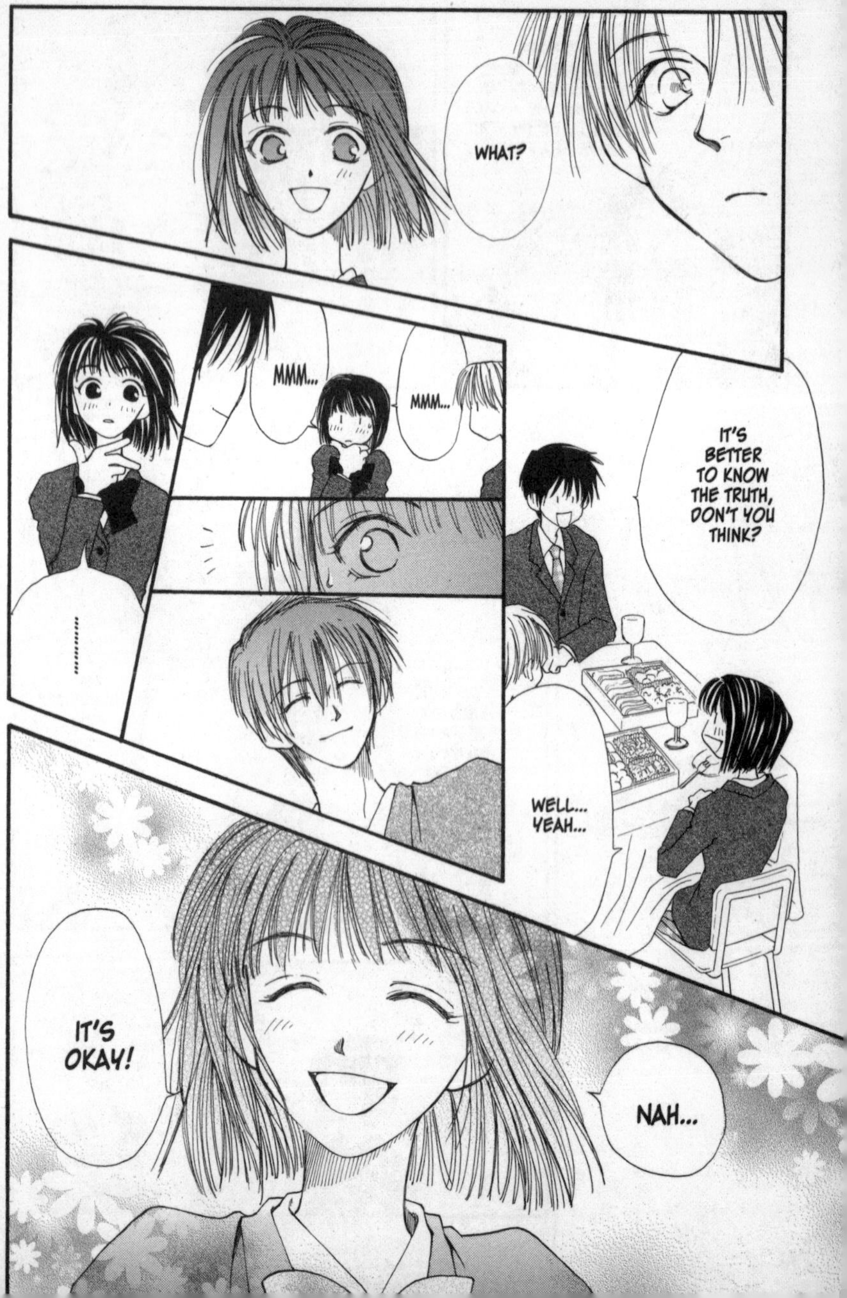
WHAT?
IT'S BETTER TO KNOW THE TRUTH, DON'T YOU THINK?
WELL... YEAH...
MMM...
MMM...
......
NAH...
IT'S OKAY!

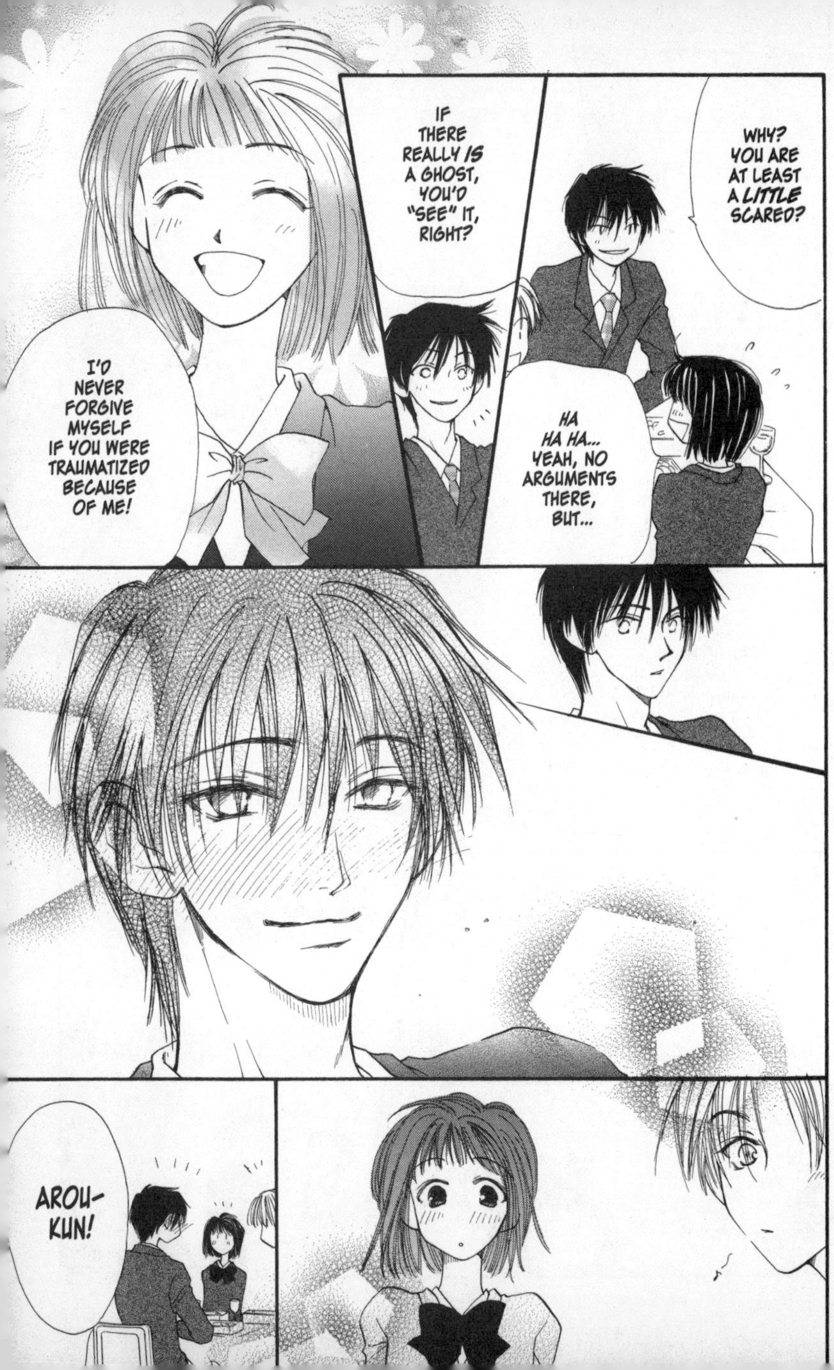
WHY? YOU ARE AT LEAST A *LITTLE* SCARED?
HA HA HA... YEAH, NO ARGUMENTS THERE, BUT...
IF THERE REALLY *IS* A GHOST, YOU'D "SEE" IT, RIGHT?
I'D NEVER FORGIVE MYSELF IF YOU WERE TRAUMATIZED BECAUSE OF ME!
AROU-KUN!

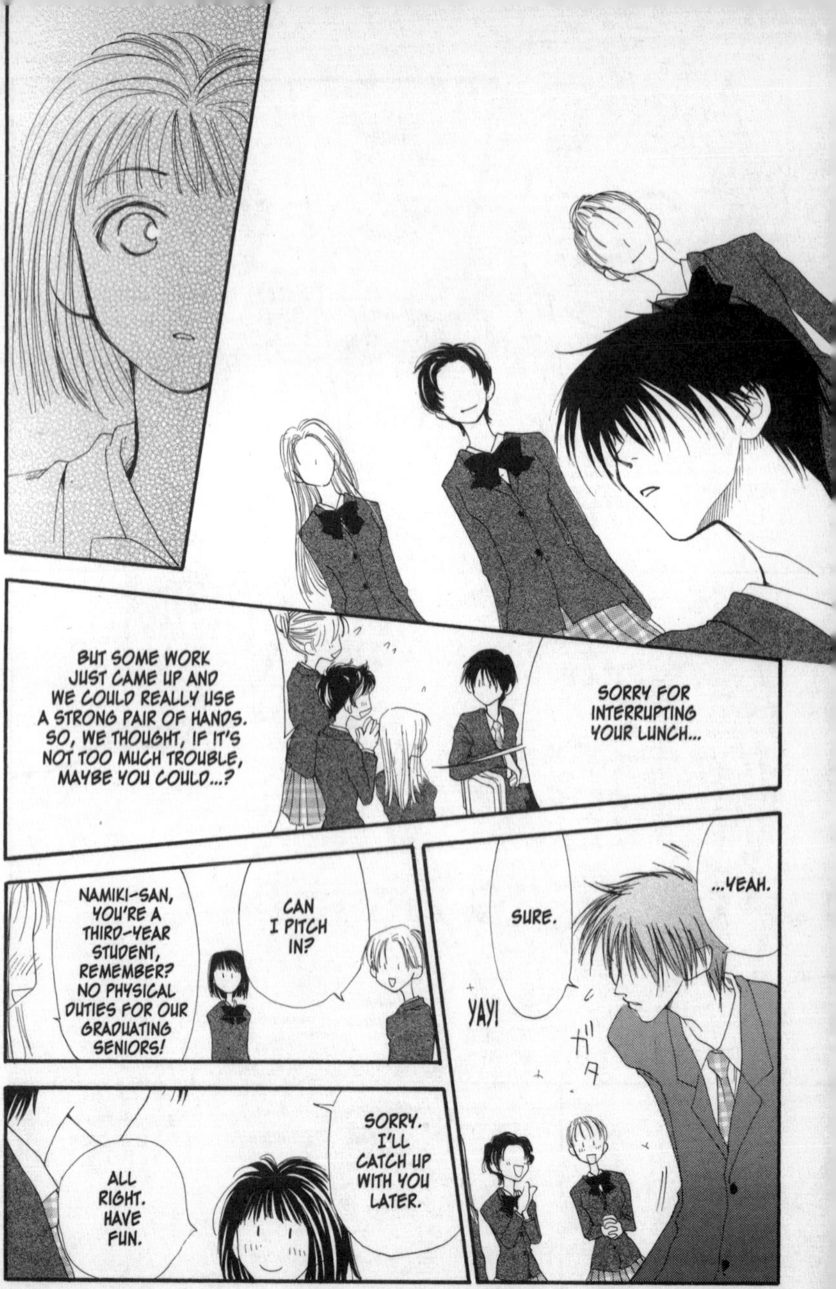
SORRY FOR INTERRUPTING YOUR LUNCH...
BUT SOME WORK JUST CAME UP AND WE COULD REALLY USE A STRONG PAIR OF HANDS. SO, WE THOUGHT, IF IT'S NOT TOO MUCH TROUBLE, MAYBE YOU COULD...?
...YEAH.
SURE.
YAY!
ガタ
CAN I PITCH IN?
NAMIKI-SAN, YOU'RE A THIRD-YEAR STUDENT, REMEMBER? NO PHYSICAL DUTIES FOR OUR GRADUATING SENIORS!
SORRY. I'LL CATCH UP WITH YOU LATER.
ALL RIGHT. HAVE FUN.

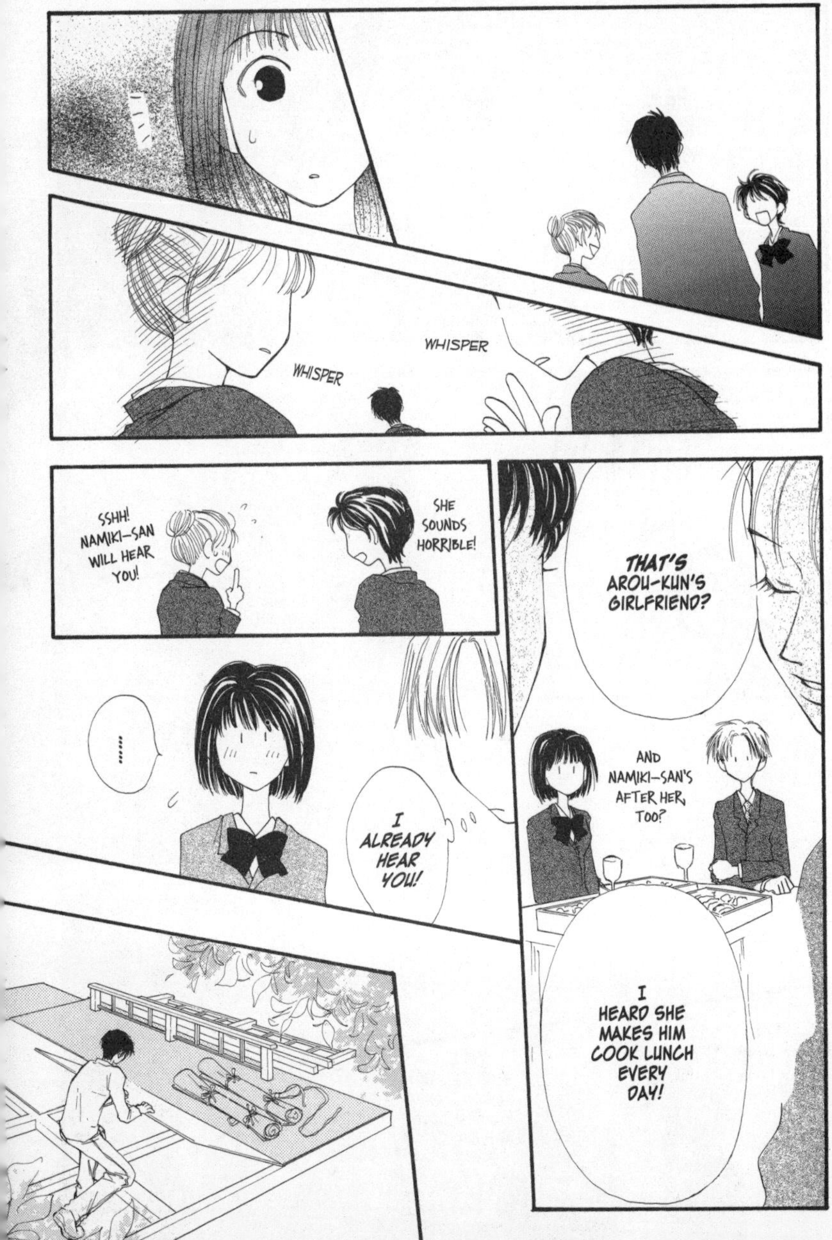
WHISPER
WHISPER
THAT'S AROU-KUN'S GIRLFRIEND?
AND NAMIKI-SAN'S AFTER HER, TOO?
I HEARD SHE MAKES HIM COOK LUNCH EVERY DAY!
SHE SOUNDS HORRIBLE!
SSHH! NAMIKI-SAN WILL HEAR YOU!
I ALREADY HEAR YOU!
......

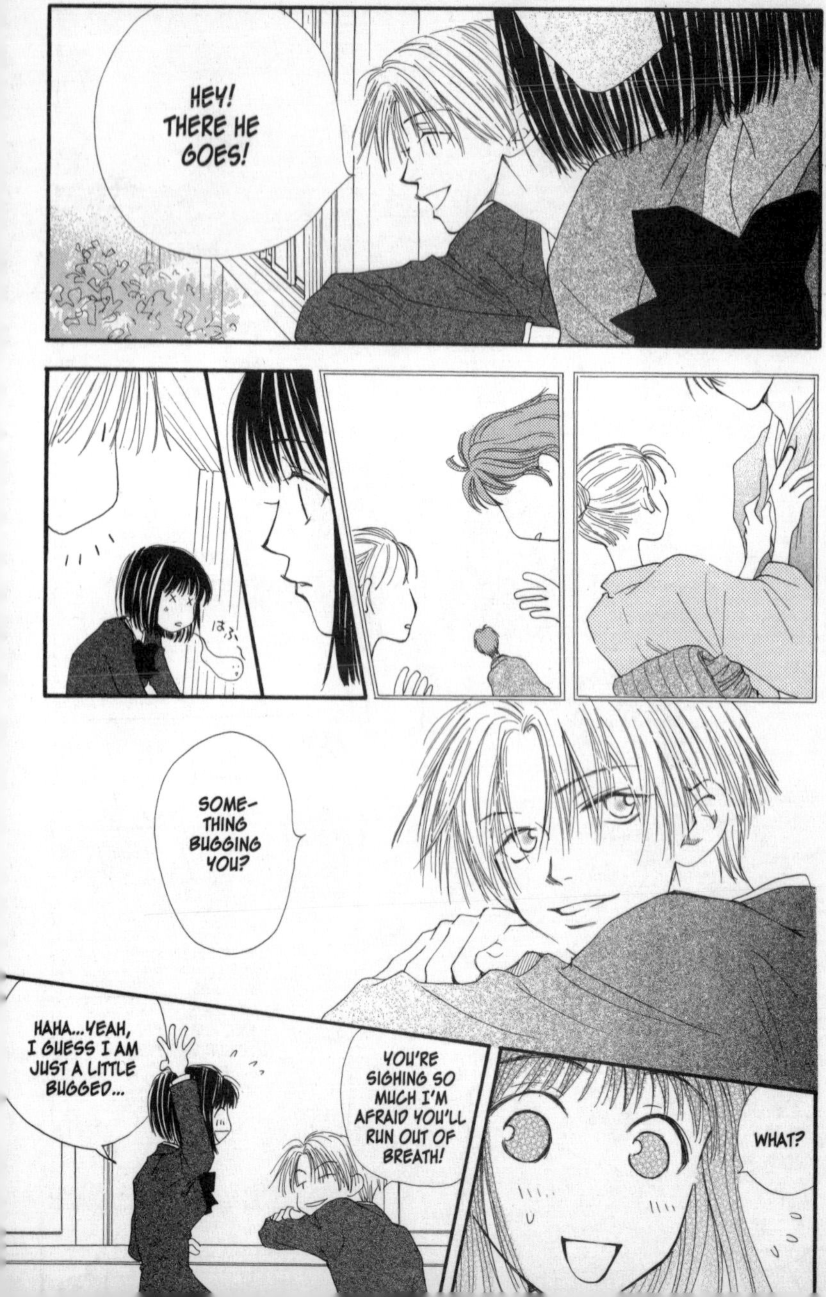
HEY! THERE HE GOES!
はふ
SOME-THING BUGGING YOU?
WHAT?
YOU'RE SIGHING SO MUCH I'M AFRAID YOU'LL RUN OUT OF BREATH!
HAHA...YEAH, I GUESS I AM JUST A LITTLE BUGGED...

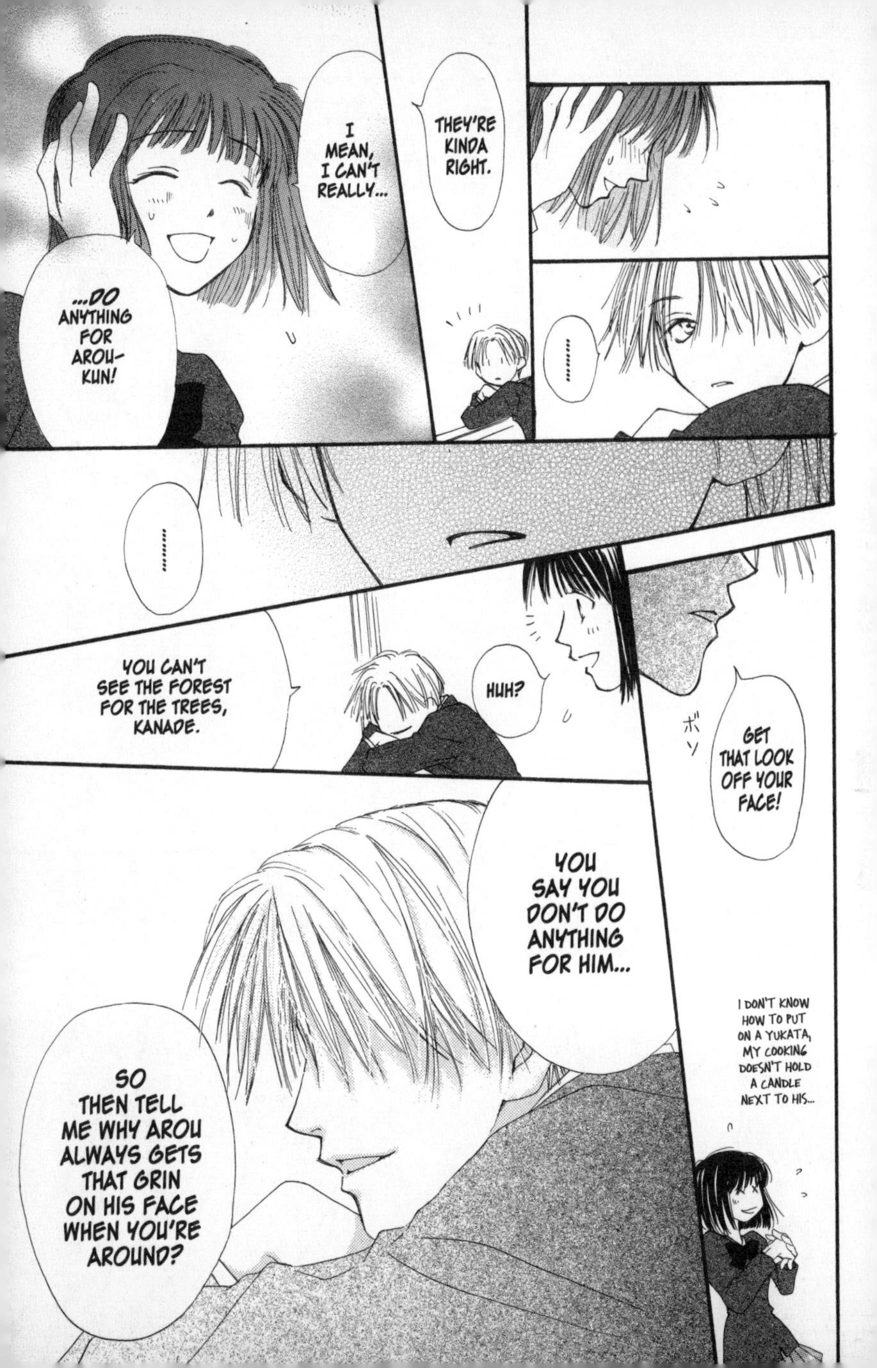

......
THEY'RE KINDA RIGHT.
I MEAN, I CAN'T REALLY...
...DO ANYTHING FOR AROU-KUN!
......
ボツ
GET THAT LOOK OFF YOUR FACE!
I DON'T KNOW HOW TO PUT ON A YUKATA, MY COOKING DOESN'T HOLD A CANDLE NEXT TO HIS...
HUH?
YOU CAN'T SEE THE FOREST FOR THE TREES, KANADE.
YOU SAY YOU DON'T DO ANYTHING FOR HIM...
SO THEN TELL ME WHY AROU ALWAYS GETS THAT GRIN ON HIS FACE WHEN YOU'RE AROUND?

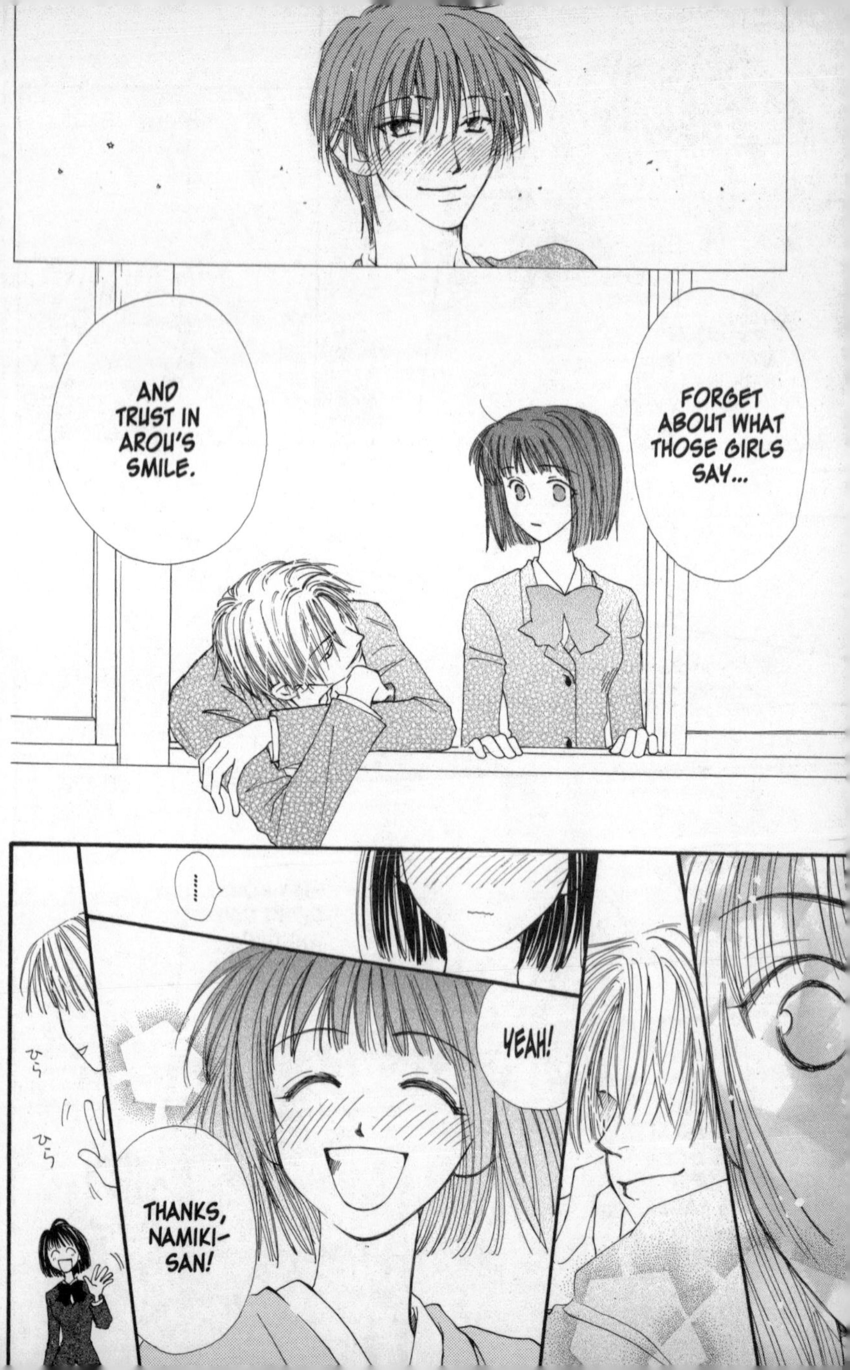
FORGET ABOUT WHAT THOSE GIRLS SAY...
AND TRUST IN AROU'S SMILE.
......
YEAH!
THANKS, NAMIKI-SAN!
ひら
ひら

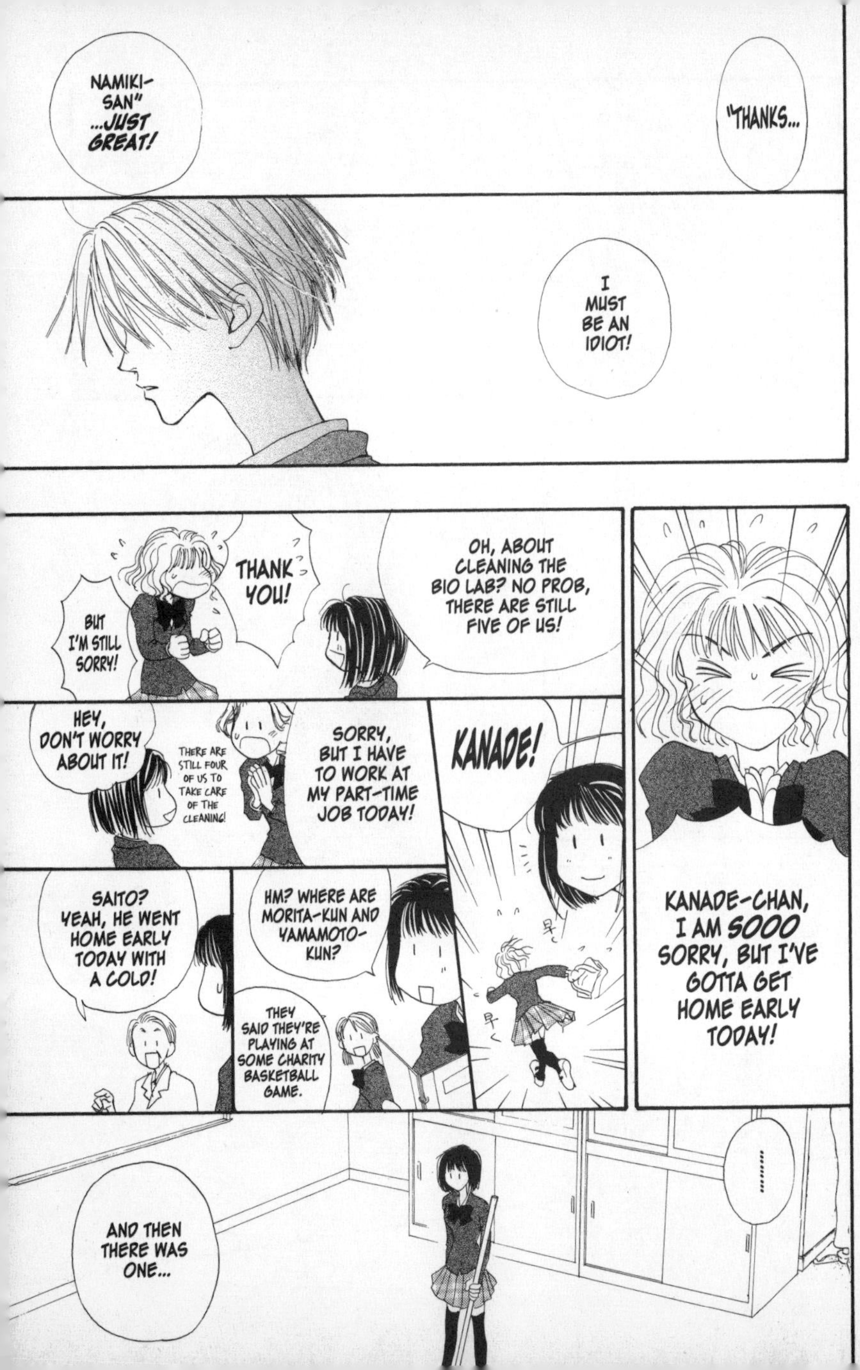
"THANKS...
NAMIKI-SAN" ...JUST GREAT!
I MUST BE AN IDIOT!
KANADE-CHAN, I AM SOOO SORRY, BUT I'VE GOTTA GET HOME EARLY TODAY!
OH, ABOUT CLEANING THE BIO LAB? NO PROB, THERE ARE STILL FIVE OF US!
THANK YOU!
BUT I'M STILL SORRY!
KANADE!
早く
早く
SORRY, BUT I HAVE TO WORK AT MY PART-TIME JOB TODAY!
HEY, DON'T WORRY ABOUT IT!
THERE ARE STILL FOUR OF US TO TAKE CARE OF THE CLEANING!
HM? WHERE ARE MORITA-KUN AND YAMAMOTO-KUN?
THEY SAID THEY'RE PLAYING AT SOME CHARITY BASKETBALL GAME.
SAITO? YEAH, HE WENT HOME EARLY TODAY WITH A COLD!
......
AND THEN THERE WAS ONE...

OKAY...

LET'S JUST GET THIS DONE.

SWEEP SWEEP

GULP

....

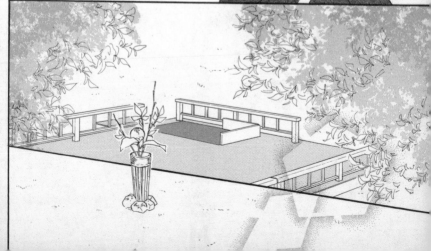

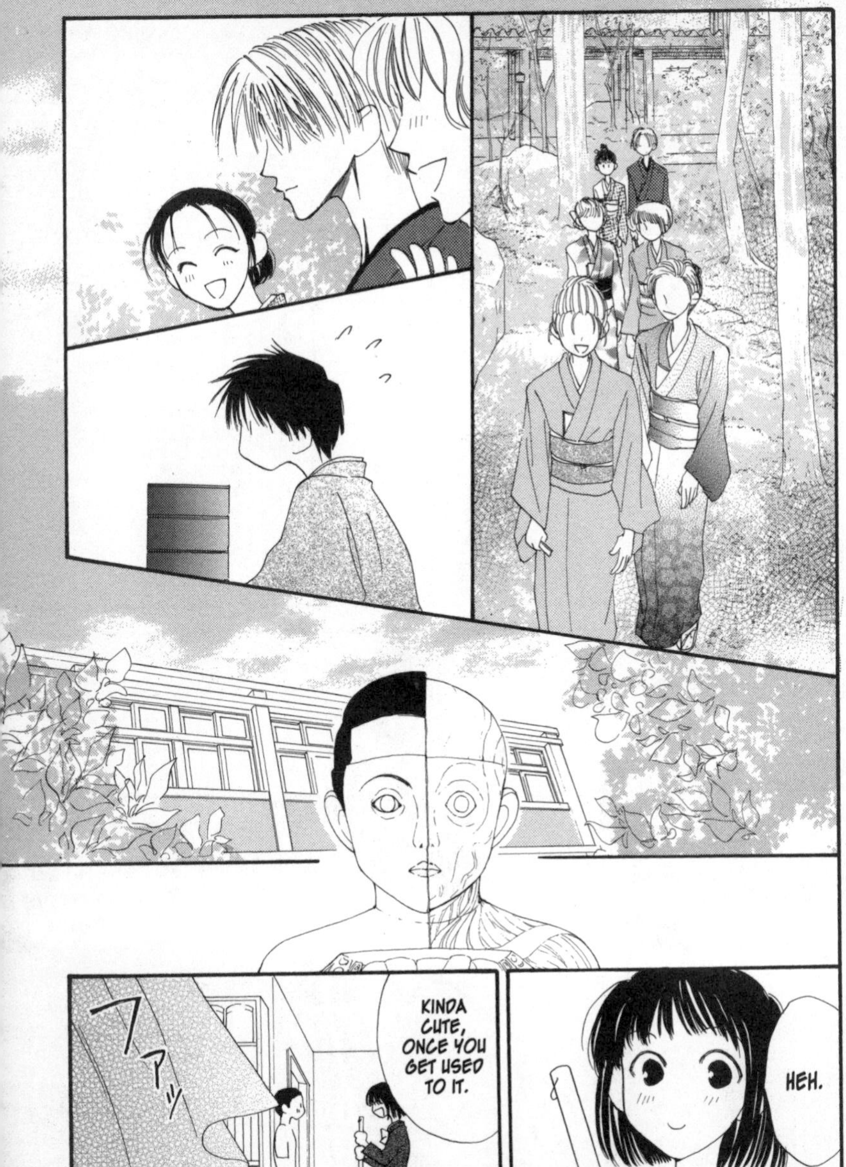
HEH.
KINDA CUTE, ONCE YOU GET USED TO IT.
ファッ

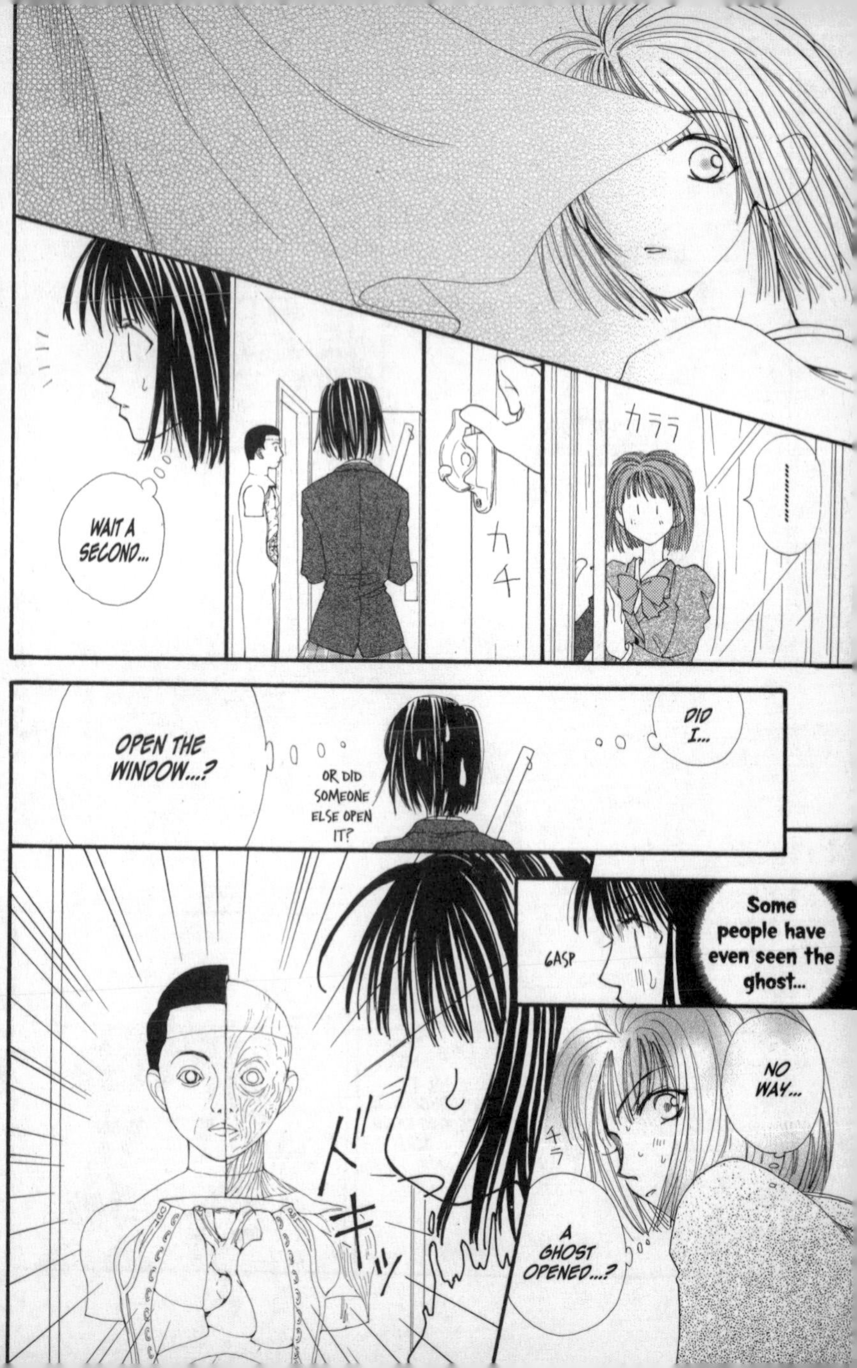
カララ
......
カチ
WAIT A SECOND...
DID I...
OPEN THE WINDOW...?
OR DID SOMEONE ELSE OPEN IT?
Some people have even seen the ghost...
GASP
NO WAY...
チラ
A GHOST OPENED...?
ドキッ

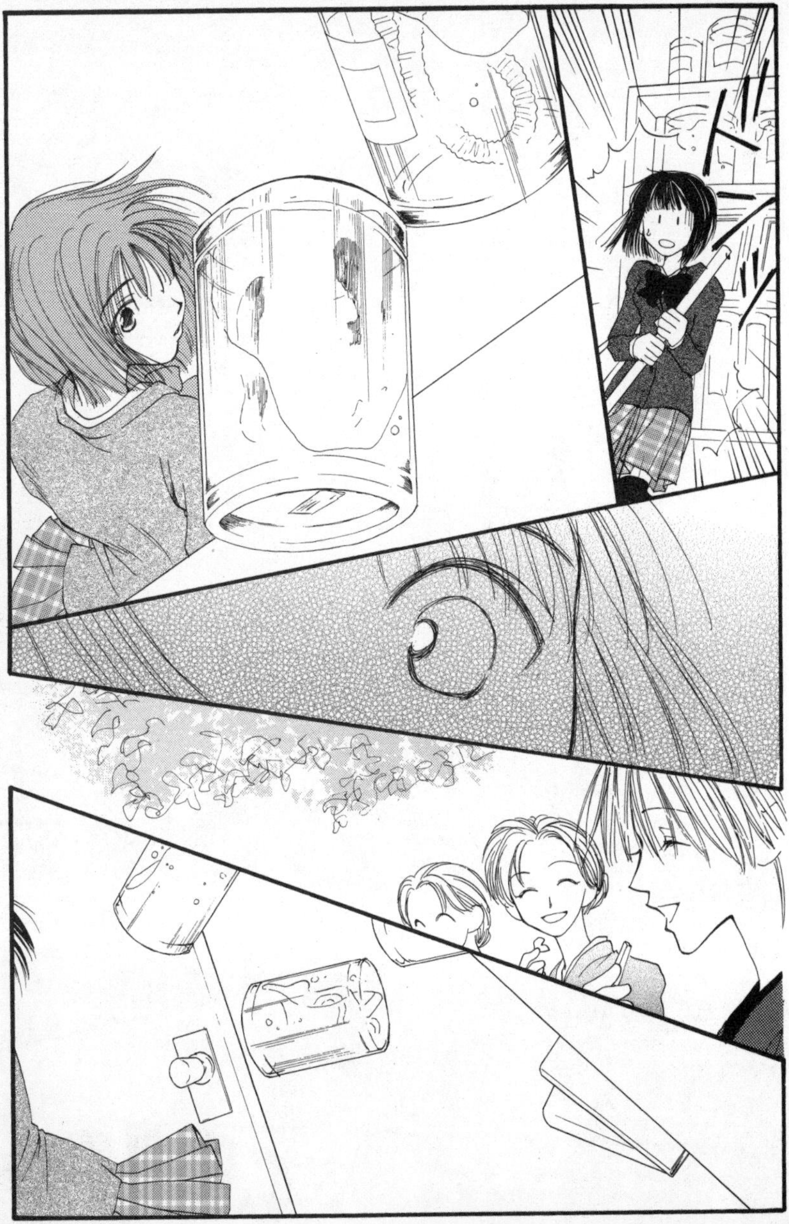
ド

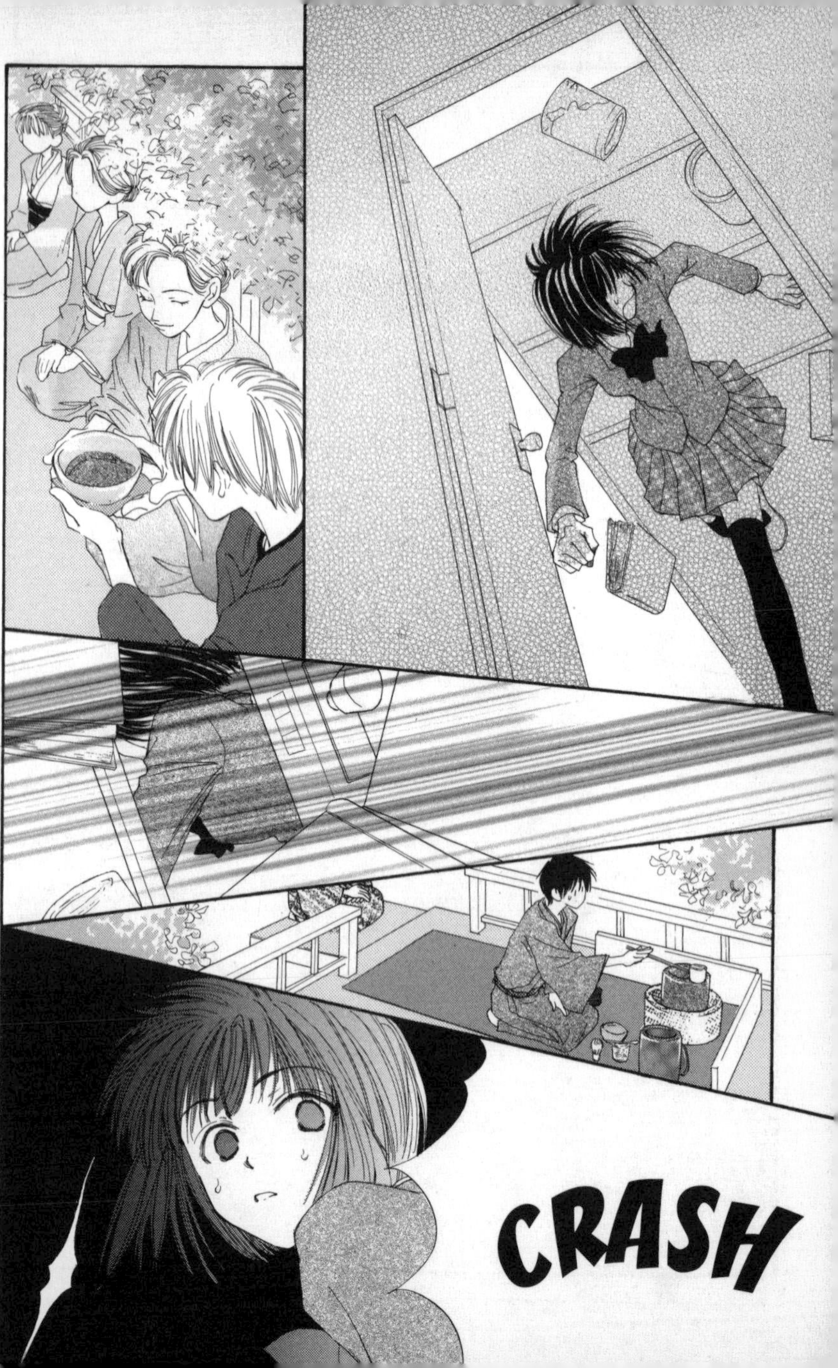
CRASH

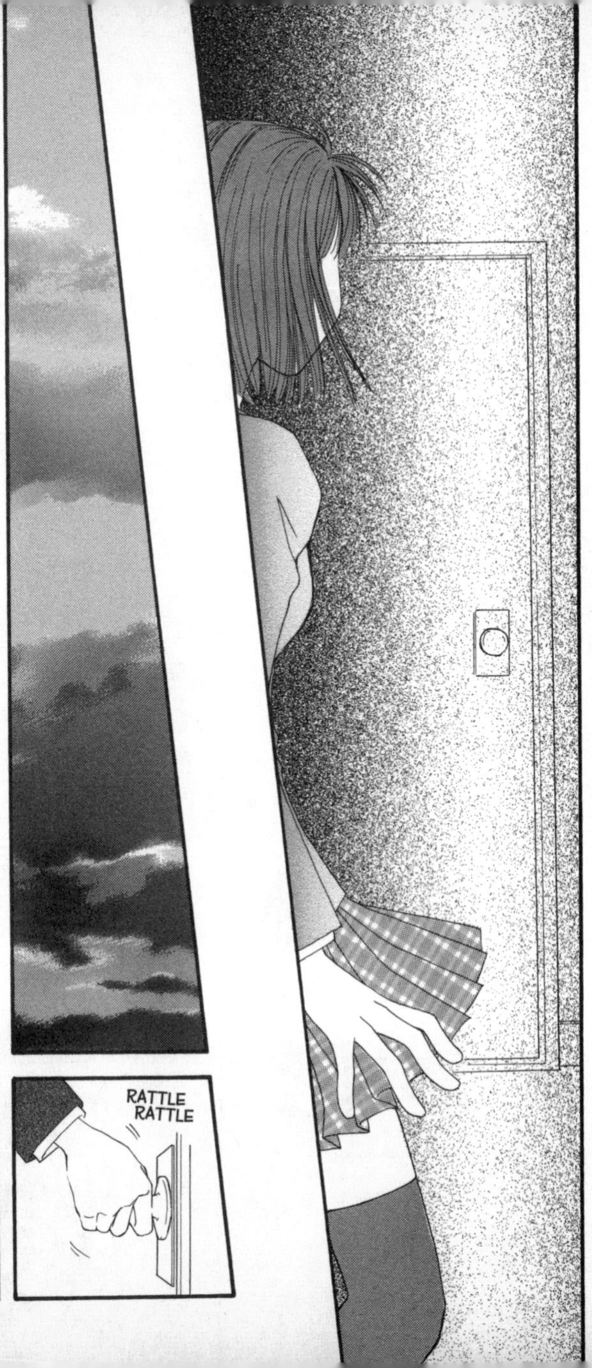
RATTLE
RATTLE

1/4 Sakura Mail

No. 3

I love tea. However, I'm a complete amateur at doing the tea ceremony, so all I ever make is green tea.
Whenever I write scripts, I have a cup of tea in front of me, but inevitably (since my debut story!), it gets knocked over.
(I know, I shouldn't set my tea down next to the script, but I wouldn't be able to write without it! So, what can you do?)
Recently, I've been managing to keep the manuscript from getting dirty, but if I do spill tea on it, I've decided to tell myself that it's like a kind of ritual.
No accidents happened to me while writing this sixth chapter, all the way up to deadline. But just when I thought, "Hey, maybe my jinx is broken!"...

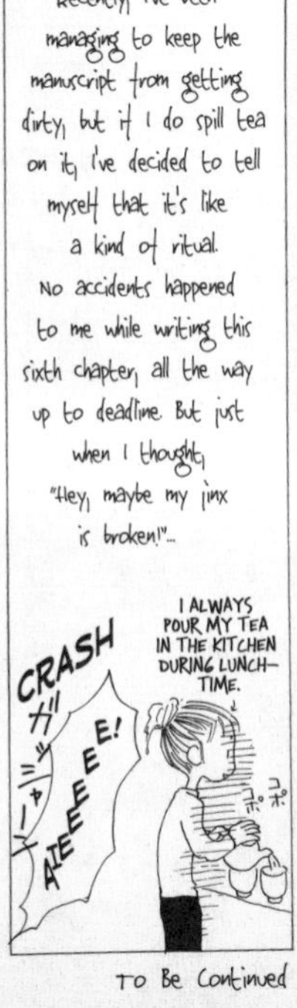
CRASH
I ALWAYS POUR MY TEA IN THE KITCHEN DURING LUNCH-TIME.
AIEEEEE!

To Be Continued

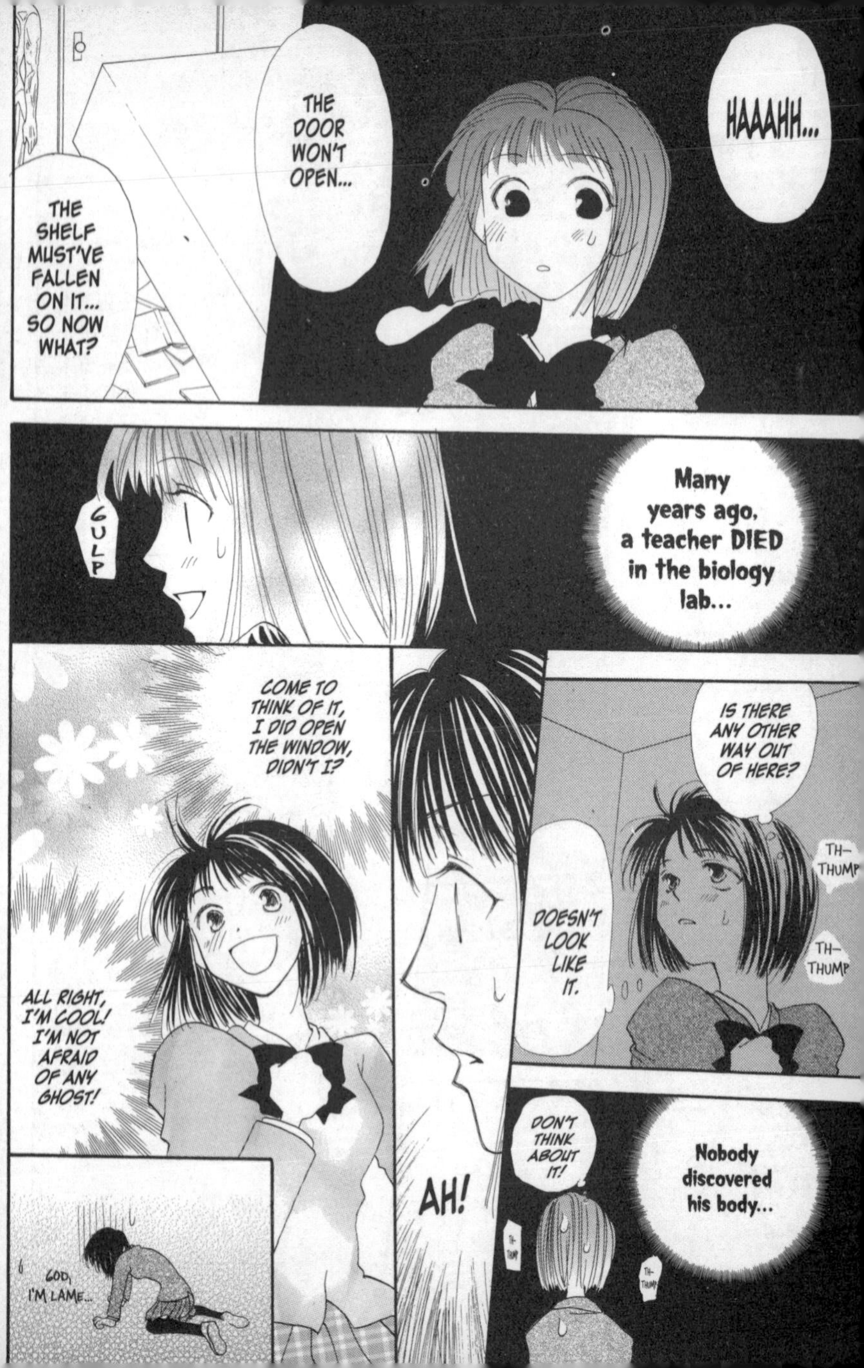
HAAAHH...
THE DOOR WON'T OPEN...
THE SHELF MUST'VE FALLEN ON IT... SO NOW WHAT?
Many years ago, a teacher DIED in the biology lab...
GULP
IS THERE ANY OTHER WAY OUT OF HERE?
TH-THUMP
TH-THUMP
DOESN'T LOOK LIKE IT.
Nobody discovered his body...
DON'T THINK ABOUT IT!
TH-THUMP
TH-THUMP
AH!
COME TO THINK OF IT, I DID OPEN THE WINDOW, DIDN'T I?
ALL RIGHT, I'M COOL! I'M NOT AFRAID OF ANY GHOST!
GOD, I'M LAME...

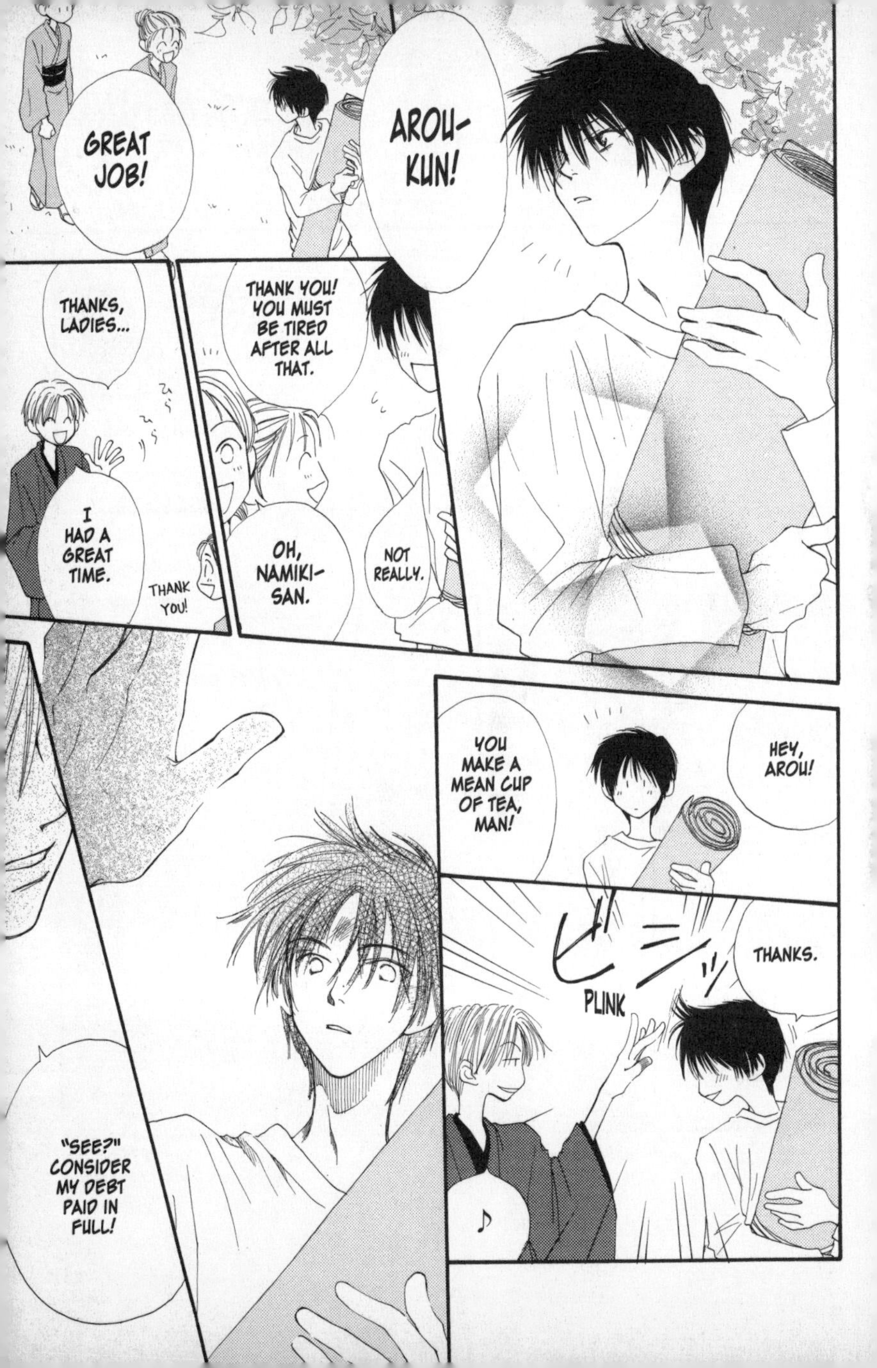
AROU-KUN!
GREAT JOB!
THANK YOU! YOU MUST BE TIRED AFTER ALL THAT.
NOT REALLY.
OH, NAMIKI-SAN.
THANKS, LADIES...
I HAD A GREAT TIME.
THANK YOU!
HEY, AROU!
YOU MAKE A MEAN CUP OF TEA, MAN!
THANKS.
PLINK
♪
"SEE?" CONSIDER MY DEBT PAID IN FULL!

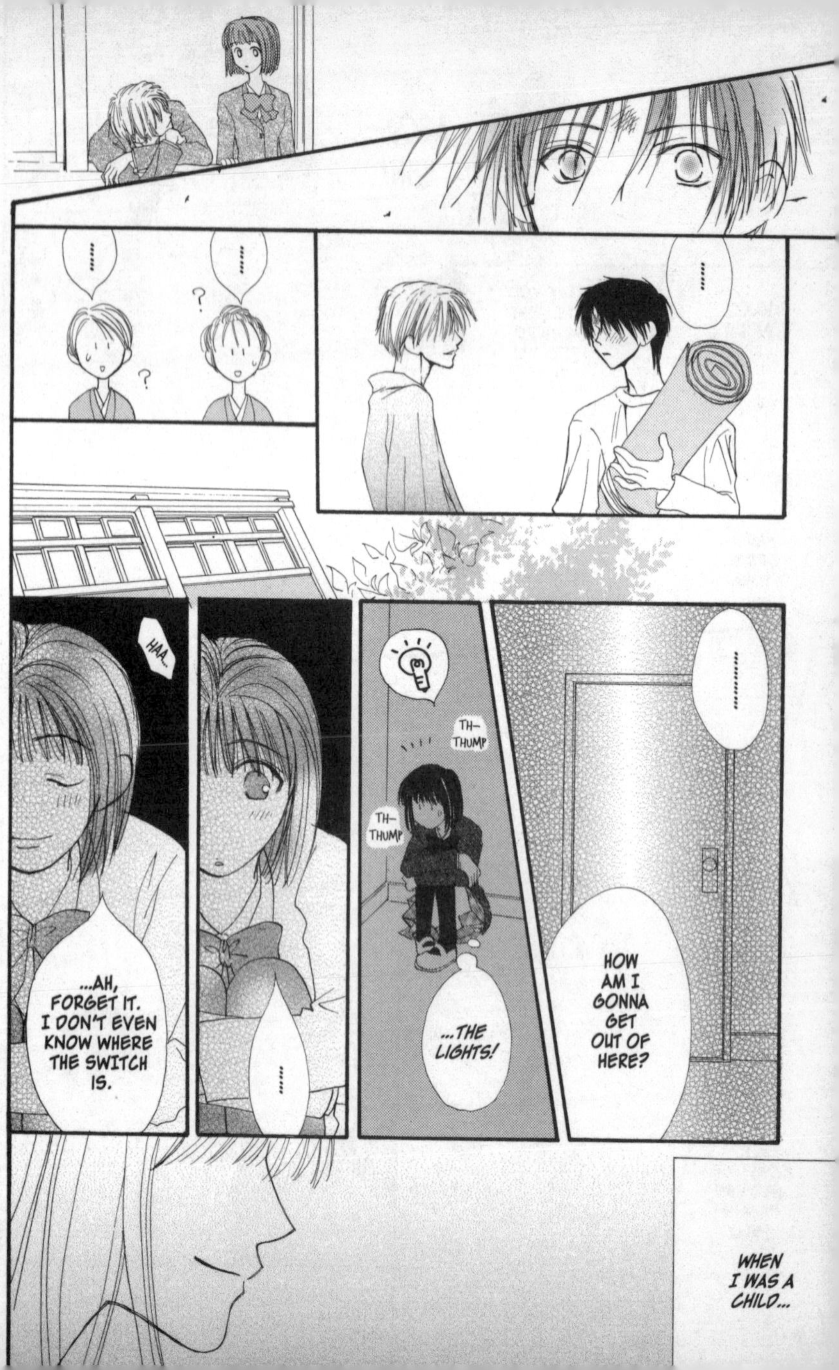
......
......
?
......
?
....
HOW AM I GONNA GET OUT OF HERE?
TH-THUMP
TH-THUMP
...THE LIGHTS!
......
HAA...
...AH, FORGET IT. I DON'T EVEN KNOW WHERE THE SWITCH IS.
WHEN I WAS A CHILD...

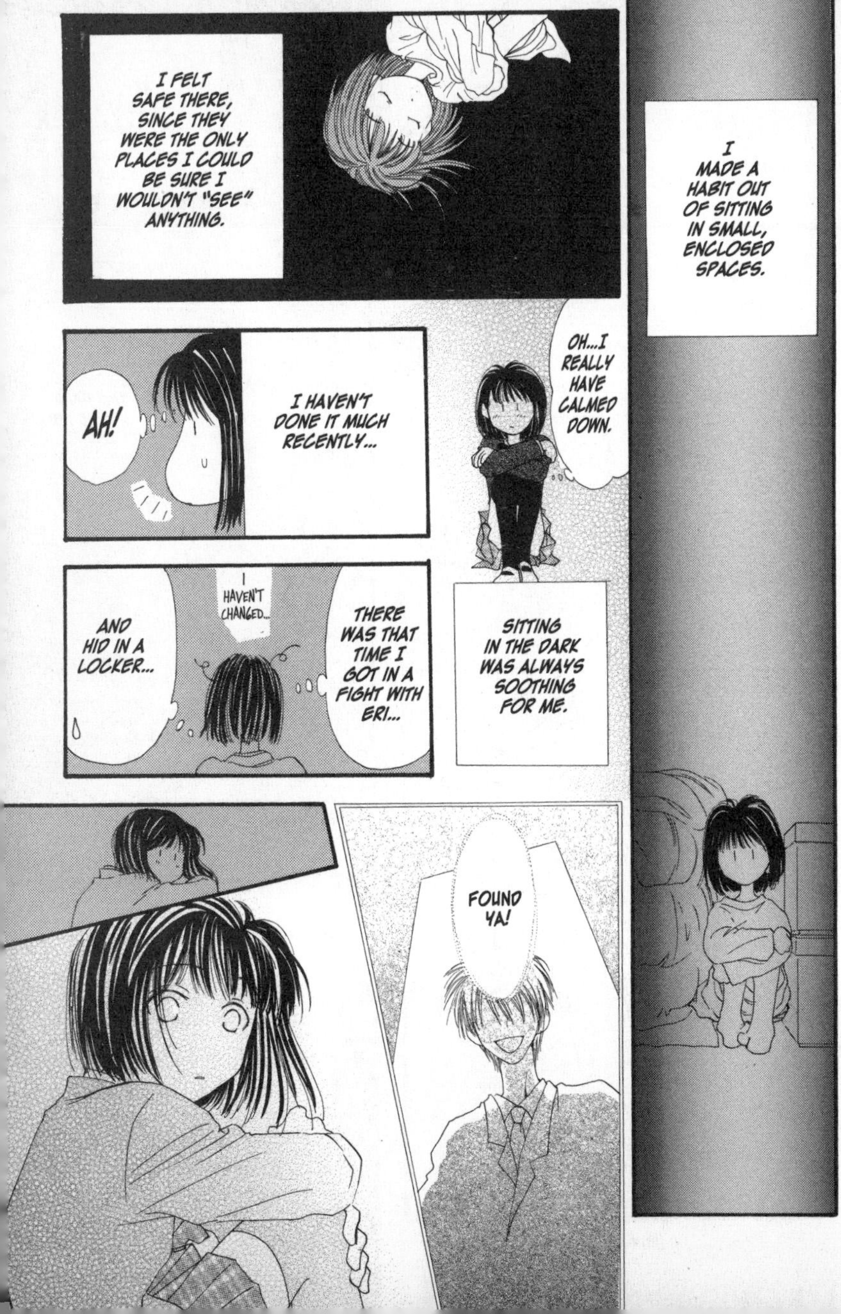
I MADE A HABIT OUT OF SITTING IN SMALL, ENCLOSED SPACES.
I FELT SAFE THERE, SINCE THEY WERE THE ONLY PLACES I COULD BE SURE I WOULDN'T "SEE" ANYTHING.
OH...I REALLY HAVE CALMED DOWN.
I HAVEN'T DONE IT MUCH RECENTLY...
AH!
SITTING IN THE DARK WAS ALWAYS SOOTHING FOR ME.
THERE WAS THAT TIME I GOT IN A FIGHT WITH ERI...
AND HID IN A LOCKER...
I HAVEN'T CHANGED...
FOUND YA!

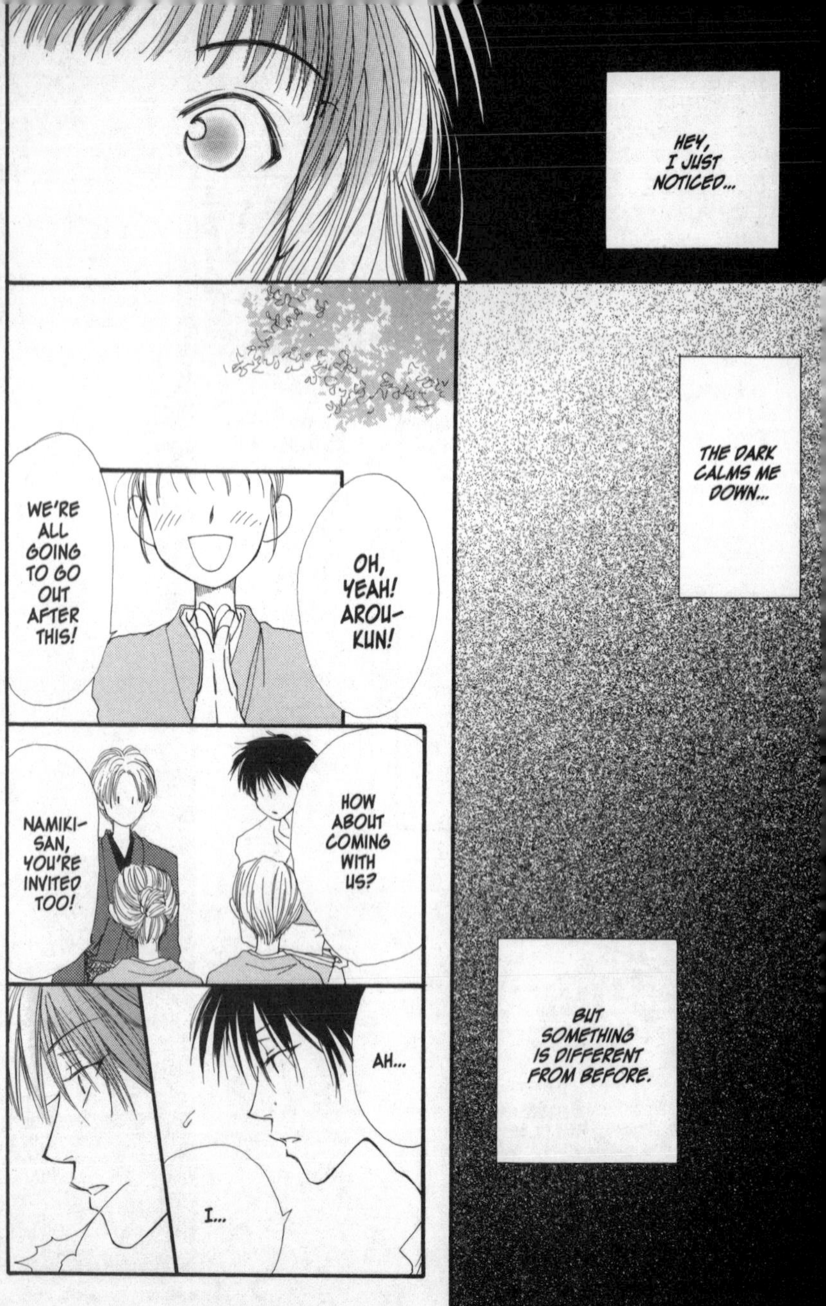
HEY, I JUST NOTICED...
THE DARK CALMS ME DOWN...
BUT SOMETHING IS DIFFERENT FROM BEFORE.
OH, YEAH! AROU-KUN!
WE'RE ALL GOING TO GO OUT AFTER THIS!
HOW ABOUT COMING WITH US?
NAMIKI-SAN, YOU'RE INVITED TOO!
AH...
I...

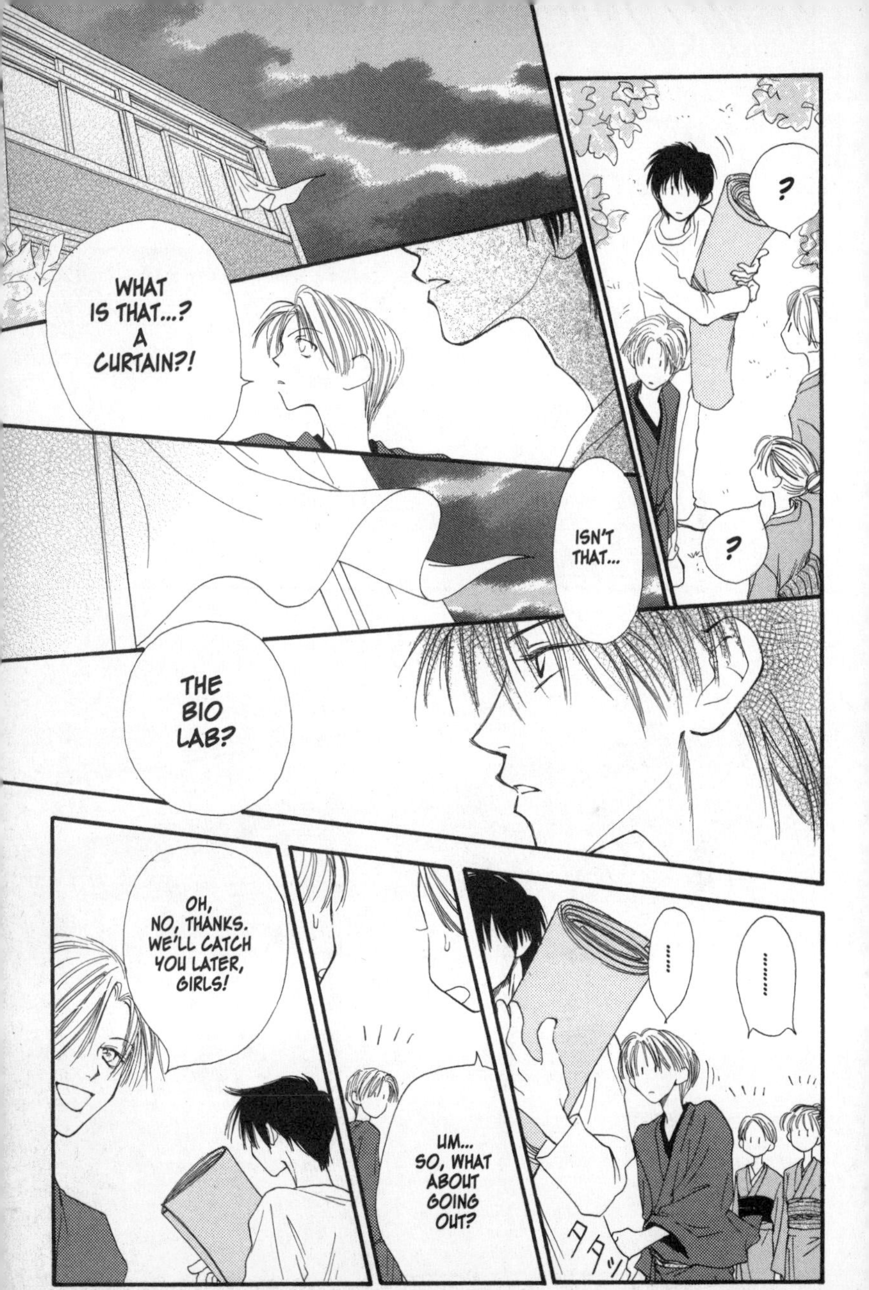
?
?
WHAT IS THAT...? A CURTAIN?!
ISN'T THAT...
THE BIO LAB?
......
......
タタッ
UM... SO, WHAT ABOUT GOING OUT?
OH, NO, THANKS. WE'LL CATCH YOU LATER, GIRLS!

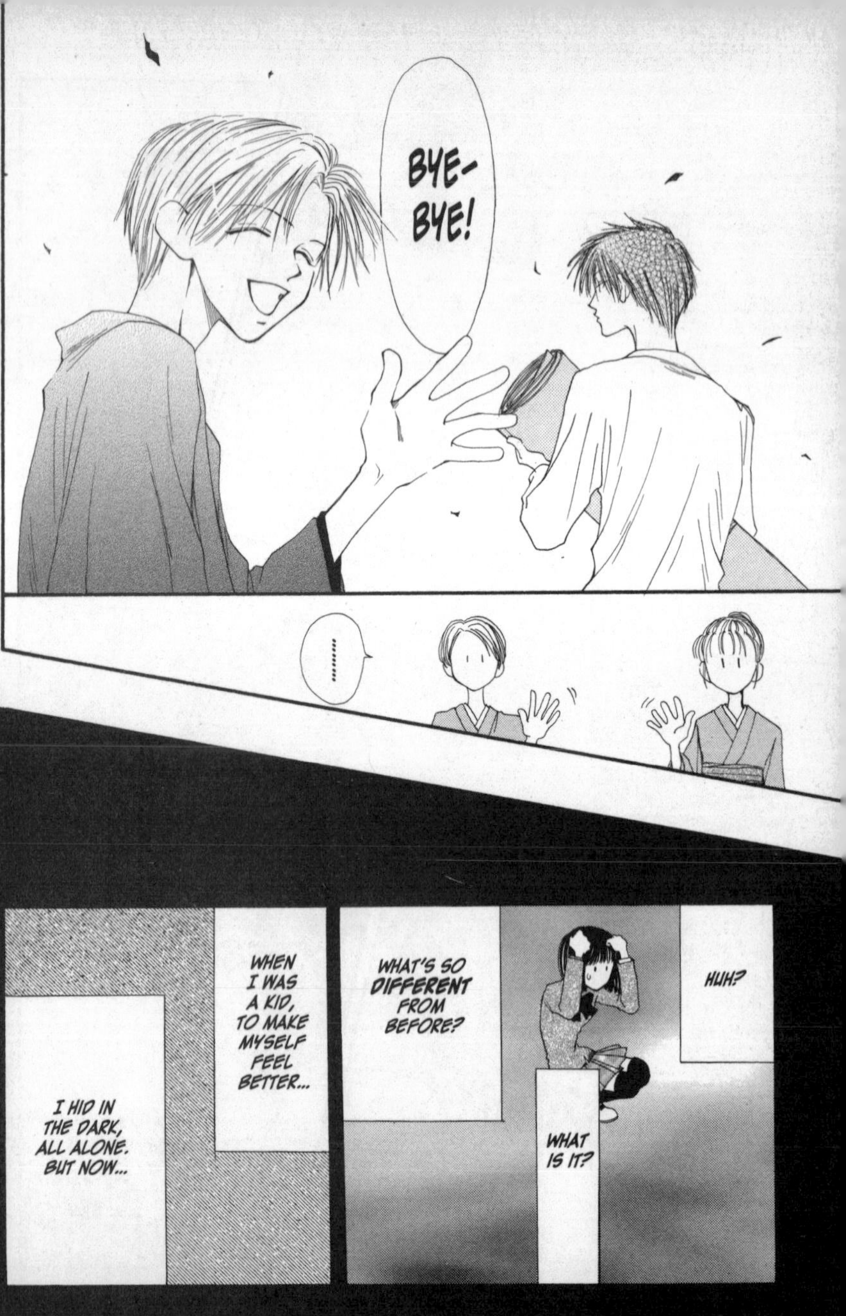
BYE-BYE!
......
HUH?
WHAT'S SO DIFFERENT FROM BEFORE?
WHAT IS IT?
WHEN I WAS A KID, TO MAKE MYSELF FEEL BETTER...
I HID IN THE DARK, ALL ALONE. BUT NOW...

OH.
THAT'S IT.
WHEN I USED TO HANG OUT IN DARK PLACES...
THAT'S WHAT'S DIFFER-ENT.
I NEVER NOTICED THAT I WAS ALONE.
KANADE!

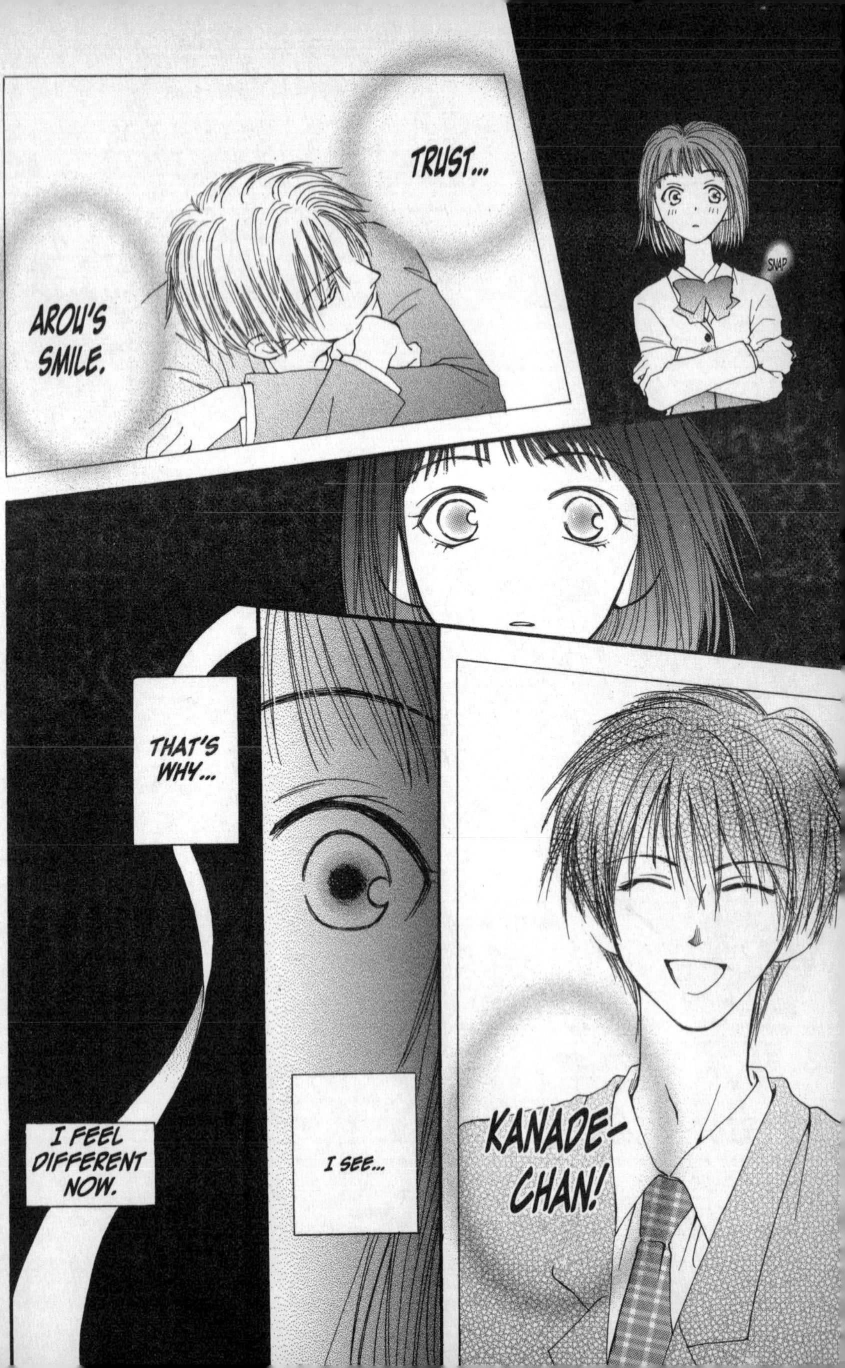
SNAP
TRUST...
AROU'S SMILE.
KANADE-CHAN!
I SEE...
THAT'S WHY...
I FEEL DIFFERENT NOW.

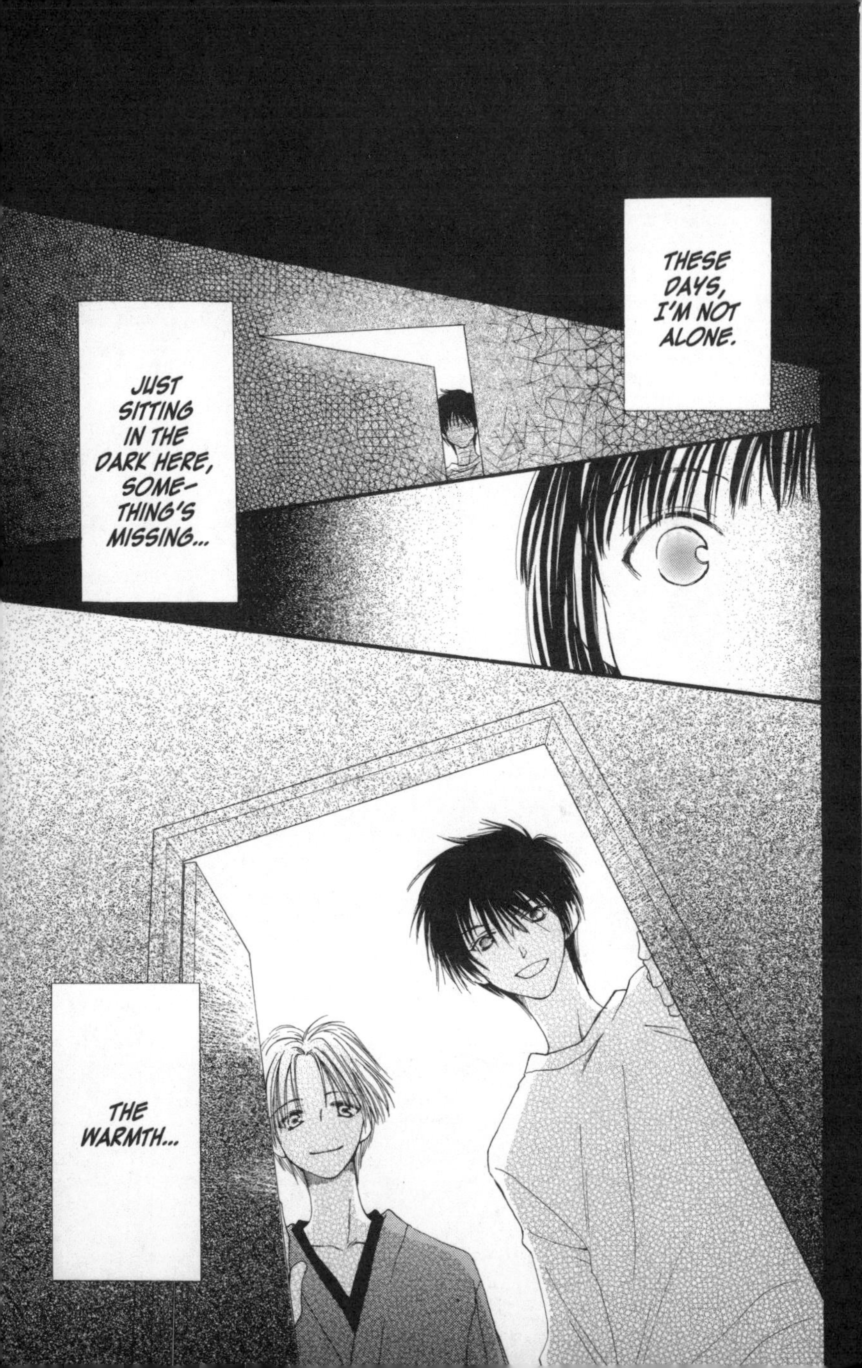
THESE DAYS, I'M NOT ALONE.
JUST SITTING IN THE DARK HERE, SOME-THING'S MISSING...
THE WARMTH...

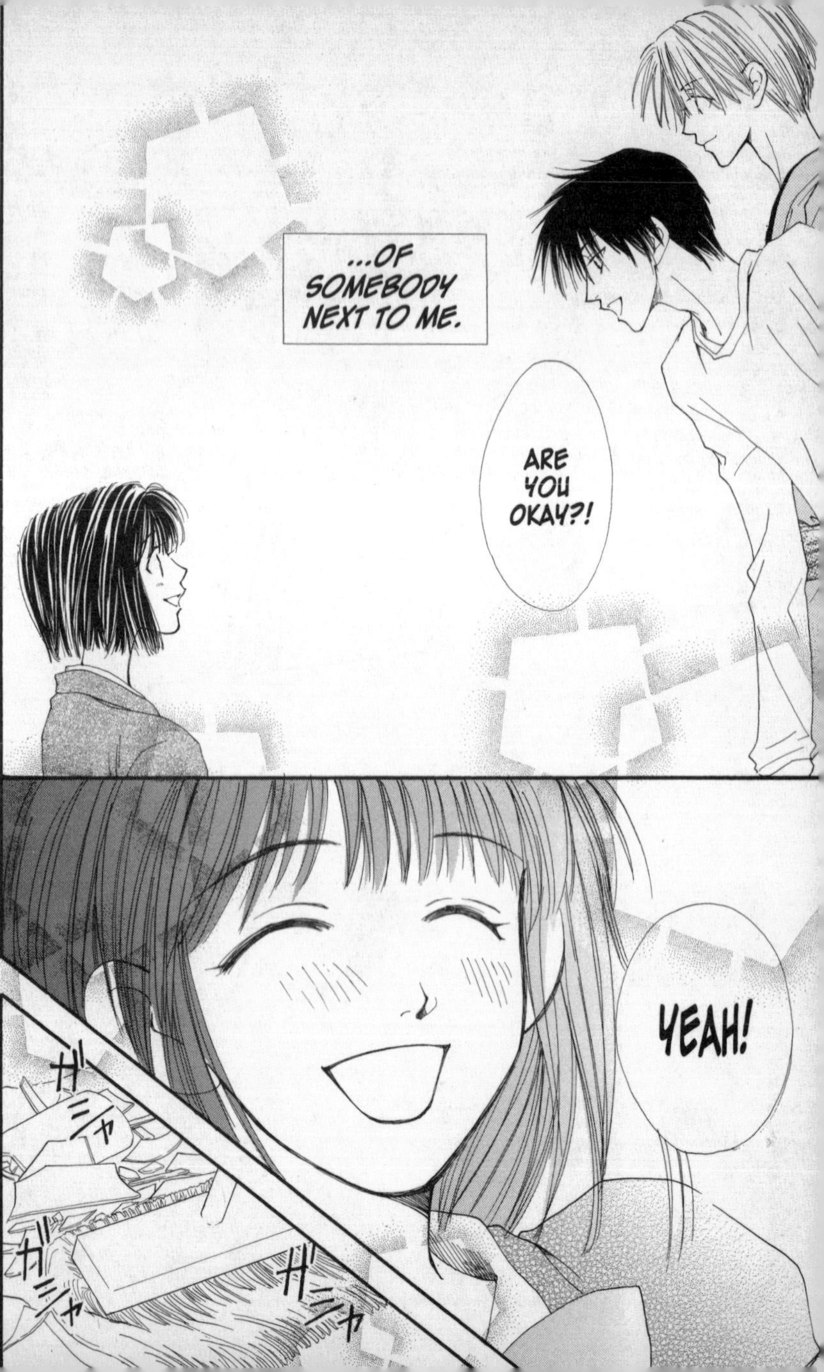
...OF SOMEBODY NEXT TO ME.
ARE YOU OKAY?!
YEAH!
ガシャ
ガシャ
ガシャ

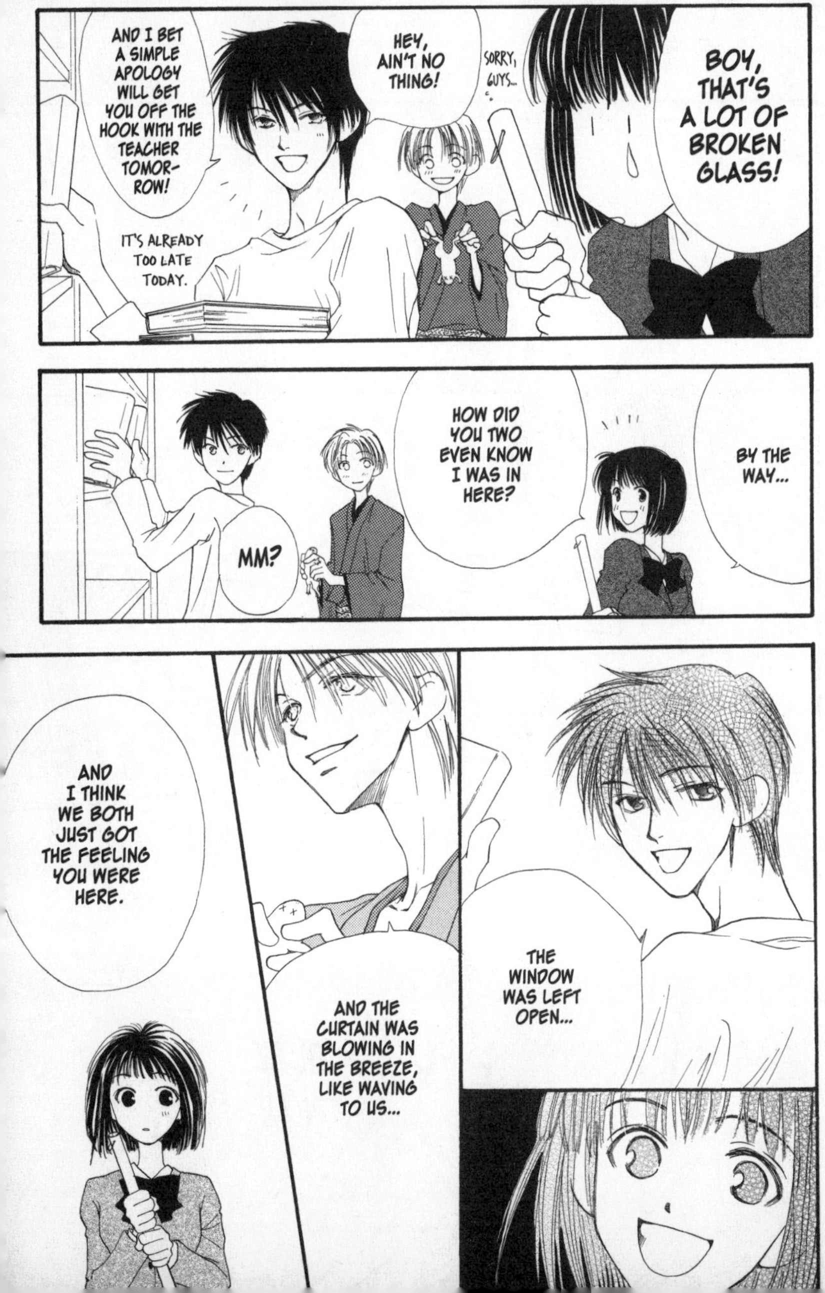
BOY, THAT'S A LOT OF BROKEN GLASS!
SORRY, GUYS...
HEY, AIN'T NO THING!
AND I BET A SIMPLE APOLOGY WILL GET YOU OFF THE HOOK WITH THE TEACHER TOMOR-ROW!
IT'S ALREADY TOO LATE TODAY.
BY THE WAY...
HOW DID YOU TWO EVEN KNOW I WAS IN HERE?
MM?
THE WINDOW WAS LEFT OPEN...
AND THE CURTAIN WAS BLOWING IN THE BREEZE, LIKE WAVING TO US...
AND I THINK WE BOTH JUST GOT THE FEELING YOU WERE HERE.

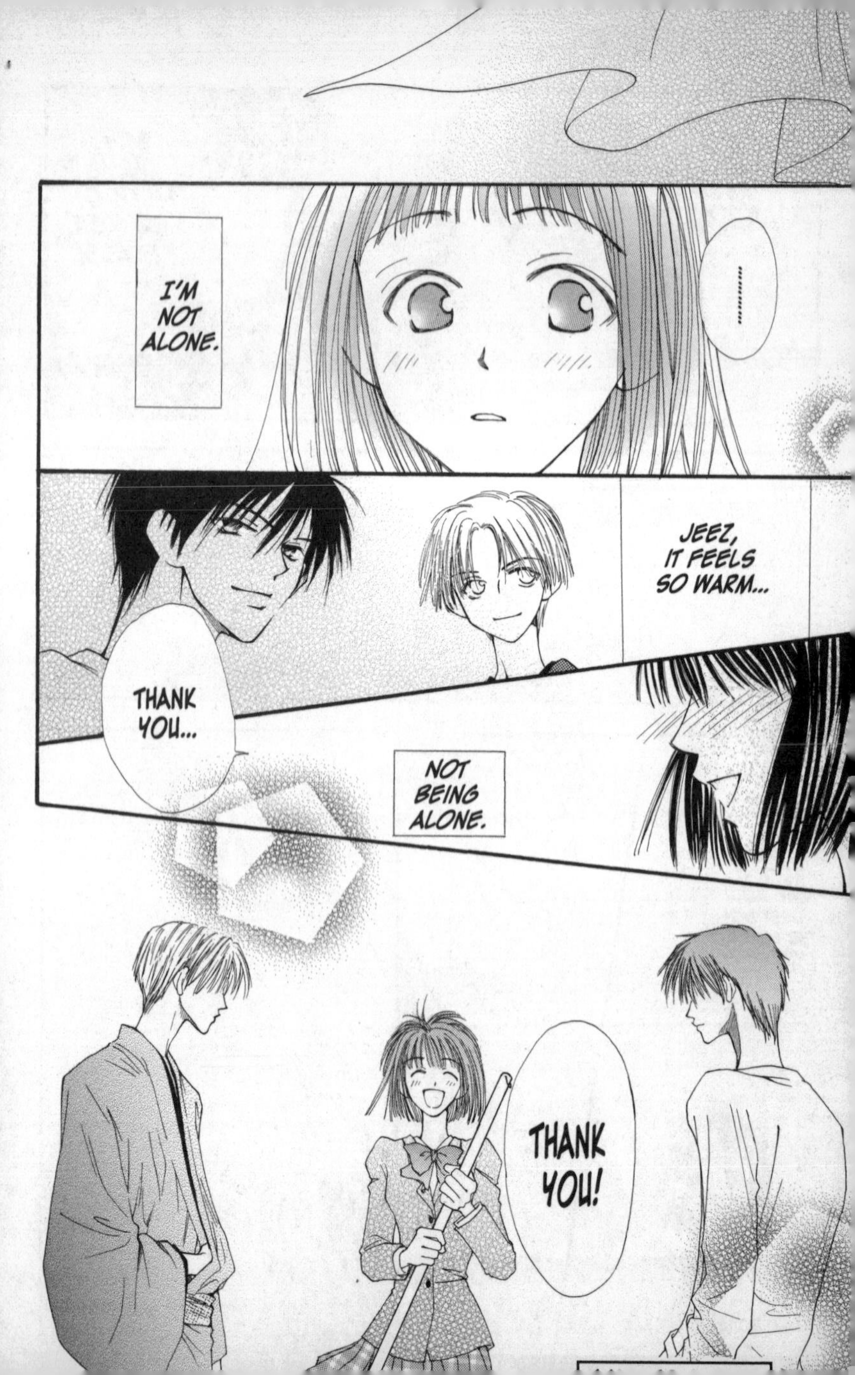
......
I'M NOT ALONE.
JEEZ, IT FEELS SO WARM...
THANK YOU...
NOT BEING ALONE.
THANK YOU!

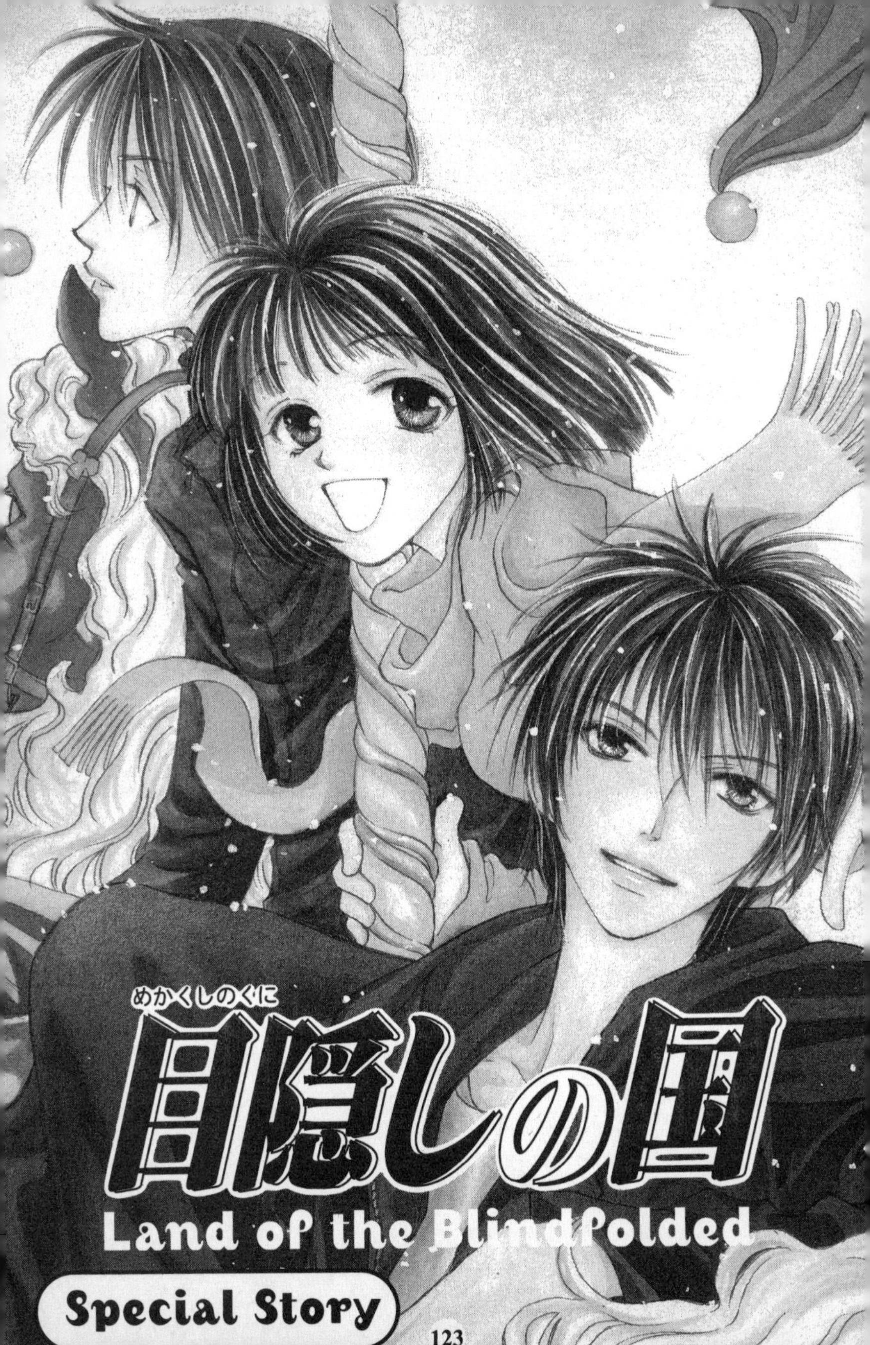

めかくしのくに
目隠しの国
Land of the Blindfolded
Special Story

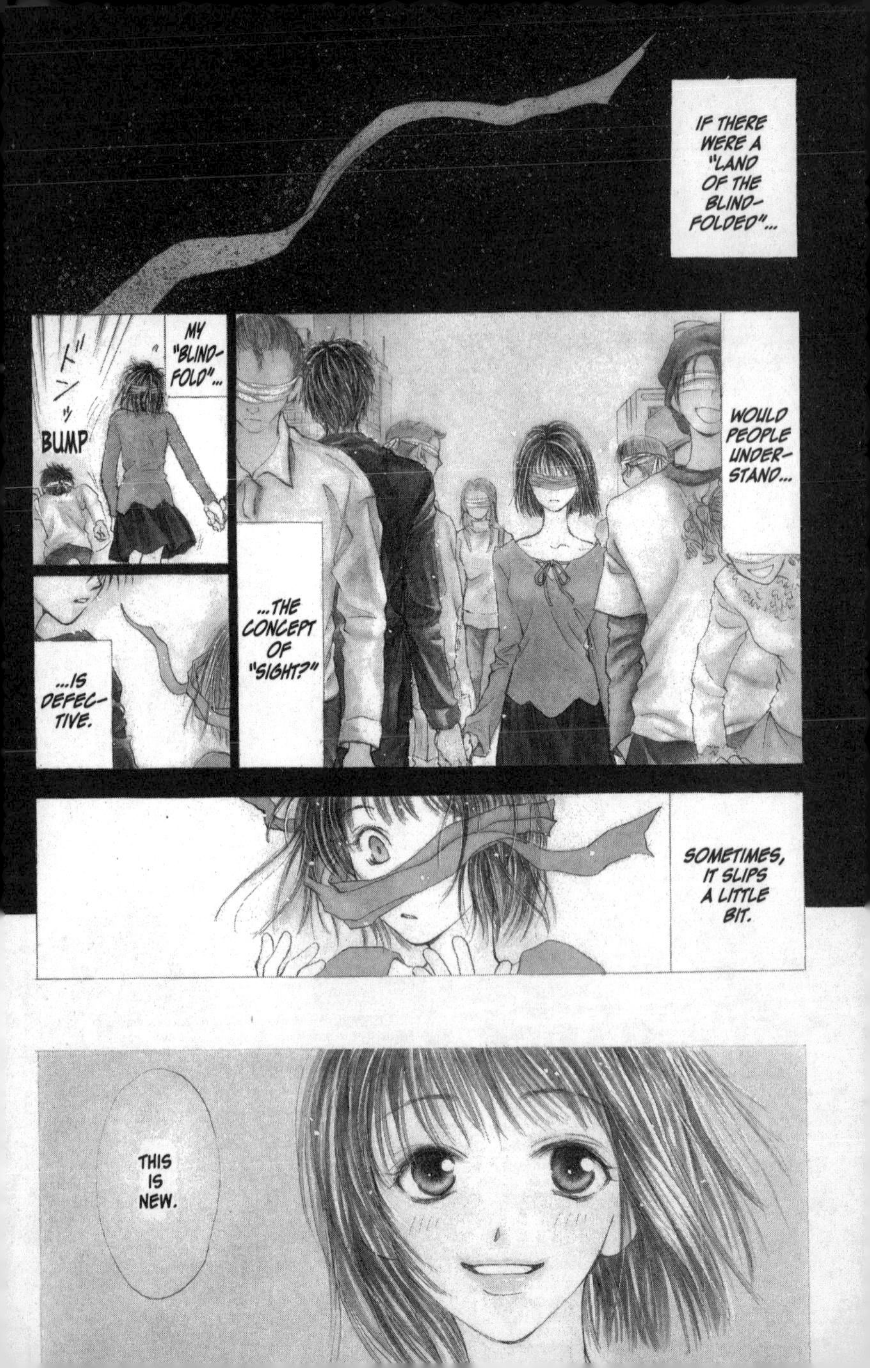
IF THERE WERE A "LAND OF THE BLIND-FOLDED"...
WOULD PEOPLE UNDER-STAND...
...THE CONCEPT OF "SIGHT?"
MY "BLIND-FOLD"...
ドンッ
BUMP
...IS DEFEC-TIVE.
SOMETIMES, IT SLIPS A LITTLE BIT.
THIS IS NEW.

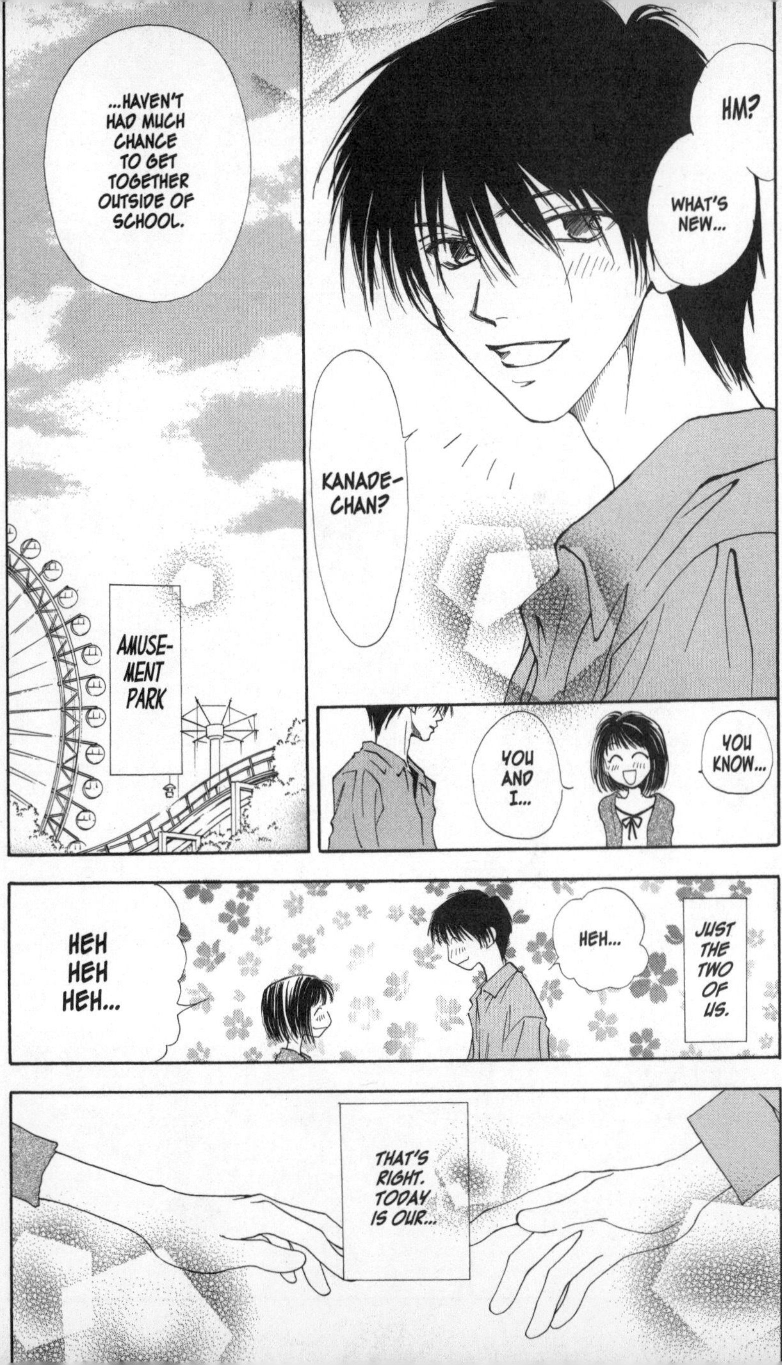
HM?
WHAT'S NEW...
KANADE-CHAN?
YOU KNOW...
YOU AND I...
...HAVEN'T HAD MUCH CHANCE TO GET TOGETHER OUTSIDE OF SCHOOL.
AMUSEMENT PARK
JUST THE TWO OF US.
HEH...
HEH HEH HEH...
THAT'S RIGHT. TODAY IS OUR...

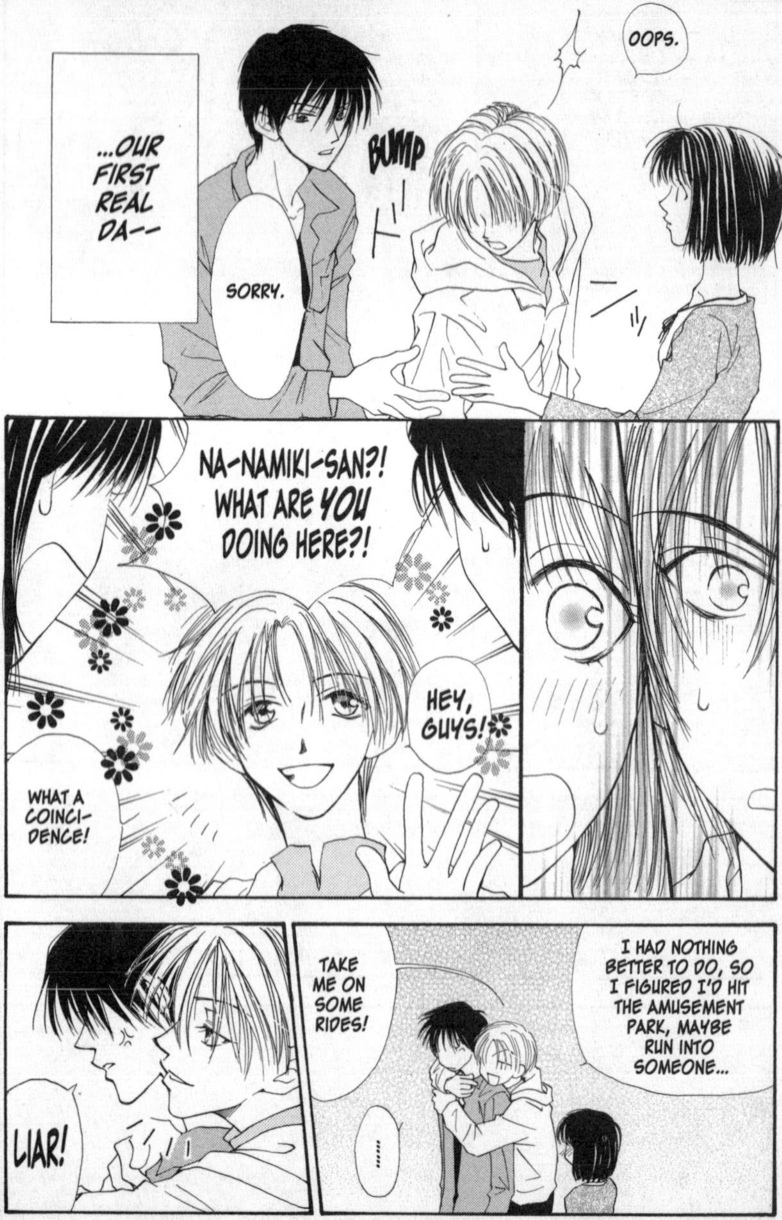
OOPS.
BUMP
...OUR FIRST REAL DA--
SORRY.
NA-NAMIKI-SAN?! WHAT ARE YOU DOING HERE?!
HEY, GUYS!
WHAT A COINCI-DENCE!
I HAD NOTHING BETTER TO DO, SO I FIGURED I'D HIT THE AMUSEMENT PARK, MAYBE RUN INTO SOMEONE...
TAKE ME ON SOME RIDES!
......
LIAR!

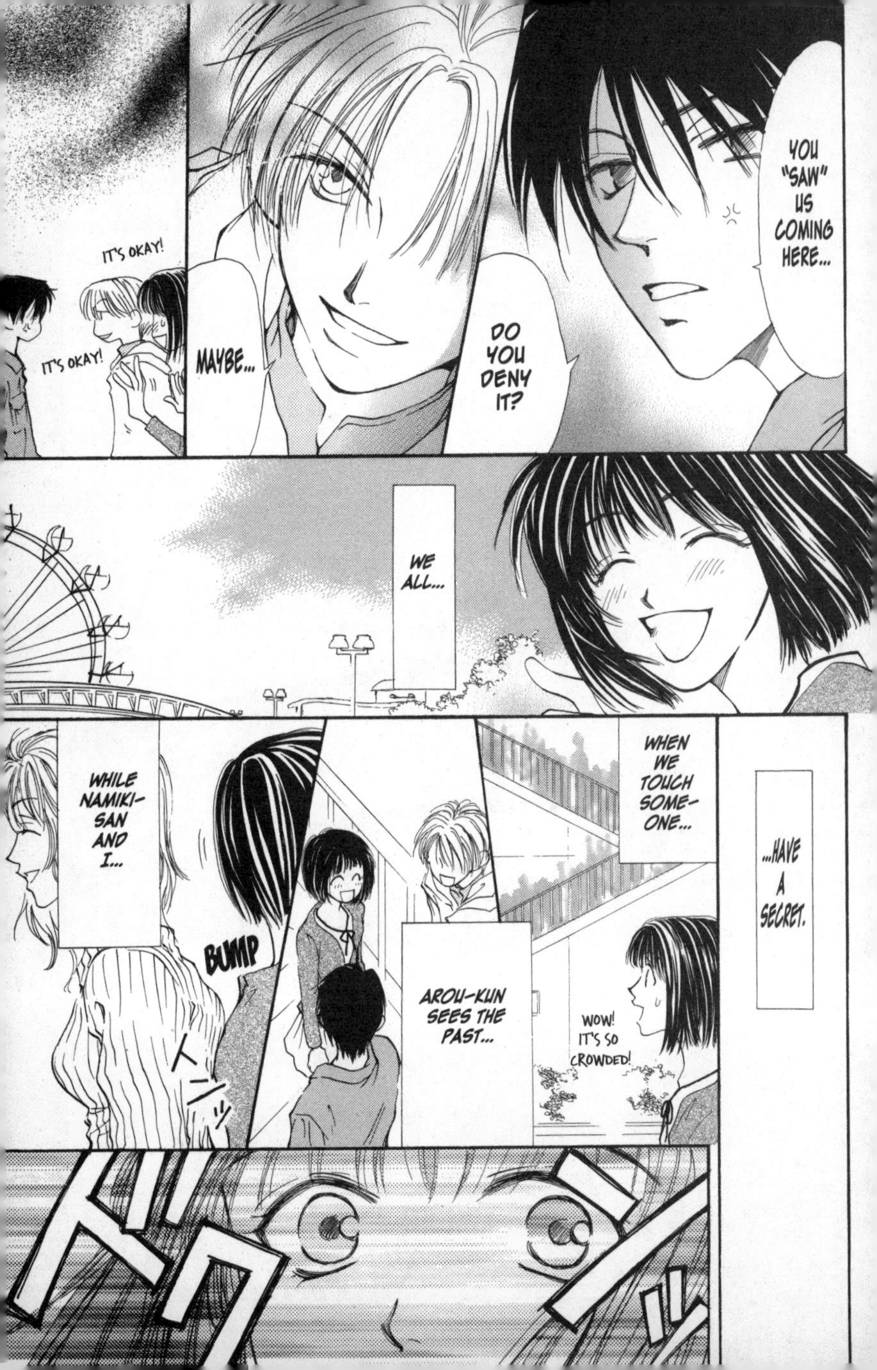
YOU "SAW" US COMING HERE...
DO YOU DENY IT?
MAYBE...
IT'S OKAY!
IT'S OKAY!
WE ALL...
...HAVE A SECRET.
WHEN WE TOUCH SOME-ONE...
AROU-KUN SEES THE PAST...
WOW! IT'S SO CROWDED!
WHILE NAMIKI-SAN AND I...
BUMP

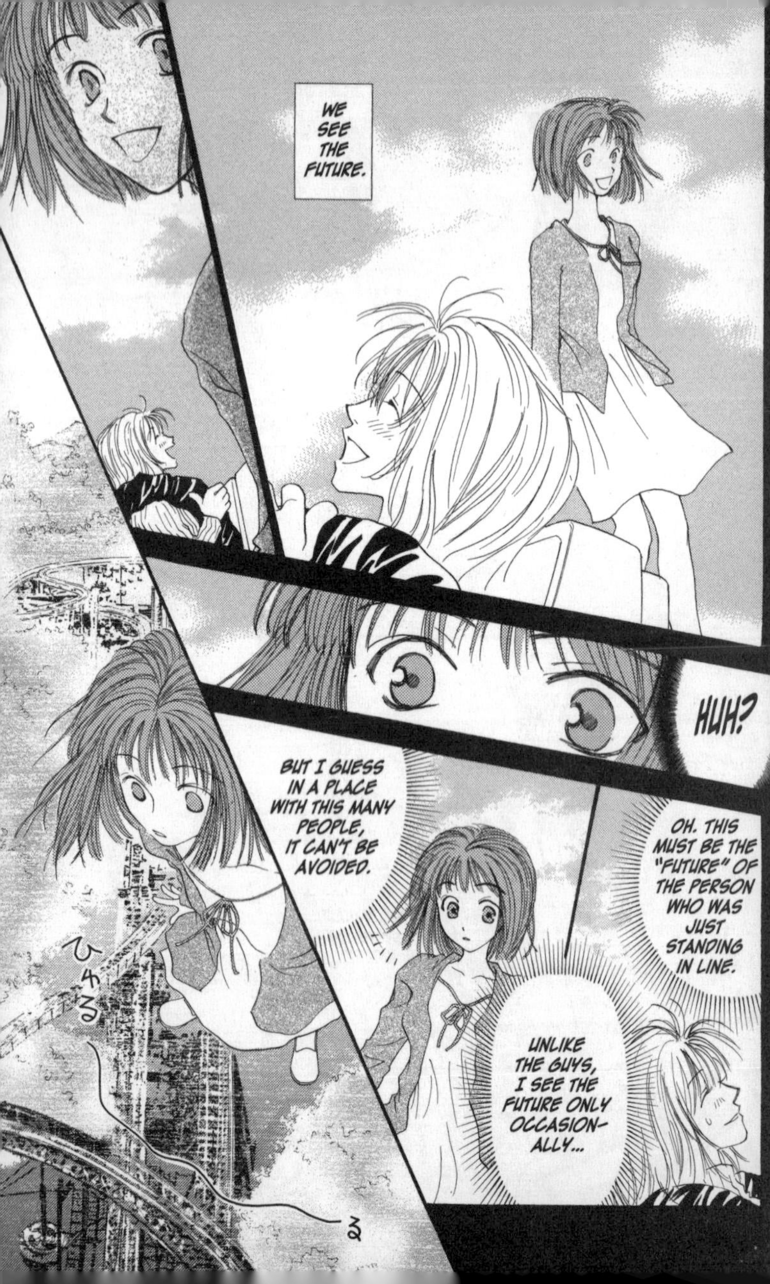
WE SEE THE FUTURE.
HUH?
OH. THIS MUST BE THE "FUTURE" OF THE PERSON WHO WAS JUST STANDING IN LINE.
UNLIKE THE GUYS, I SEE THE FUTURE ONLY OCCASION-ALLY...
BUT I GUESS IN A PLACE WITH THIS MANY PEOPLE, IT CAN'T BE AVOIDED.
ひゅるる

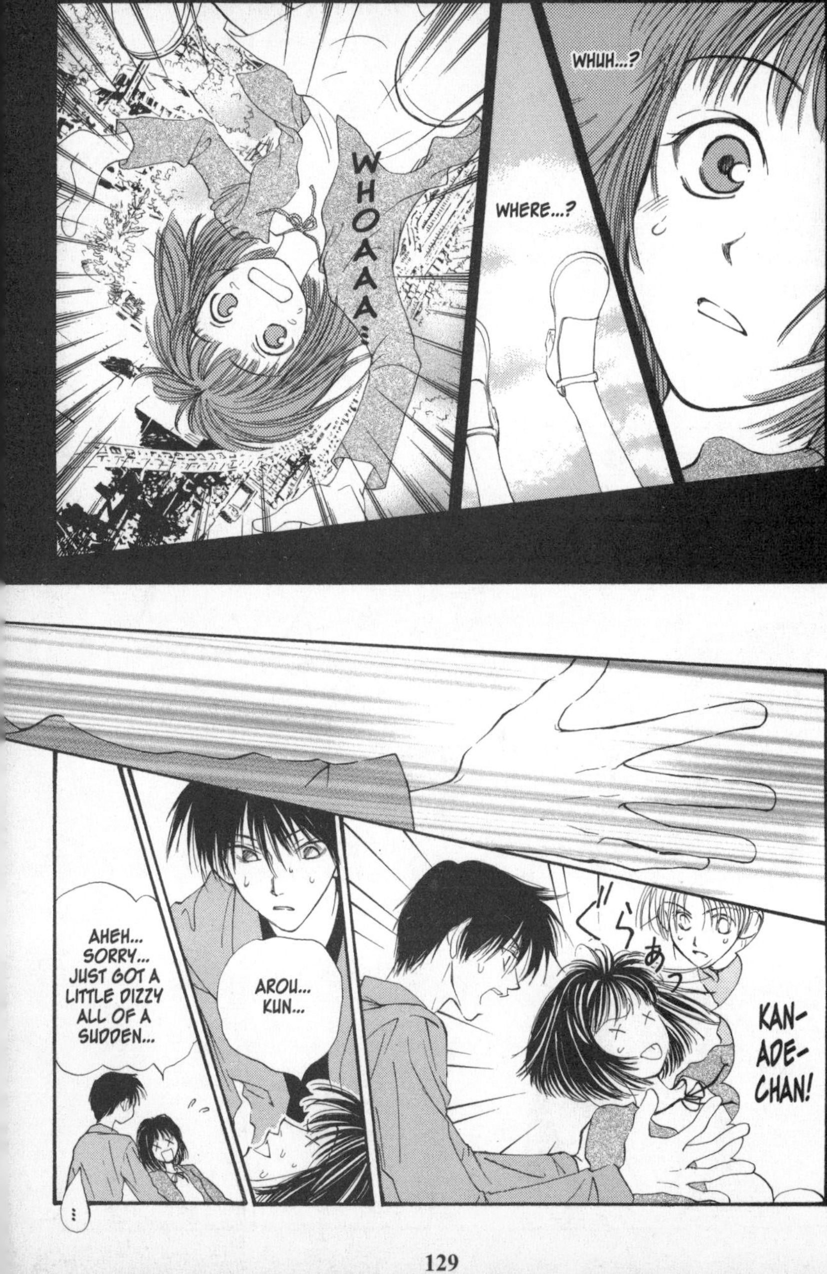
WHUH...?
WHERE...?
WHOAAA...!
ぐらぁっ
KAN-ADE-CHAN!
AROU... KUN...
AHEH... SORRY... JUST GOT A LITTLE DIZZY ALL OF A SUDDEN...
...

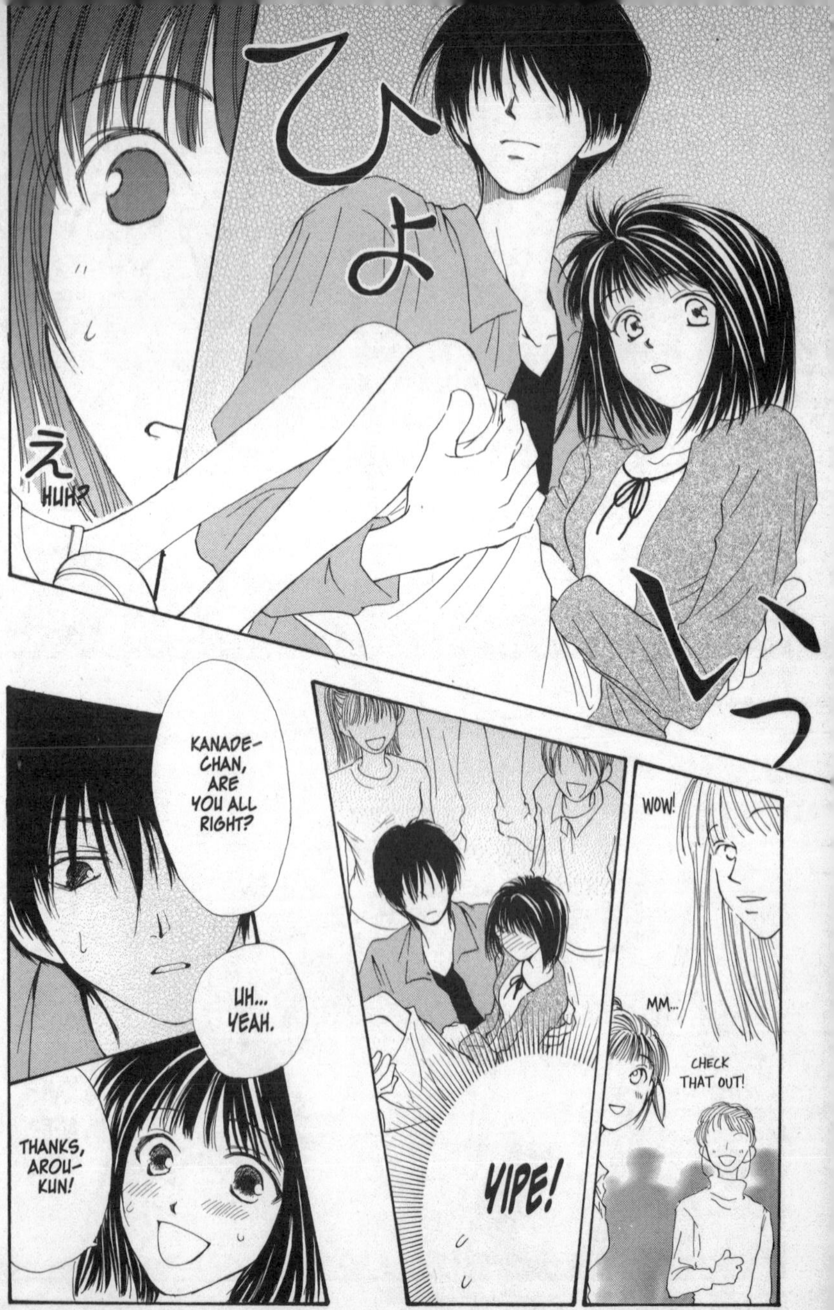
ひよいっ
え
HUH?
WOW!
MM...
CHECK THAT OUT!
YIPE!
KANADE-CHAN, ARE YOU ALL RIGHT?
UH... YEAH.
THANKS, AROU-KUN!

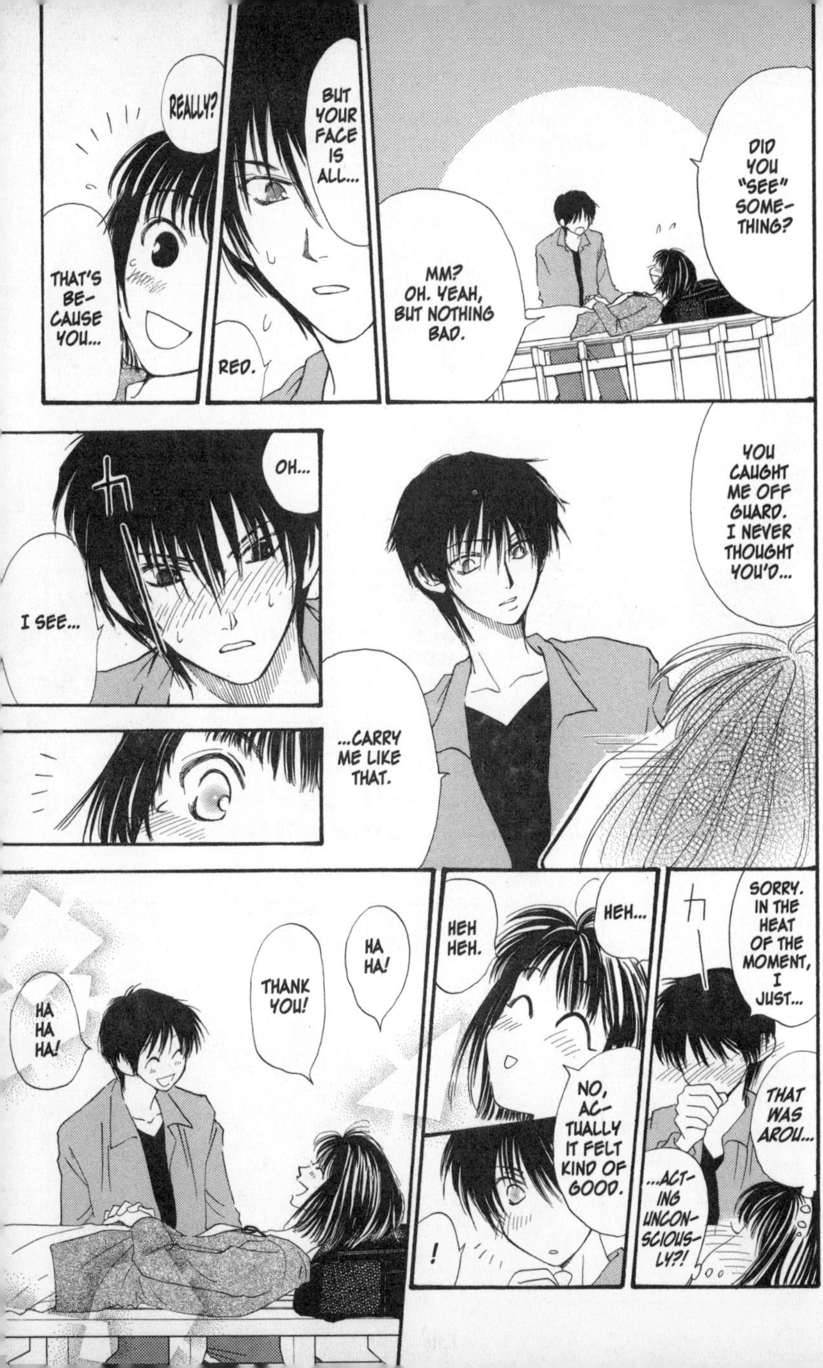
DID YOU "SEE" SOMETHING?
MM? OH. YEAH, BUT NOTHING BAD.
BUT YOUR FACE IS ALL...
RED.
REALLY?
THAT'S BE-CAUSE YOU...
YOU CAUGHT ME OFF GUARD. I NEVER THOUGHT YOU'D...
...CARRY ME LIKE THAT.
OH...
I SEE...
SORRY. IN THE HEAT OF THE MOMENT, I JUST...
THAT WAS AROU...
...ACT-ING UNCON-SCIOUS-LY?!
HEH...
HEH HEH.
NO, AC-TUALLY IT FELT KIND OF GOOD.
!
HA HA!
THANK YOU!
HA HA HA!

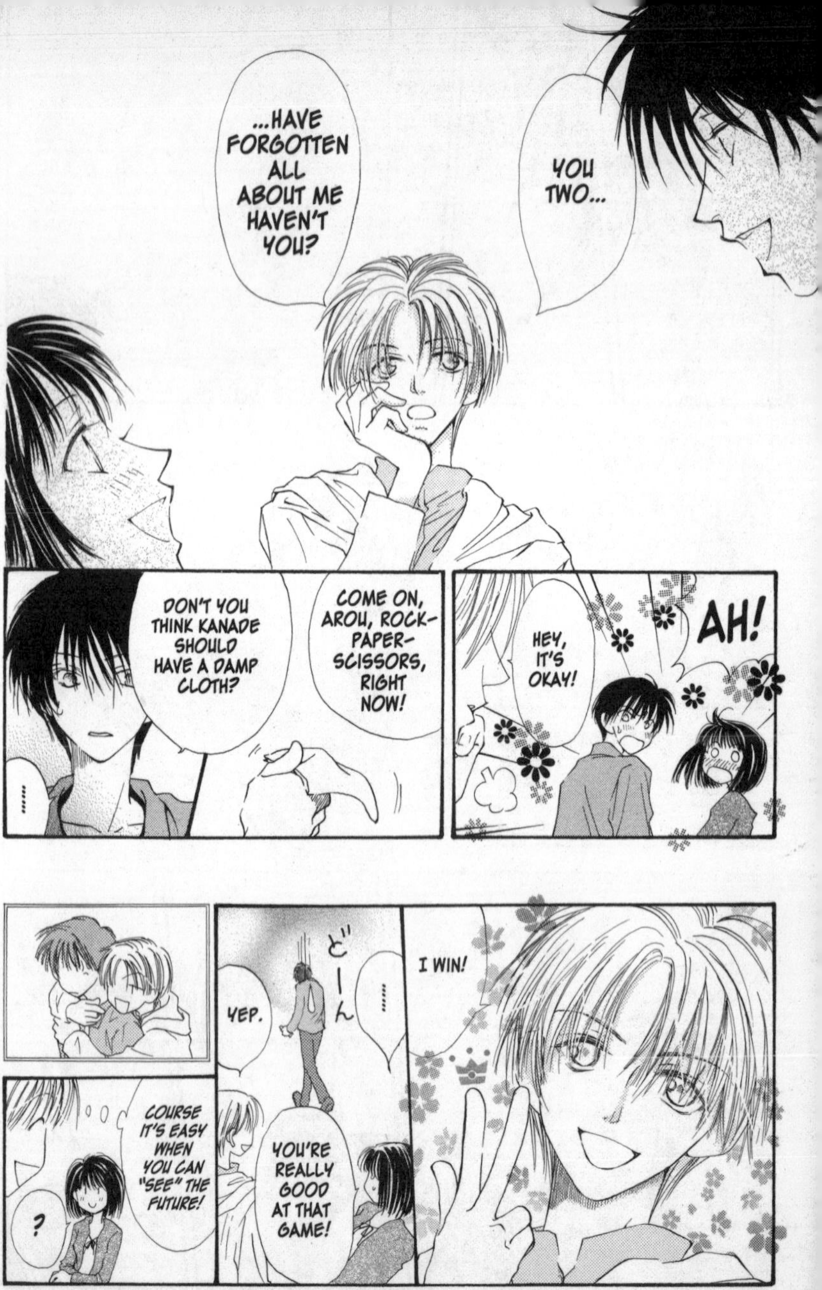
YOU TWO...
...HAVE FORGOTTEN ALL ABOUT ME HAVEN'T YOU?
AH!
HEY, IT'S OKAY!
COME ON, AROU, ROCK-PAPER-SCISSORS, RIGHT NOW!
DON'T YOU THINK KANADE SHOULD HAVE A DAMP CLOTH?
......
I WIN!
......
どーん
YEP.
YOU'RE REALLY GOOD AT THAT GAME!
COURSE IT'S EASY WHEN YOU CAN "SEE" THE FUTURE!
?

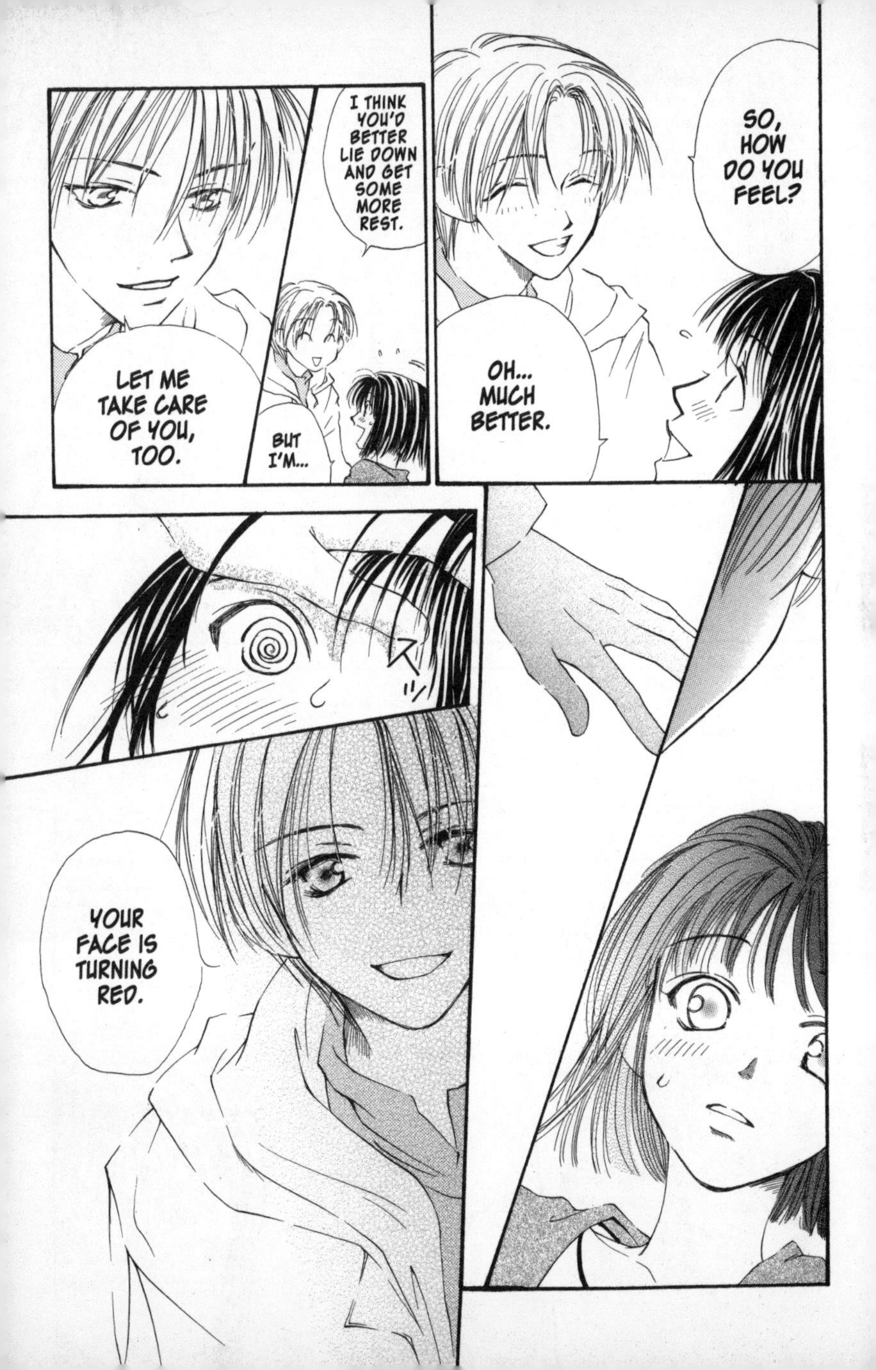
SO, HOW DO YOU FEEL?
OH... MUCH BETTER.
I THINK YOU'D BETTER LIE DOWN AND GET SOME MORE REST.
BUT I'M...
LET ME TAKE CARE OF YOU, TOO.
YOUR FACE IS TURNING RED.

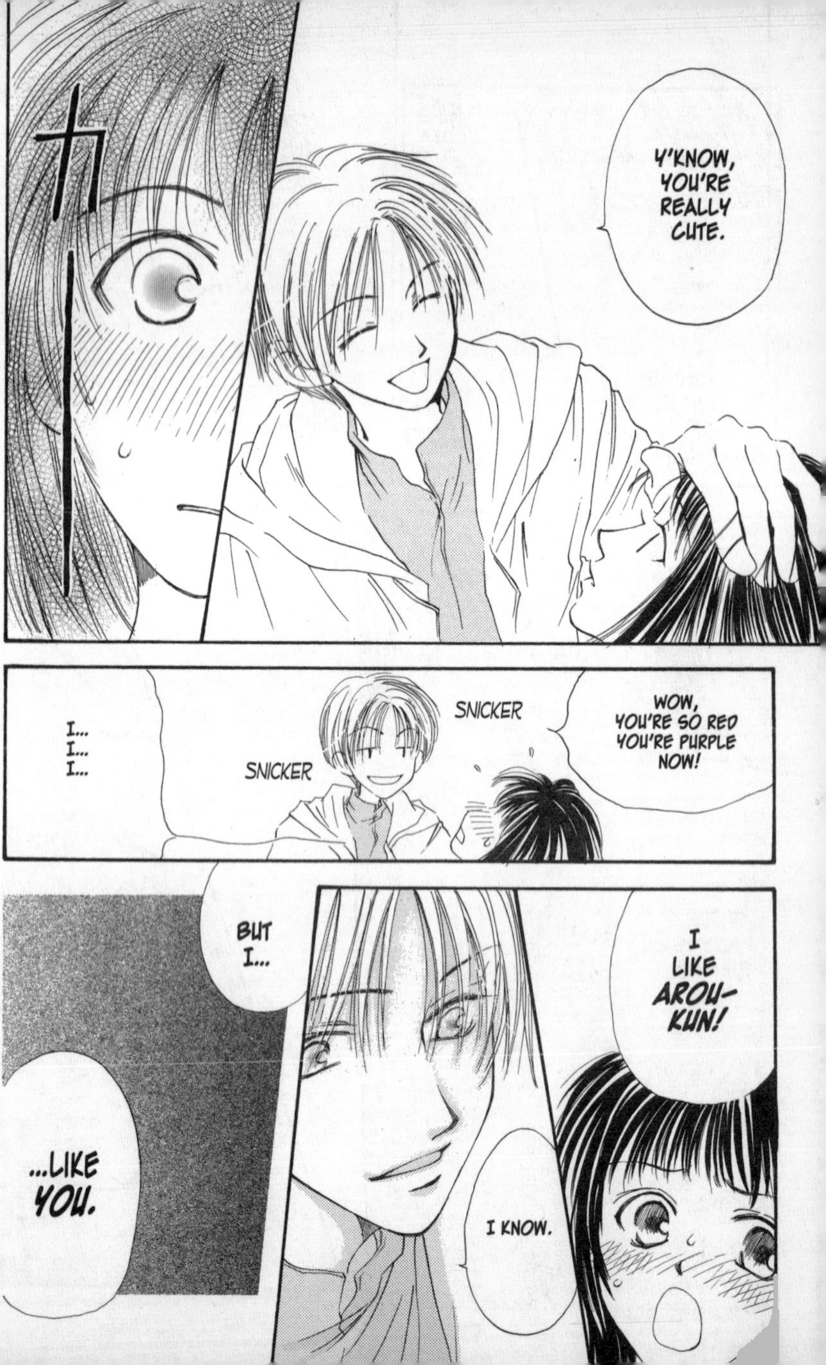
Y'KNOW, YOU'RE REALLY CUTE.
カ
WOW, YOU'RE SO RED YOU'RE PURPLE NOW!
SNICKER
SNICKER
I... I... I...
I LIKE AROU-KUN!
BUT I...
I KNOW.
...LIKE YOU.

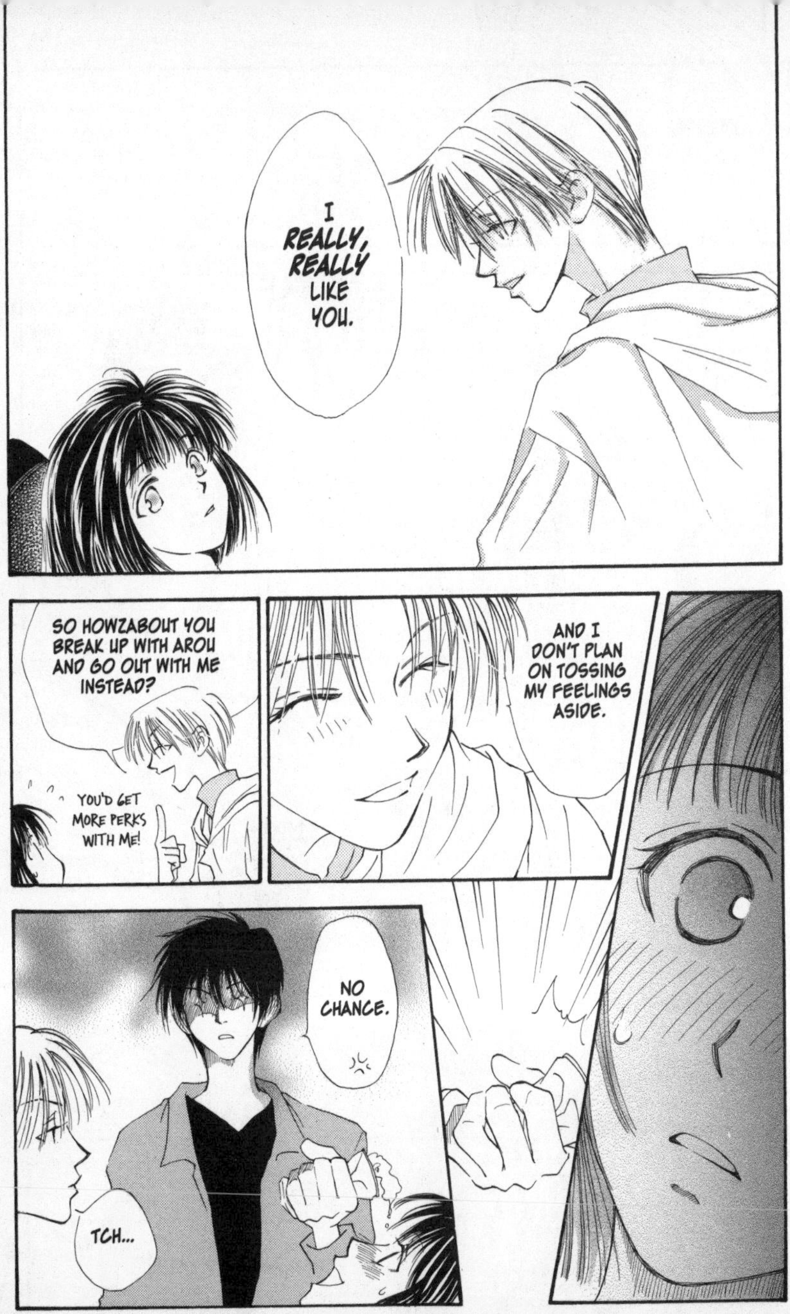
I REALLY, REALLY LIKE YOU.
AND I DON'T PLAN ON TOSSING MY FEELINGS ASIDE.
SO HOWZABOUT YOU BREAK UP WITH AROU AND GO OUT WITH ME INSTEAD?
YOU'D GET MORE PERKS WITH ME!
NO CHANCE.
TCH...

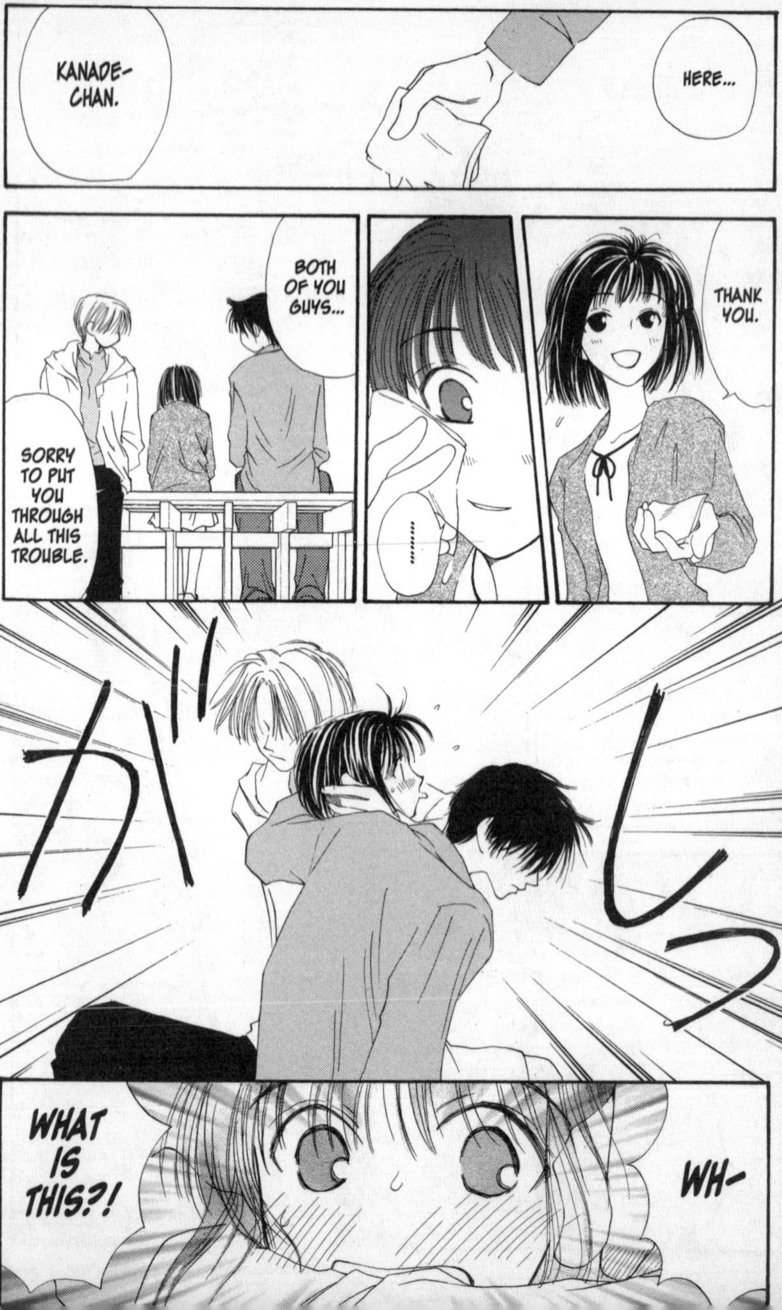
HERE...
KANADE-CHAN.
THANK YOU.
......
BOTH OF YOU GUYS...
SORRY TO PUT YOU THROUGH ALL THIS TROUBLE.
がしっ
WH-
WHAT IS THIS?!

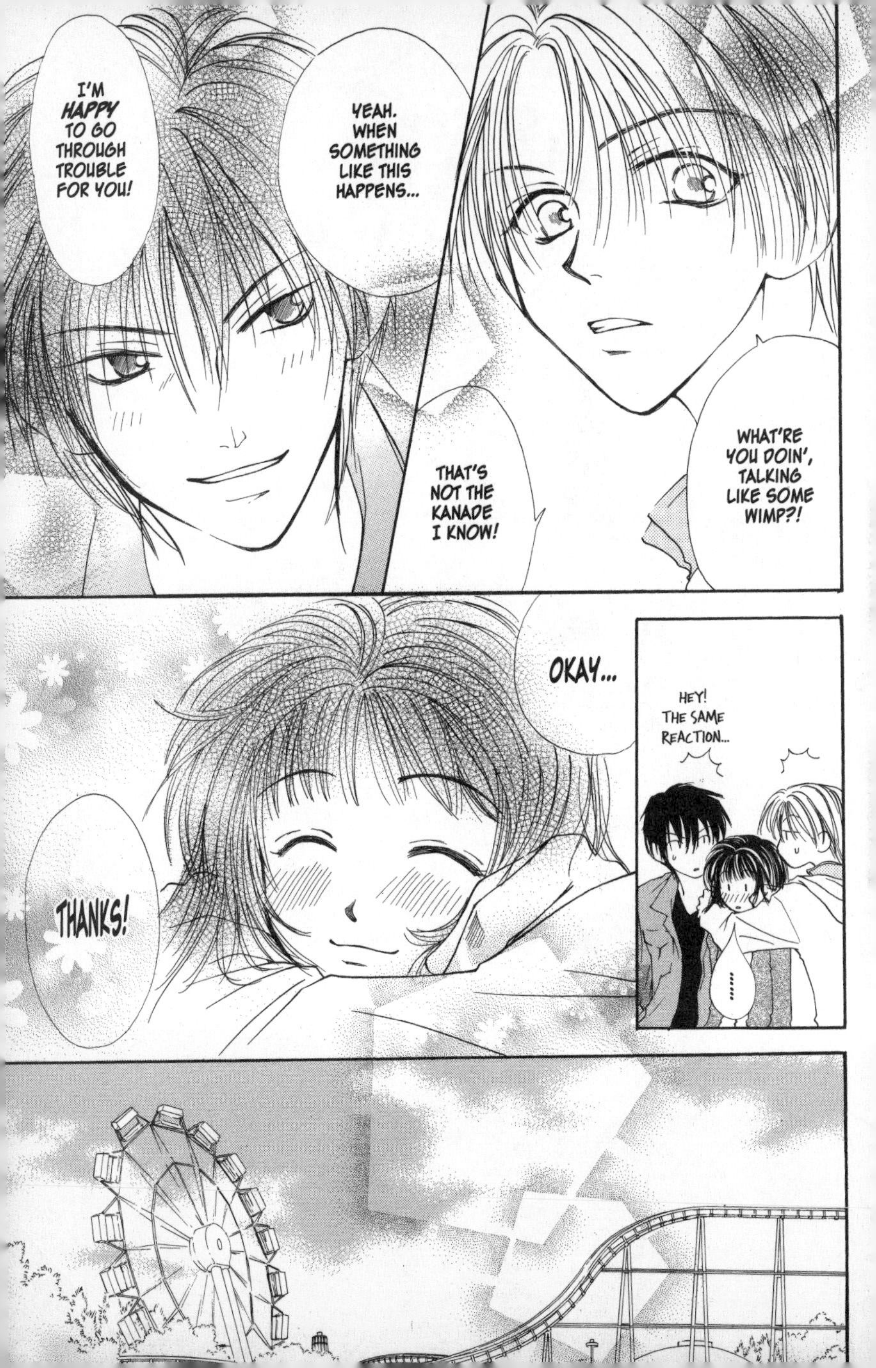
WHAT'RE YOU DOIN', TALKING LIKE SOME WIMP?!
THAT'S NOT THE KANADE I KNOW!
YEAH. WHEN SOMETHING LIKE THIS HAPPENS...
I'M *HAPPY* TO GO THROUGH TROUBLE FOR YOU!
HEY! THE SAME REACTION...
......
OKAY...
THANKS!

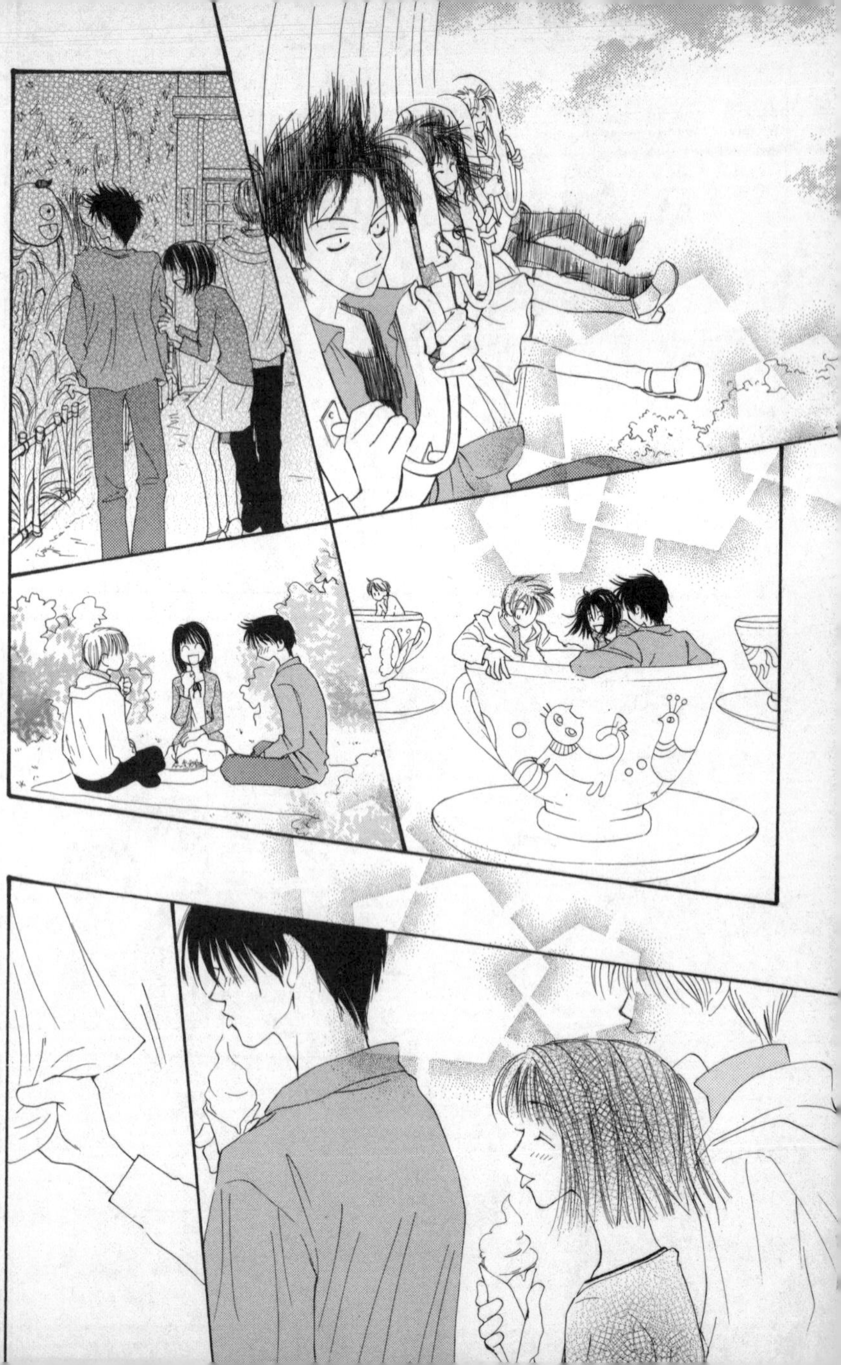

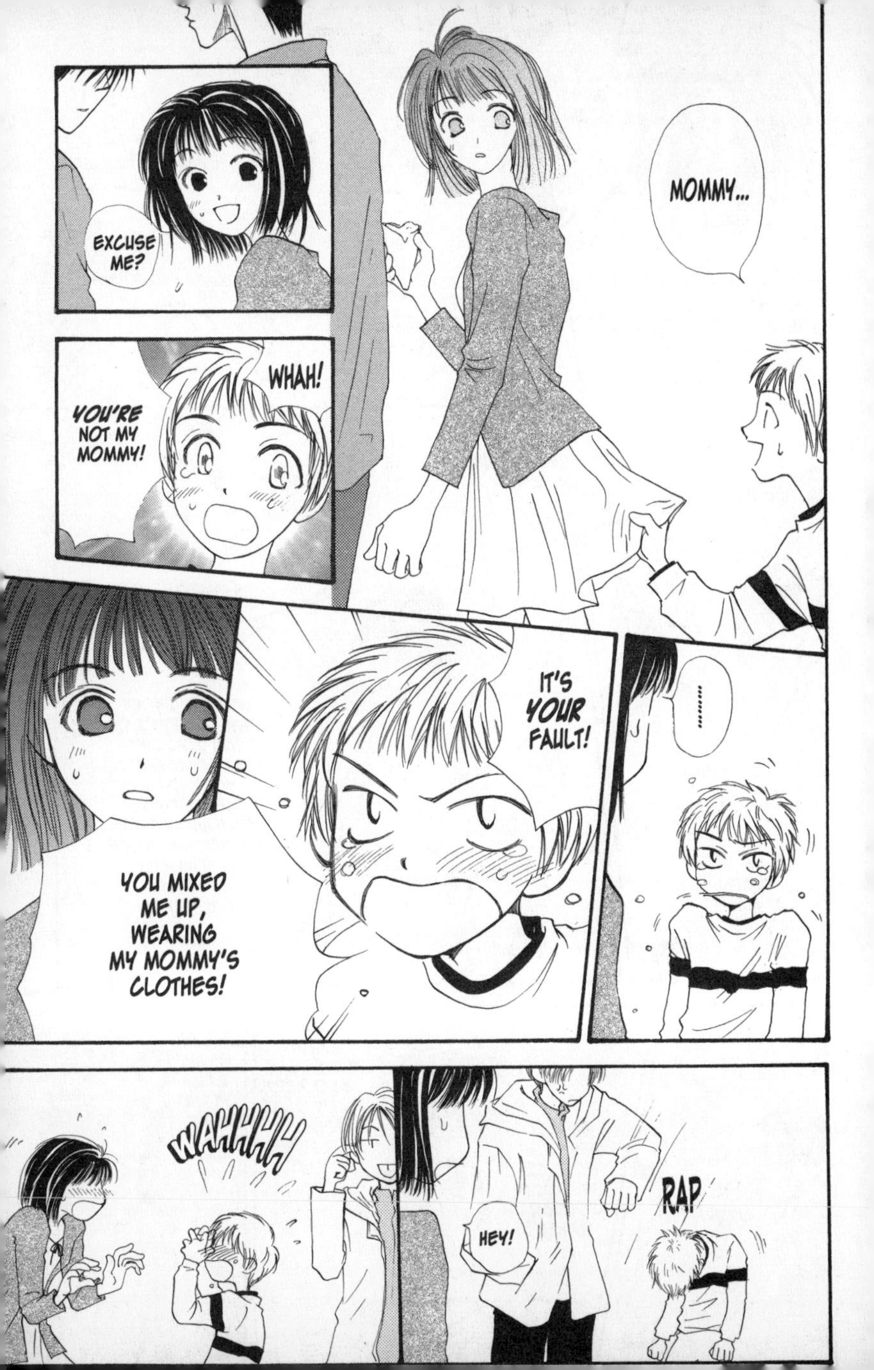
MOMMY...
EXCUSE ME?
WHAH!
YOU'RE NOT MY MOMMY!
......
IT'S YOUR FAULT!
YOU MIXED ME UP, WEARING MY MOMMY'S CLOTHES!
RAP
HEY!
WAHHHH

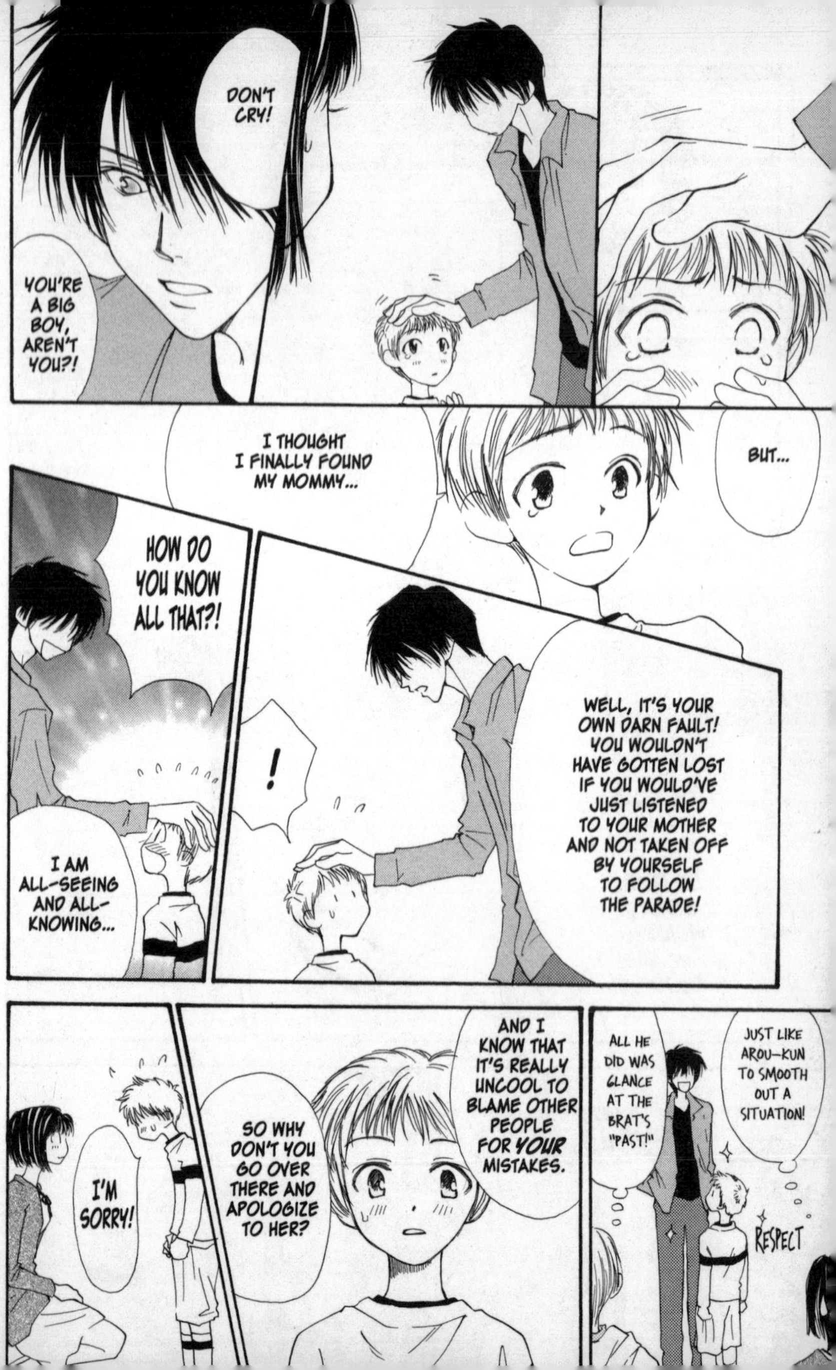
DON'T CRY!
YOU'RE A BIG BOY, AREN'T YOU?!
BUT...
I THOUGHT I FINALLY FOUND MY MOMMY...
WELL, IT'S YOUR OWN DARN FAULT! YOU WOULDN'T HAVE GOTTEN LOST IF YOU WOULD'VE JUST LISTENED TO YOUR MOTHER AND NOT TAKEN OFF BY YOURSELF TO FOLLOW THE PARADE!
!
HOW DO YOU KNOW ALL THAT?!
I AM ALL-SEEING AND ALL-KNOWING...
JUST LIKE AROU-KUN TO SMOOTH OUT A SITUATION!
ALL HE DID WAS GLANCE AT THE BRAT'S "PAST!"
RESPECT
AND I KNOW THAT IT'S REALLY UNCOOL TO BLAME OTHER PEOPLE FOR *YOUR* MISTAKES.
SO WHY DON'T YOU GO OVER THERE AND APOLOGIZE TO HER?
I'M SORRY!

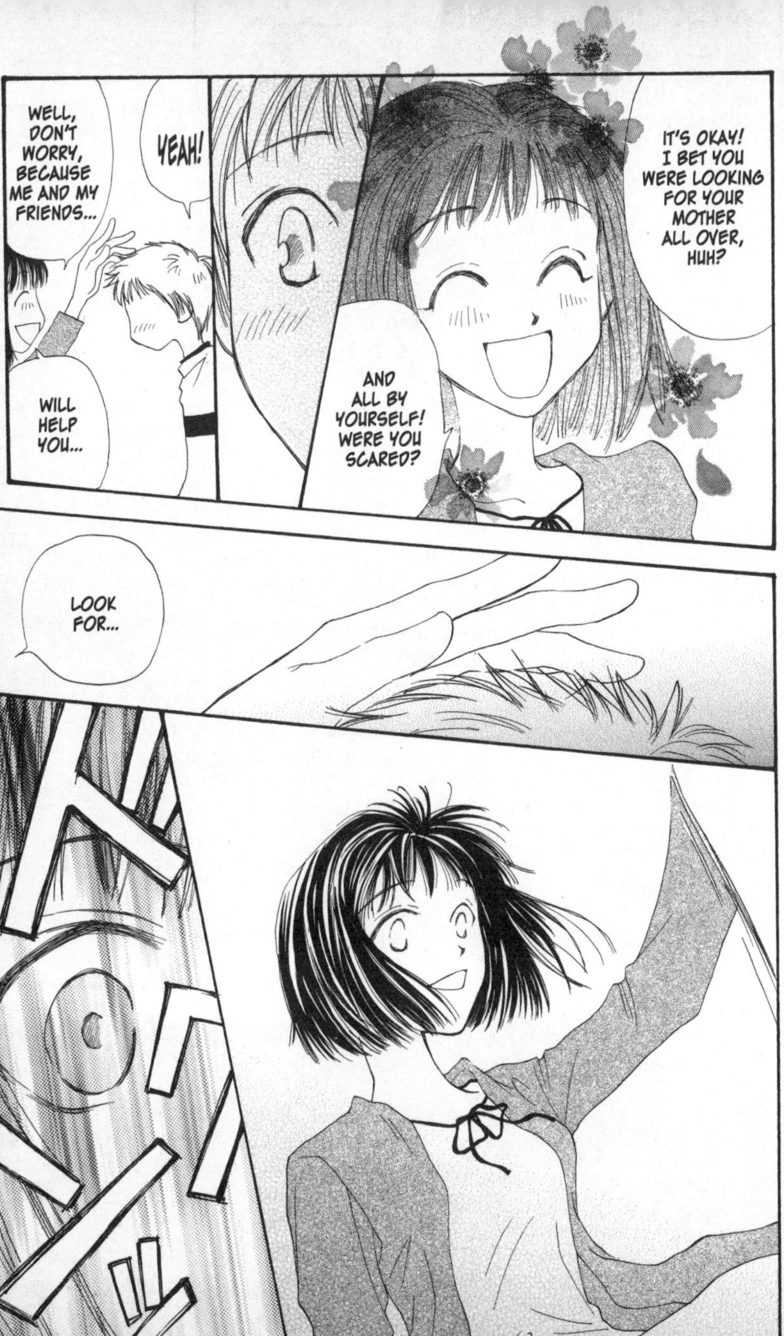
IT'S OKAY! I BET YOU WERE LOOKING FOR YOUR MOTHER ALL OVER, HUH?
AND ALL BY YOURSELF! WERE YOU SCARED?
YEAH!
WELL, DON'T WORRY, BECAUSE ME AND MY FRIENDS...
WILL HELP YOU...
LOOK FOR...

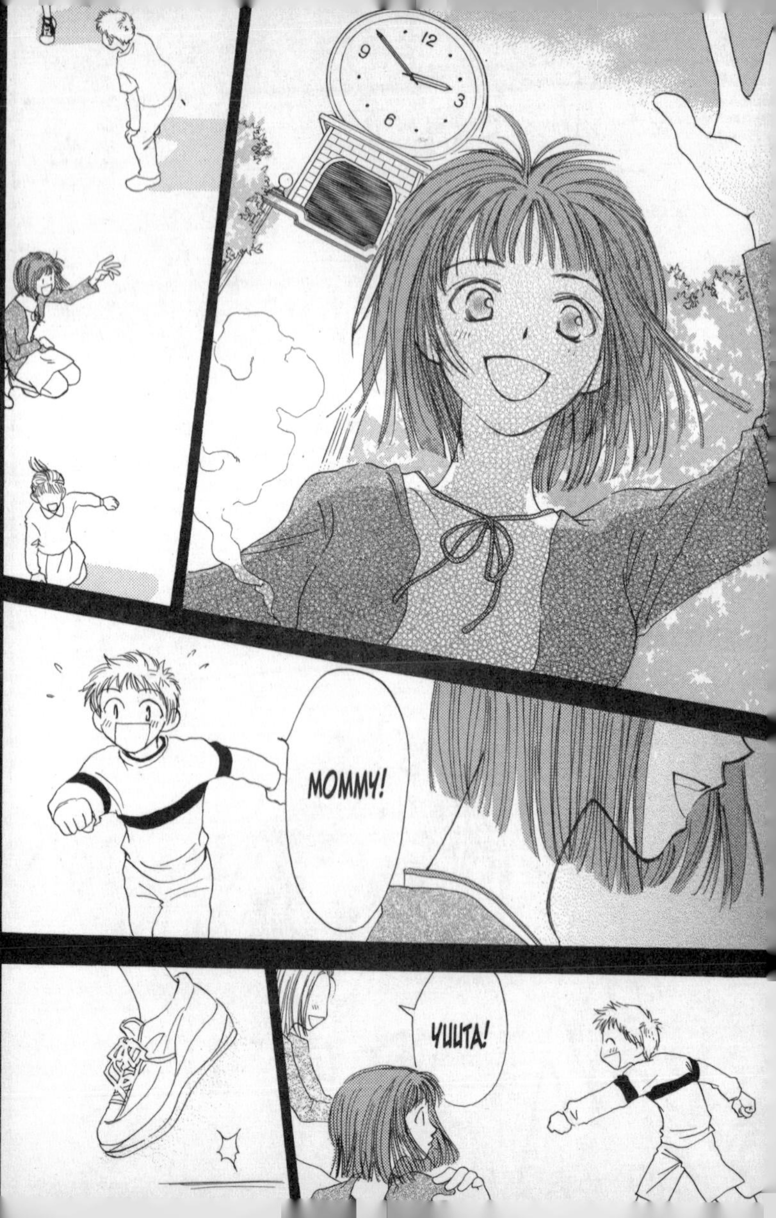
MOMMY!
YUUTA!

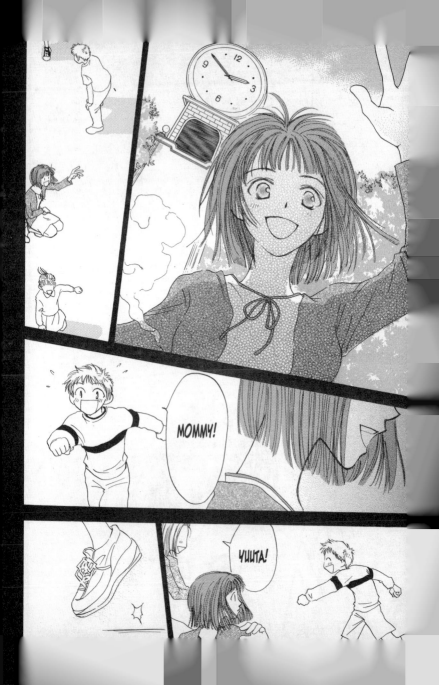

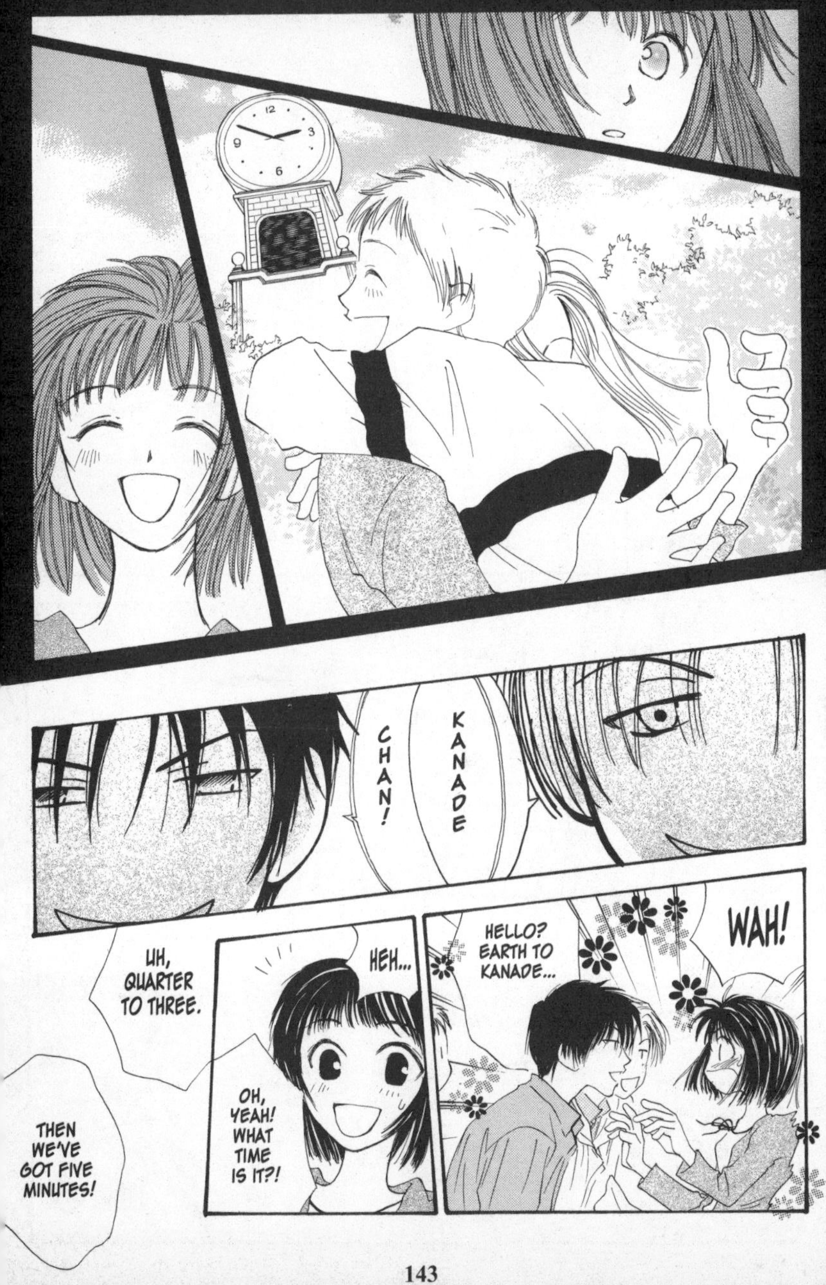
KANADE CHAN!
WAH!
HELLO? EARTH TO KANADE...
HEH...
OH, YEAH! WHAT TIME IS IT?!
UH, QUARTER TO THREE.
THEN WE'VE GOT FIVE MINUTES!

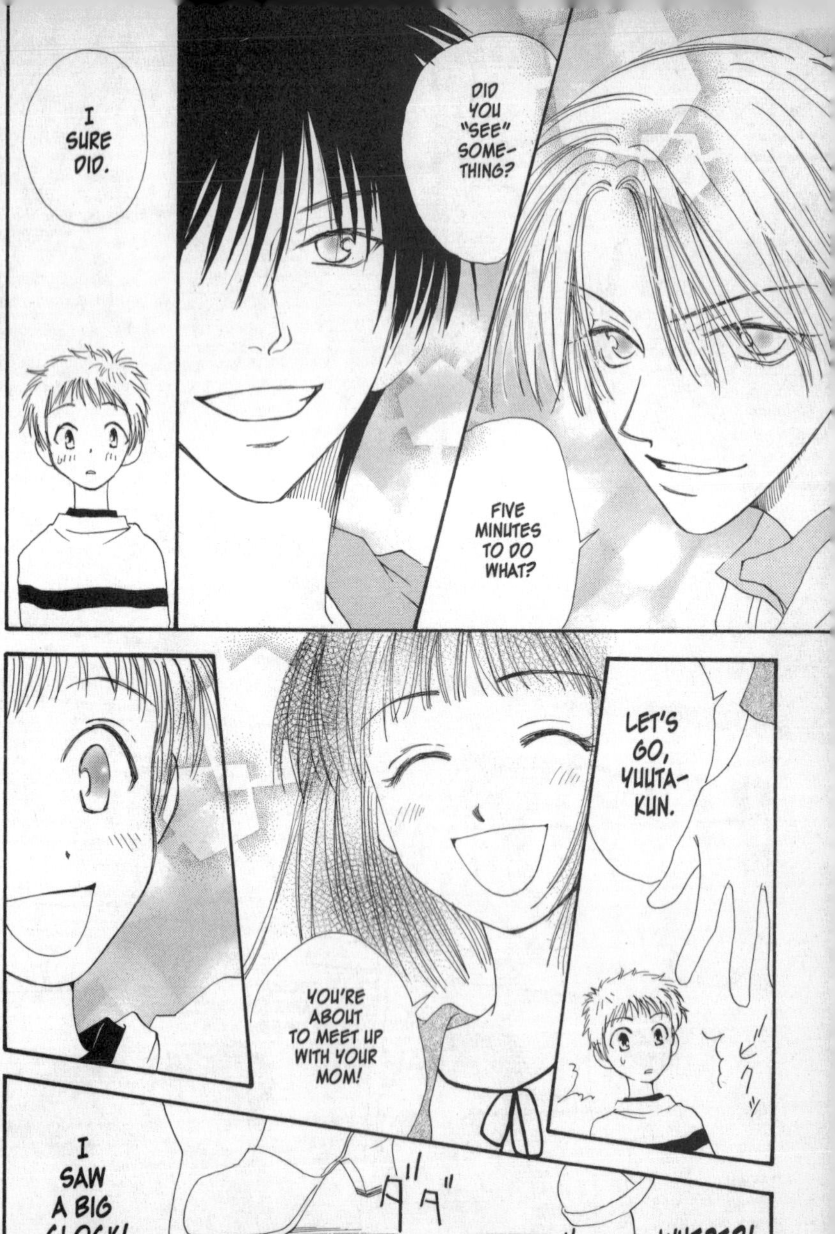

DID YOU "SEE" SOME-THING?
FIVE MINUTES TO DO WHAT?
I SURE DID.
LET'S GO, YUUTA-KUN.
ビクッ
YOU'RE ABOUT TO MEET UP WITH YOUR MOM!
WHERE?!
ダバ
ダダ
I SAW A BIG CLOCK!

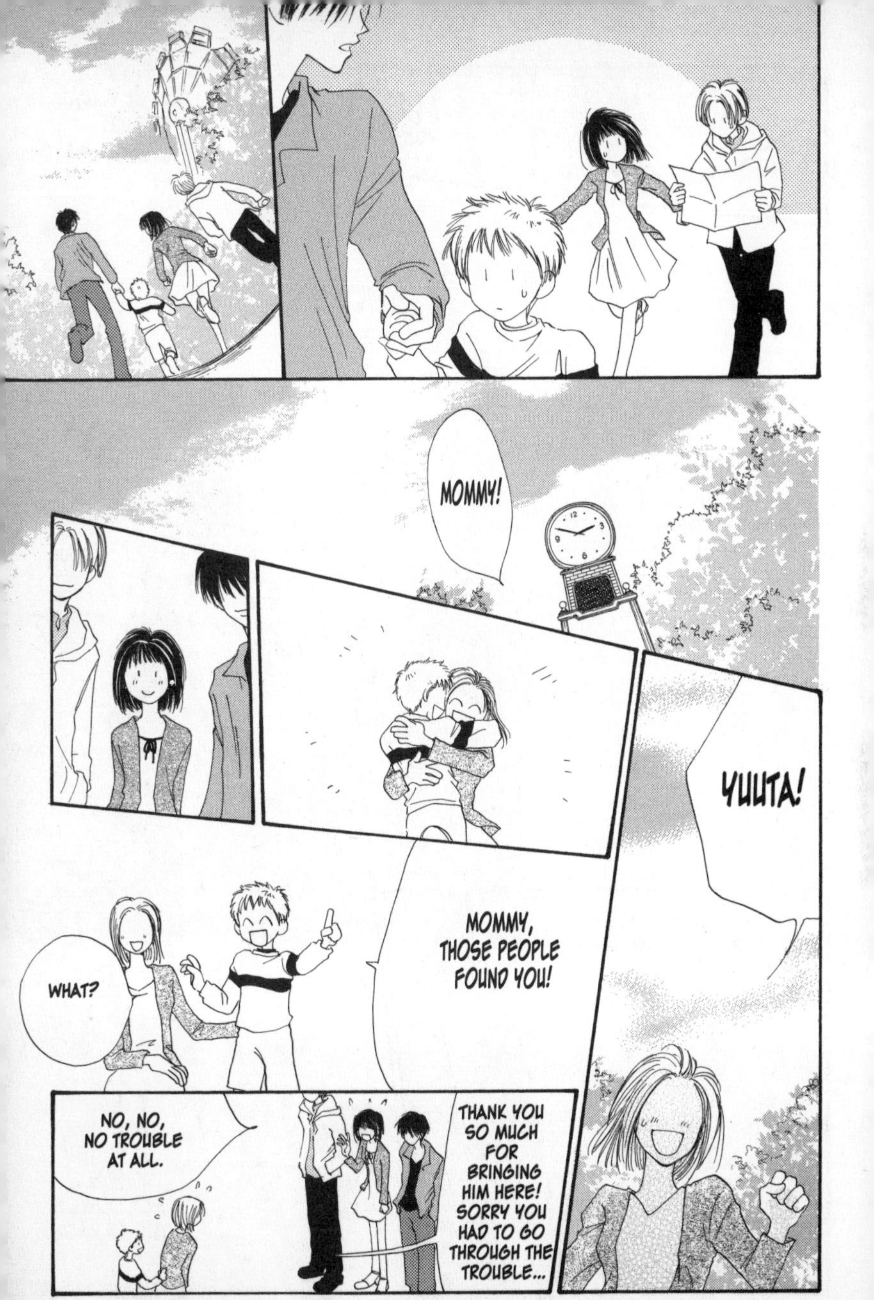
MOMMY!
YUUTA!
MOMMY, THOSE PEOPLE FOUND YOU!
WHAT?
THANK YOU SO MUCH FOR BRINGING HIM HERE! SORRY YOU HAD TO GO THROUGH THE TROUBLE...
NO, NO, NO TROUBLE AT ALL.

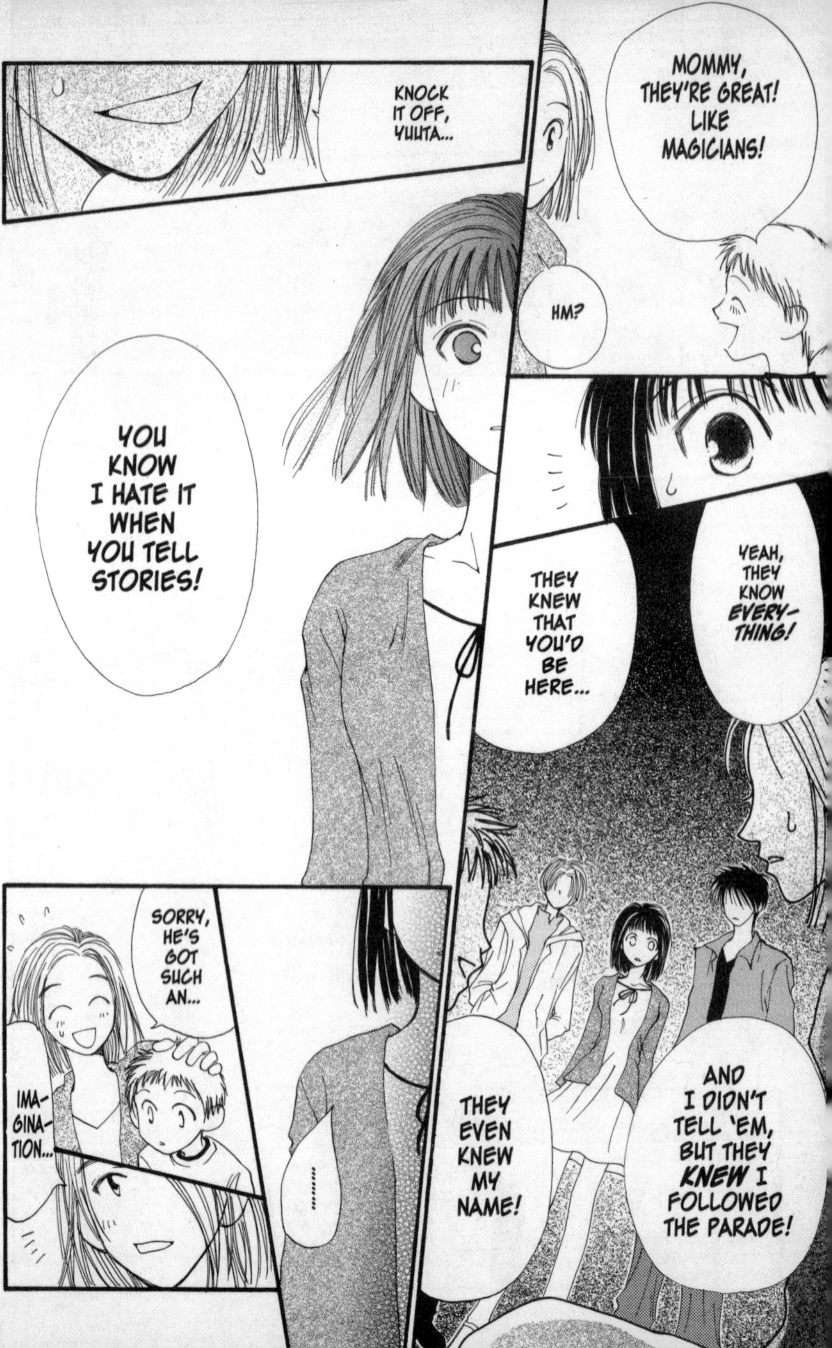
MOMMY, THEY'RE GREAT! LIKE MAGICIANS!
HM?
KNOCK IT OFF, YUUTA...
YOU KNOW I HATE IT WHEN YOU TELL STORIES!
THEY KNEW THAT YOU'D BE HERE...
YEAH, THEY KNOW *EVERYTHING!*
THEY EVEN KNEW MY NAME!
AND I DIDN'T TELL 'EM, BUT THEY *KNEW* I FOLLOWED THE PARADE!
SORRY, HE'S GOT SUCH AN...
IMAGINATION...
......

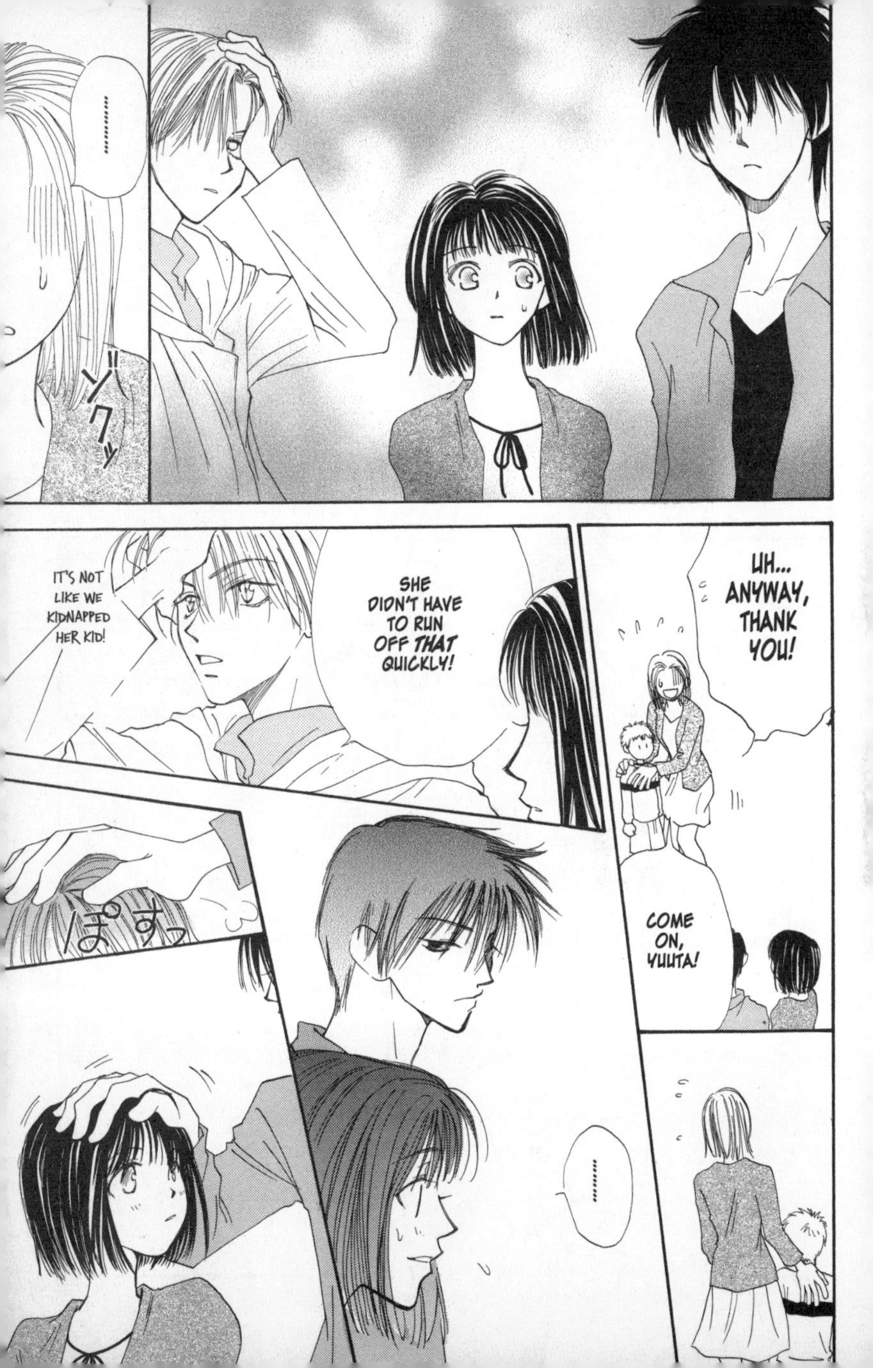
......
ゾクッ
UH... ANYWAY, THANK YOU!
COME ON, YUUTA!
SHE DIDN'T HAVE TO RUN OFF *THAT* QUICKLY!
IT'S NOT LIKE WE KIDNAPPED HER KID!
ぽすっ
......

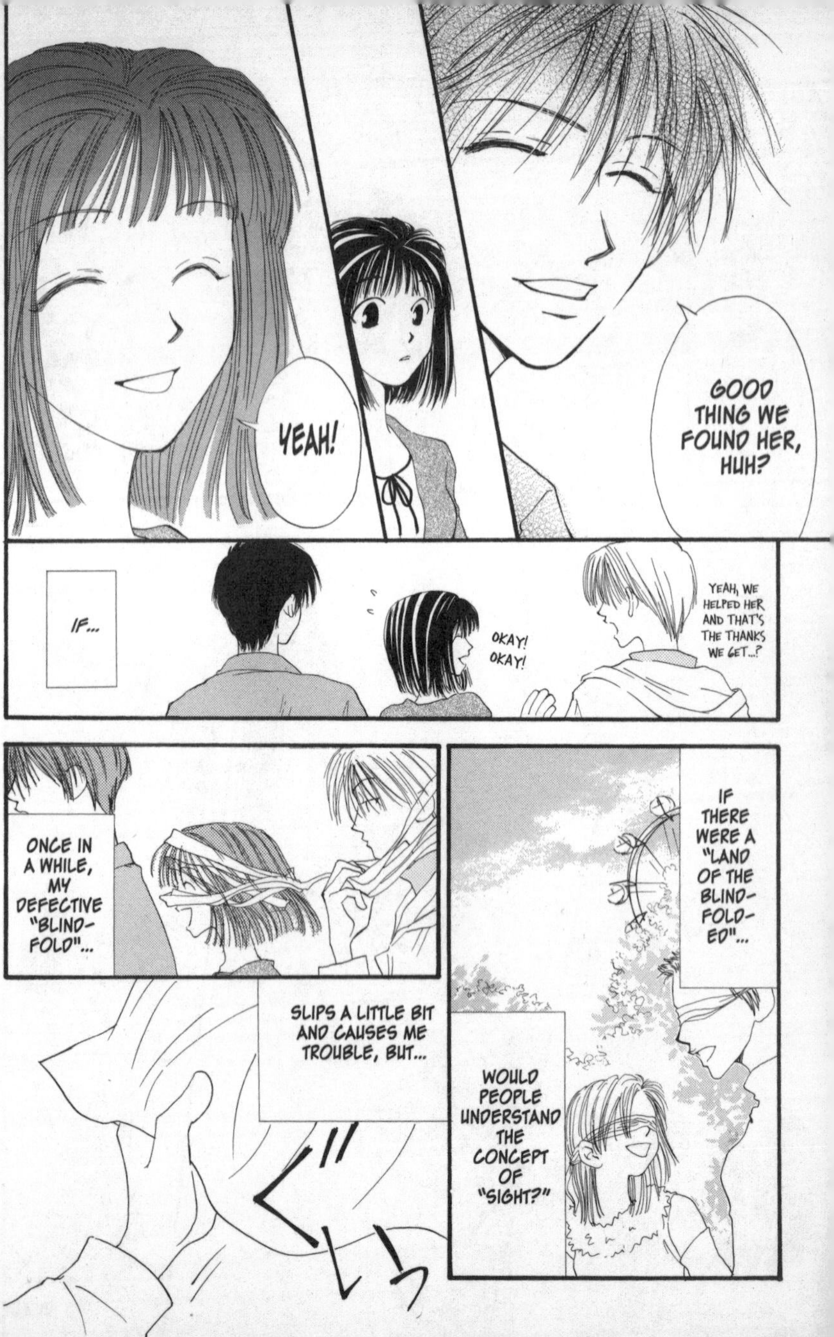
GOOD THING WE FOUND HER, HUH?
YEAH!
YEAH, WE HELPED HER AND THAT'S THE THANKS WE GET...?
OKAY! OKAY!
IF...
IF THERE WERE A "LAND OF THE BLIND-FOLD-ED"...
WOULD PEOPLE UNDERSTAND THE CONCEPT OF "SIGHT?"
ONCE IN A WHILE, MY DEFECTIVE "BLIND-FOLD"...
SLIPS A LITTLE BIT AND CAUSES ME TROUBLE, BUT...
ぐいっ

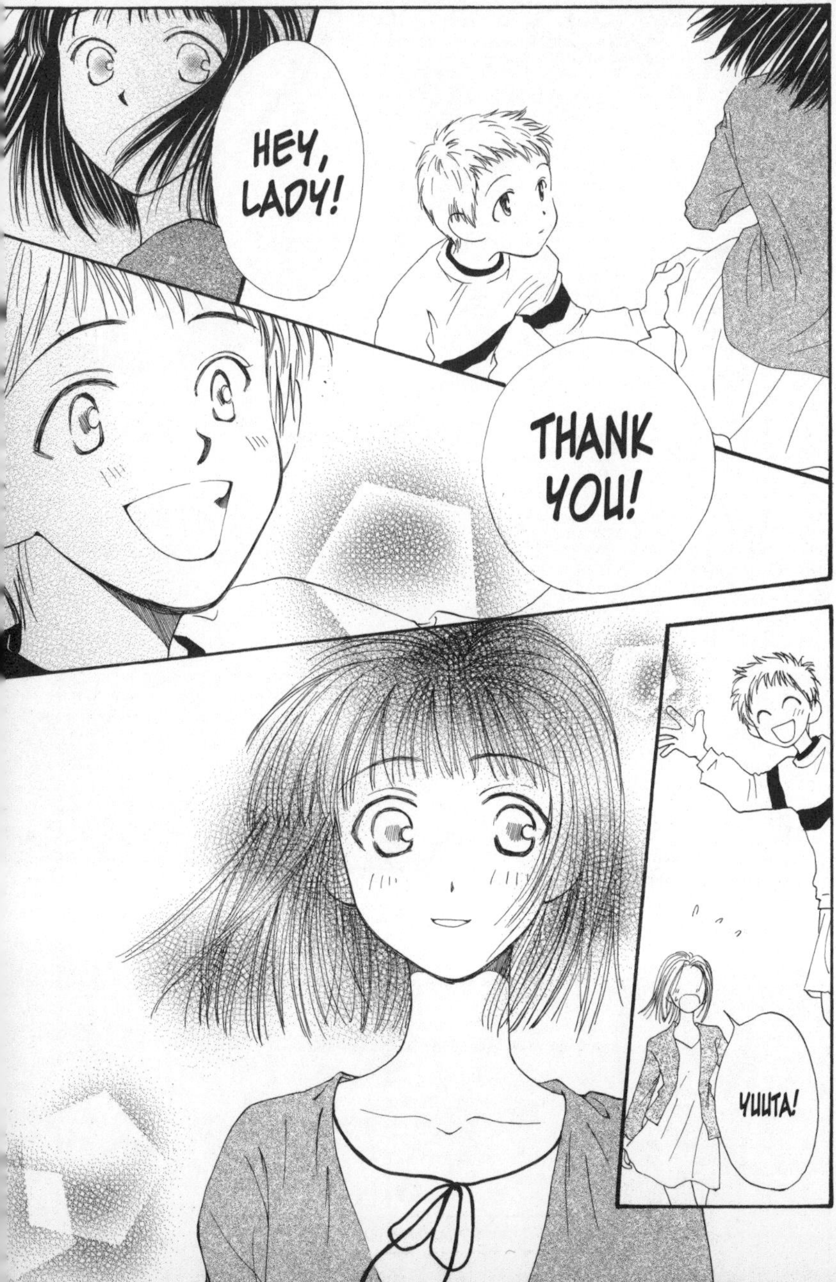
HEY, LADY!
THANK YOU!
YUUTA!

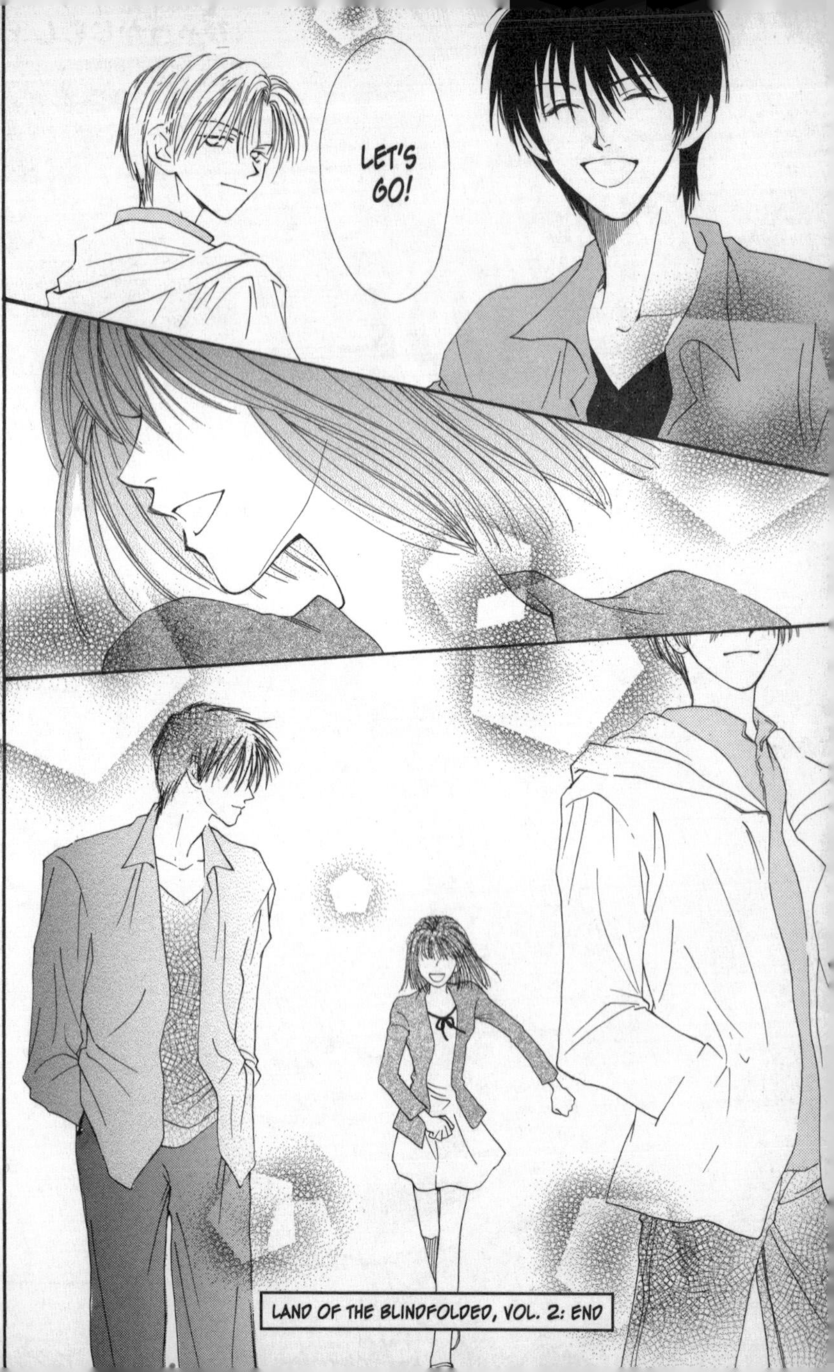
LET'S GO!
LAND OF THE BLINDFOLDED, VOL. 2: END

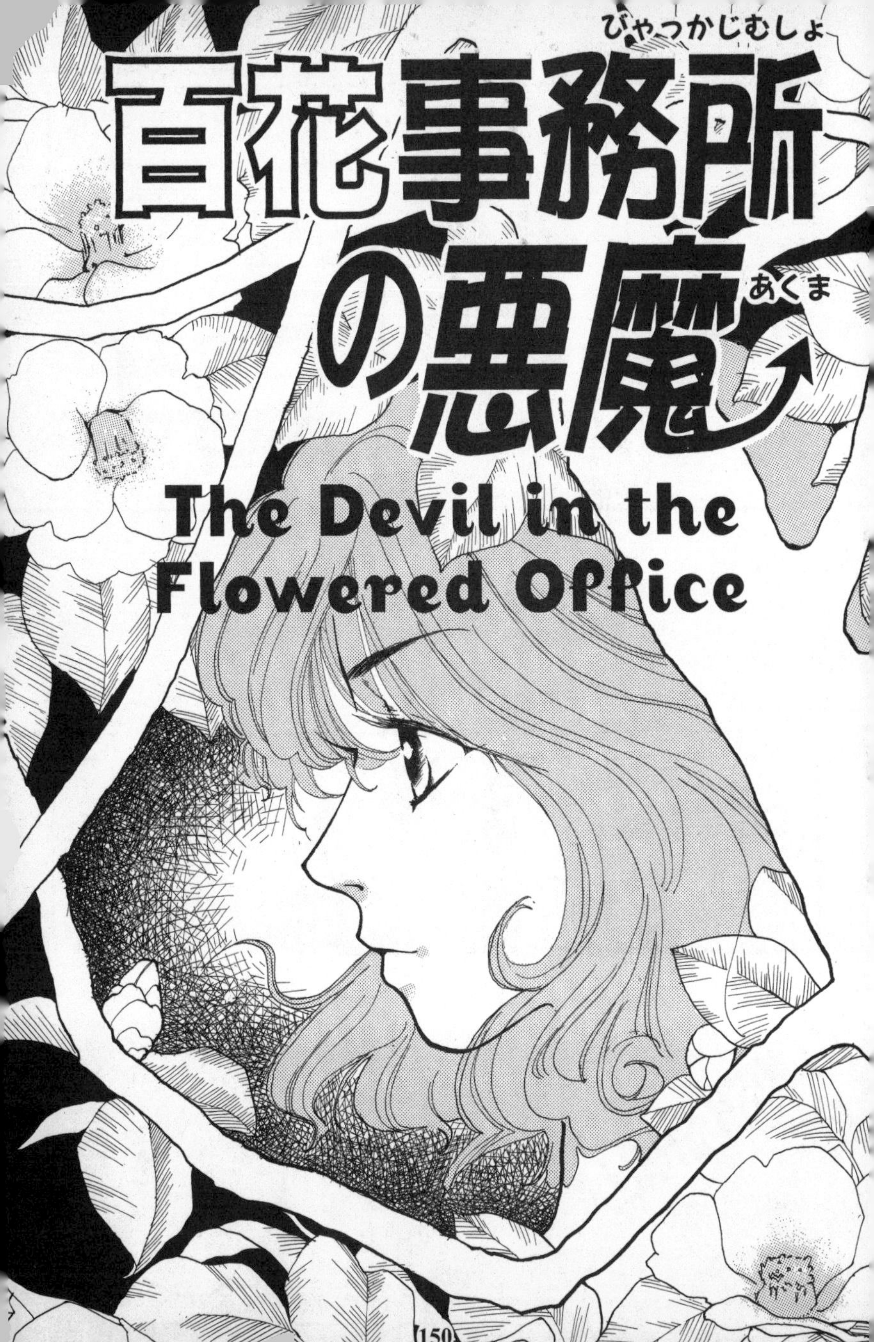
びゃっかじむしょ
百花事務所の悪魔
あくま
The Devil in the Flowered Office

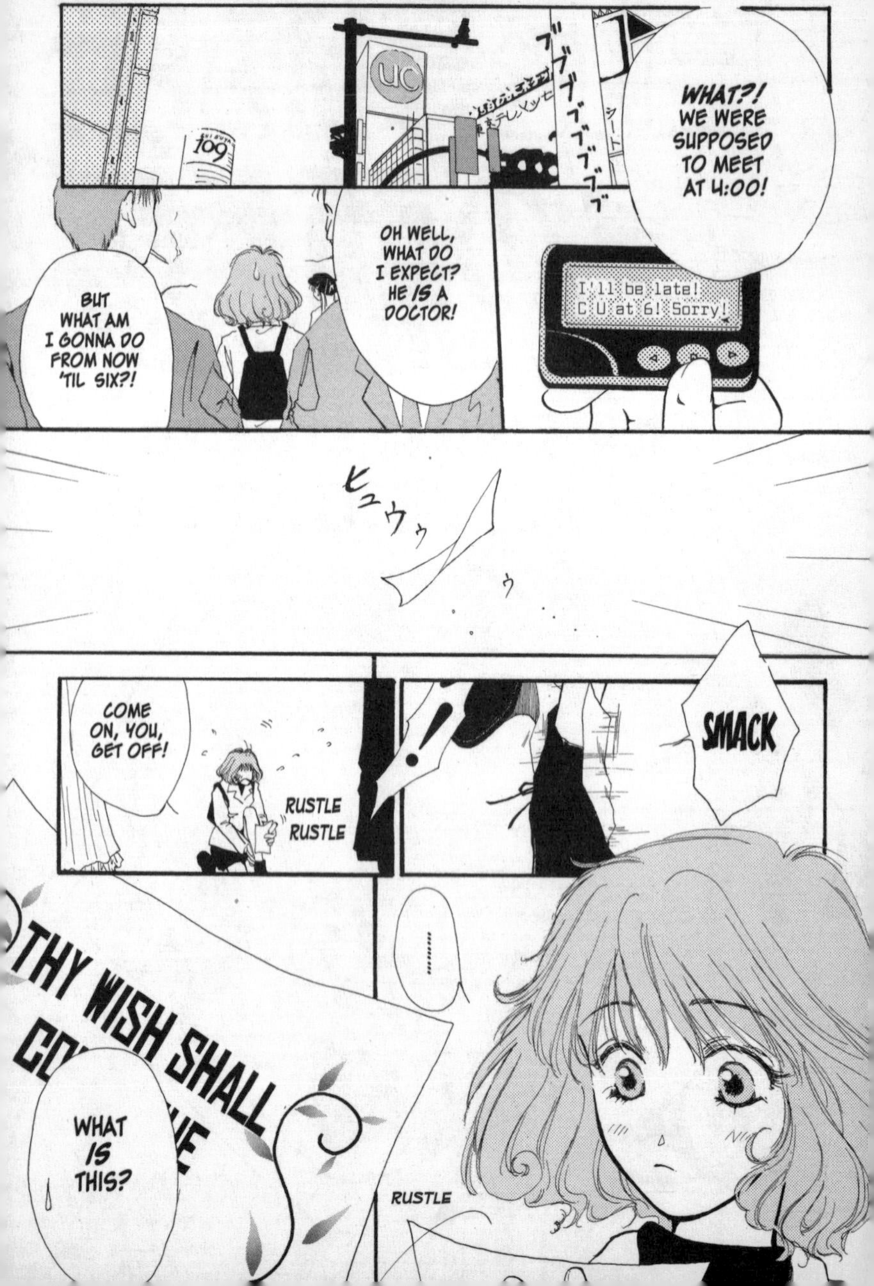

ブブブブブブブブブ
109
UC
WHAT?! WE WERE SUPPOSED TO MEET AT 4:00!
I'll be late! C U at 6! Sorry!
OH WELL, WHAT DO I EXPECT? HE IS A DOCTOR!
BUT WHAT AM I GONNA DO FROM NOW 'TIL SIX?!
ヒュウゥ
ウ
SMACK
!
COME ON, YOU, GET OFF!
RUSTLE RUSTLE
......
THY WISH SHALL
WHAT IS THIS?
RUSTLE

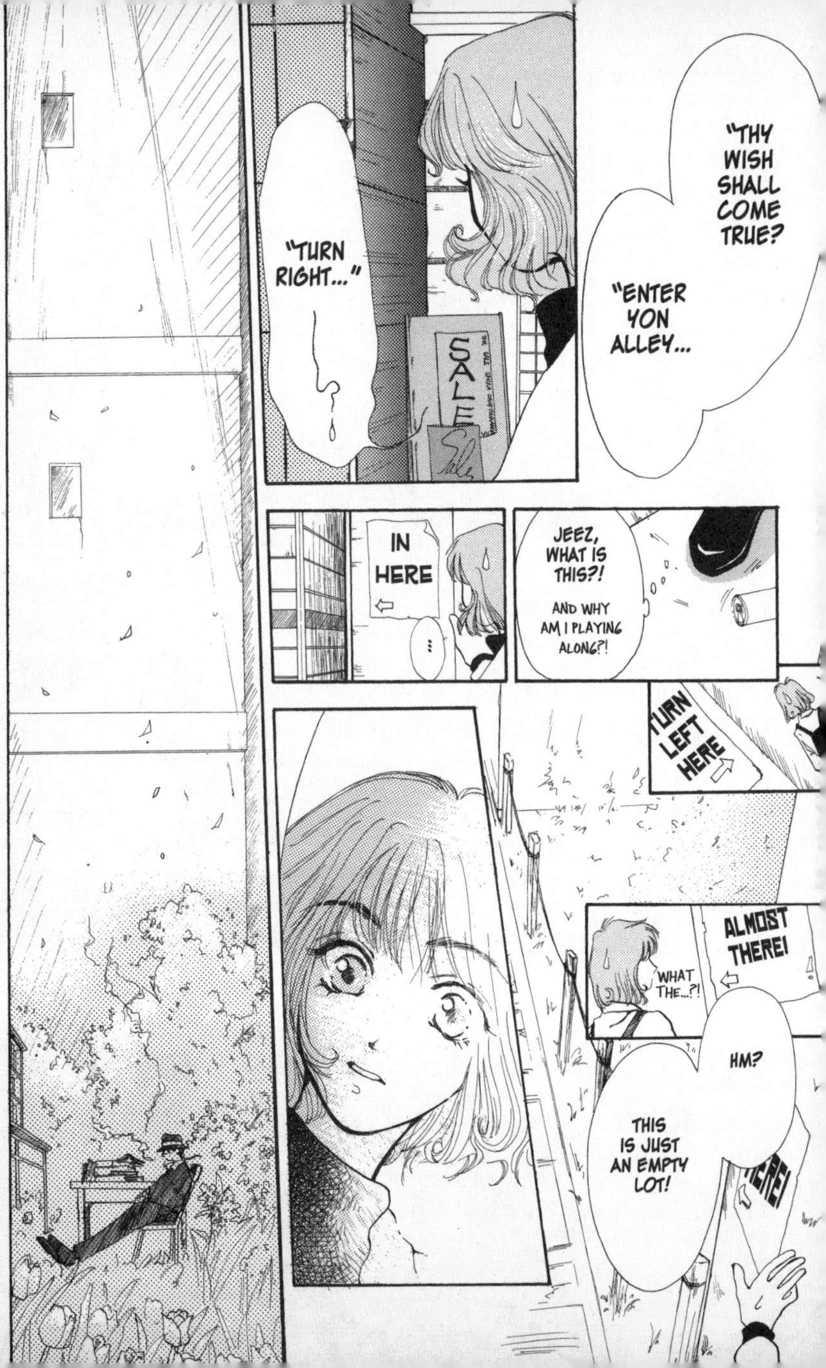
"THY WISH SHALL COME TRUE?
"ENTER YON ALLEY...
"TURN RIGHT..."
SALE
JEEZ, WHAT IS THIS?!
AND WHY AM I PLAYING ALONG?!
IN HERE
...
TURN LEFT HERE
ALMOST THERE!
WHAT THE...?!
HM?
THIS IS JUST AN EMPTY LOT!
THERE!

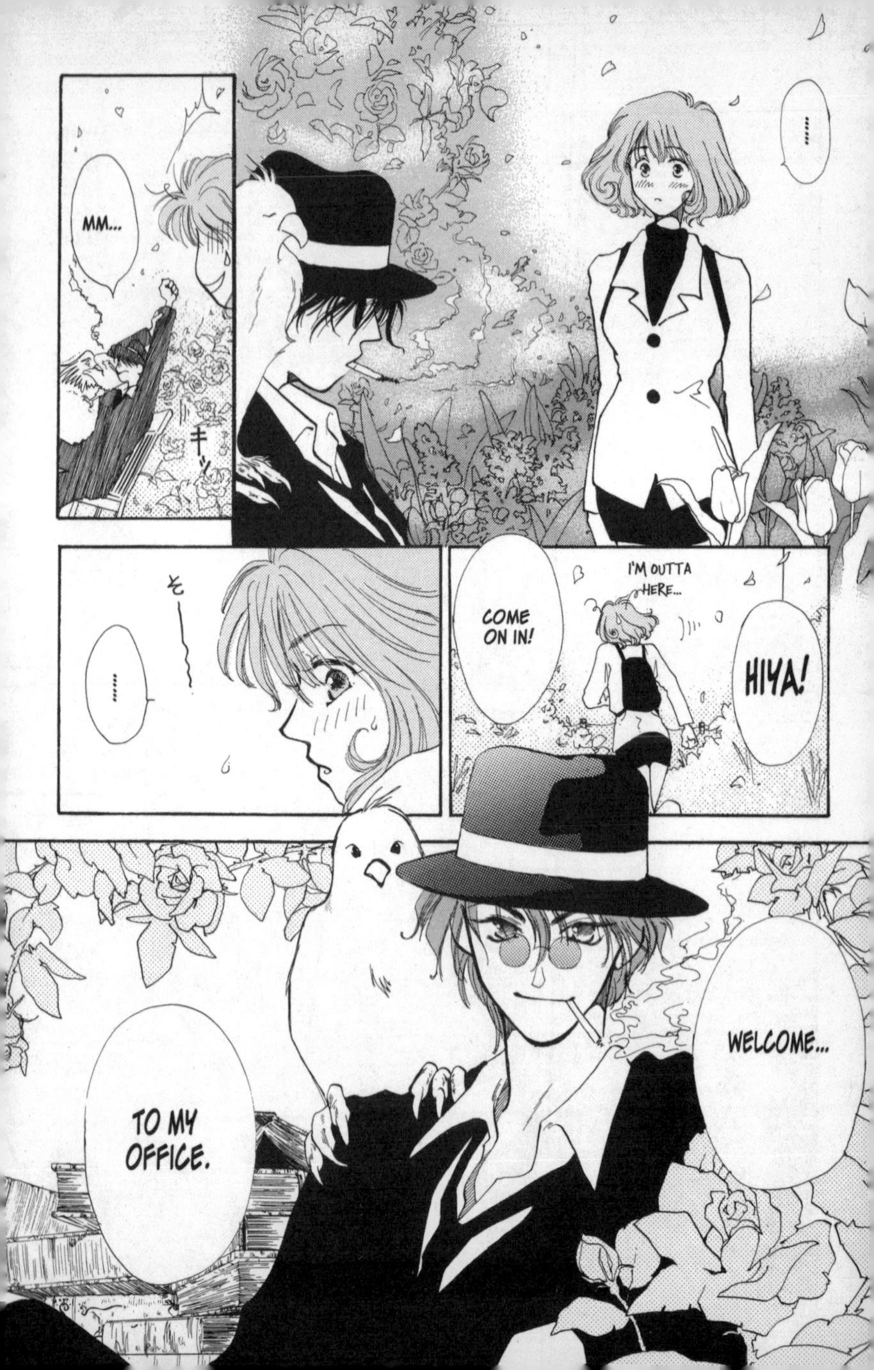
......
MM...
キッ
HIYA!
I'M OUTTA HERE...
COME ON IN!
そ～
......
WELCOME...
TO MY OFFICE.

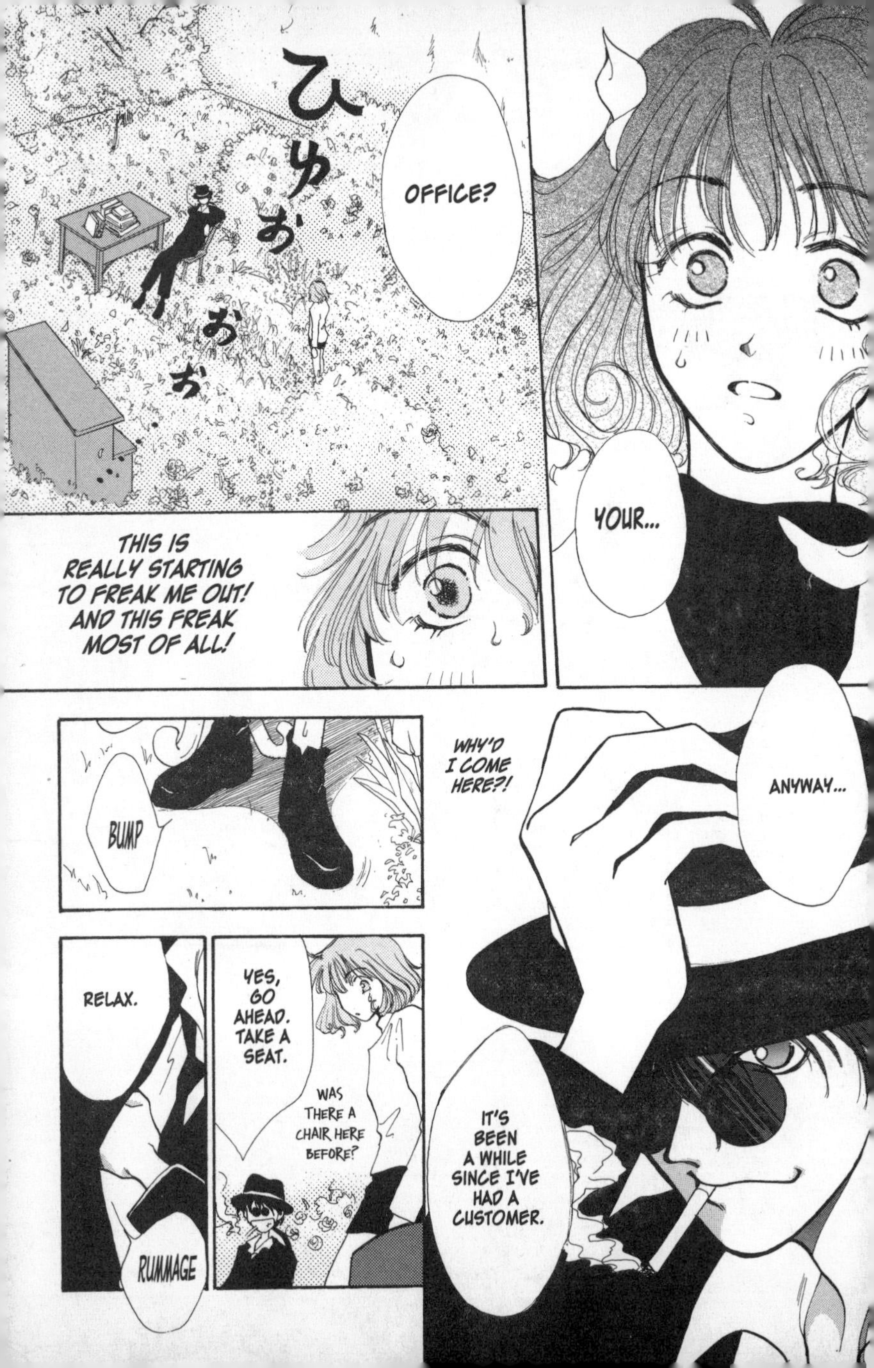
YOUR...
OFFICE?
ひゅおおお
THIS IS REALLY STARTING TO FREAK ME OUT! AND THIS FREAK MOST OF ALL!
ANYWAY...
IT'S BEEN A WHILE SINCE I'VE HAD A CUSTOMER.
WHY'D I COME HERE?!
BUMP
YES, GO AHEAD. TAKE A SEAT.
WAS THERE A CHAIR HERE BEFORE?
RELAX.
RUMMAGE

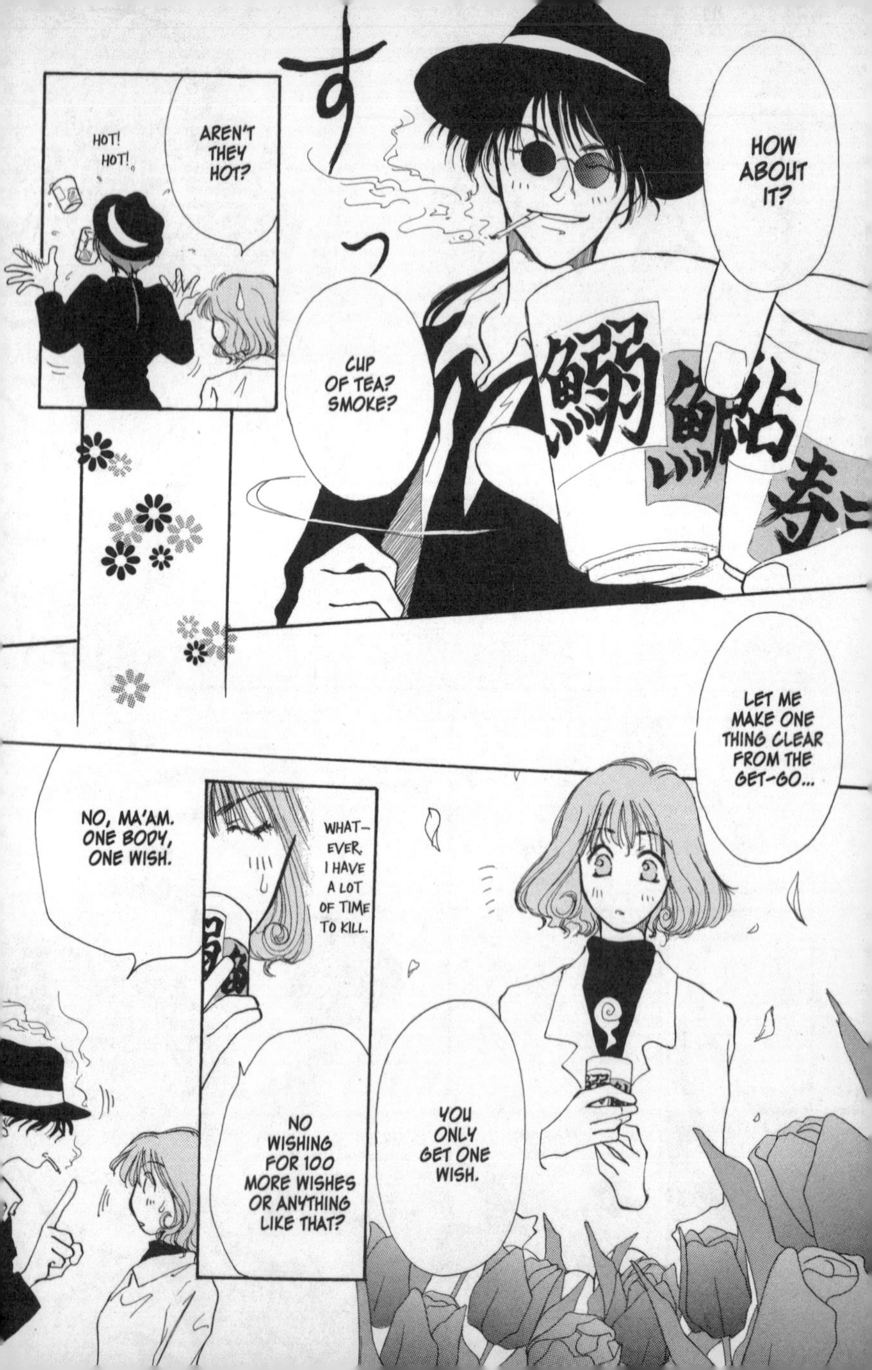
すっ
HOW ABOUT IT?
CUP OF TEA? SMOKE?
鰯
ARE'NT THEY HOT?
HOT! HOT!
LET ME MAKE ONE THING CLEAR FROM THE GET-GO...
YOU ONLY GET ONE WISH.
NO WISHING FOR 100 MORE WISHES OR ANYTHING LIKE THAT?
NO, MA'AM. ONE BODY, ONE WISH.
WHAT-EVER. I HAVE A LOT OF TIME TO KILL.

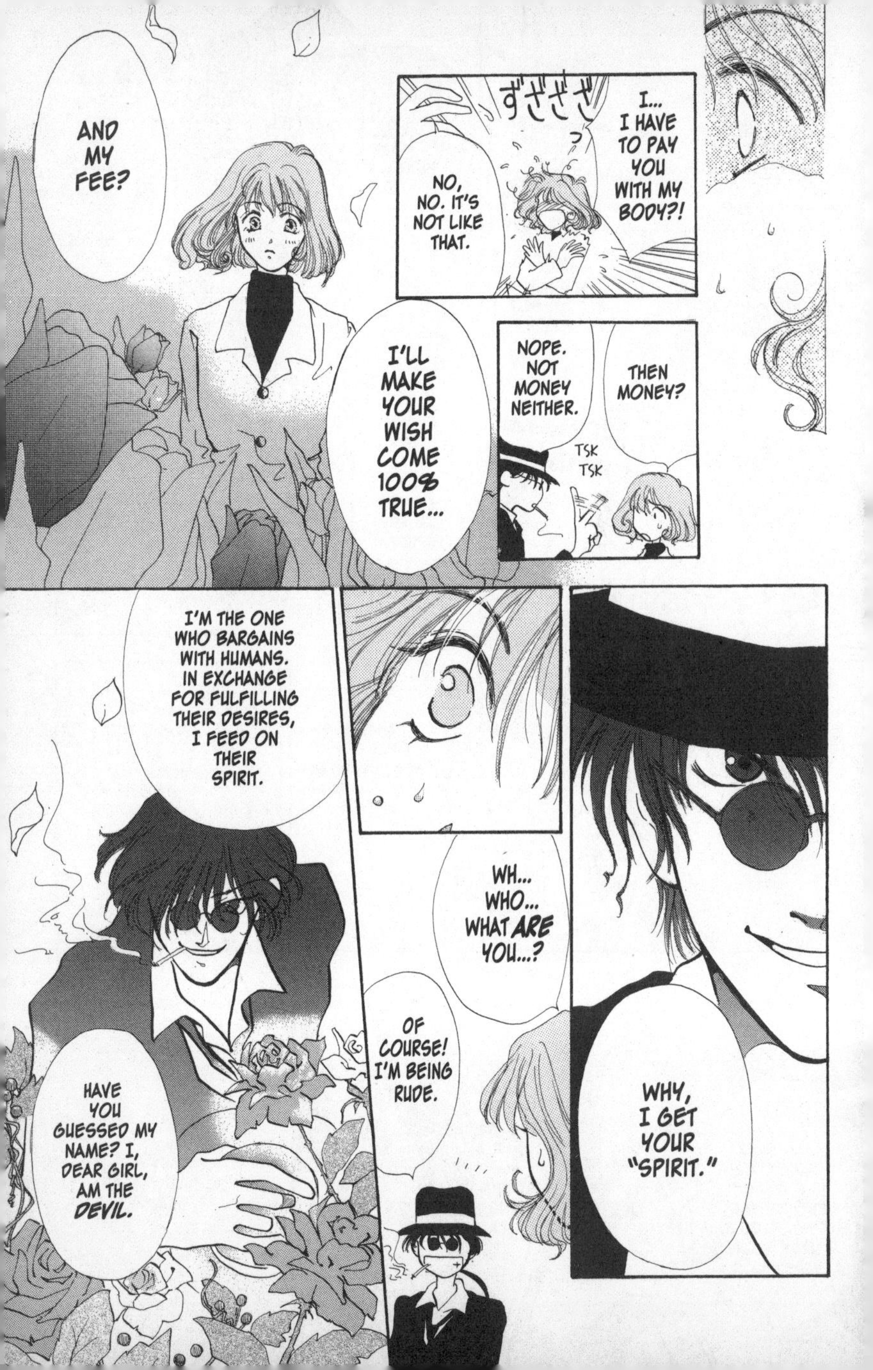
ずざざざ
I... I HAVE TO PAY YOU WITH MY BODY?!
NO, NO. IT'S NOT LIKE THAT.
THEN MONEY?
NOPE. NOT MONEY NEITHER.
TSK TSK
I'LL MAKE YOUR WISH COME 100% TRUE...
AND MY FEE?
WHY, I GET YOUR "SPIRIT."
WH... WHO... WHAT ARE YOU...?
OF COURSE! I'M BEING RUDE.
I'M THE ONE WHO BARGAINS WITH HUMANS. IN EXCHANGE FOR FULFILLING THEIR DESIRES, I FEED ON THEIR SPIRIT.
HAVE YOU GUESSED MY NAME? I, DEAR GIRL, AM THE DEVIL.

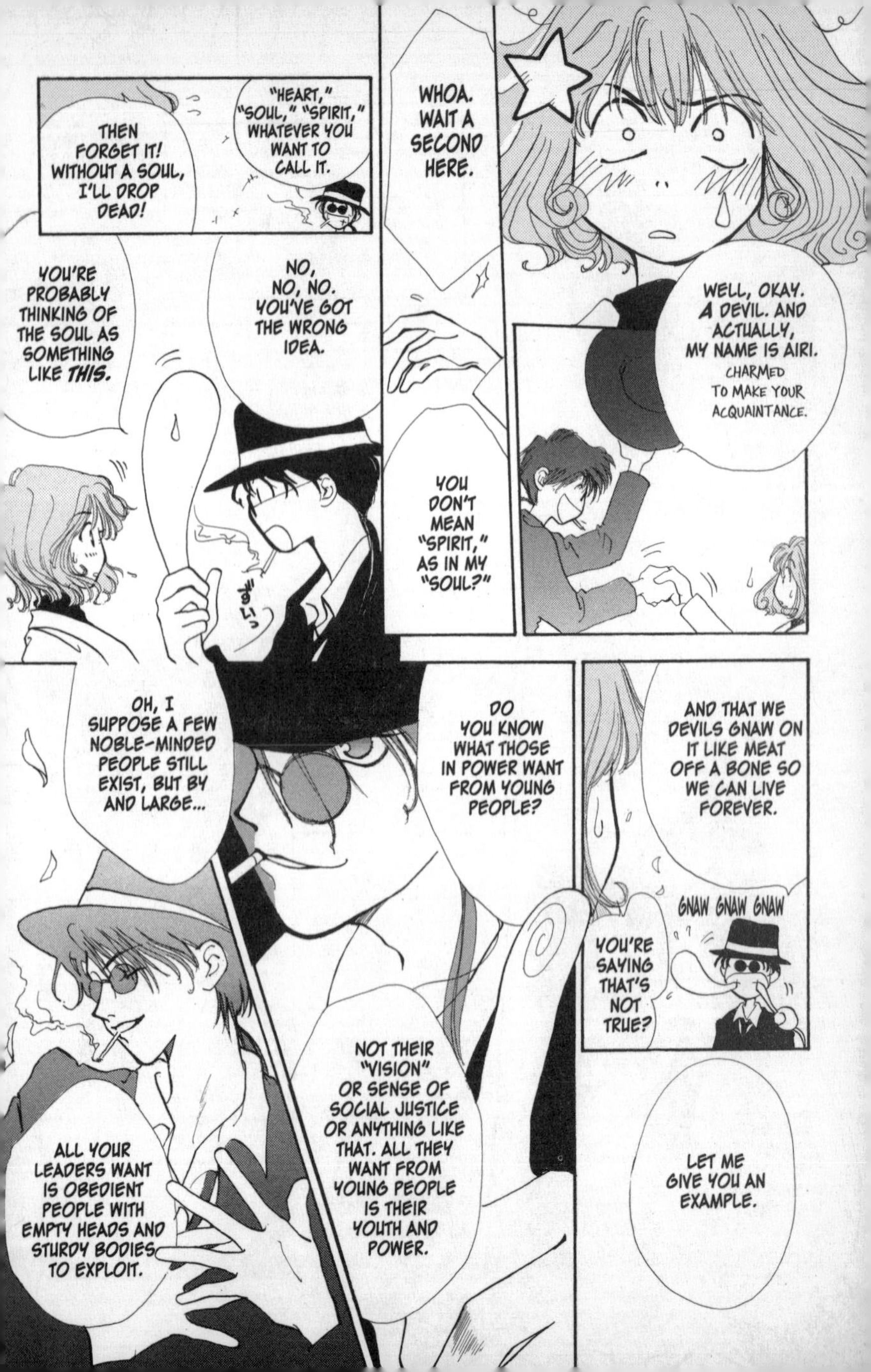
WELL, OKAY. A DEVIL. AND ACTUALLY, MY NAME IS AIRI. CHARMED TO MAKE YOUR ACQUAINTANCE.
WHOA. WAIT A SECOND HERE.
YOU DON'T MEAN "SPIRIT," AS IN MY "SOUL?"
"HEART," "SOUL," "SPIRIT," WHATEVER YOU WANT TO CALL IT.
THEN FORGET IT! WITHOUT A SOUL, I'LL DROP DEAD!
NO, NO, NO. YOU'VE GOT THE WRONG IDEA.
YOU'RE PROBABLY THINKING OF THE SOUL AS SOMETHING LIKE *THIS*.
ずいっ
AND THAT WE DEVILS GNAW ON IT LIKE MEAT OFF A BONE SO WE CAN LIVE FOREVER.
GNAW GNAW GNAW
YOU'RE SAYING THAT'S NOT TRUE?
DO YOU KNOW WHAT THOSE IN POWER WANT FROM YOUNG PEOPLE?
OH, I SUPPOSE A FEW NOBLE-MINDED PEOPLE STILL EXIST, BUT BY AND LARGE...
NOT THEIR "VISION" OR SENSE OF SOCIAL JUSTICE OR ANYTHING LIKE THAT. ALL THEY WANT FROM YOUNG PEOPLE IS THEIR YOUTH AND POWER.
ALL YOUR LEADERS WANT IS OBEDIENT PEOPLE WITH EMPTY HEADS AND STURDY BODIES TO EXPLOIT.
LET ME GIVE YOU AN EXAMPLE.

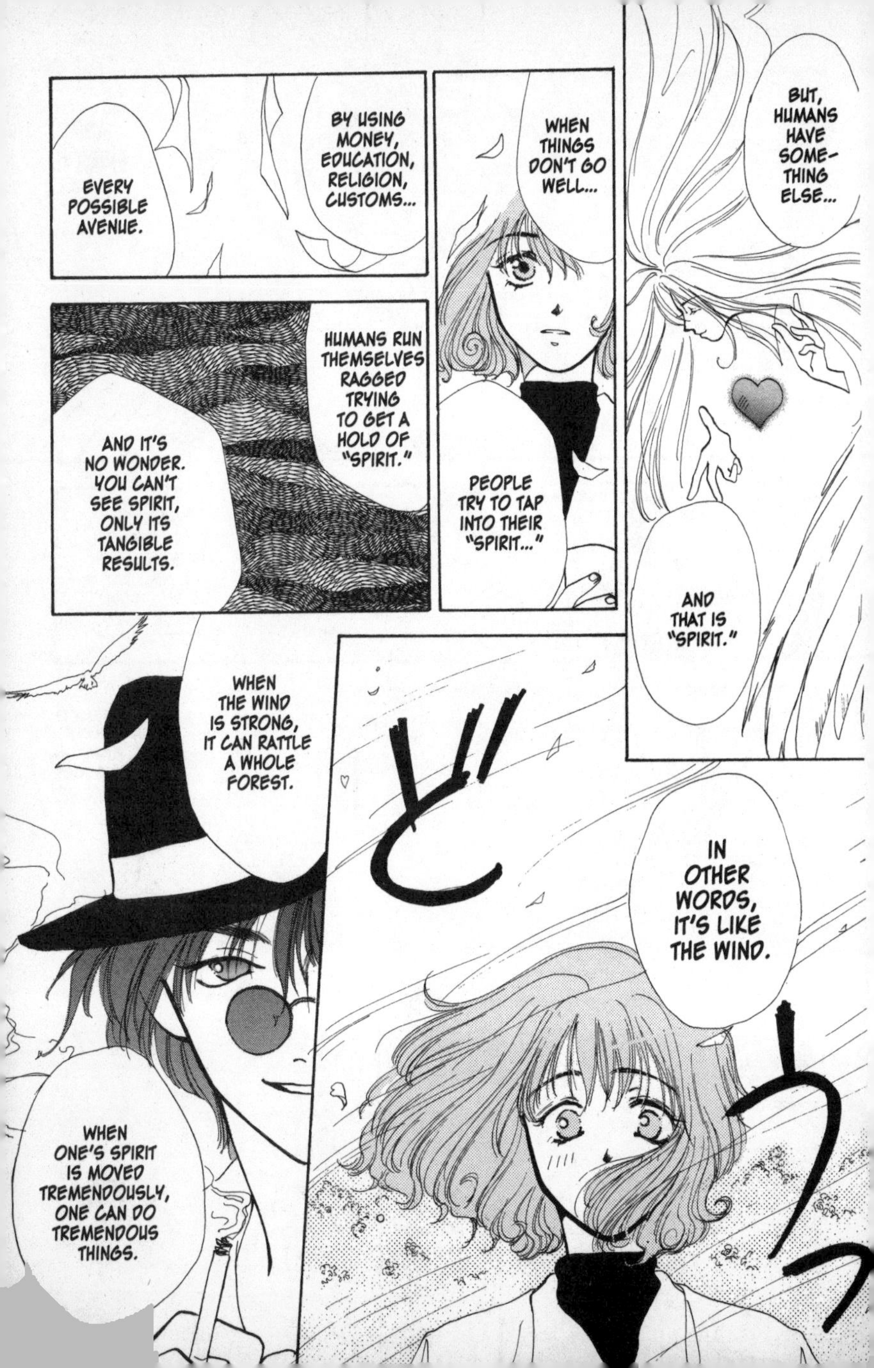
BUT, HUMANS HAVE SOME-THING ELSE...
AND THAT IS "SPIRIT."
WHEN THINGS DON'T GO WELL...
PEOPLE TRY TO TAP INTO THEIR "SPIRIT..."
BY USING MONEY, EDUCATION, RELIGION, CUSTOMS...
EVERY POSSIBLE AVENUE.
HUMANS RUN THEMSELVES RAGGED TRYING TO GET A HOLD OF "SPIRIT."
AND IT'S NO WONDER. YOU CAN'T SEE SPIRIT, ONLY ITS TANGIBLE RESULTS.
IN OTHER WORDS, IT'S LIKE THE WIND.
WHEN THE WIND IS STRONG, IT CAN RATTLE A WHOLE FOREST.
WHEN ONE'S SPIRIT IS MOVED TREMENDOUSLY, ONE CAN DO TREMENDOUS THINGS.

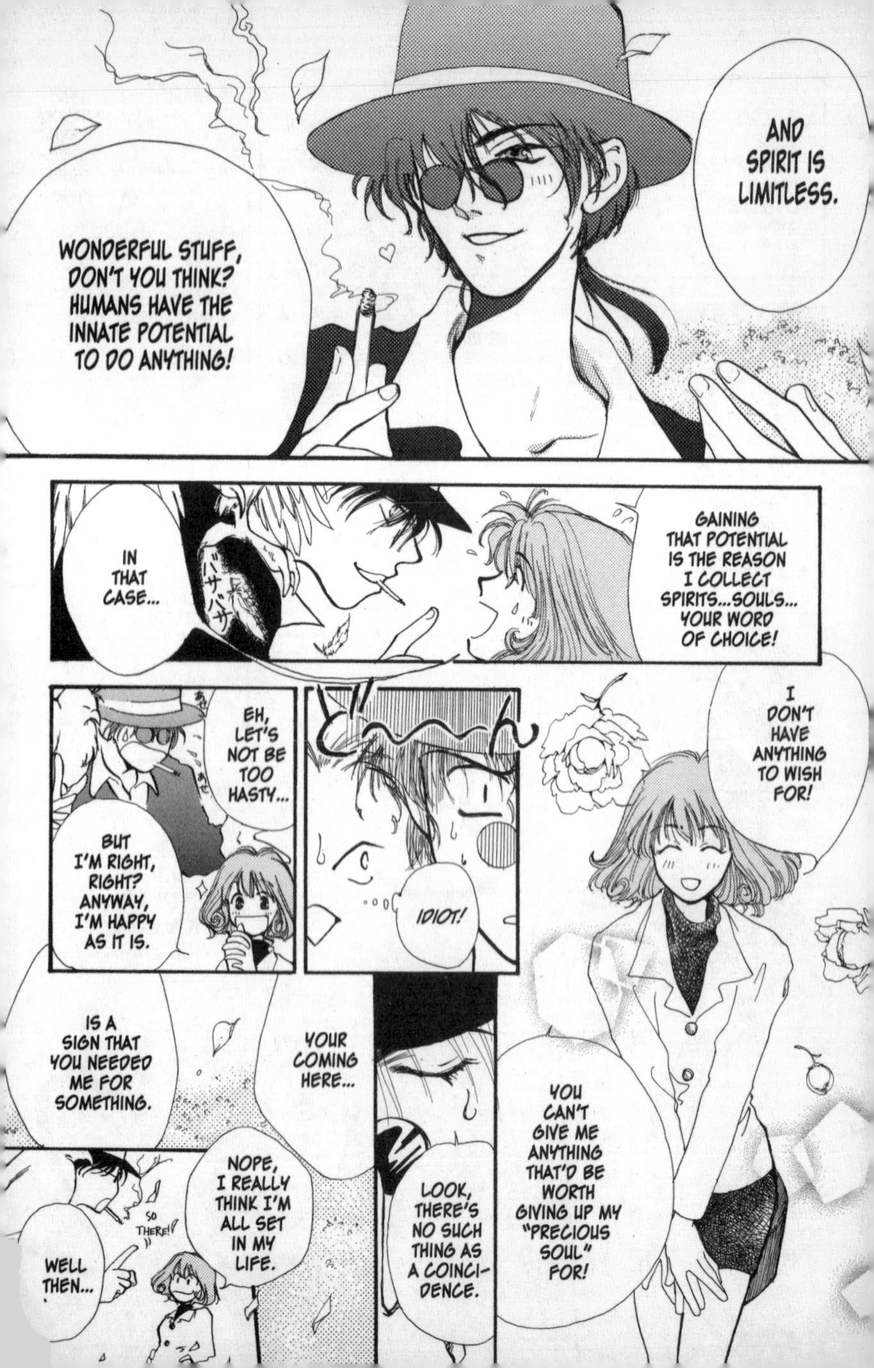
AND SPIRIT IS LIMITLESS.
WONDERFUL STUFF, DON'T YOU THINK? HUMANS HAVE THE INNATE POTENTIAL TO DO ANYTHING!
GAINING THAT POTENTIAL IS THE REASON I COLLECT SPIRITS...SOULS... YOUR WORD OF CHOICE!
バサバサ
IN THAT CASE...
I DON'T HAVE ANYTHING TO WISH FOR!
YOU CAN'T GIVE ME ANYTHING THAT'D BE WORTH GIVING UP MY "PRECIOUS SOUL" FOR!
IDIOT!
EH, LET'S NOT BE TOO HASTY...
BUT I'M RIGHT, RIGHT? ANYWAY, I'M HAPPY AS IT IS.
YOUR COMING HERE...
IS A SIGN THAT YOU NEEDED ME FOR SOMETHING.
LOOK, THERE'S NO SUCH THING AS A COINCIDENCE.
NOPE, I REALLY THINK I'M ALL SET IN MY LIFE.
SO THERE!
WELL THEN...

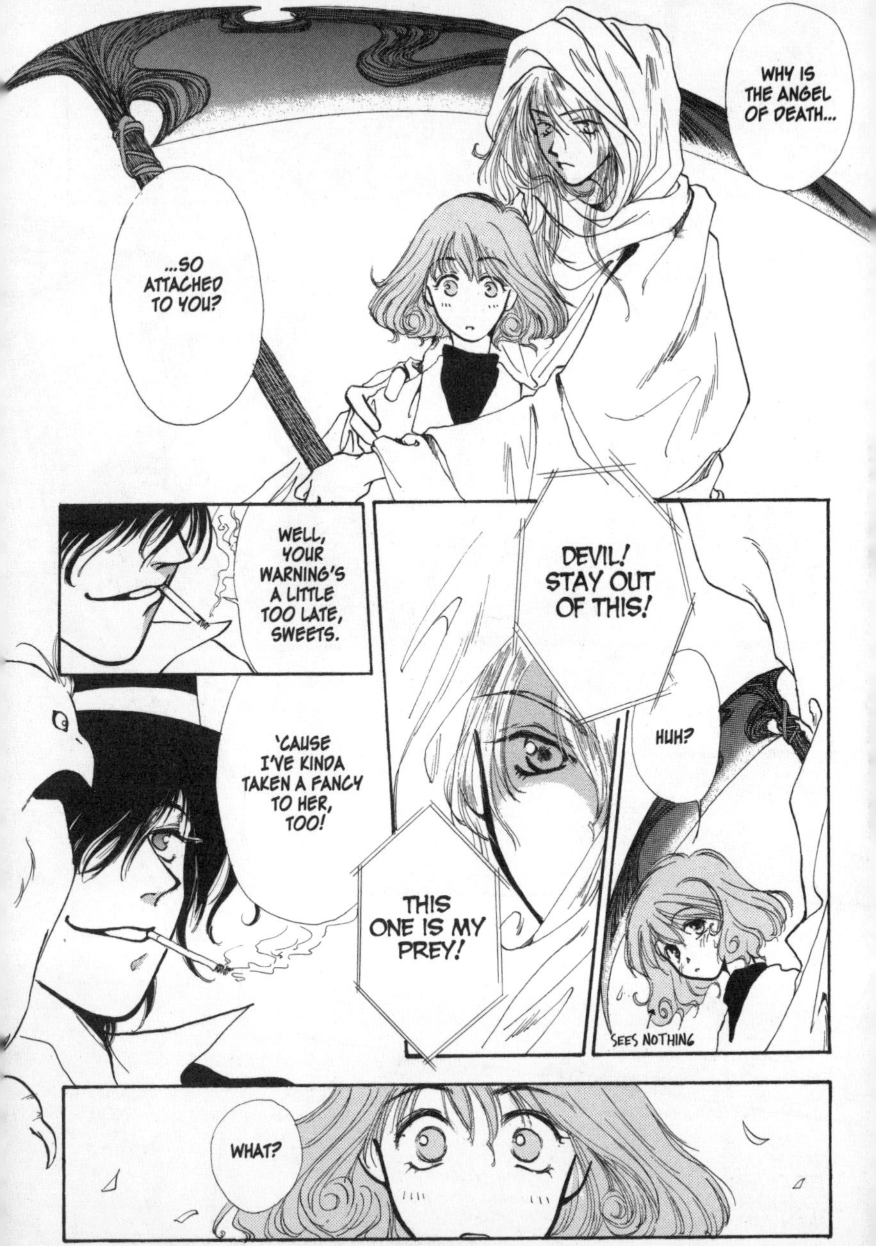
WHY IS THE ANGEL OF DEATH...
...SO ATTACHED TO YOU?
HUH?
SEES NOTHING
DEVIL! STAY OUT OF THIS!
THIS ONE IS MY PREY!
WELL, YOUR WARNING'S A LITTLE TOO LATE, SWEETS.
'CAUSE I'VE KINDA TAKEN A FANCY TO HER, TOO!
WHAT?

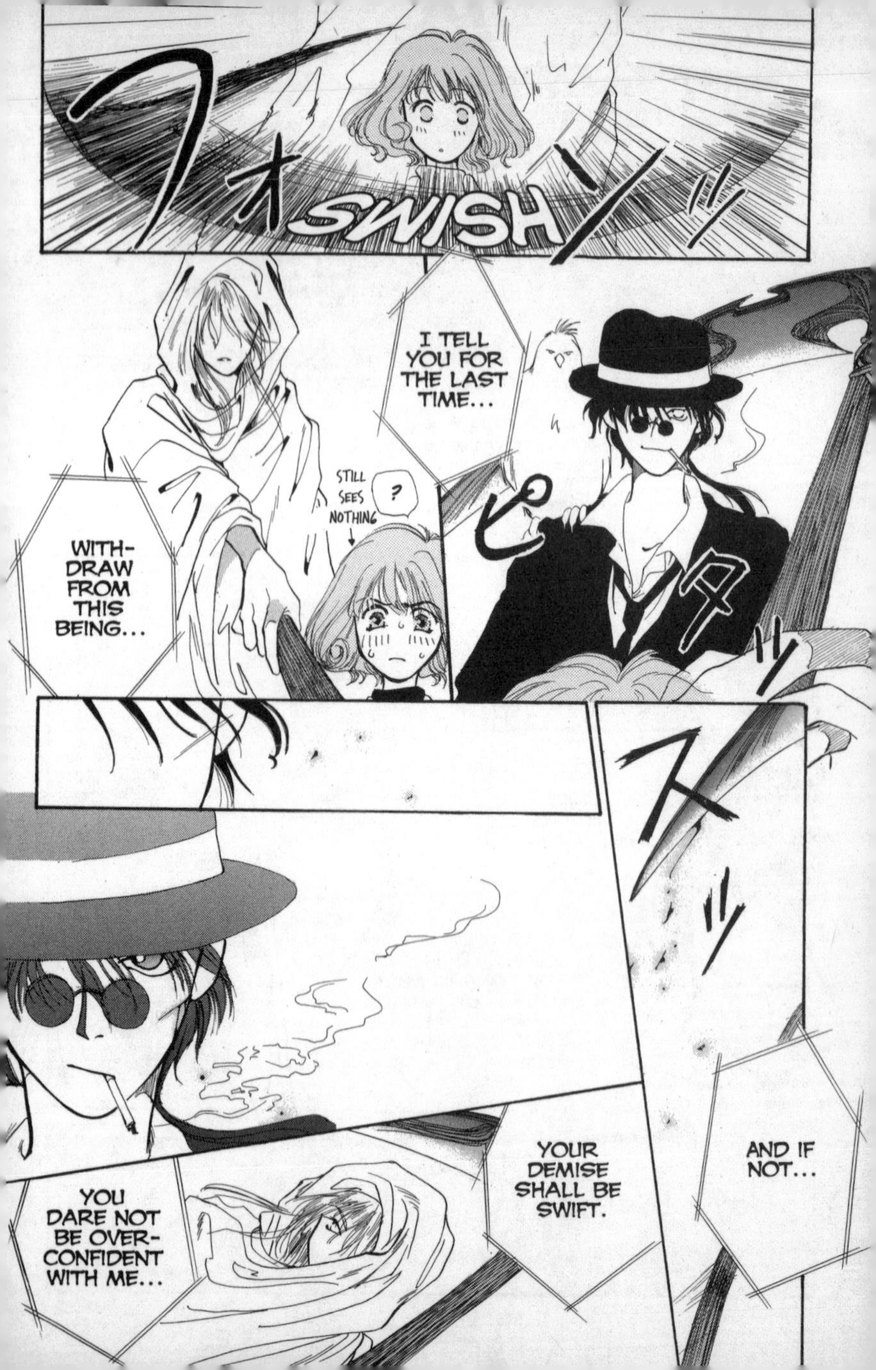
SWISH
I TELL YOU FOR THE LAST TIME...
?
STILL SEES NOTHING
WITH-DRAW FROM THIS BEING...
AND IF NOT...
YOUR DEMISE SHALL BE SWIFT.
YOU DARE NOT BE OVER-CONFIDENT WITH ME...

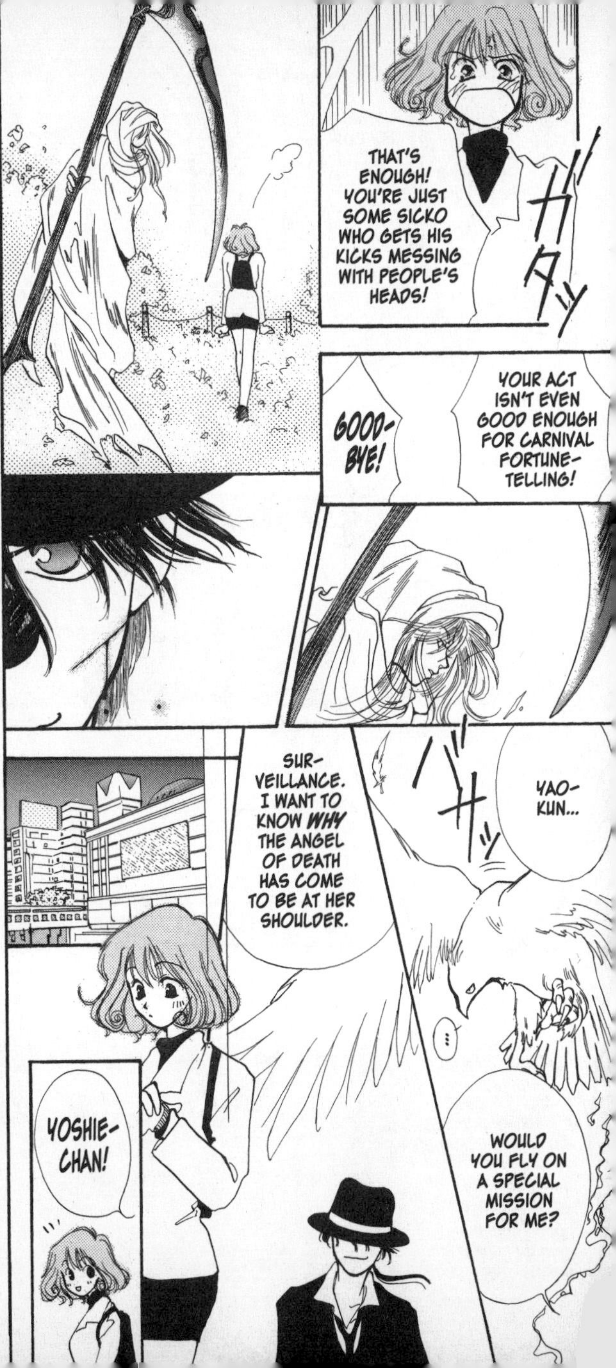
THAT'S ENOUGH! YOU'RE JUST SOME SICKO WHO GETS HIS KICKS MESSING WITH PEOPLE'S HEADS!
ガタッ
YOUR ACT ISN'T EVEN GOOD ENOUGH FOR CARNIVAL FORTUNE-TELLING!
GOOD-BYE!
YAO-KUN...
バサッ
...
WOULD YOU FLY ON A SPECIAL MISSION FOR ME?
SUR-VEILLANCE. I WANT TO KNOW *WHY* THE ANGEL OF DEATH HAS COME TO BE AT HER SHOULDER.
YOSHIE-CHAN!

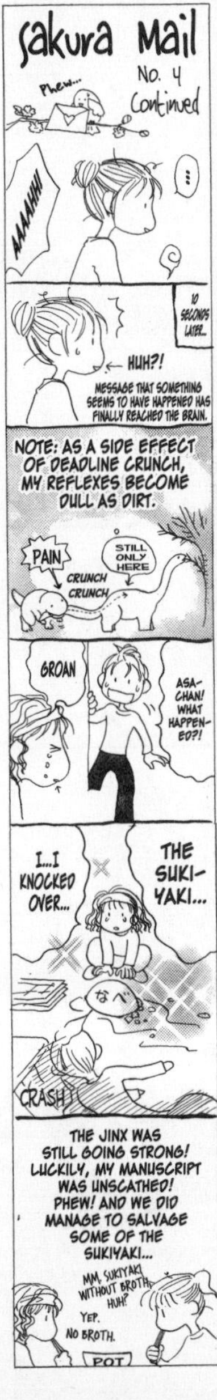
Sakura Mail
No. 4
Continued
Phew...
...
AAAAHH!
10 SECONDS LATER...
HUH?!
MESSAGE THAT SOMETHING SEEMS TO HAVE HAPPENED HAS FINALLY REACHED THE BRAIN.
NOTE: AS A SIDE EFFECT OF DEADLINE CRUNCH, MY REFLEXES BECOME DULL AS DIRT.
STILL ONLY HERE
PAIN
CRUNCH CRUNCH
ASA-CHAN! WHAT HAPPENED?!
GROAN
THE SUKI-YAKI...
I...I KNOCKED OVER...
なべ
CRASH
THE JINX WAS STILL GOING STRONG! LUCKILY, MY MANUSCRIPT WAS UNSCATHED! PHEW! AND WE DID MANAGE TO SALVAGE SOME OF THE SUKIYAKI...
MM, SUKIYAKI WITHOUT BROTH, HUH?
YEP. NO BROTH.
POT

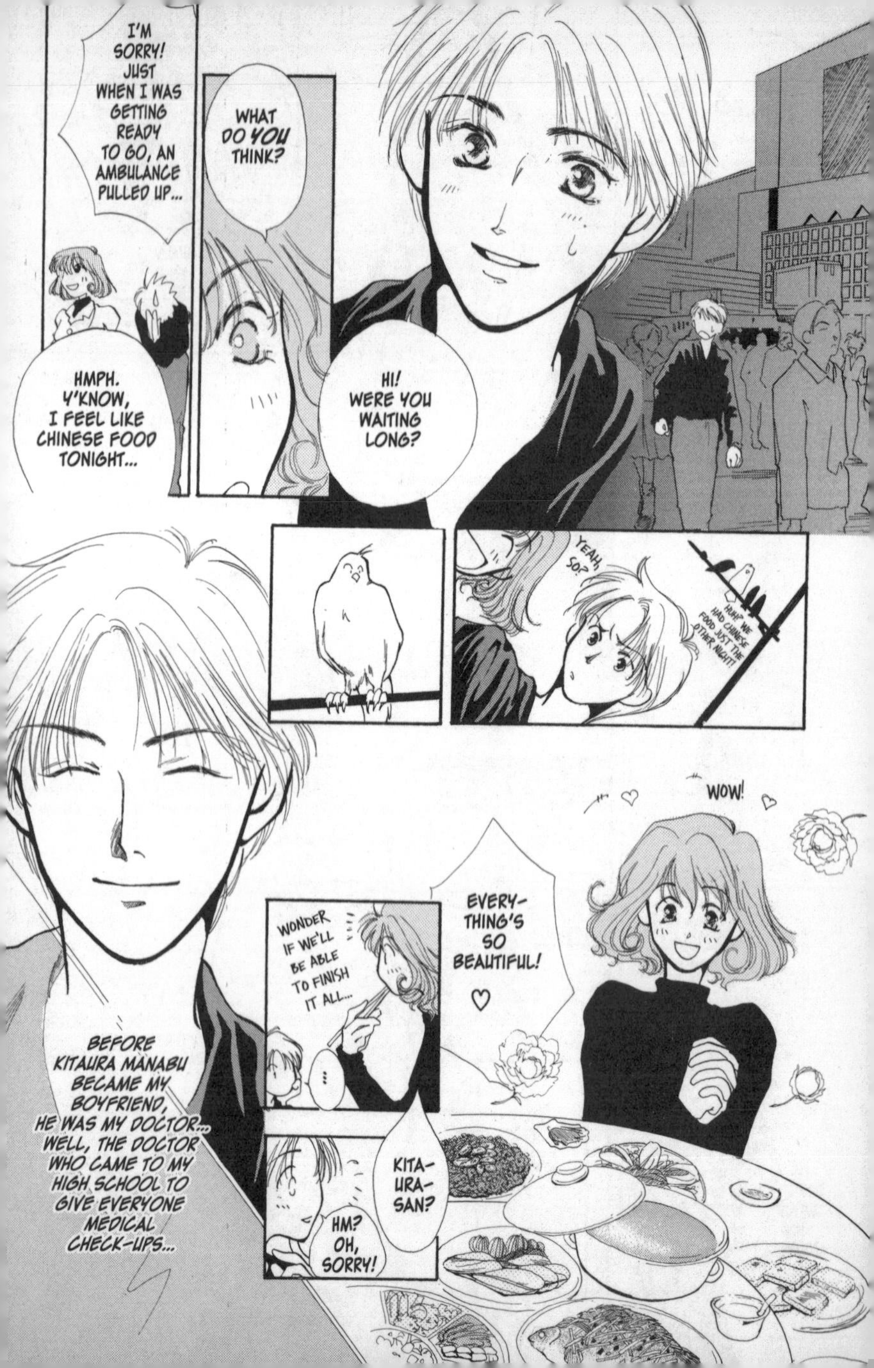
HI! WERE YOU WAITING LONG?
WHAT DO YOU THINK?
I'M SORRY! JUST WHEN I WAS GETTING READY TO GO, AN AMBULANCE PULLED UP...
HMPH. Y'KNOW, I FEEL LIKE CHINESE FOOD TONIGHT...
HUH? WE HAD CHINESE FOOD JUST THE OTHER NIGHT!
YEAH, SO?
WOW!
EVERY-THING'S SO BEAUTIFUL!
WONDER IF WE'LL BE ABLE TO FINISH IT ALL...
...
KITA-URA-SAN?
HM? OH, SORRY!
BEFORE KITAURA MANABU BECAME MY BOYFRIEND, HE WAS MY DOCTOR... WELL, THE DOCTOR WHO CAME TO MY HIGH SCHOOL TO GIVE EVERYONE MEDICAL CHECK-UPS...

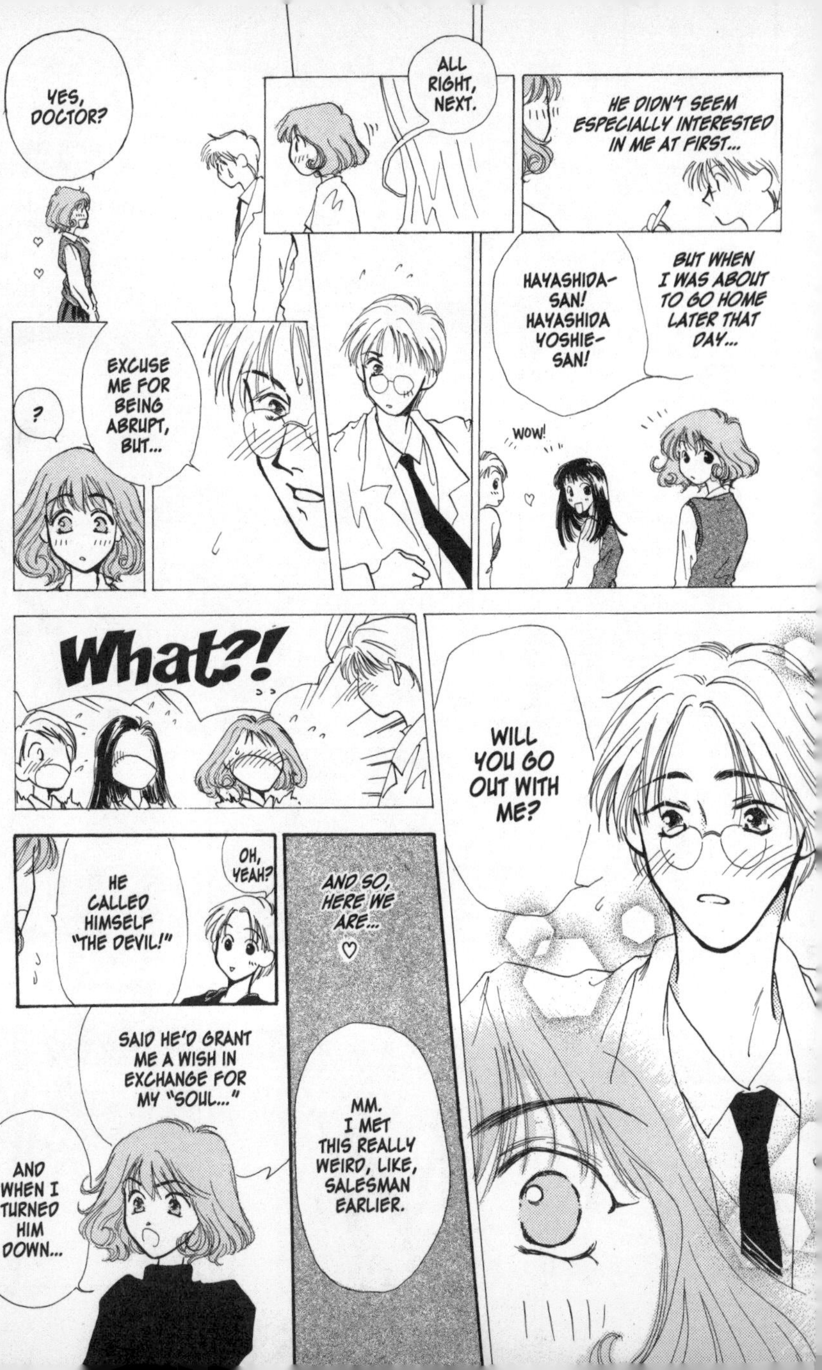
HE DIDN'T SEEM ESPECIALLY INTERESTED IN ME AT FIRST...
ALL RIGHT, NEXT.
YES, DOCTOR?
BUT WHEN I WAS ABOUT TO GO HOME LATER THAT DAY...
HAYASHIDA-SAN! HAYASHIDA YOSHIE-SAN!
WOW!
EXCUSE ME FOR BEING ABRUPT, BUT...
?
WILL YOU GO OUT WITH ME?
What?!
AND SO, HERE WE ARE...
MM. I MET THIS REALLY WEIRD, LIKE, SALESMAN EARLIER.
OH, YEAH?
HE CALLED HIMSELF "THE DEVIL!"
SAID HE'D GRANT ME A WISH IN EXCHANGE FOR MY "SOUL..."
AND WHEN I TURNED HIM DOWN...

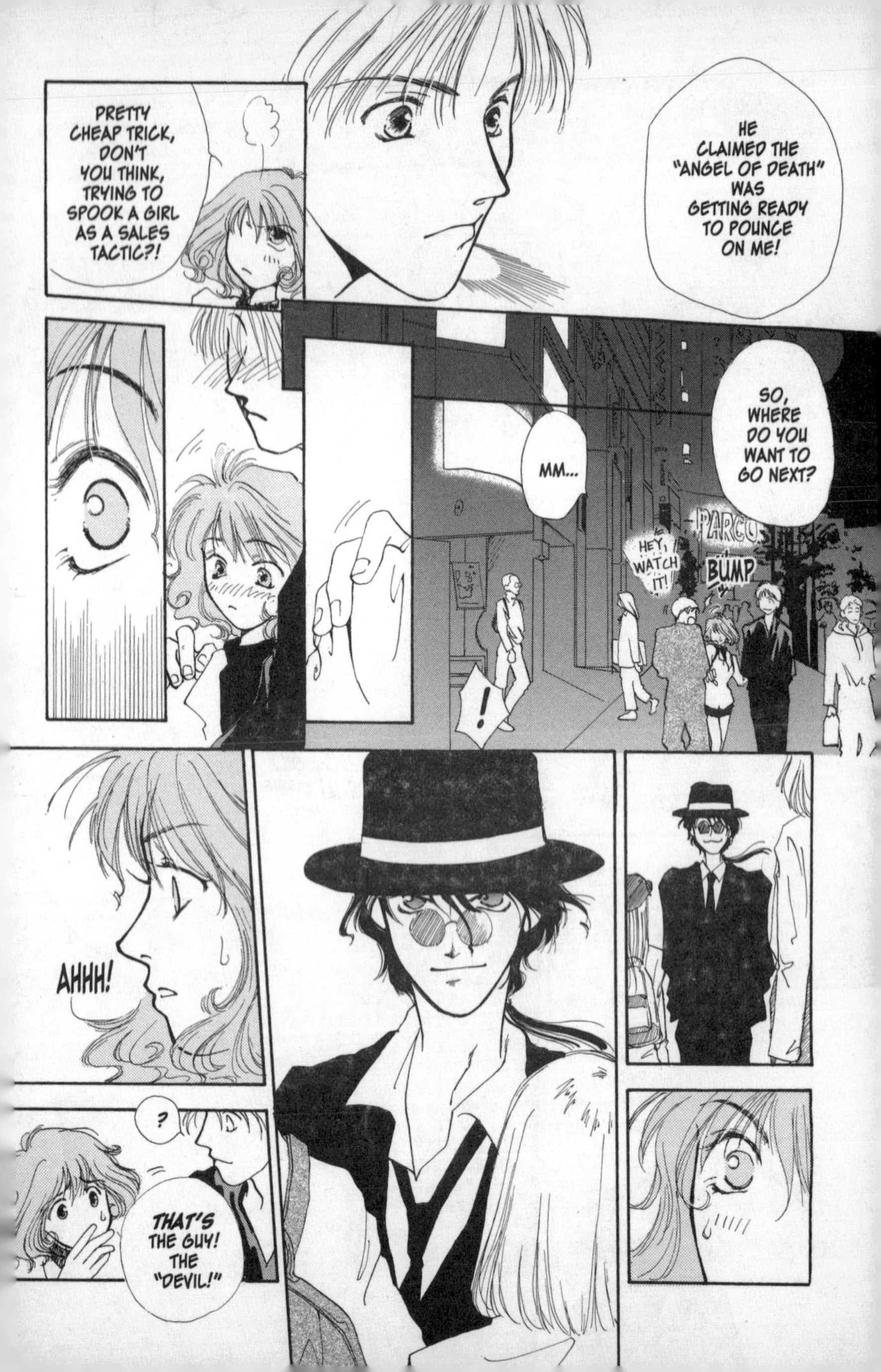
HE CLAIMED THE "ANGEL OF DEATH" WAS GETTING READY TO POUNCE ON ME!
PRETTY CHEAP TRICK, DON'T YOU THINK, TRYING TO SPOOK A GIRL AS A SALES TACTIC?!
SO, WHERE DO YOU WANT TO GO NEXT?
MM...
PARCO
BUMP
HEY, WATCH IT!
!
AHHH!
?
THAT'S THE GUY! THE "DEVIL!"

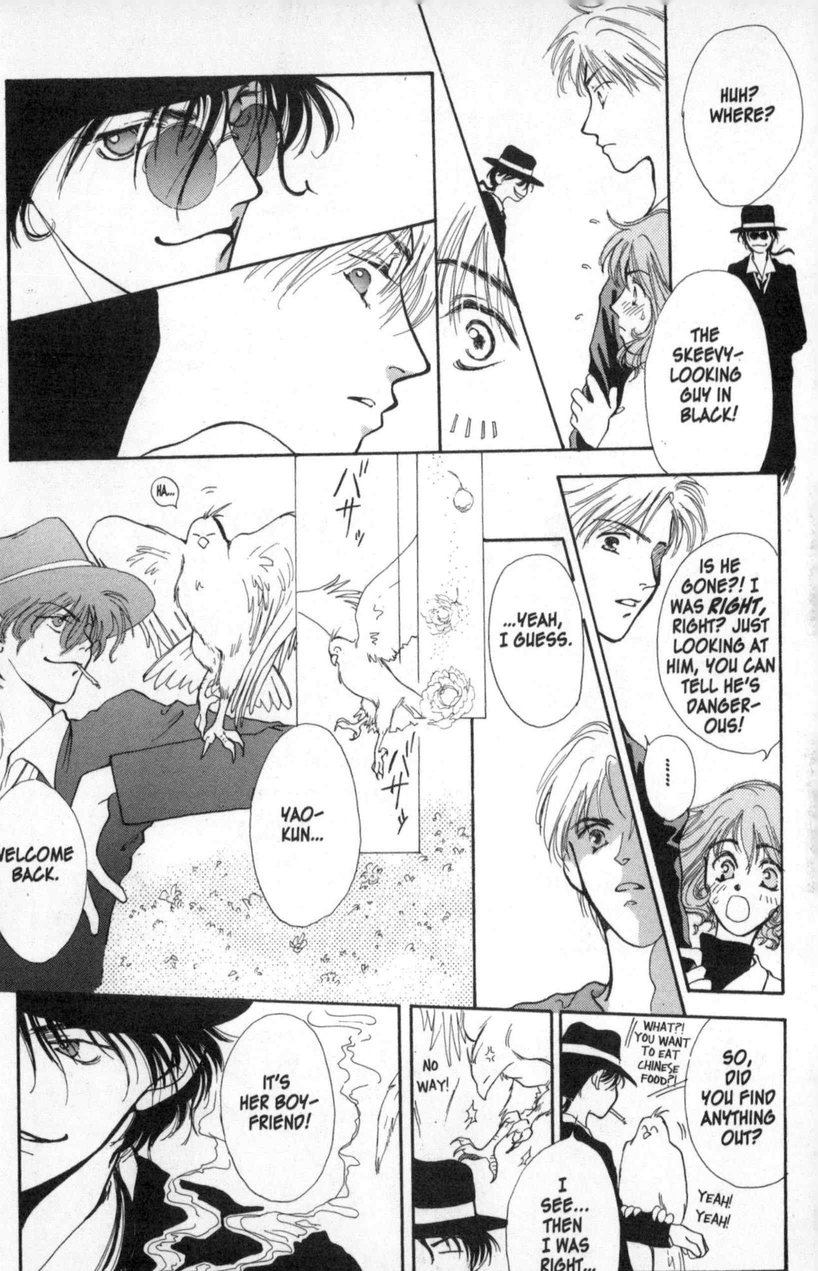
HUH? WHERE?
THE SKEEVY-LOOKING GUY IN BLACK!
IS HE GONE?! I WAS *RIGHT*, RIGHT? JUST LOOKING AT HIM, YOU CAN TELL HE'S DANGER-OUS!
......
...YEAH, I GUESS.
YAO-KUN...
HA...
WELCOME BACK.
SO, DID YOU FIND ANYTHING OUT?
WHAT?! YOU WANT TO EAT CHINESE FOOD?!
YEAH! YEAH!
I SEE... THEN I WAS RIGHT...
NO WAY!
IT'S HER BOY-FRIEND!

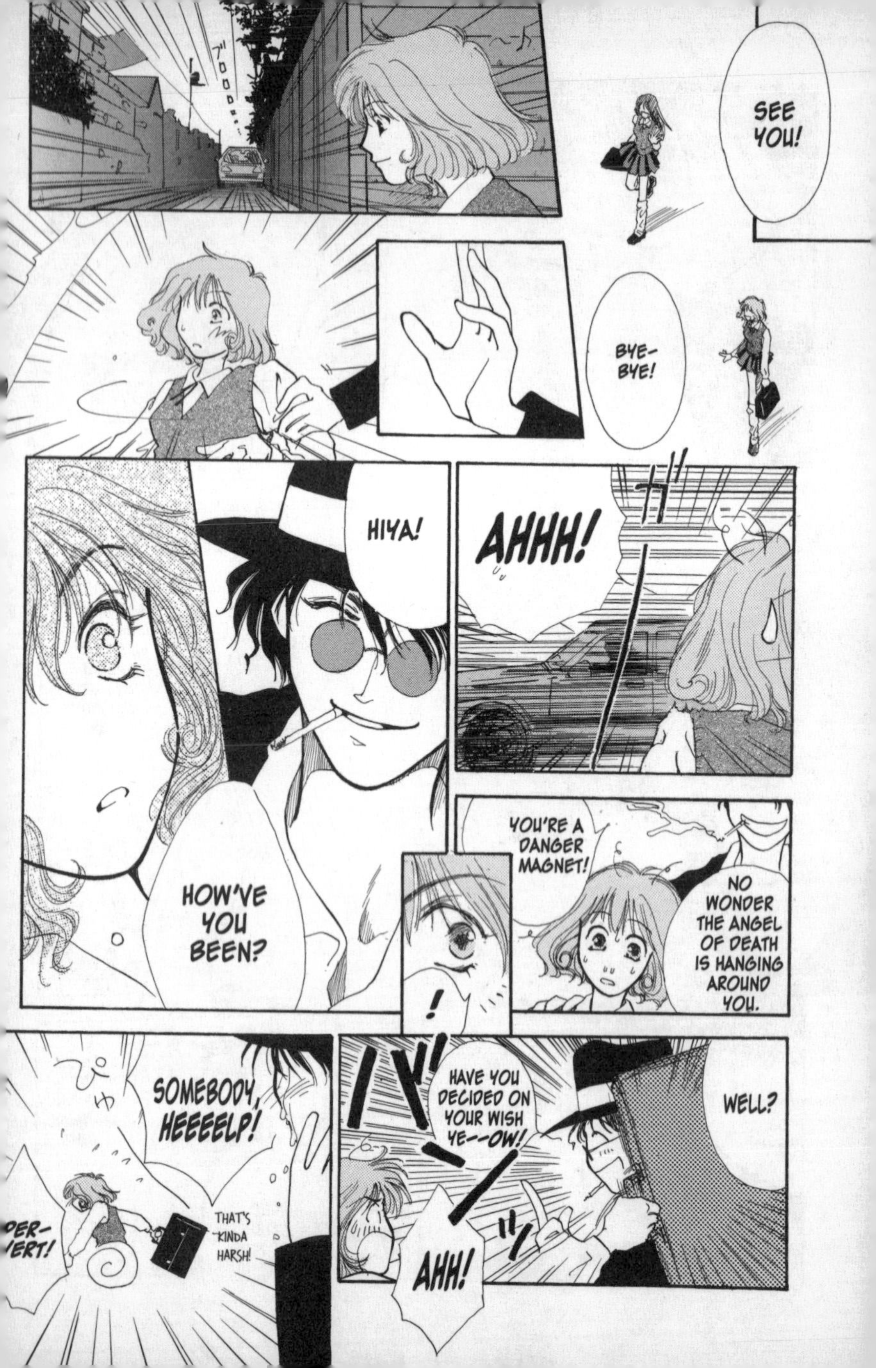
SEE YOU!
ブロロロロ…
BYE-BYE!
AHHH!
YOU'RE A DANGER MAGNET!
NO WONDER THE ANGEL OF DEATH IS HANGING AROUND YOU.
!
HIYA!
HOW'VE YOU BEEN?
WELL?
HAVE YOU DECIDED ON YOUR WISH YE--OW!
AHH!
ぴゅ
SOMEBODY, HEEEELP!
THAT'S KINDA HARSH!
PER-
ERT!

Sakura Mail

No. 5

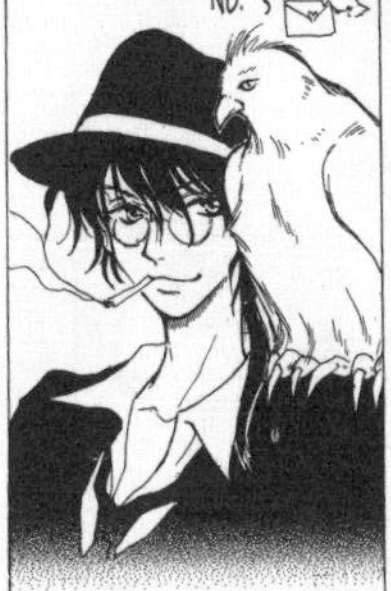

I created "Flowered Office" just so I could draw a really flashy story. I started working with this image in my head of a lot of flowers, but no matter how much I drew, I couldn't seem to fill up the panels with enough flowers. I was a little overwhelmed by how many flowers I had to draw, but at least, along the way, my flower-drawing prowess slightly improved...

By the way, yao-kun is Airi's familiar and is a bird of prey. Just to clarify for those who think (and there have been many) he's a pigeon...

Sorry, yao-kun!

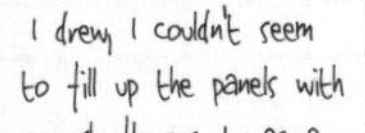
I'M SORRY!

Well, I'm running out of space, so I'll sign off here until next time.

Sakura

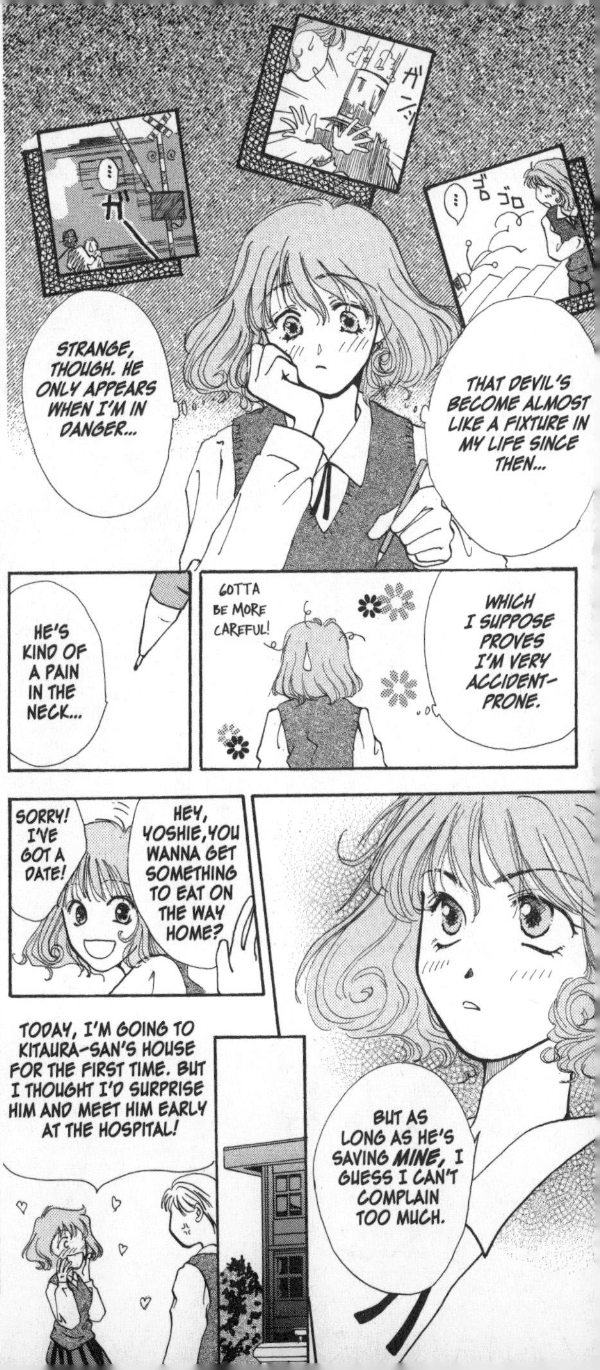
THAT DEVIL'S BECOME ALMOST LIKE A FIXTURE IN MY LIFE SINCE THEN...
STRANGE, THOUGH. HE ONLY APPEARS WHEN I'M IN DANGER...
WHICH I SUPPOSE PROVES I'M VERY ACCIDENT-PRONE.
GOTTA BE MORE CAREFUL!
HE'S KIND OF A PAIN IN THE NECK...
BUT AS LONG AS HE'S SAVING MINE, I GUESS I CAN'T COMPLAIN TOO MUCH.
HEY, YOSHIE, YOU WANNA GET SOMETHING TO EAT ON THE WAY HOME?
SORRY! I'VE GOT A DATE!
TODAY, I'M GOING TO KITAURA-SAN'S HOUSE FOR THE FIRST TIME. BUT I THOUGHT I'D SURPRISE HIM AND MEET HIM EARLY AT THE HOSPITAL!

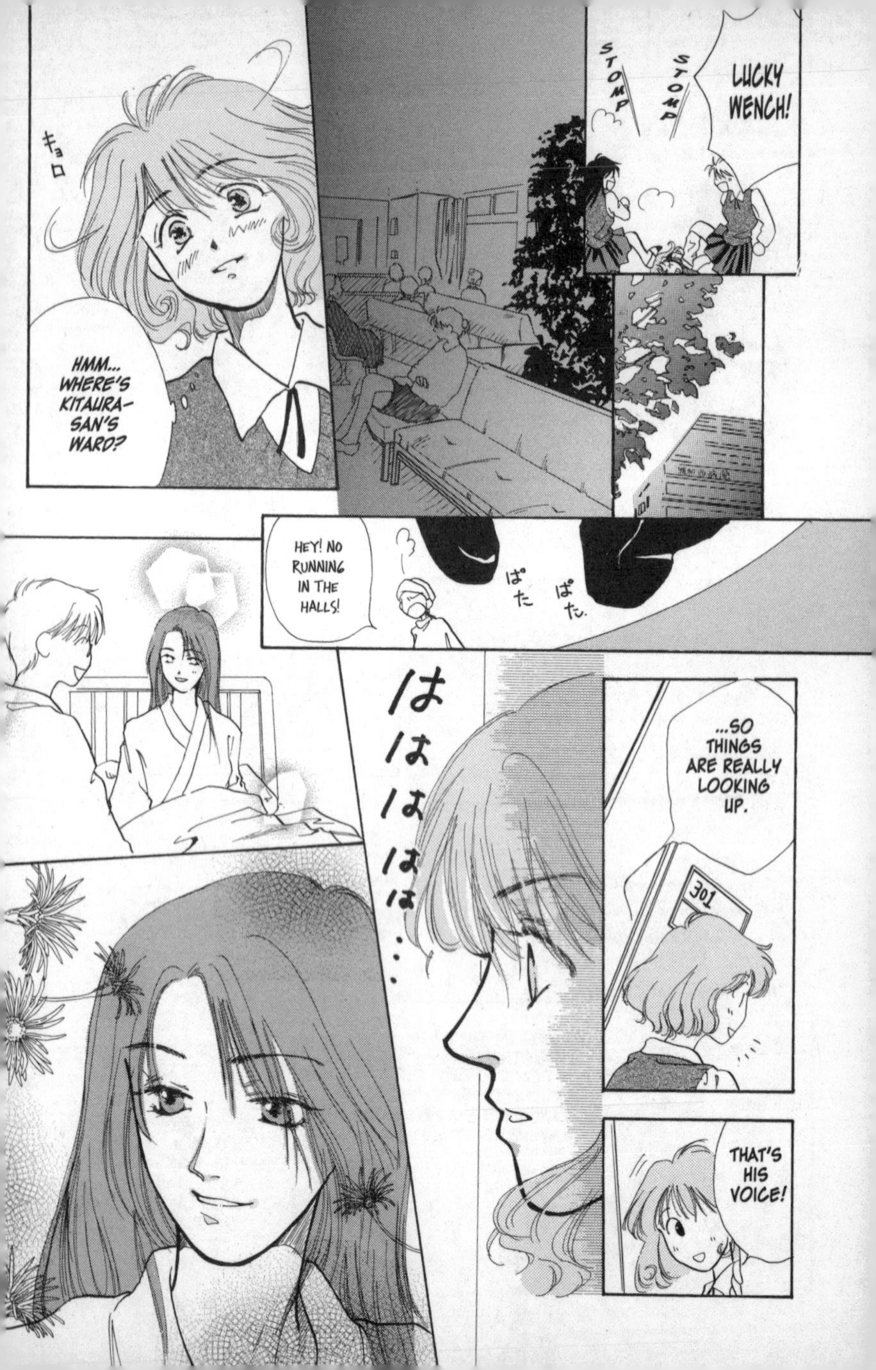
LUCKY WENCH!
STOMP
STOMP
キョロ
HMM... WHERE'S KITAURA-SAN'S WARD?
ぱた ぱた
HEY! NO RUNNING IN THE HALLS!
...SO THINGS ARE REALLY LOOKING UP.
301
THAT'S HIS VOICE!
ははははは…

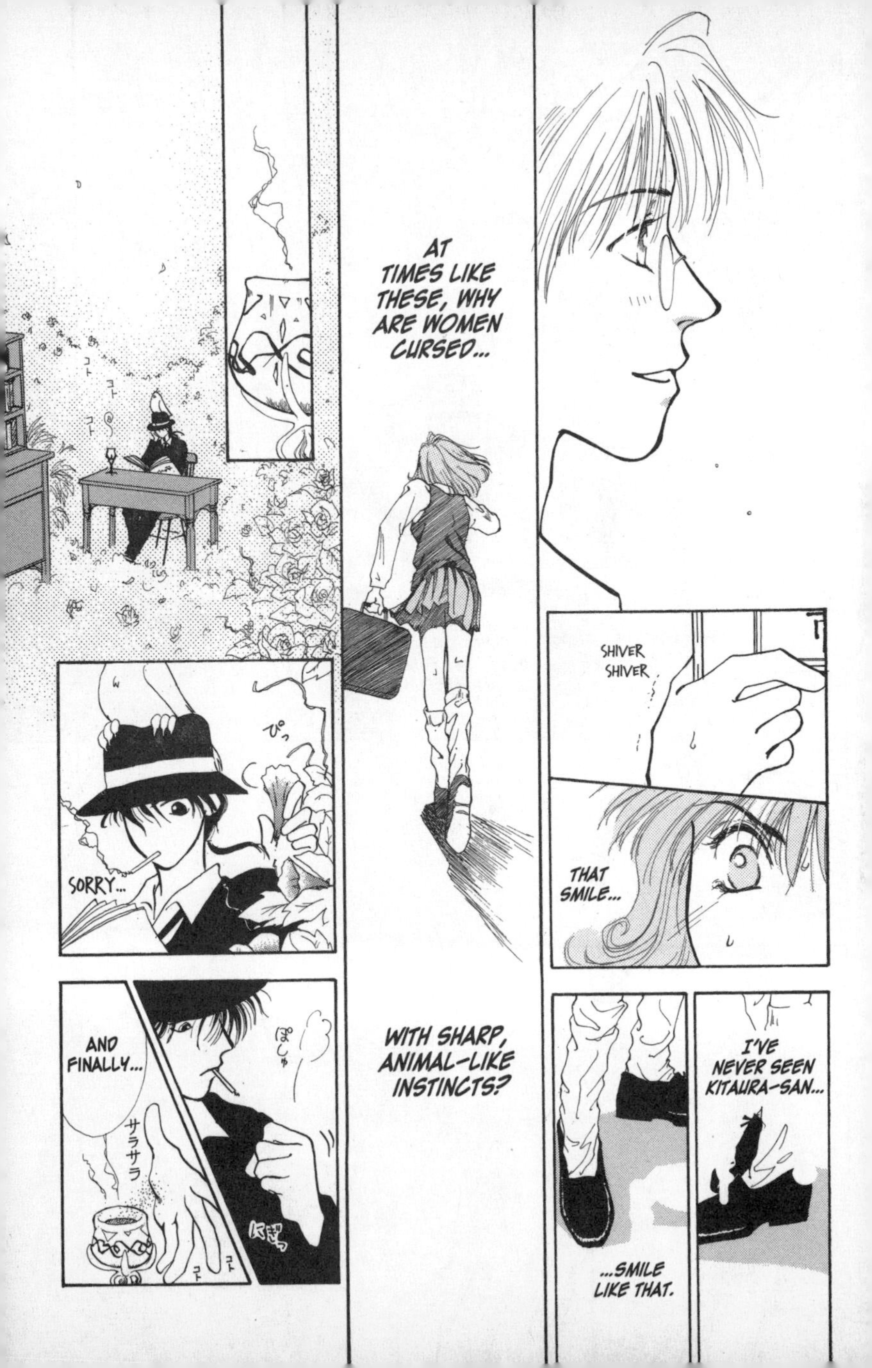
SHIVER SHIVER
THAT SMILE...
I'VE NEVER SEEN KITAURA-SAN...
...SMILE LIKE THAT.
AT TIMES LIKE THESE, WHY ARE WOMEN CURSED...
WITH SHARP, ANIMAL-LIKE INSTINCTS?
コト
コト
コト
ぴっ
SORRY...
ぽしゅ
AND FINALLY...
サラサラ
コト
コト

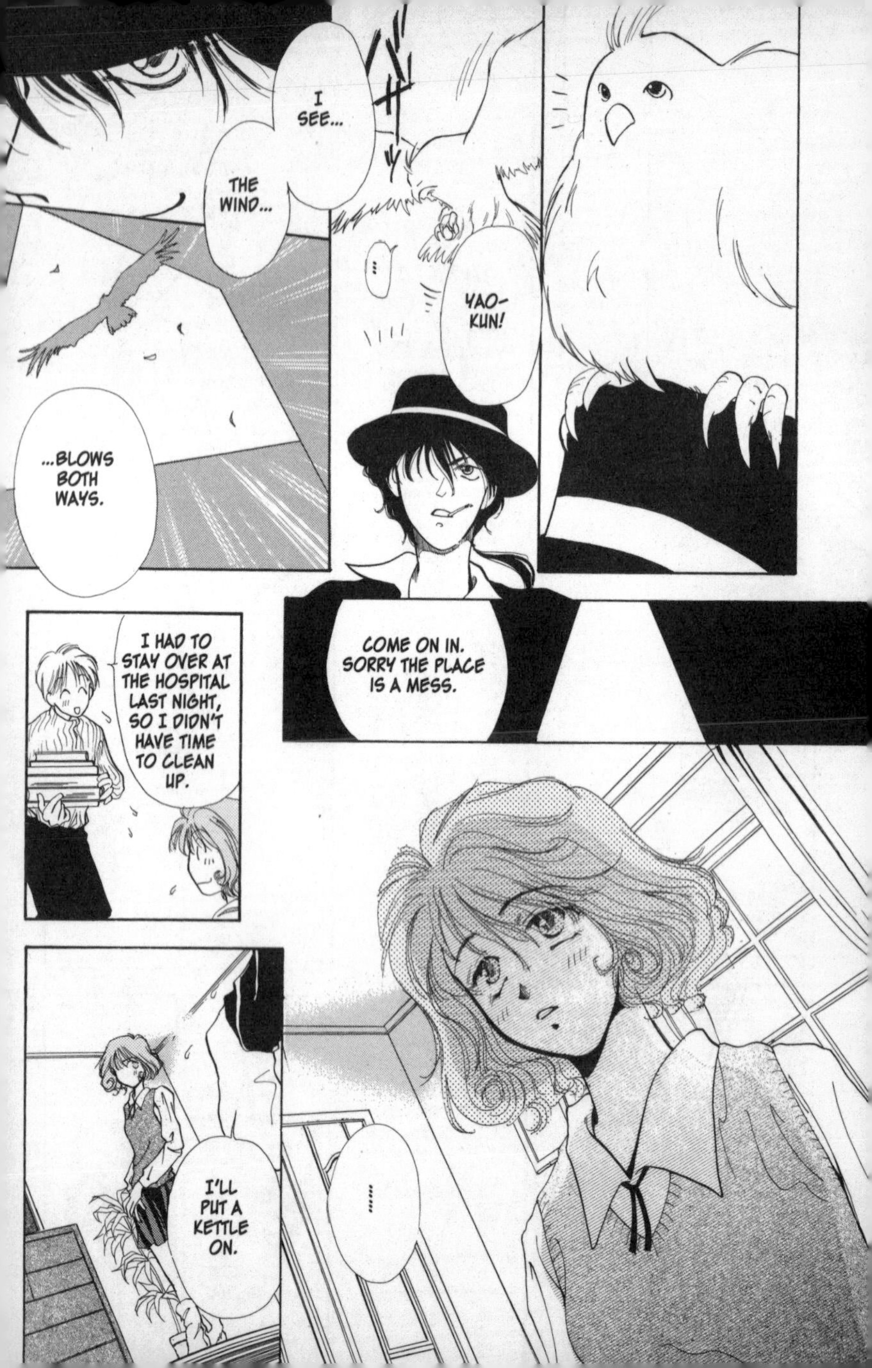
...
YAO-KUN!
I SEE...
THE WIND...
...BLOWS BOTH WAYS.
COME ON IN. SORRY THE PLACE IS A MESS.
I HAD TO STAY OVER AT THE HOSPITAL LAST NIGHT, SO I DIDN'T HAVE TIME TO CLEAN UP.
.....
I'LL PUT A KETTLE ON.

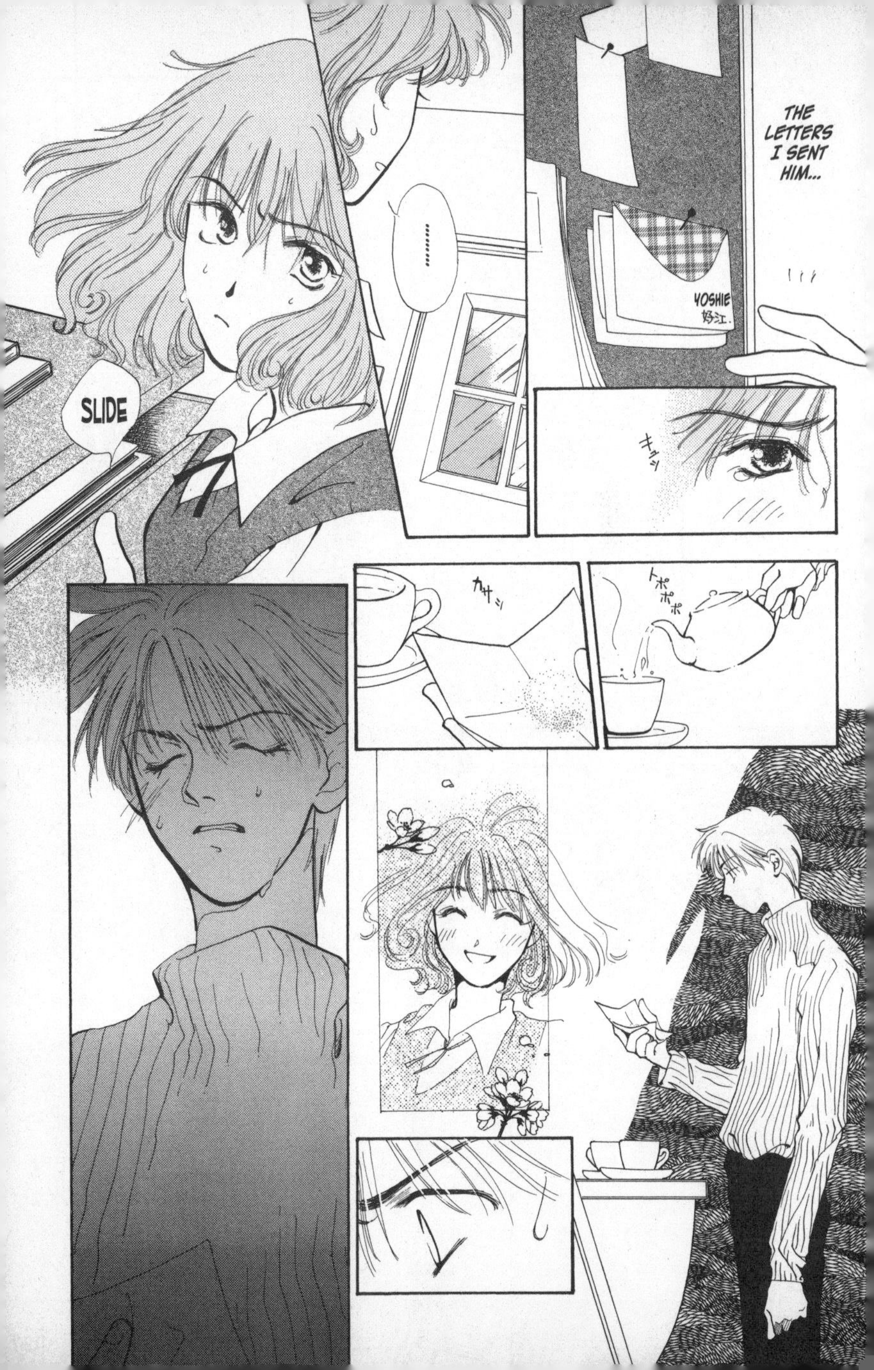
THE LETTERS I SENT HIM...
YOSHIE
好江.
......
SLIDE
トポポポ
カサッ

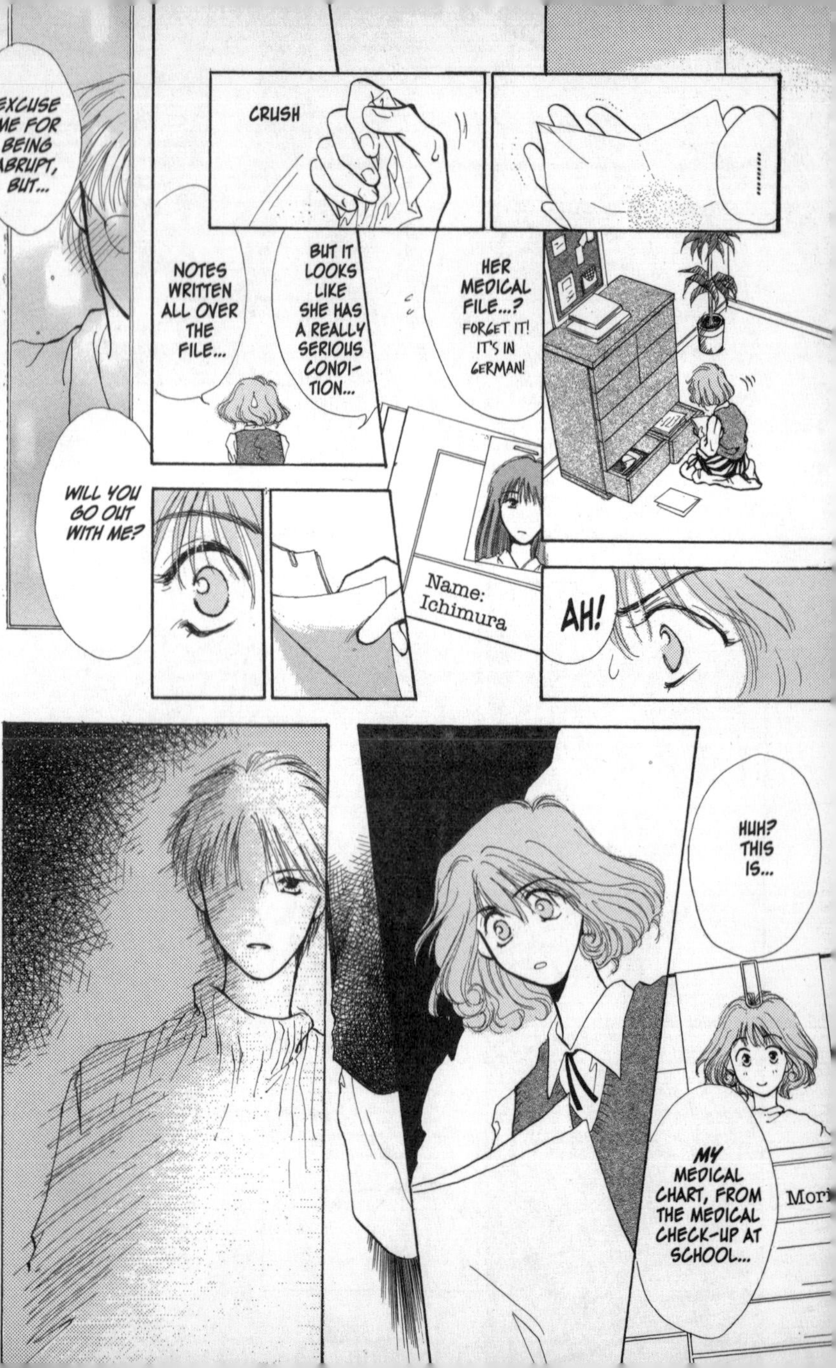

......
CRUSH
HER MEDICAL FILE...? FORGET IT! IT'S IN GERMAN!
BUT IT LOOKS LIKE SHE HAS A REALLY SERIOUS CONDITION...
NOTES WRITTEN ALL OVER THE FILE...
AH!
Name: Ichimura
EXCUSE ME FOR BEING ABRUPT, BUT...
WILL YOU GO OUT WITH ME?
HUH? THIS IS...
MY MEDICAL CHART, FROM THE MEDICAL CHECK-UP AT SCHOOL...
Mori

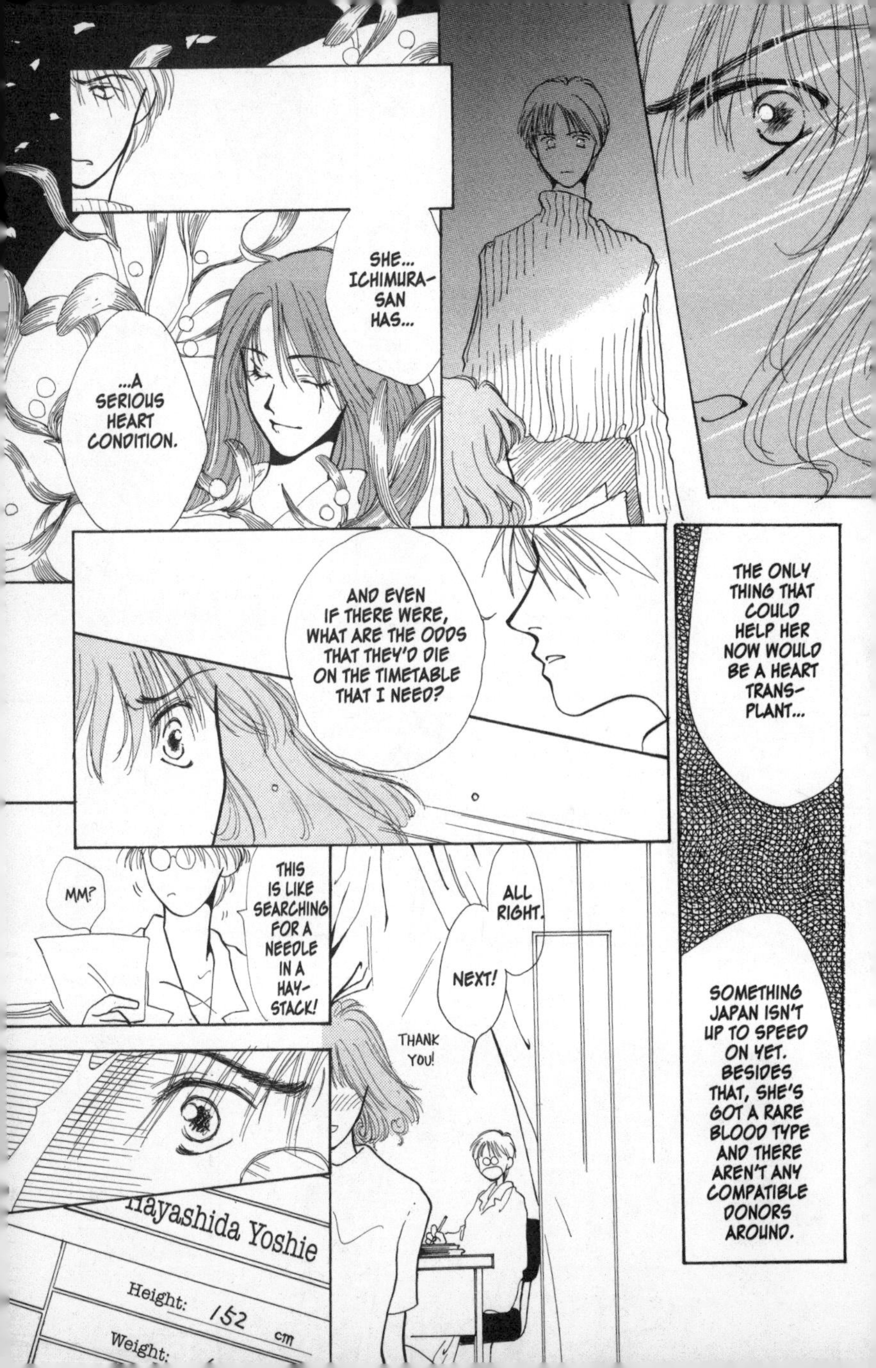
SHE... ICHIMURA-SAN HAS...
...A SERIOUS HEART CONDITION.
THE ONLY THING THAT COULD HELP HER NOW WOULD BE A HEART TRANS-PLANT...
SOMETHING JAPAN ISN'T UP TO SPEED ON YET. BESIDES THAT, SHE'S GOT A RARE BLOOD TYPE AND THERE AREN'T ANY COMPATIBLE DONORS AROUND.
AND EVEN IF THERE WERE, WHAT ARE THE ODDS THAT THEY'D DIE ON THE TIMETABLE THAT I NEED?
ALL RIGHT.
NEXT!
THANK YOU!
THIS IS LIKE SEARCHING FOR A NEEDLE IN A HAY-STACK!
MM?
Hayashida Yoshie
Height: 152 cm
Weight:

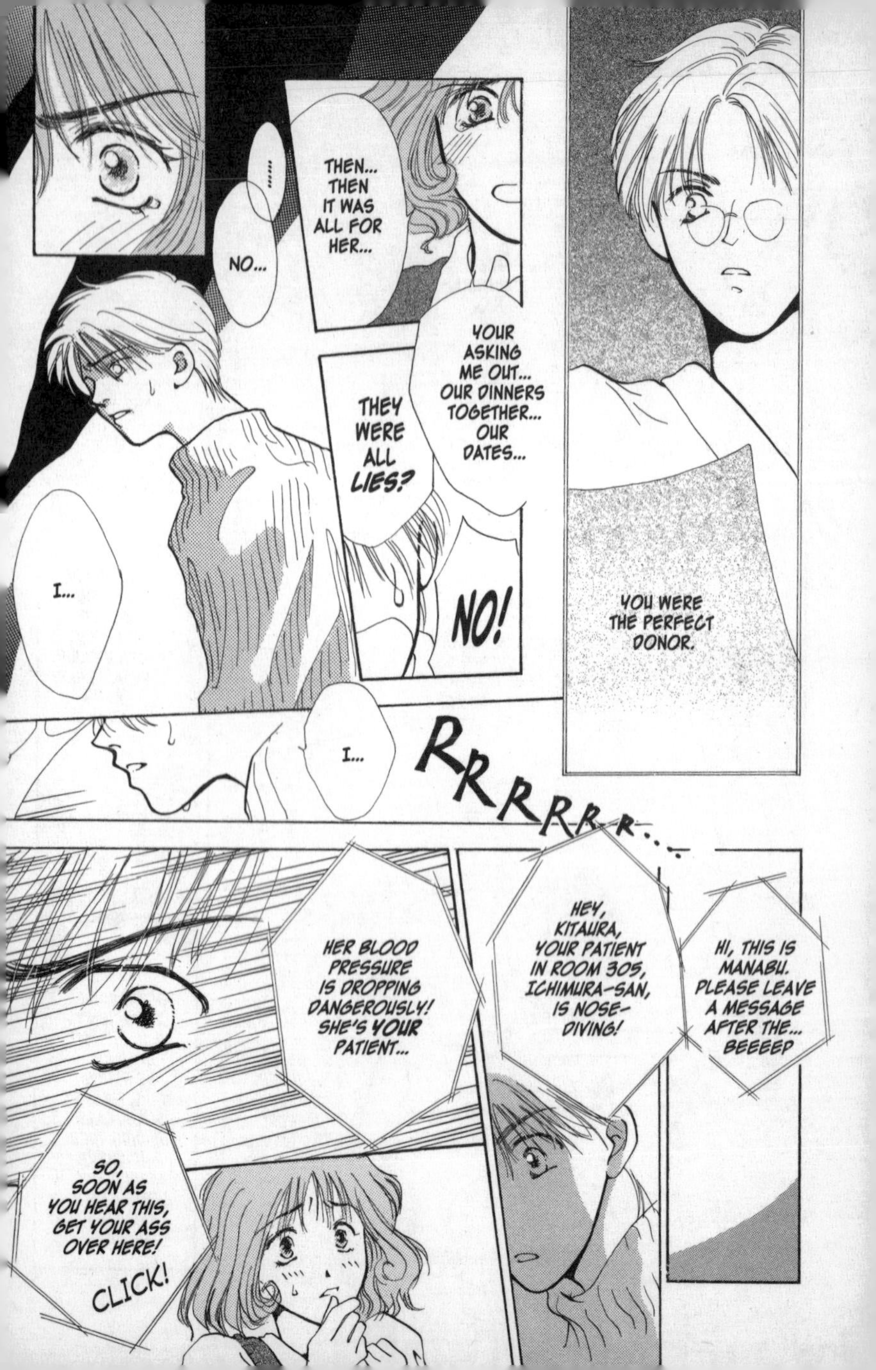
YOU WERE THE PERFECT DONOR.
THEN... THEN IT WAS ALL FOR HER...
......
NO...
YOUR ASKING ME OUT... OUR DINNERS TOGETHER... OUR DATES...
THEY WERE ALL LIES?
NO!
I...
I...
RRRRRRR...
HI, THIS IS MANABU. PLEASE LEAVE A MESSAGE AFTER THE... BEEEEP
HEY, KITAURA, YOUR PATIENT IN ROOM 305, ICHIMURA-SAN, IS NOSE-DIVING!
HER BLOOD PRESSURE IS DROPPING DANGEROUSLY! SHE'S YOUR PATIENT...
SO, SOON AS YOU HEAR THIS, GET YOUR ASS OVER HERE!
CLICK!

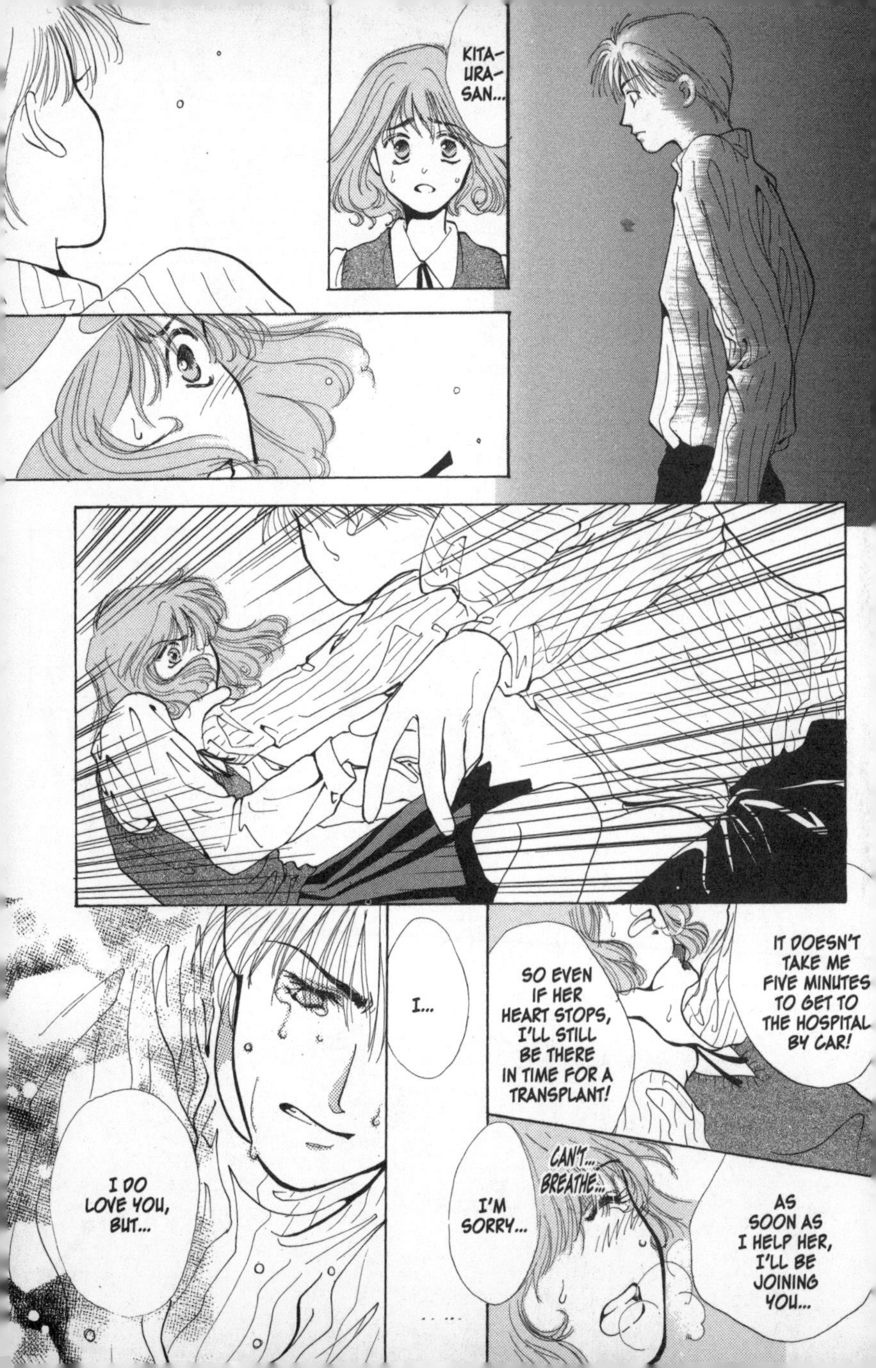
KITA-URA-SAN...
IT DOESN'T TAKE ME FIVE MINUTES TO GET TO THE HOSPITAL BY CAR!
SO EVEN IF HER HEART STOPS, I'LL STILL BE THERE IN TIME FOR A TRANSPLANT!
AS SOON AS I HELP HER, I'LL BE JOINING YOU...
CAN'T... BREATHE...
I...
I'M SORRY...
I DO LOVE YOU, BUT...

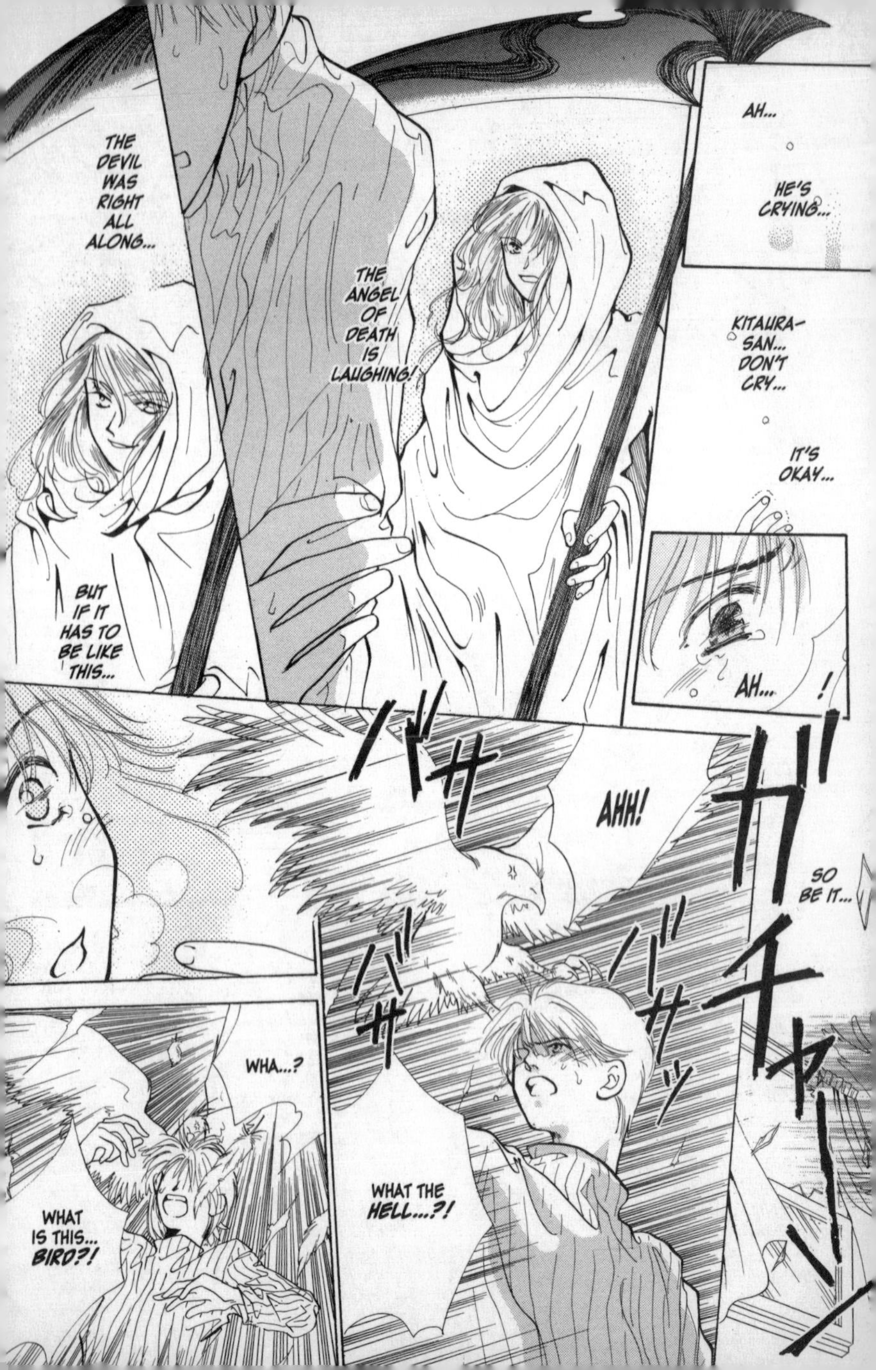
AH...
HE'S CRYING...
KITAURA-SAN... DON'T CRY...
IT'S OKAY...
AH... !
THE ANGEL OF DEATH IS LAUGHING!
THE DEVIL WAS RIGHT ALL ALONG...
BUT IF IT HAS TO BE LIKE THIS...
SO BE IT...
ガシャーン
バサ
AHH!
バサッ
バサ
WHAT THE HELL...?!
WHA...?
WHAT IS THIS... BIRD?!

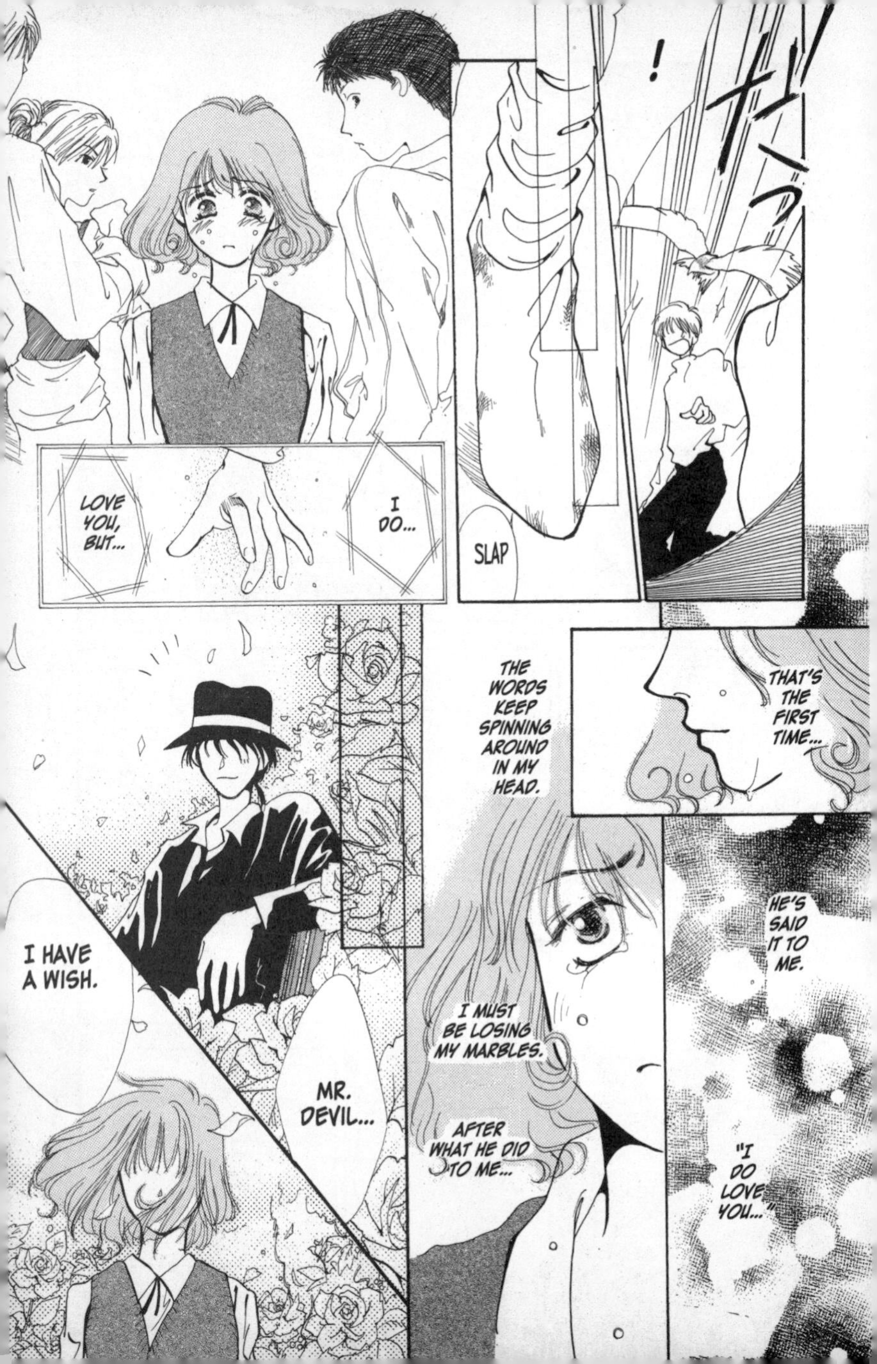
!
SLAP
I DO...
LOVE YOU, BUT...
THAT'S THE FIRST TIME...
HE'S SAID IT TO ME.
"I DO LOVE YOU..."
THE WORDS KEEP SPINNING AROUND IN MY HEAD.
I MUST BE LOSING MY MARBLES.
AFTER WHAT HE DID TO ME...
MR. DEVIL...
I HAVE A WISH.

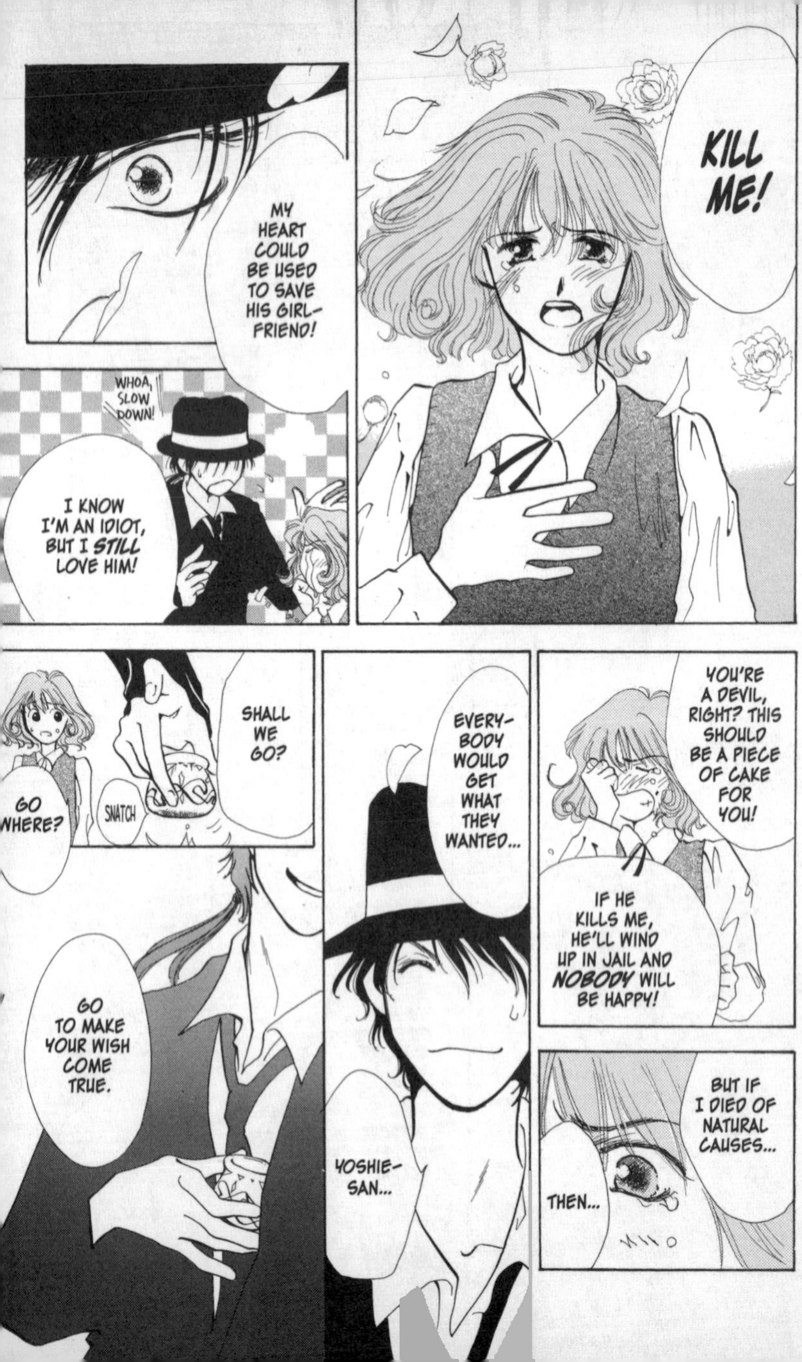
KILL ME!
MY HEART COULD BE USED TO SAVE HIS GIRL-FRIEND!
WHOA, SLOW DOWN!
I KNOW I'M AN IDIOT, BUT I STILL LOVE HIM!
YOU'RE A DEVIL, RIGHT? THIS SHOULD BE A PIECE OF CAKE FOR YOU!
IF HE KILLS ME, HE'LL WIND UP IN JAIL AND NOBODY WILL BE HAPPY!
BUT IF I DIED OF NATURAL CAUSES...
THEN...
EVERY-BODY WOULD GET WHAT THEY WANTED...
YOSHIE-SAN...
SHALL WE GO?
SNATCH
GO WHERE?
GO TO MAKE YOUR WISH COME TRUE.

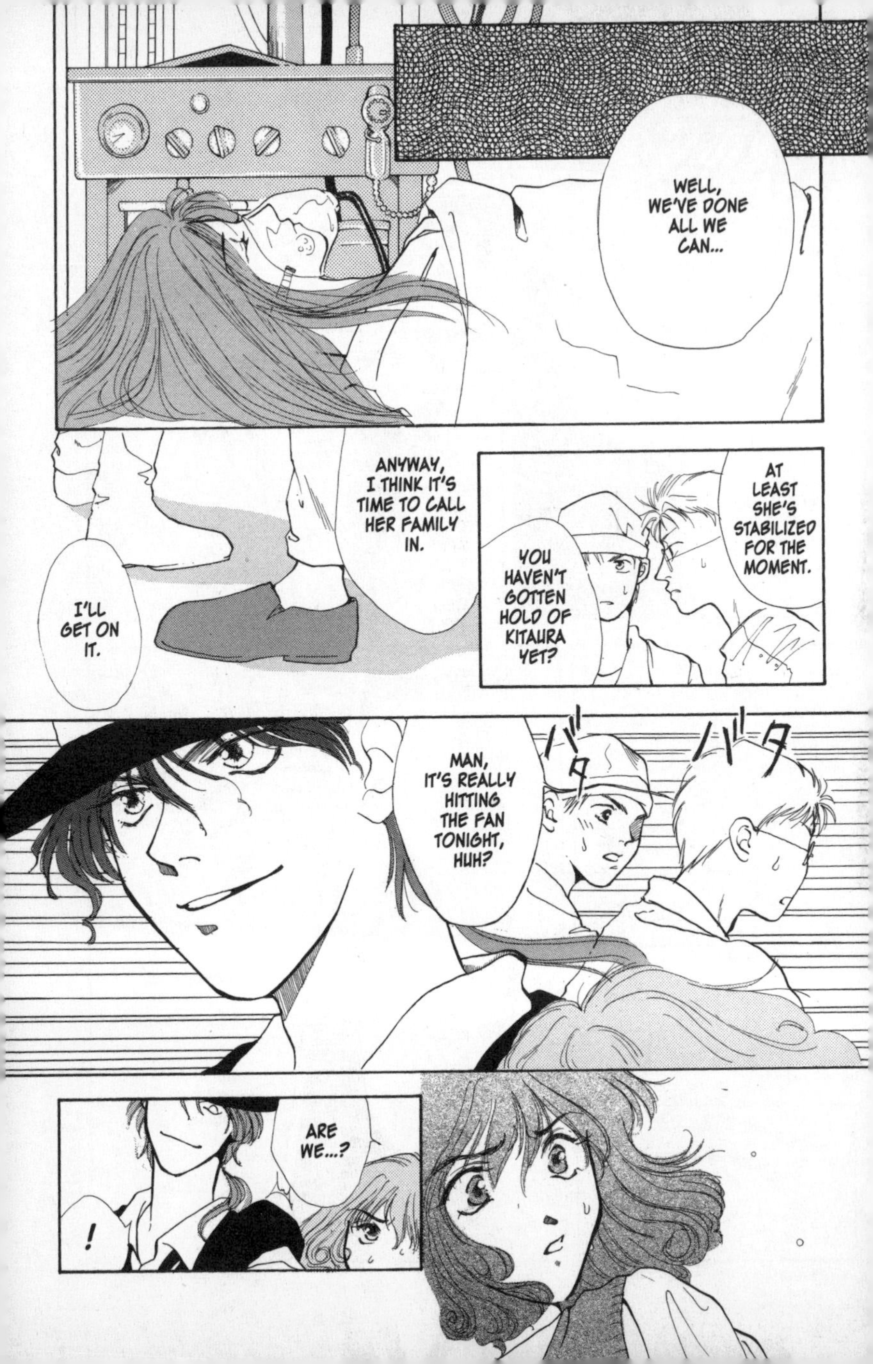
WELL, WE'VE DONE ALL WE CAN...
AT LEAST SHE'S STABILIZED FOR THE MOMENT.
YOU HAVEN'T GOTTEN HOLD OF KITAURA YET?
ANYWAY, I THINK IT'S TIME TO CALL HER FAMILY IN.
I'LL GET ON IT.
バタ
バタ
MAN, IT'S REALLY HITTING THE FAN TONIGHT, HUH?
ARE WE...?
!

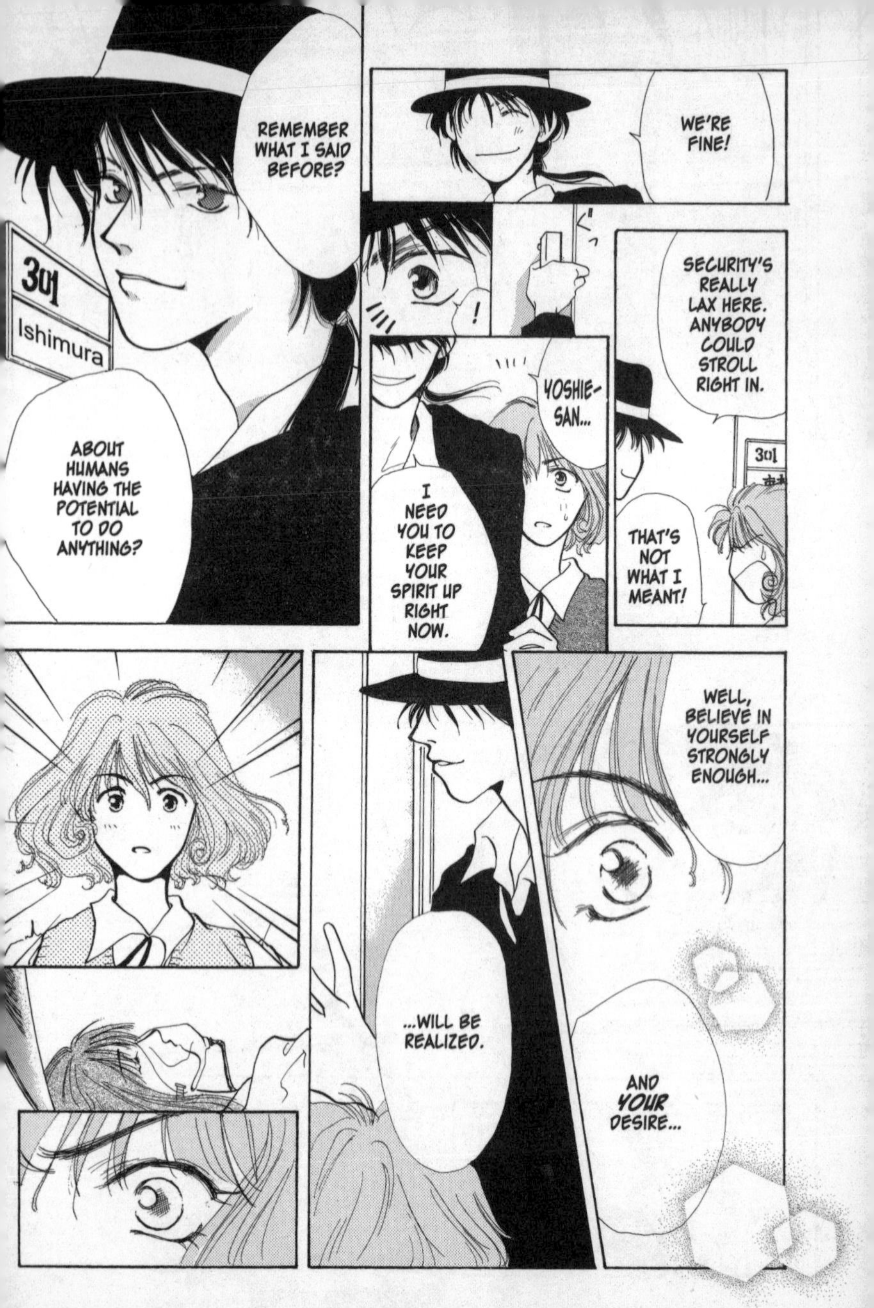
WE'RE FINE!
!
SECURITY'S REALLY LAX HERE. ANYBODY COULD STROLL RIGHT IN.
301
THAT'S NOT WHAT I MEANT!
YOSHIE-SAN...
I NEED YOU TO KEEP YOUR SPIRIT UP RIGHT NOW.
REMEMBER WHAT I SAID BEFORE?
301
Ishimura
ABOUT HUMANS HAVING THE POTENTIAL TO DO ANYTHING?
WELL, BELIEVE IN YOURSELF STRONGLY ENOUGH...
AND YOUR DESIRE...
...WILL BE REALIZED.

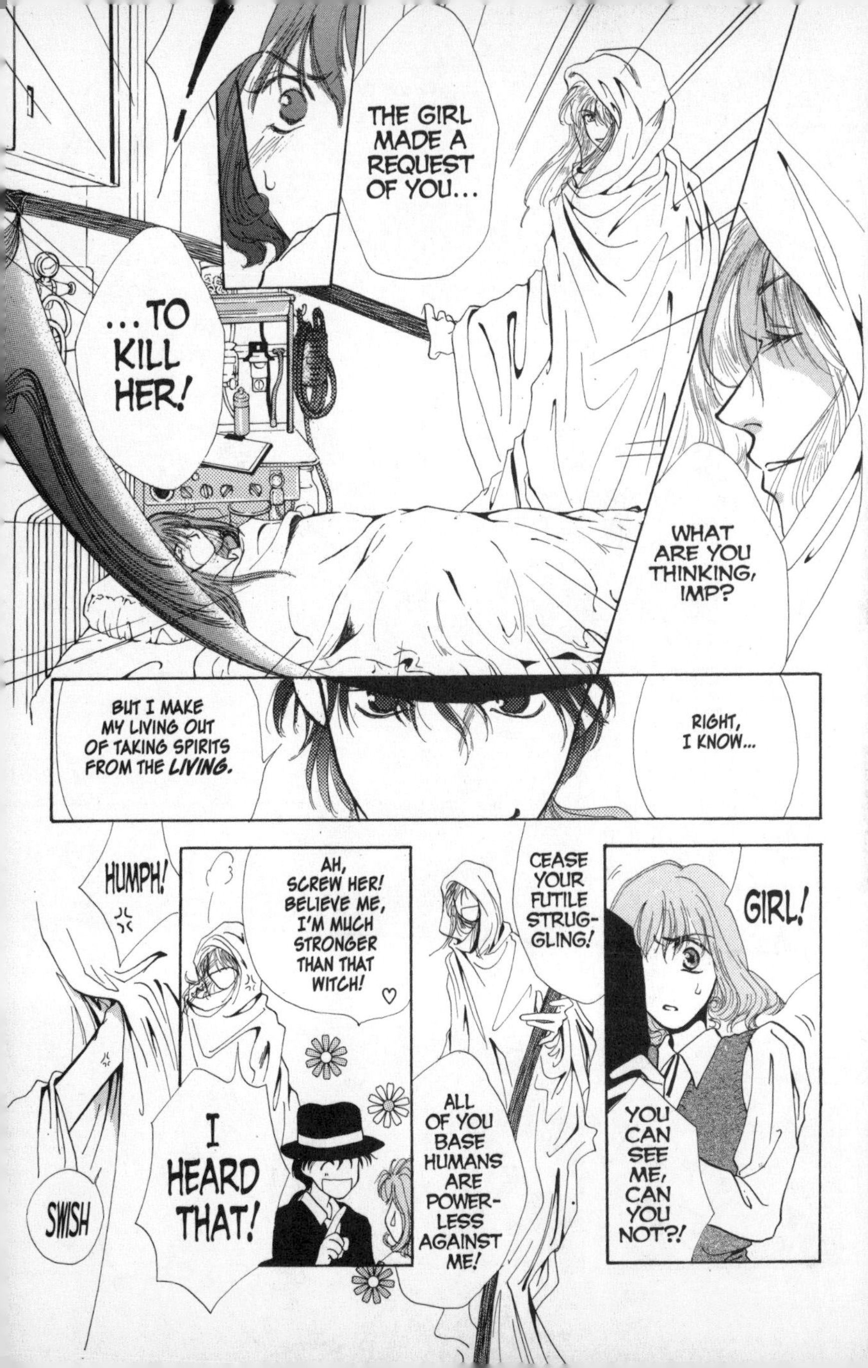
THE GIRL MADE A REQUEST OF YOU...
...TO KILL HER!
WHAT ARE YOU THINKING, IMP?
RIGHT, I KNOW...
BUT I MAKE MY LIVING OUT OF TAKING SPIRITS FROM THE *LIVING.*
GIRL!
YOU CAN SEE ME, CAN YOU NOT?!
CEASE YOUR FUTILE STRUG-GLING!
ALL OF YOU BASE HUMANS ARE POWER-LESS AGAINST ME!
AH, SCREW HER! BELIEVE ME, I'M MUCH STRONGER THAN THAT WITCH! ♡
I HEARD THAT!
HUMPH!
SWISH

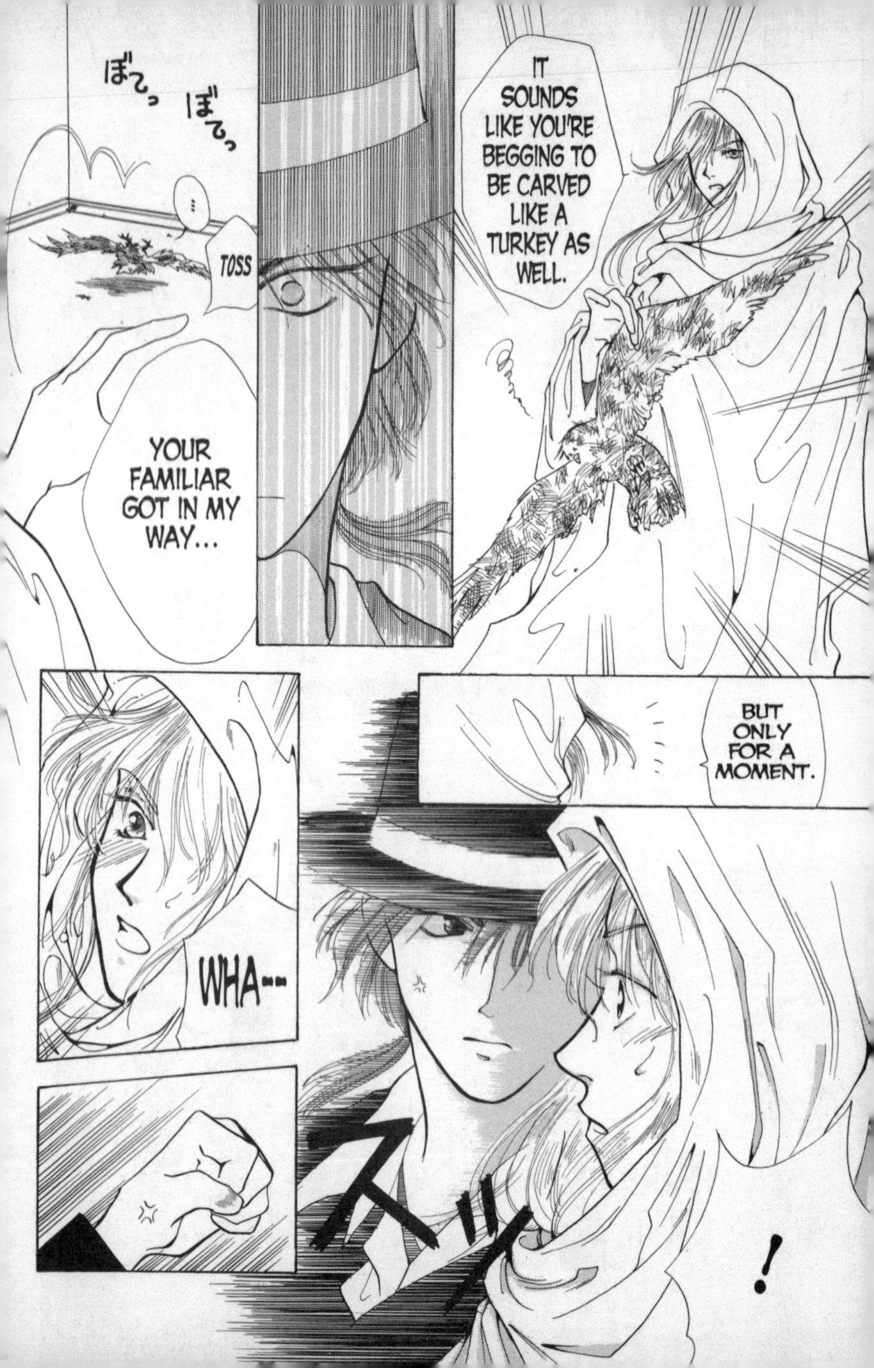
IT SOUNDS LIKE YOU'RE BEGGING TO BE CARVED LIKE A TURKEY AS WELL.
ぼてっ ぼてっ
...
TOSS
YOUR FAMILIAR GOT IN MY WAY...
BUT ONLY FOR A MOMENT.
!
WHA--

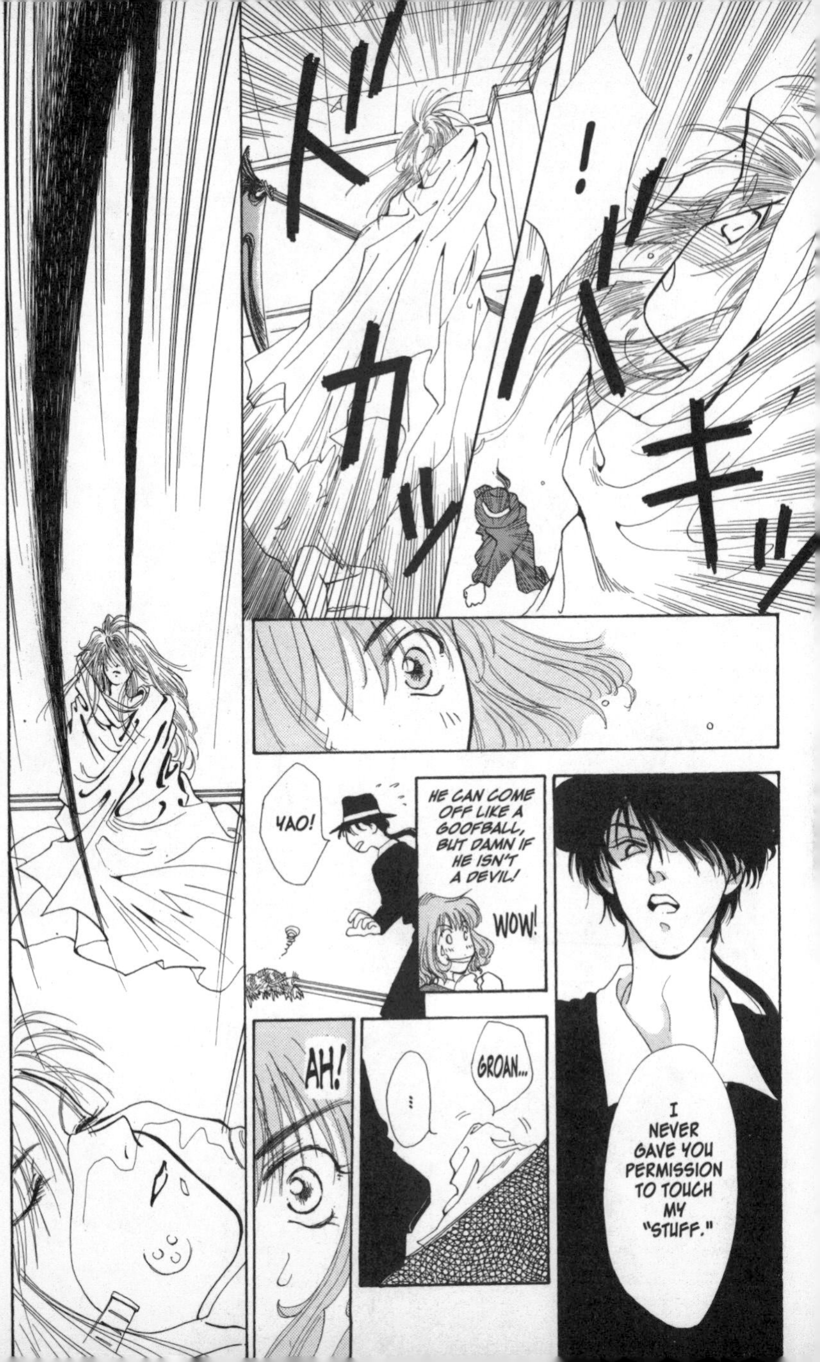
!
バキッ
ドカッ
I NEVER GAVE YOU PERMISSION TO TOUCH MY "STUFF."
HE CAN COME OFF LIKE A GOOFBALL, BUT DAMN IF HE ISN'T A DEVIL!
WOW!
YAO!
GROAN...
...
AH!

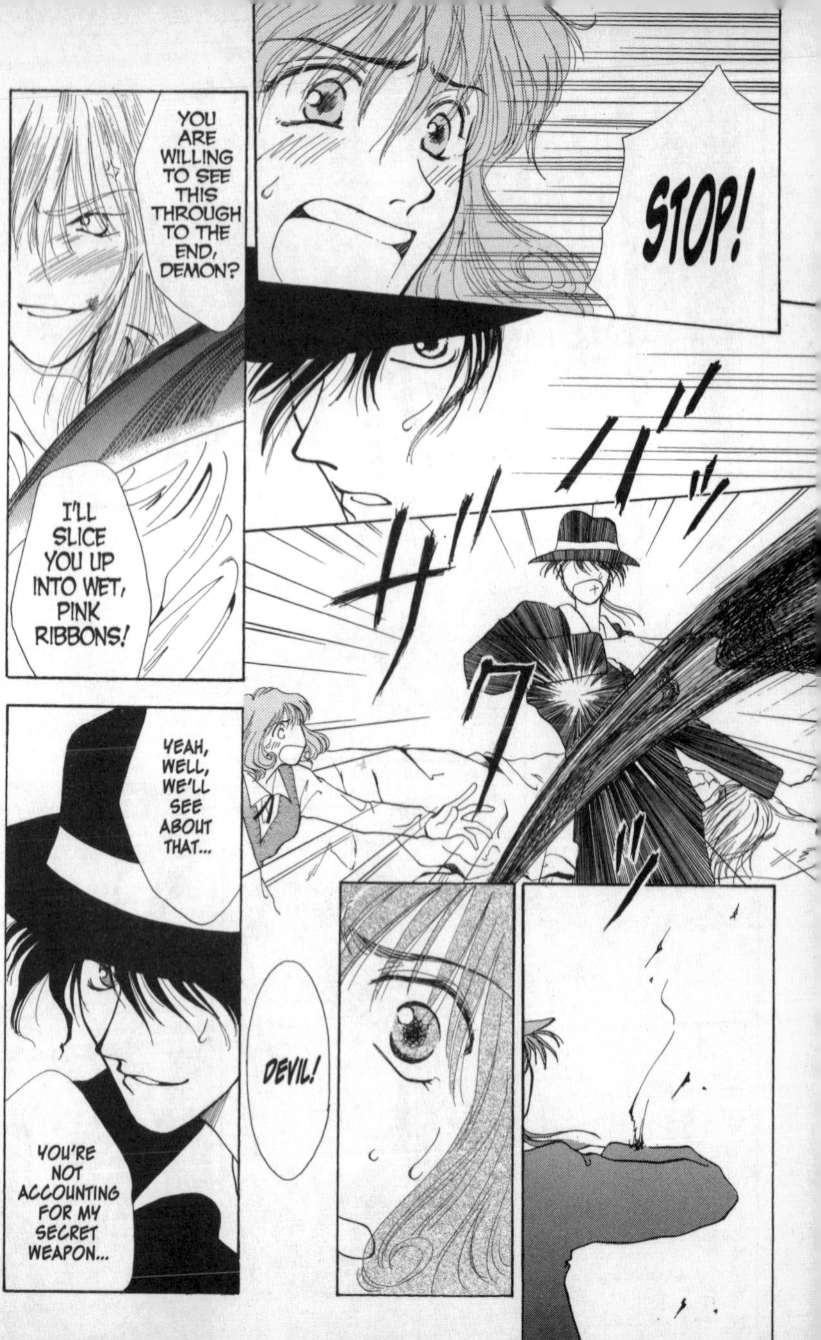
STOP!
YOU ARE WILLING TO SEE THIS THROUGH TO THE END, DEMON?
I'LL SLICE YOU UP INTO WET, PINK RIBBONS!
YEAH, WELL, WE'LL SEE ABOUT THAT...
YOU'RE NOT ACCOUNTING FOR MY SECRET WEAPON...
DEVIL!

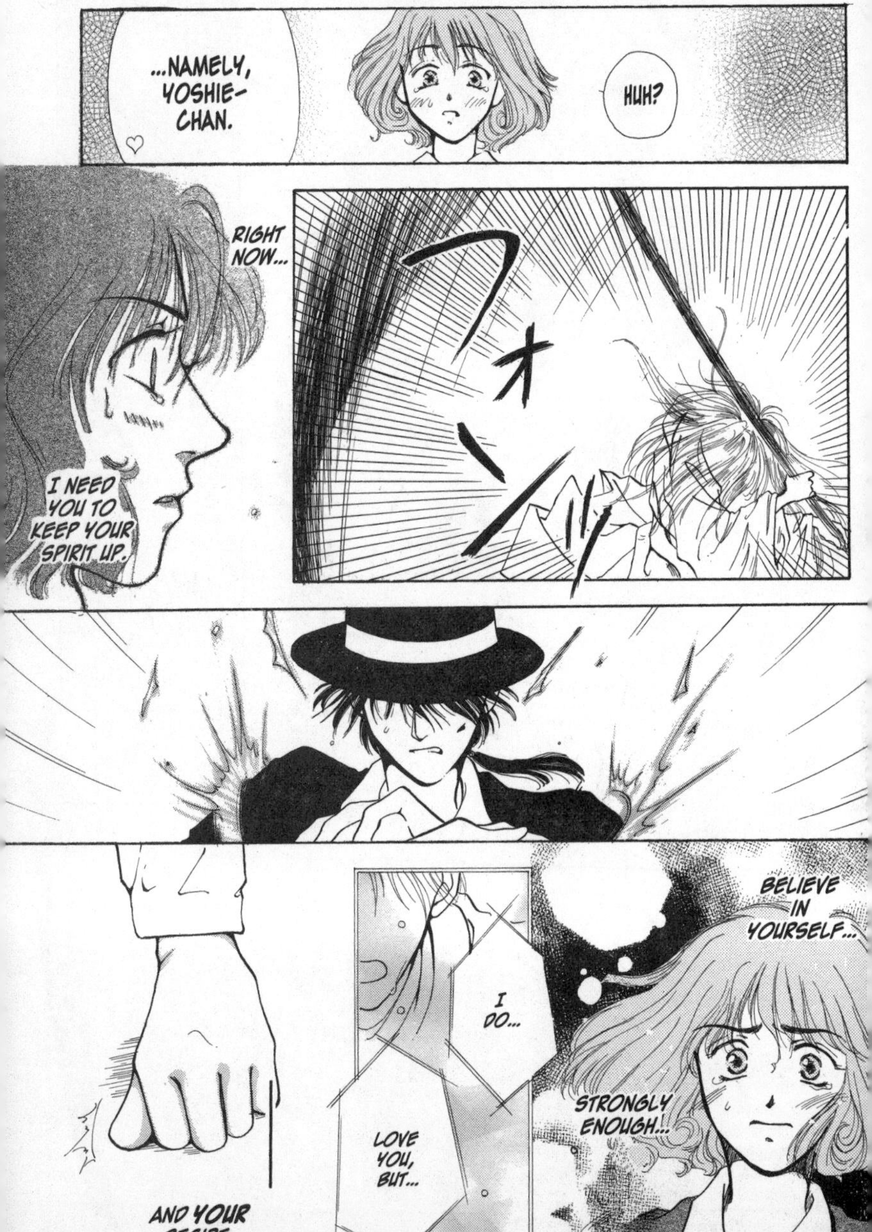
...NAMELY, YOSHIE-CHAN.
HUH?
フォン
RIGHT NOW...
I NEED YOU TO KEEP YOUR SPIRIT UP.
BELIEVE IN YOURSELF...
STRONGLY ENOUGH...
I DO...
LOVE YOU, BUT...
AND YOUR DESIRE...

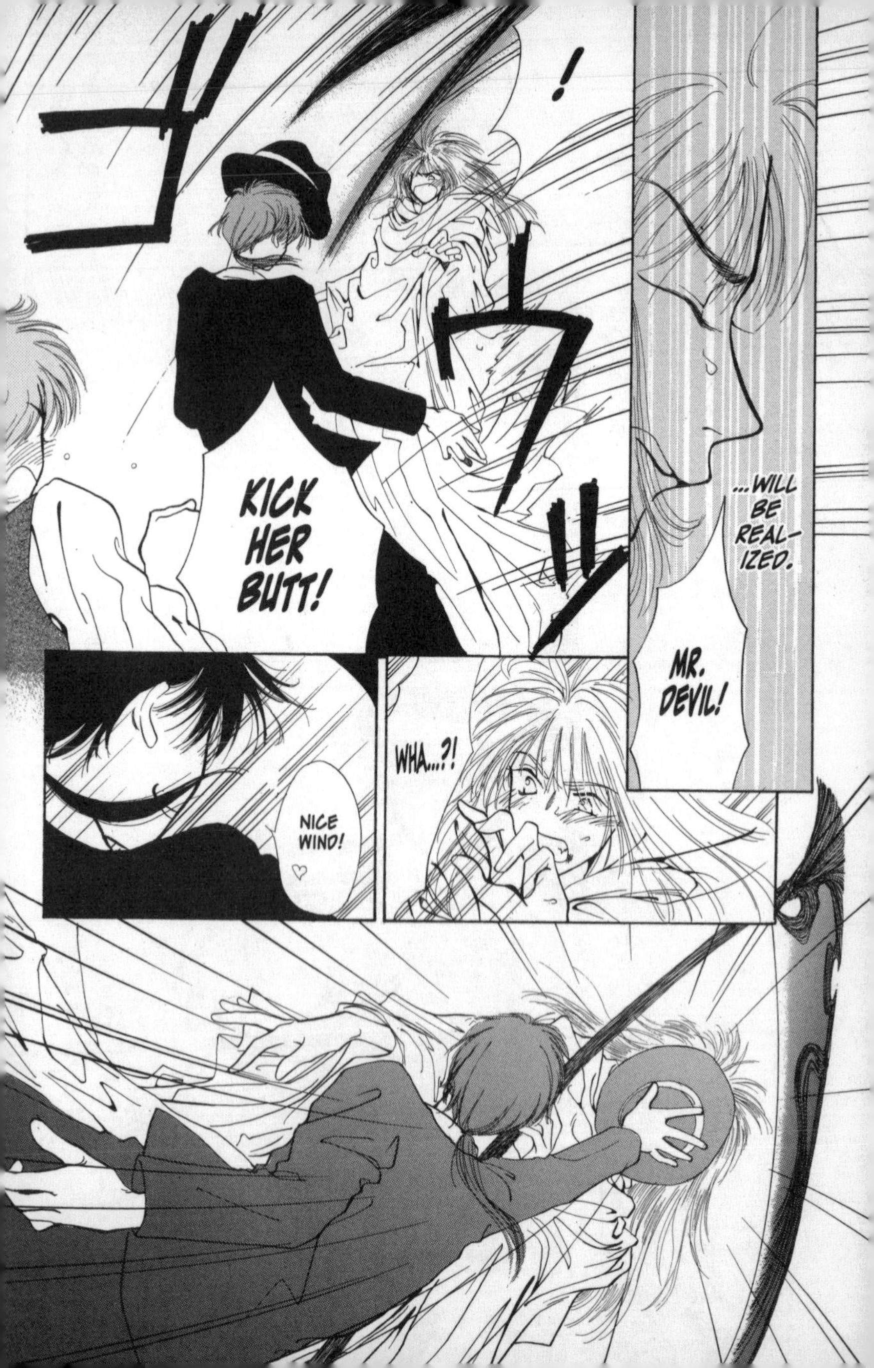
...WILL BE REALIZED.
MR. DEVIL!
!
KICK HER BUTT!
WHA...?!
NICE WIND! ♡

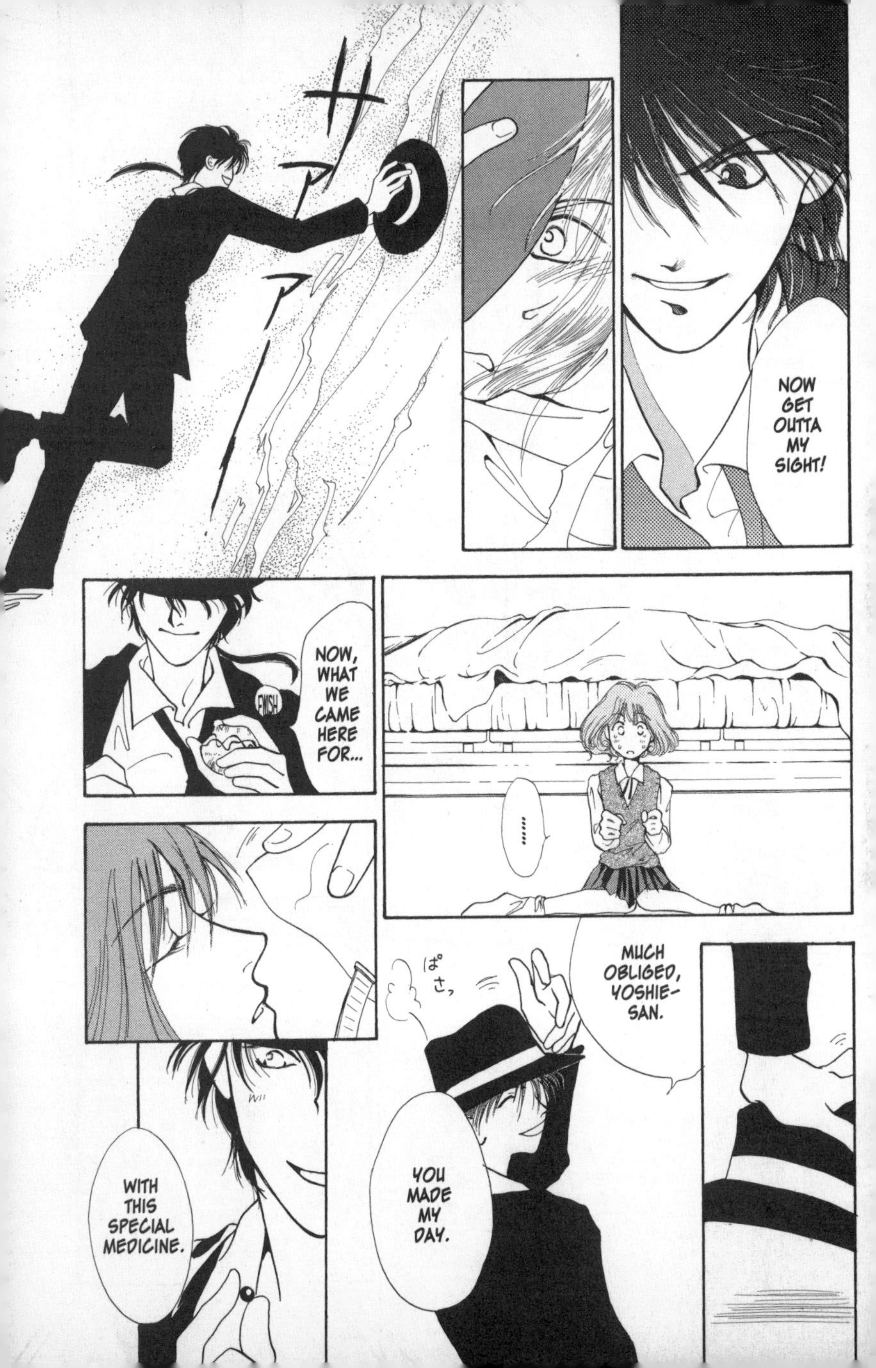
NOW GET OUTTA MY SIGHT!
......
NOW, WHAT WE CAME HERE FOR...
FWISH
MUCH OBLIGED, YOSHIE-SAN.
ぱさっ
YOU MADE MY DAY.
WITH THIS SPECIAL MEDICINE.

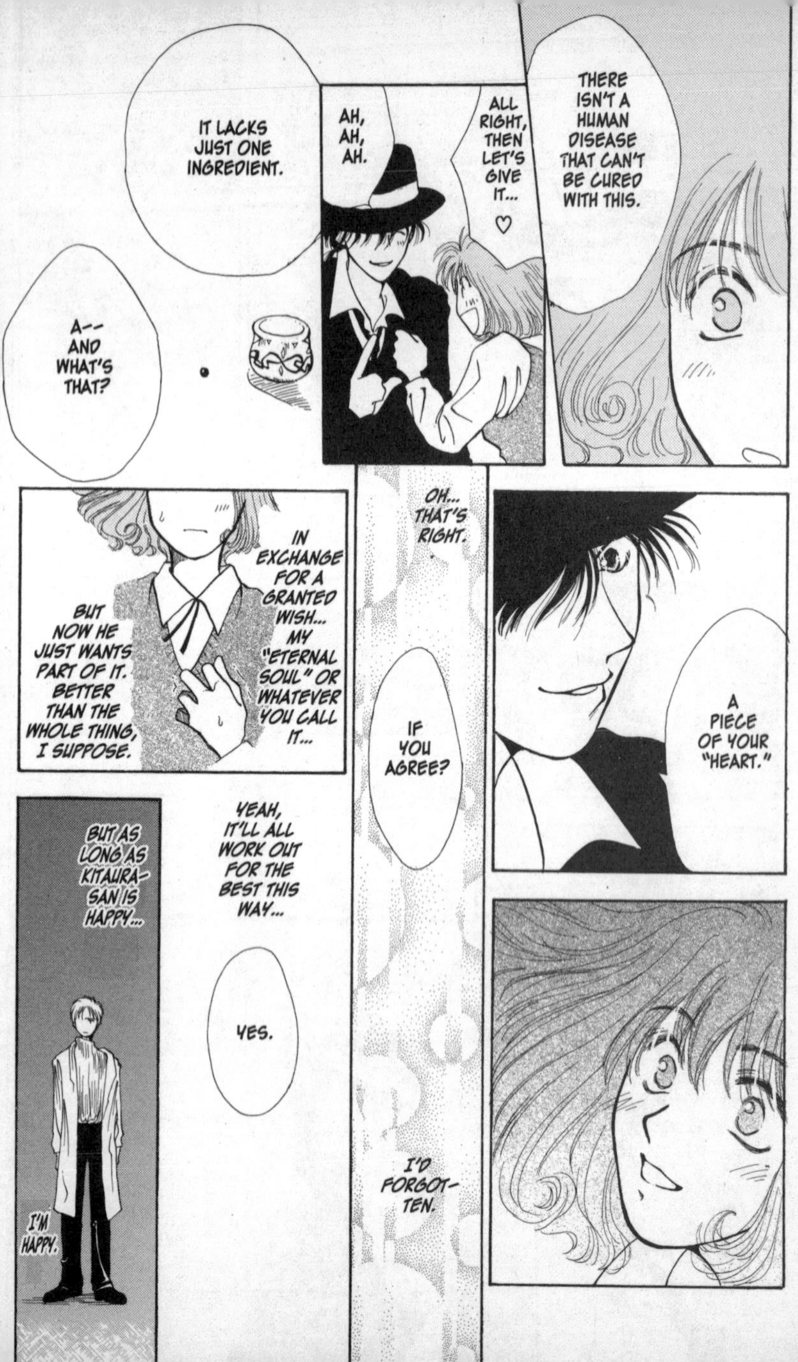
THERE ISN'T A HUMAN DISEASE THAT CAN'T BE CURED WITH THIS.
ALL RIGHT, THEN LET'S GIVE IT... ♡
AH, AH, AH.
IT LACKS JUST ONE INGREDIENT.
A-- AND WHAT'S THAT?
OH... THAT'S RIGHT.
A PIECE OF YOUR "HEART."
IF YOU AGREE?
IN EXCHANGE FOR A GRANTED WISH... MY "ETERNAL SOUL" OR WHATEVER YOU CALL IT...
BUT NOW HE JUST WANTS PART OF IT. BETTER THAN THE WHOLE THING, I SUPPOSE.
I'D FORGOT-TEN.
YES.
YEAH, IT'LL ALL WORK OUT FOR THE BEST THIS WAY...
BUT AS LONG AS KITAURA-SAN IS HAPPY...
I'M HAPPY.

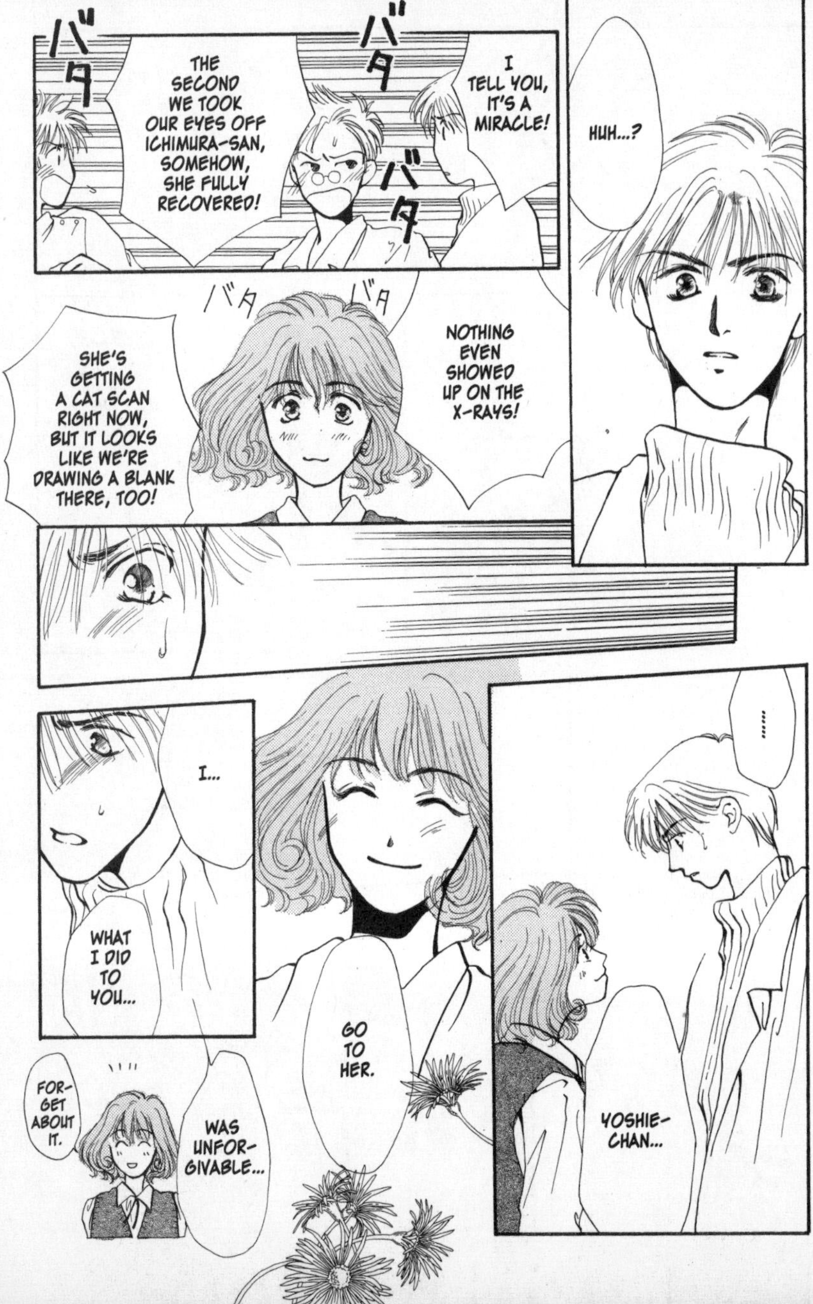
HUH...?
I TELL YOU, IT'S A MIRACLE!
バタ
バタ
THE SECOND WE TOOK OUR EYES OFF ICHIMURA-SAN, SOMEHOW, SHE FULLY RECOVERED!
バタ
NOTHING EVEN SHOWED UP ON THE X-RAYS!
バタ
バタ
SHE'S GETTING A CAT SCAN RIGHT NOW, BUT IT LOOKS LIKE WE'RE DRAWING A BLANK THERE, TOO!
.....
YOSHIE-CHAN...
I...
WHAT I DID TO YOU...
WAS UNFORGIVABLE...
FOR-GET ABOUT IT.
GO TO HER.

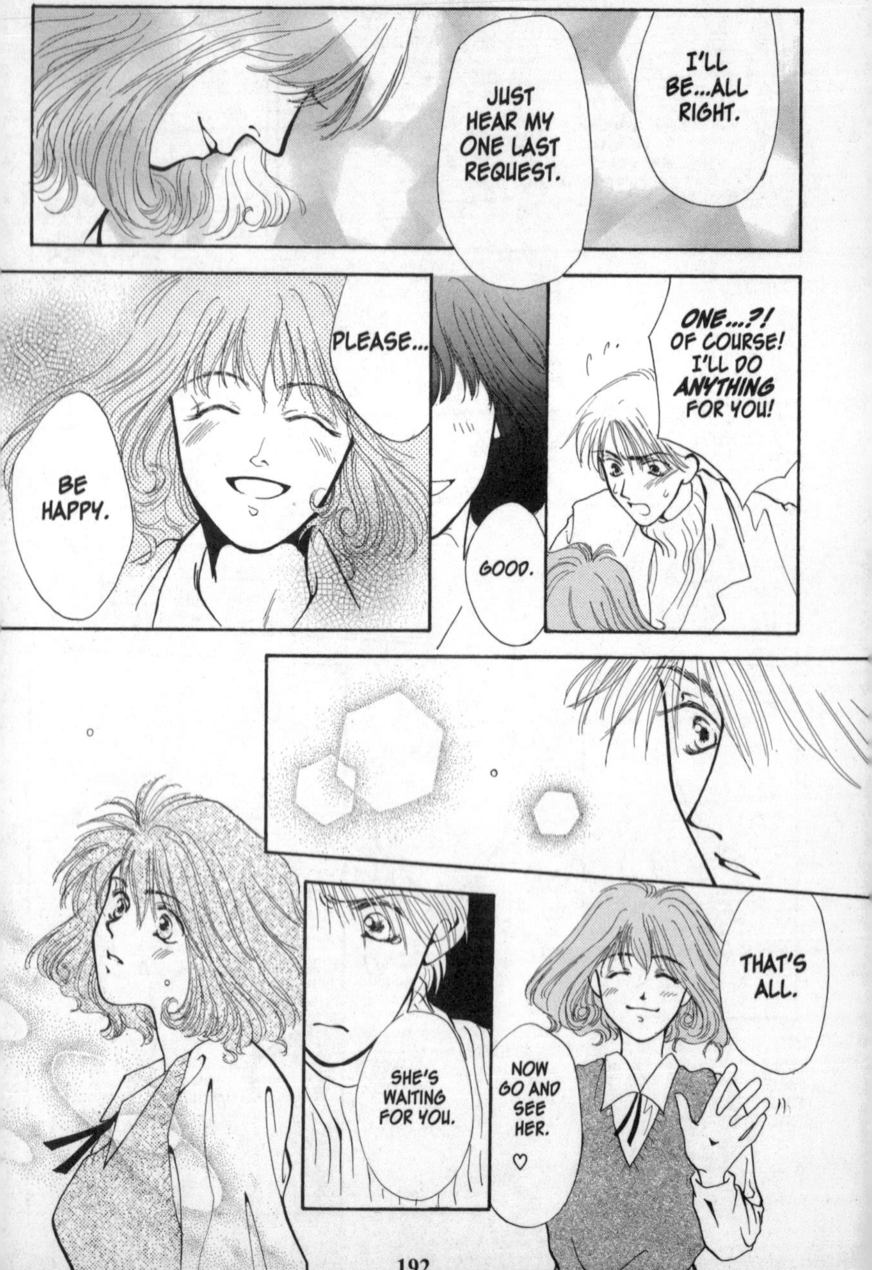
I'LL BE...ALL RIGHT.
JUST HEAR MY ONE LAST REQUEST.
ONE...?! OF COURSE! I'LL DO *ANYTHING* FOR YOU!
GOOD.
PLEASE...
BE HAPPY.
THAT'S ALL.
NOW GO AND SEE HER. ♡
SHE'S WAITING FOR YOU.

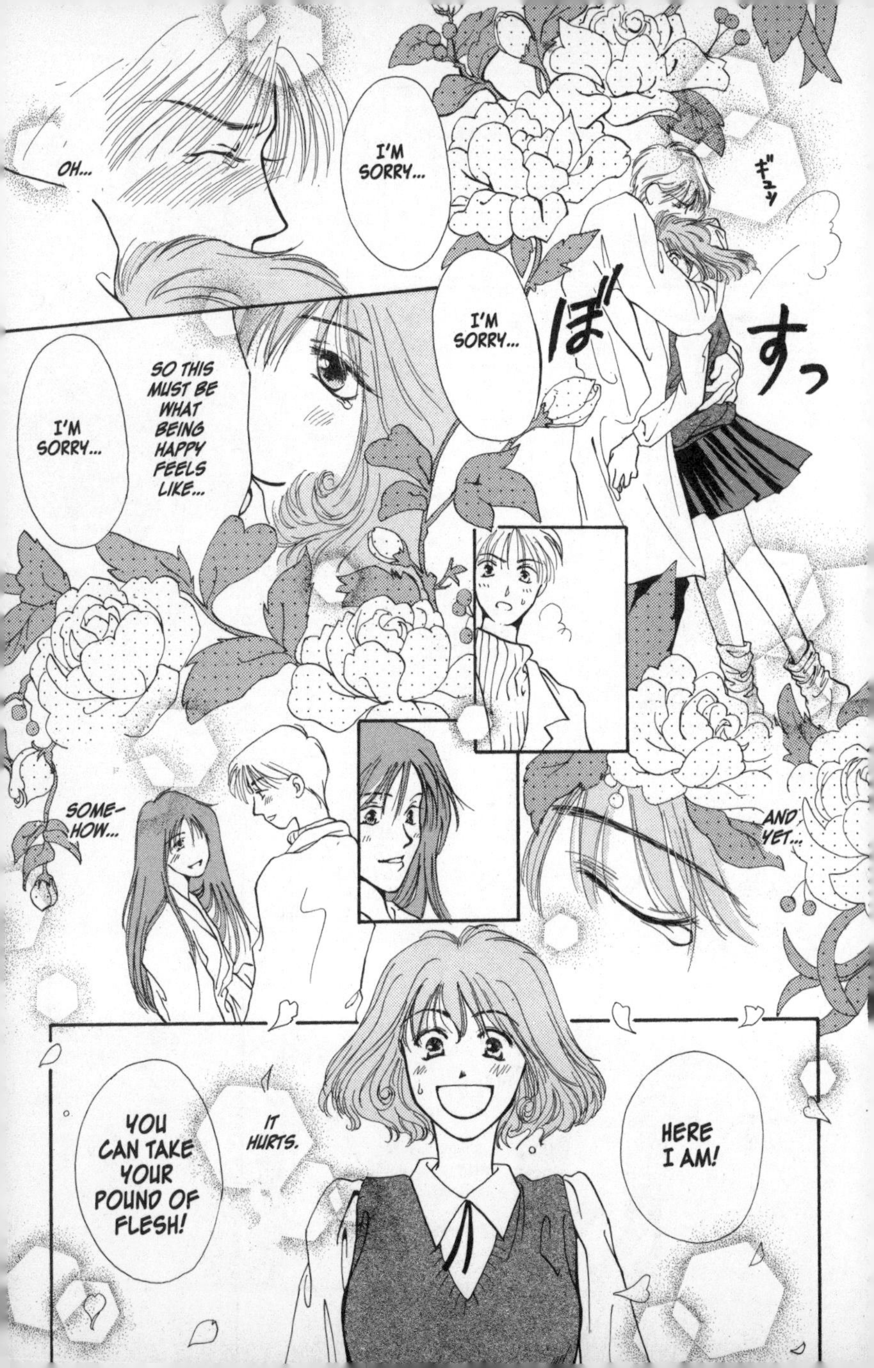
ギュッ
ぼすっ
I'M SORRY...
OH...
I'M SORRY...
SO THIS MUST BE WHAT BEING HAPPY FEELS LIKE...
I'M SORRY...
AND YET...
SOME-HOW...
HERE I AM!
IT HURTS.
YOU CAN TAKE YOUR POUND OF FLESH!

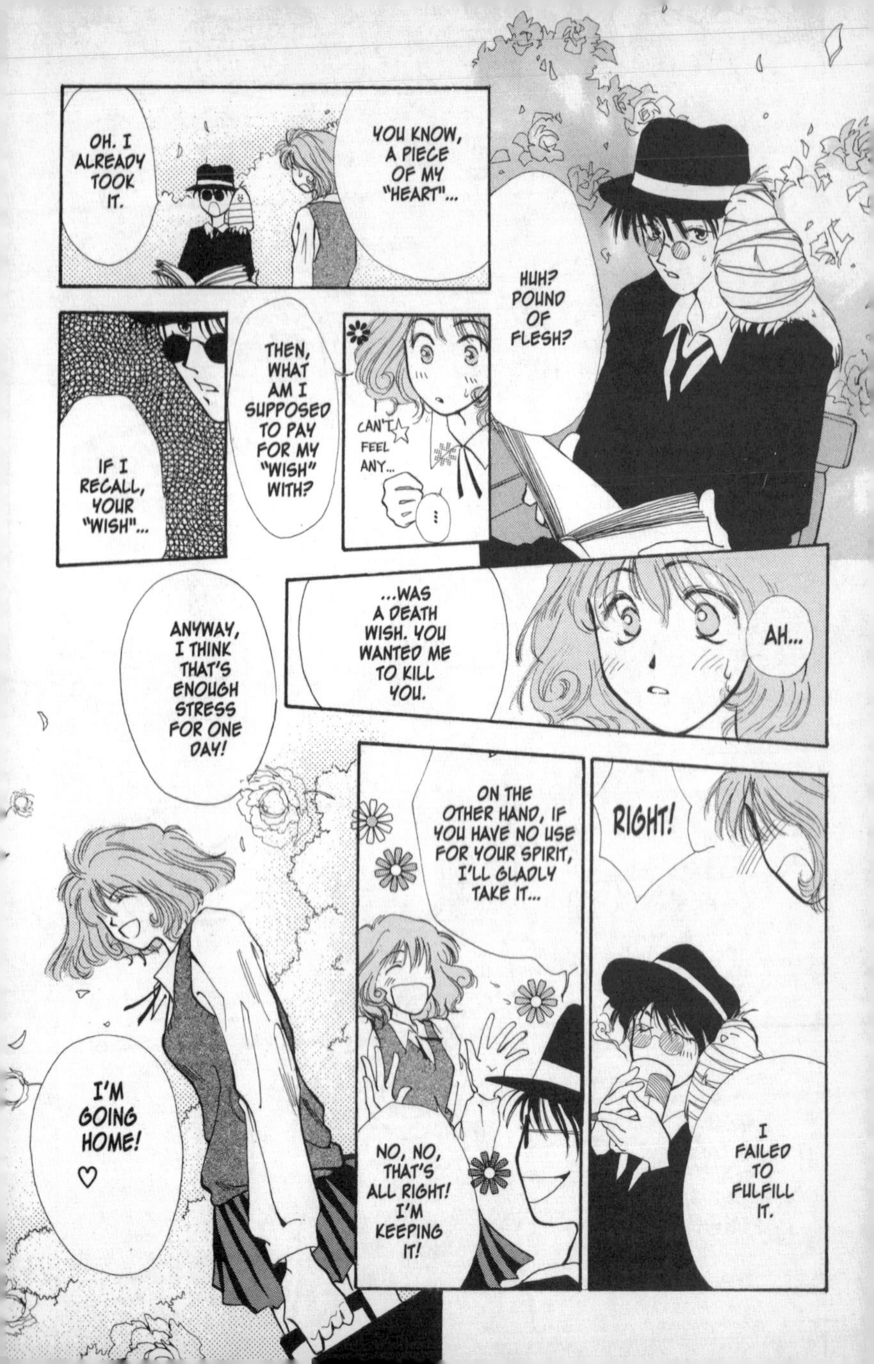
HUH? POUND OF FLESH?
YOU KNOW, A PIECE OF MY "HEART"...
OH. I ALREADY TOOK IT.
THEN, WHAT AM I SUPPOSED TO PAY FOR MY "WISH" WITH?
CAN'T FEEL ANY...
...
IF I RECALL, YOUR "WISH"...
...WAS A DEATH WISH. YOU WANTED ME TO KILL YOU.
AH...
RIGHT!
I FAILED TO FULFILL IT.
ON THE OTHER HAND, IF YOU HAVE NO USE FOR YOUR SPIRIT, I'LL GLADLY TAKE IT...
NO, NO, THAT'S ALL RIGHT! I'M KEEPING IT!
ANYWAY, I THINK THAT'S ENOUGH STRESS FOR ONE DAY!
I'M GOING HOME! ♡

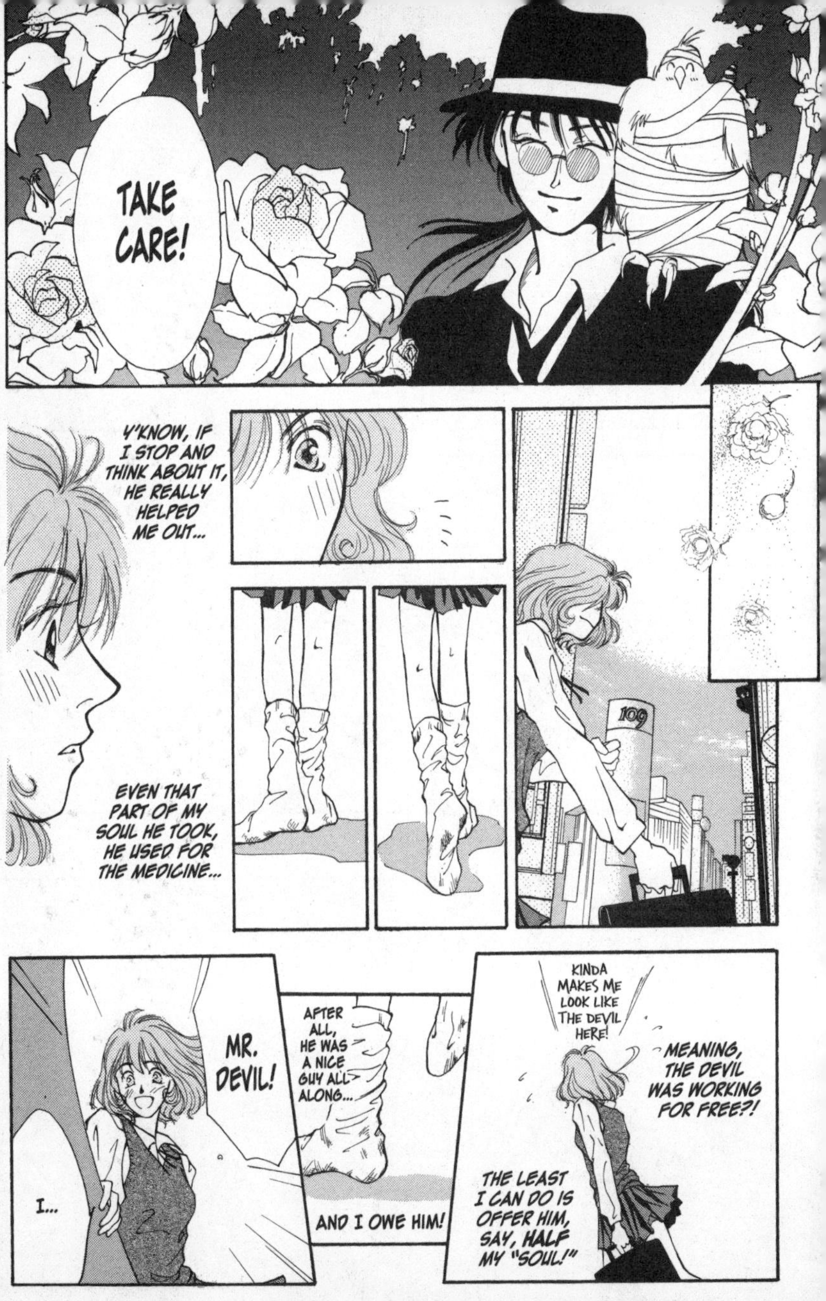
TAKE CARE!
109
Y'KNOW, IF I STOP AND THINK ABOUT IT, HE REALLY HELPED ME OUT...
EVEN THAT PART OF MY SOUL HE TOOK, HE USED FOR THE MEDICINE...
MEANING, THE DEVIL WAS WORKING FOR FREE?!
KINDA MAKES ME LOOK LIKE THE DEVIL HERE!
THE LEAST I CAN DO IS OFFER HIM, SAY, HALF MY "SOUL!"
AFTER ALL, HE WAS A NICE GUY ALL ALONG...
AND I OWE HIM!
MR. DEVIL!
I...

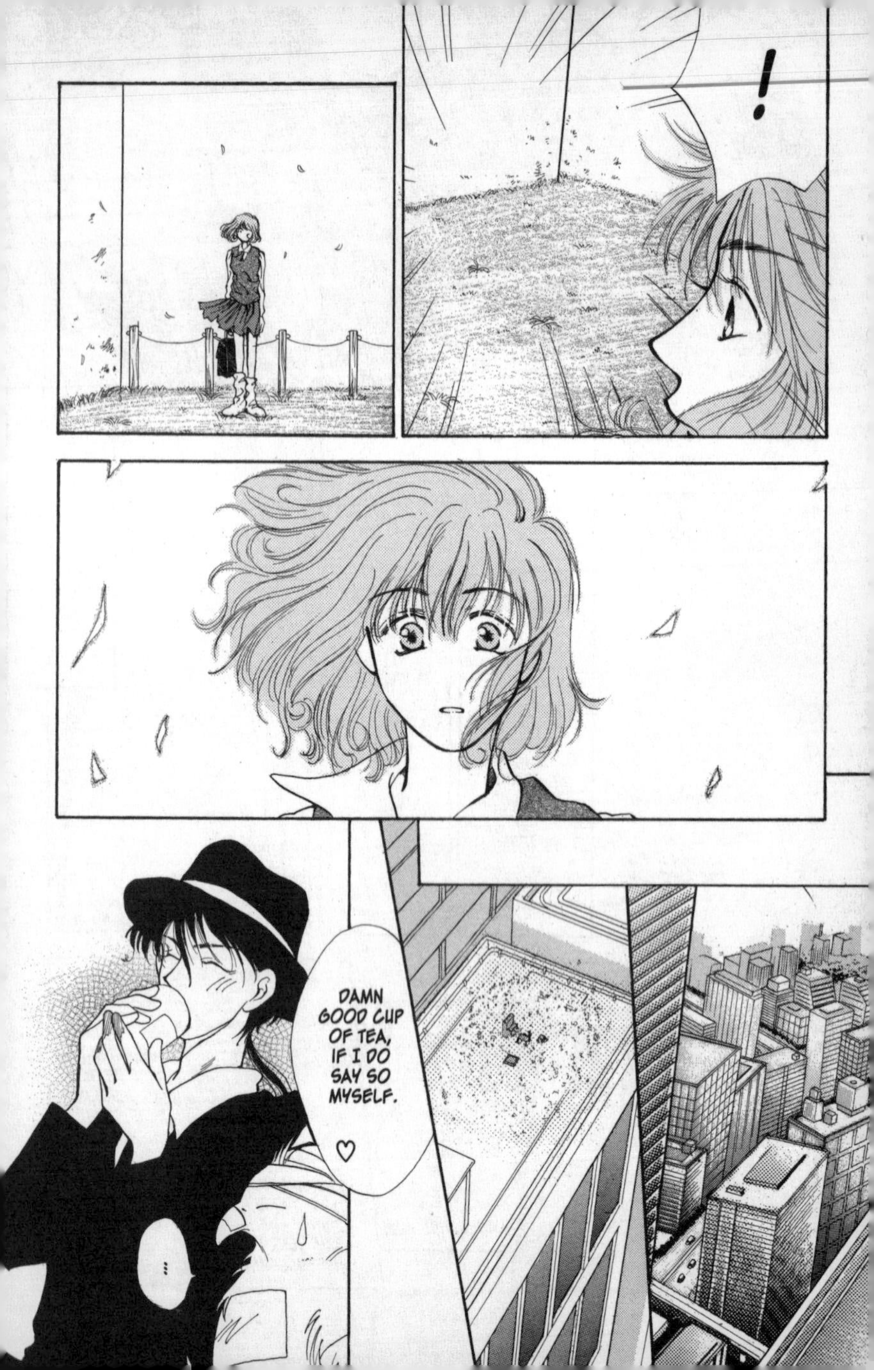
!
DAMN GOOD CUP OF TEA, IF I DO SAY SO MYSELF. ♡
...

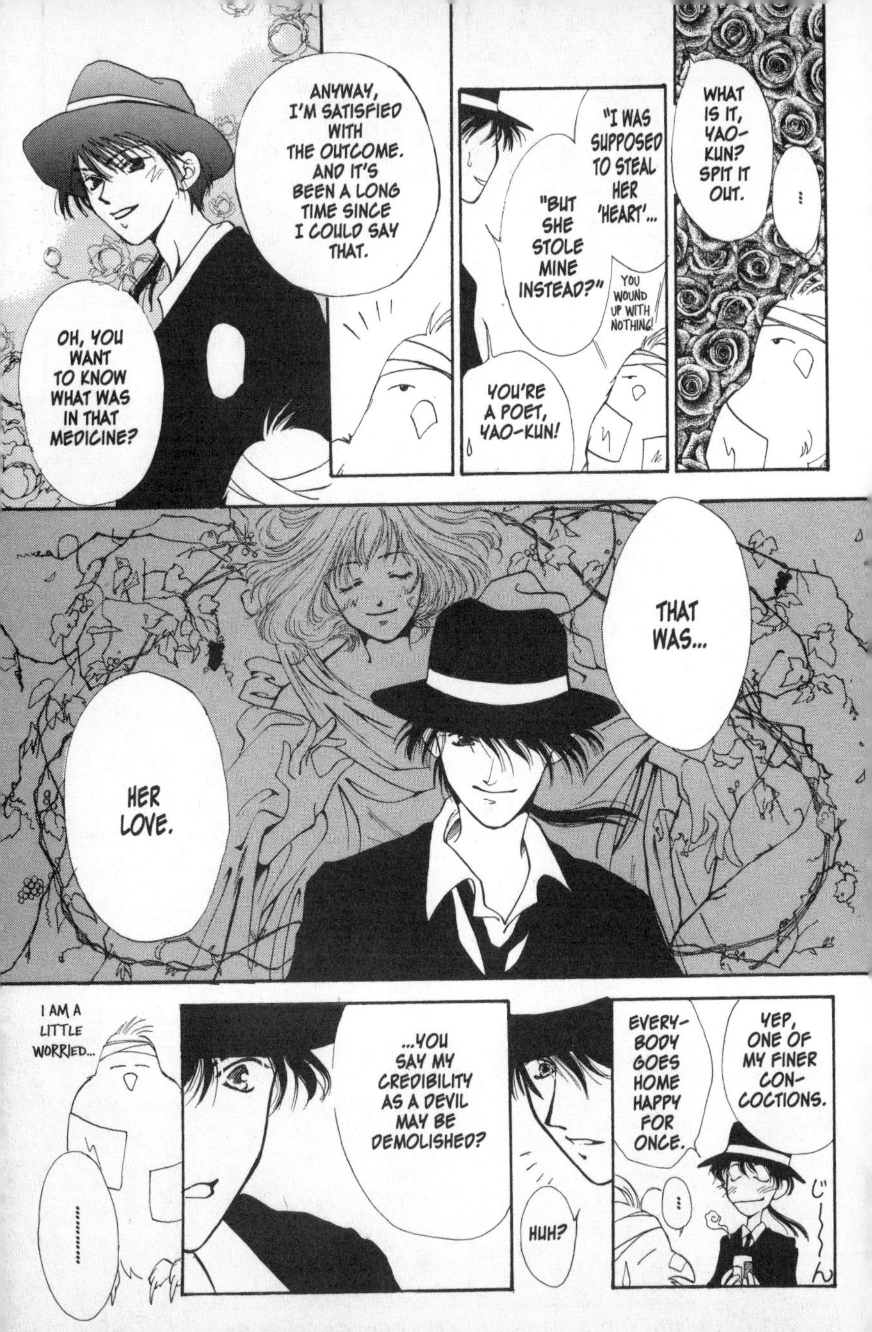
WHAT IS IT, YAO-KUN? SPIT IT OUT.
...
"I WAS SUPPOSED TO STEAL HER 'HEART'...
"BUT SHE STOLE MINE INSTEAD?"
YOU WOUND UP WITH NOTHING!
YOU'RE A POET, YAO-KUN!
ANYWAY, I'M SATISFIED WITH THE OUTCOME. AND IT'S BEEN A LONG TIME SINCE I COULD SAY THAT.
OH, YOU WANT TO KNOW WHAT WAS IN THAT MEDICINE?
THAT WAS...
HER LOVE.
YEP, ONE OF MY FINER CON-COCTIONS.
EVERY-BODY GOES HOME HAPPY FOR ONCE.
...
じ～～ん
...YOU SAY MY CREDIBILITY AS A DEVIL MAY BE DEMOLISHED?
HUH?
I AM A LITTLE WORRIED...
....

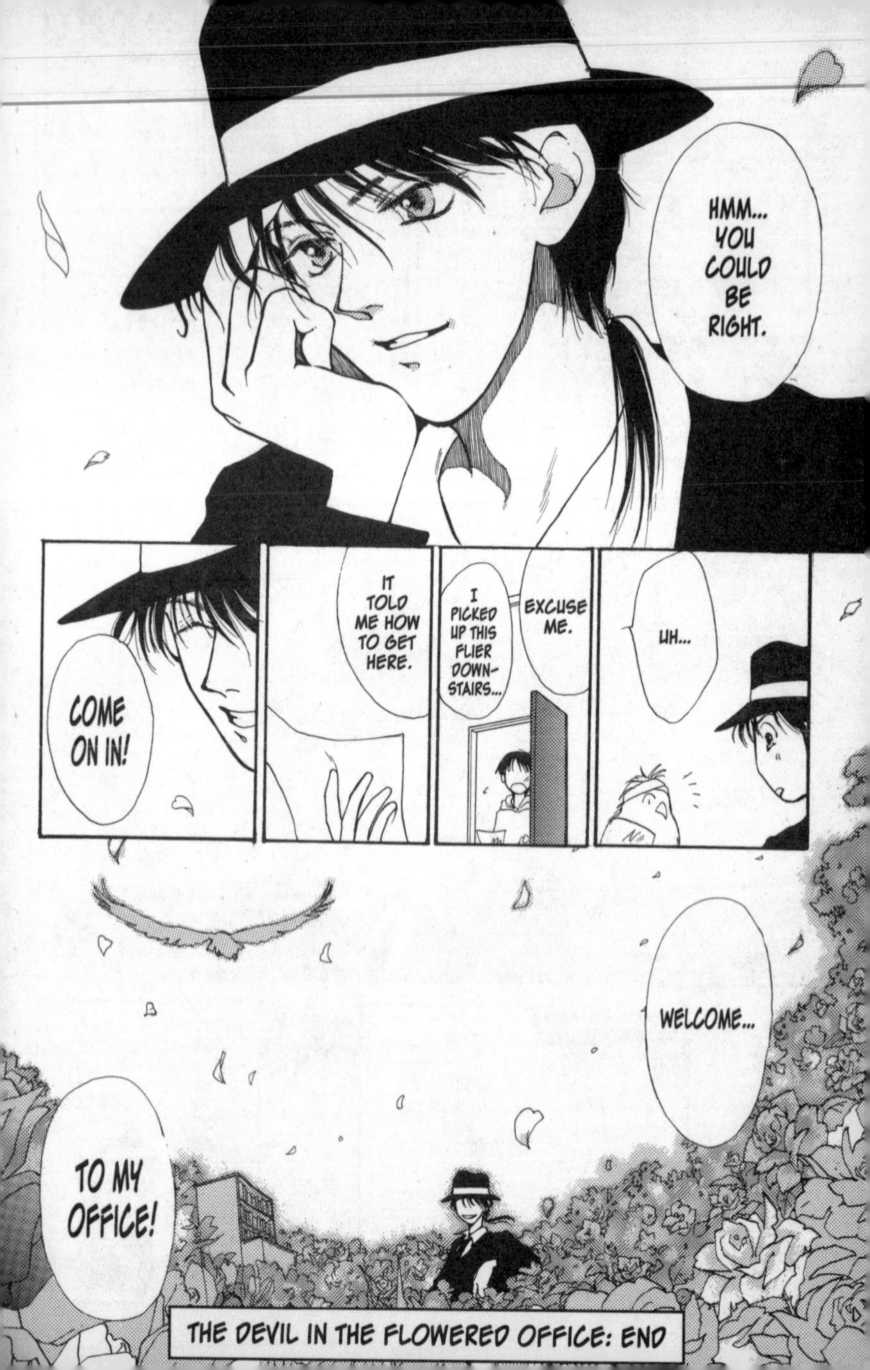
HMM... YOU COULD BE RIGHT.
UH...
EXCUSE ME.
I PICKED UP THIS FLIER DOWN-STAIRS...
IT TOLD ME HOW TO GET HERE.
COME ON IN!
WELCOME...
TO MY OFFICE!
THE DEVIL IN THE FLOWERED OFFICE: END

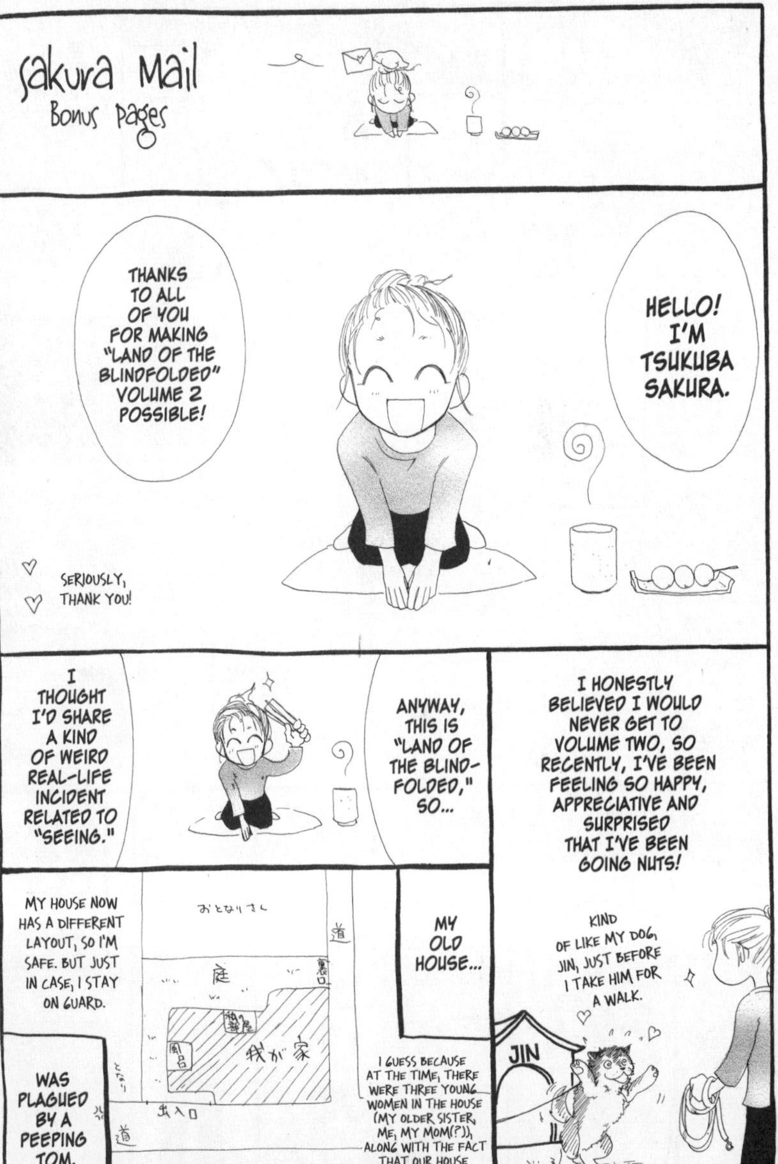
Sakura Mail
Bonus Pages
HELLO! I'M TSUKUBA SAKURA.
THANKS TO ALL OF YOU FOR MAKING "LAND OF THE BLINDFOLDED" VOLUME 2 POSSIBLE!
SERIOUSLY, THANK YOU!
I HONESTLY BELIEVED I WOULD NEVER GET TO VOLUME TWO, SO RECENTLY, I'VE BEEN FEELING SO HAPPY, APPRECIATIVE AND SURPRISED THAT I'VE BEEN GOING NUTS!
ANYWAY, THIS IS "LAND OF THE BLIND-FOLDED," SO...
I THOUGHT I'D SHARE A KIND OF WEIRD REAL-LIFE INCIDENT RELATED TO "SEEING."
KIND OF LIKE MY DOG, JIN, JUST BEFORE I TAKE HIM FOR A WALK.
JIN
MY OLD HOUSE...
WAS PLAGUED BY A PEEPING TOM.
I GUESS BECAUSE AT THE TIME, THERE WERE THREE YOUNG WOMEN IN THE HOUSE (MY OLDER SISTER, ME, MY MOM(?)), ALONG WITH THE FACT THAT OUR HOUSE WAS ON A CORNER, MAKING IT EASY TO ESCAPE.
MY HOUSE NOW HAS A DIFFERENT LAYOUT, SO I'M SAFE. BUT JUST IN CASE, I STAY ON GUARD.
おとなりさん
道
庭
裏口
私の部屋
風呂
我が家
出入口
道

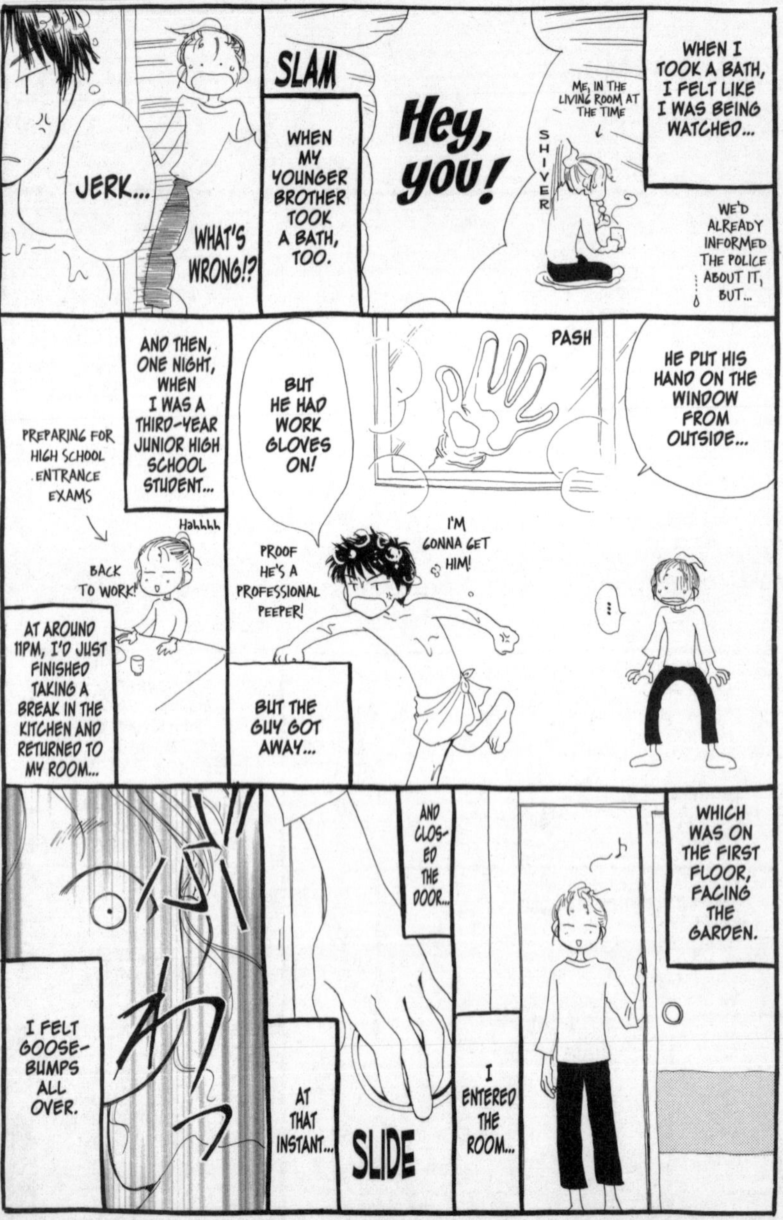
WHEN I TOOK A BATH, I FELT LIKE I WAS BEING WATCHED...
ME, IN THE LIVING ROOM AT THE TIME
SHIVER
WE'D ALREADY INFORMED THE POLICE ABOUT IT, BUT...
Hey, you!
SLAM
WHEN MY YOUNGER BROTHER TOOK A BATH, TOO.
WHAT'S WRONG!?
JERK...
HE PUT HIS HAND ON THE WINDOW FROM OUTSIDE...
PASH
BUT HE HAD WORK GLOVES ON!
I'M GONNA GET HIM!
PROOF HE'S A PROFESSIONAL PEEPER!
...
BUT THE GUY GOT AWAY...
AND THEN, ONE NIGHT, WHEN I WAS A THIRD-YEAR JUNIOR HIGH SCHOOL STUDENT...
PREPARING FOR HIGH SCHOOL ENTRANCE EXAMS
Hahhhh
BACK TO WORK!
AT AROUND 11PM, I'D JUST FINISHED TAKING A BREAK IN THE KITCHEN AND RETURNED TO MY ROOM...
WHICH WAS ON THE FIRST FLOOR, FACING THE GARDEN.
I ENTERED THE ROOM...
AND CLOS-ED THE DOOR...
SLIDE
AT THAT INSTANT...
I FELT GOOSE-BUMPS ALL OVER.

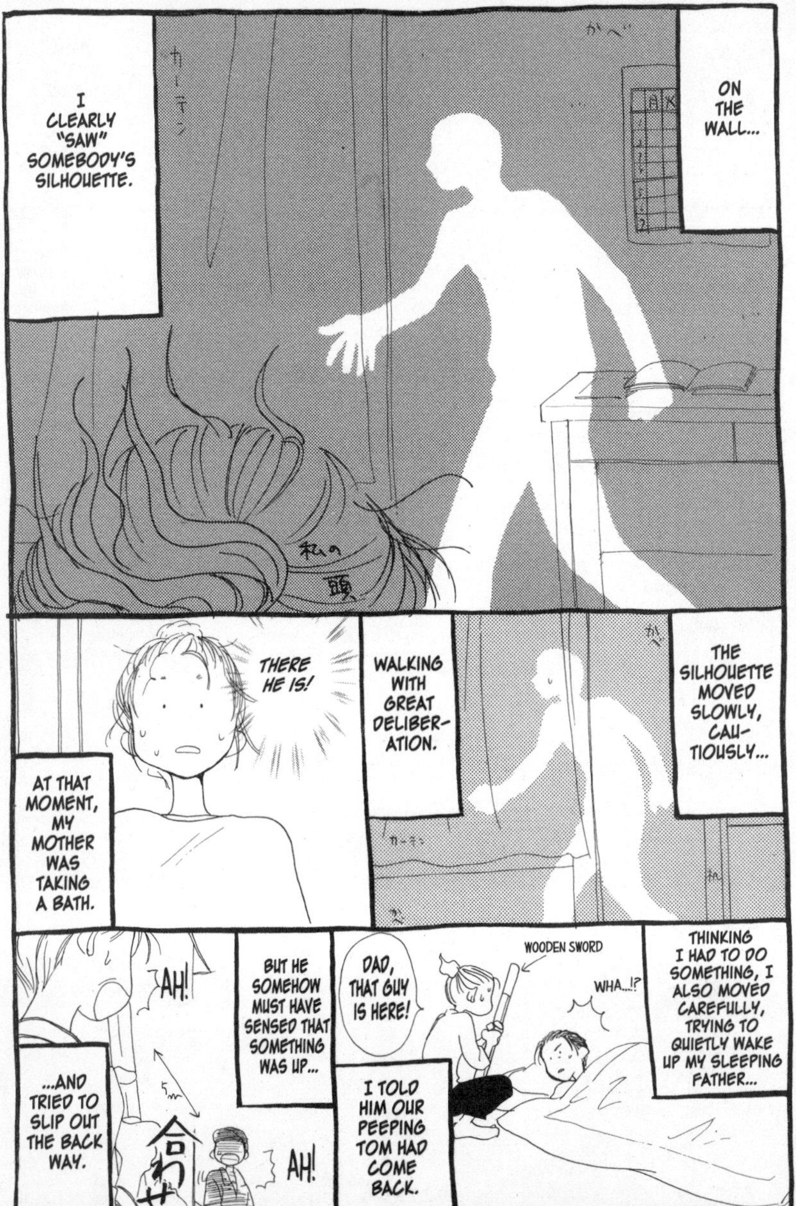
ON THE WALL...
かべ
カーテン
I CLEARLY "SAW" SOMEBODY'S SILHOUETTE.
私の頭
THE SILHOUETTE MOVED SLOWLY, CAU-TIOUSLY...
WALKING WITH GREAT DELIBER-ATION.
THERE HE IS!
AT THAT MOMENT, MY MOTHER WAS TAKING A BATH.
THINKING I HAD TO DO SOMETHING, I ALSO MOVED CAREFULLY, TRYING TO QUIETLY WAKE UP MY SLEEPING FATHER...
WHA...!?
WOODEN SWORD
DAD, THAT GUY IS HERE!
I TOLD HIM OUR PEEPING TOM HAD COME BACK.
BUT HE SOMEHOW MUST HAVE SENSED THAT SOMETHING WAS UP...
AH!
...AND TRIED TO SLIP OUT THE BACK WAY.
合わせ
AH!

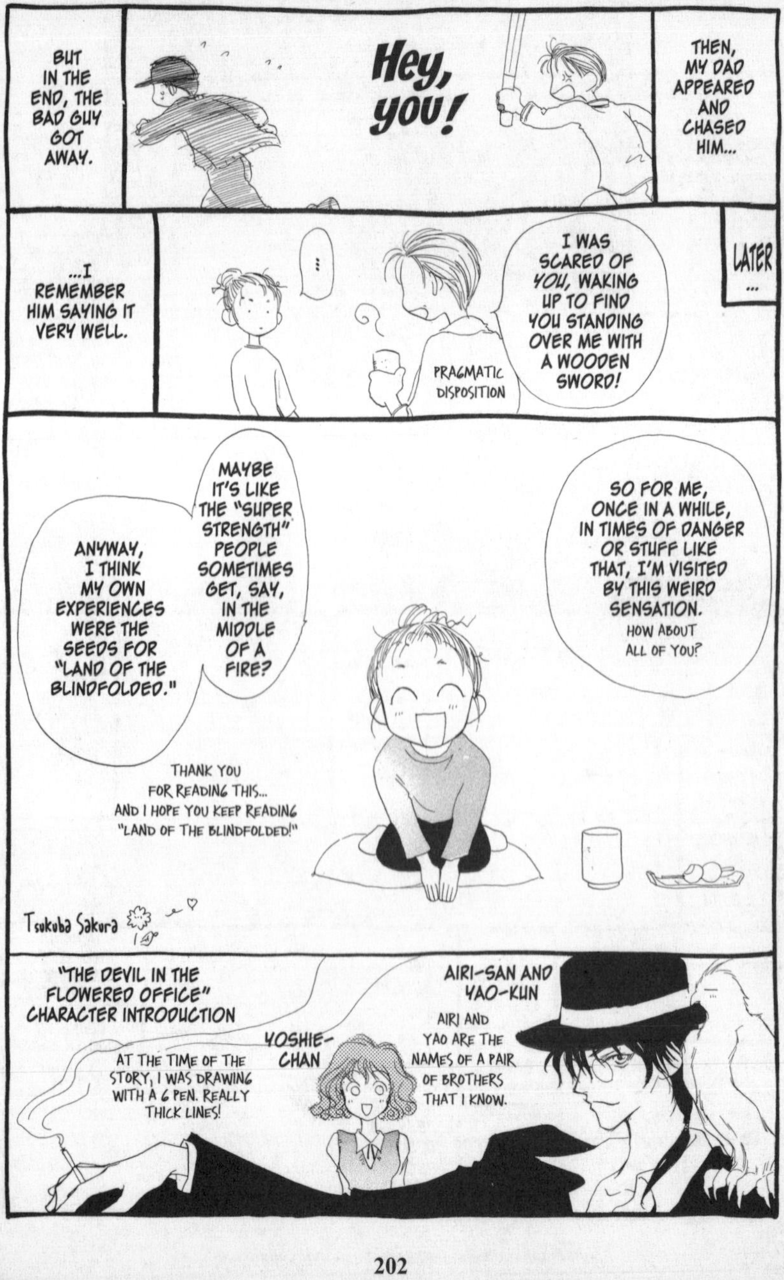
THEN, MY DAD APPEARED AND CHASED HIM...
Hey, you!
BUT IN THE END, THE BAD GUY GOT AWAY.
LATER...
I WAS SCARED OF *YOU*, WAKING UP TO FIND YOU STANDING OVER ME WITH A WOODEN SWORD!
PRAGMATIC DISPOSITION
...
...I REMEMBER HIM SAYING IT VERY WELL.
SO FOR ME, ONCE IN A WHILE, IN TIMES OF DANGER OR STUFF LIKE THAT, I'M VISITED BY THIS WEIRD SENSATION.
HOW ABOUT ALL OF YOU?
MAYBE IT'S LIKE THE "SUPER STRENGTH" PEOPLE SOMETIMES GET, SAY, IN THE MIDDLE OF A FIRE?
ANYWAY, I THINK MY OWN EXPERIENCES WERE THE SEEDS FOR "LAND OF THE BLINDFOLDED."
THANK YOU FOR READING THIS... AND I HOPE YOU KEEP READING "LAND OF THE BLINDFOLDED!"
Tsukuba Sakura
AIRI-SAN AND YAO-KUN
AIRI AND YAO ARE THE NAMES OF A PAIR OF BROTHERS THAT I KNOW.
YOSHIE-CHAN
"THE DEVIL IN THE FLOWERED OFFICE" CHARACTER INTRODUCTION
AT THE TIME OF THE STORY, I WAS DRAWING WITH A G PEN. REALLY THICK LINES!

Land of the Blindfolded

Volume 3

By Sakura Tsukuba. After risking her life to help someone, Kanade confides a secret to Arou and Namiki: when she was a young girl just discovering her supernatural talent, she "saw" her beloved grandfather die in a fire. Was it her intervention that changed his fate? Then, through a careless mistake, the school doctor realizes that Kanade can sometimes glimpse the future. But why is he so intent on stopping her from changing destiny?

MEKAKUSHI NO KUNI © 1998 Sakura Tsukuba/HAKUSENSHA, INC.

IF YOU LIKE *LAND OF THE BLINDFOLDED*, YOU'LL LOVE THESE OTHER SERIES, TOO!

By Sakura Tsukuba
2 Volumes Available

By Toru Fujieda
4 Volumes Available

By D. Kishi & T. Ichinose
1 Volume Available

By Nari Kusakawa
3 Volumes Available

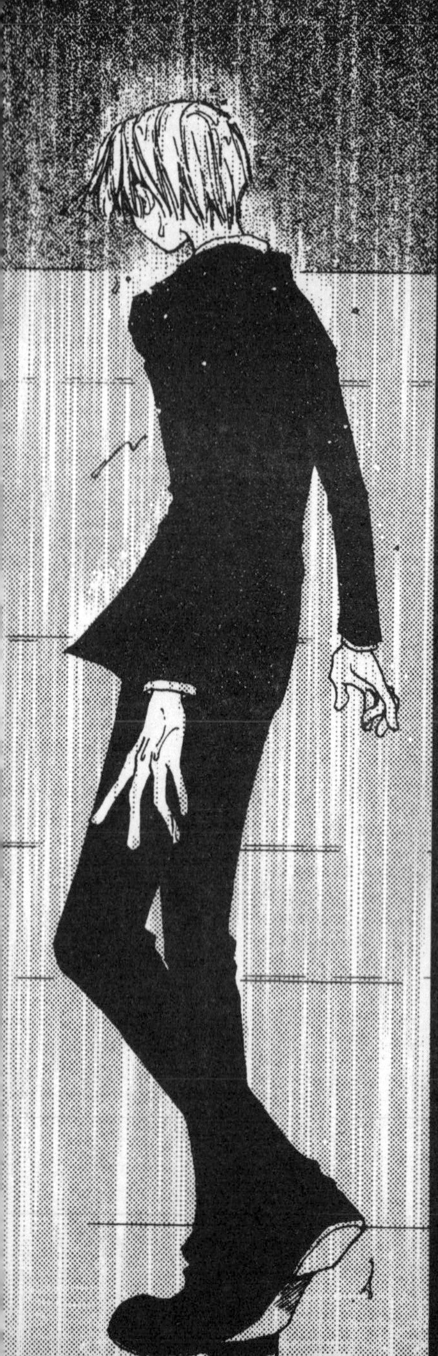

KNOW WHAT'S INSIDE

With the wide variety of manga available, CMX understands it can be confusing to determine age-appropriate material. We rate our books in four categories: EVERYONE, TEEN, TEEN + and MATURE. For the TEEN, TEEN + and MATURE categories, we include additional, specific descriptions to assist consumers in determining if the book is age appropriate. (Our MATURE books are shipped shrink-wrapped with a Parental Advisory sticker affixed to the wrapper.)

E

EVERYONE

Titles with this rating are appropriate for all age readers. They contain no offensive material. They may contain mild violence and/or some comic mischief.

T

TEEN

Titles with this rating are appropriate for a teen audience and older. They may contain some violent content, language, and/or suggestive themes.

T+

TEEN PLUS

Titles with this rating are appropriate for an audience of 16 and older. They may contain partial nudity, mild profanity and more intense violence.

M

MATURE

Titles with this rating are appropriate only for mature readers. They may contain graphic violence, nudity, sex and content suitable only for older readers.

CMX

MEKAKUSHI NO KUNI Volume 2 © 1996 Sakura Tsukuba.
All Rights Reserved. First published in Japan in 2000 by
HAKUSENSHA, INC., Tokyo.

LAND OF THE BLINDFOLDED Volume 2, published by
WildStorm Productions, an imprint of DC Comics, 888
Prospect St. #240, La Jolla, CA 92037. English Translation
© 2004. All Rights Reserved. English language translation
rights in the United States of America and Canada arranged
with HAKUSENSHA, INC., Tokyo, through Tuttle-Mori
Agency, Inc., Tokyo. The stories, characters, and incidents
mentioned in this magazine are entirely fictional. Printed on
recyclable paper. WildStorm does not read or accept unso-
licited submissions of ideas, stories or artwork. Printed in
Canada. SECOND PRINTING.

DC Comics, A Warner Bros. Entertainment Company.

Sheldon Drzka – Translation and Adaptation
Tom B. Long – Lettering
Larry Berry – Design
Jonathan Tarbox – Editor

ISBN:1-4012-0525-9
ISBN-13: 978-1-4012-0525-6

All the pages in this book were created—and are printed here—in Japanese RIGHT-to-LEFT format. No artwork has been reversed or altered, so you can read the stories the way the creators meant for them to be read.

RIGHT TO LEFT?!

Traditional Japanese manga starts at the upper right-hand corner, and moves right-to-left as it goes down the page. Follow this guide for an easy understanding.

For more information and sneak previews, visit cmxmanga.com. Call 1-800-COMIC BOOK for the nearest comics shop or head to your local book store.